Applications of Statistical Sampling to Auditing

Applications of Statistical Sampling to Auditing

ALVIN A. ARENS, PhD, CPA

Price Waterhouse Auditing Professor
Michigan State University

JAMES K. LOEBBECKE, CPA

Professor
Graduate School of Business
University of Utah

Prentice-Hall, Inc., Englewood Cliffs, New Jersey 07632

Library of Congress Cataloging in Publication Data

ARENS, ALVIN A
   Applications of statistical sampling to auditing.

   Includes index.
   1.–Auditing. 2.–Sampling (Statistics)
I.–Loebbecke, James K., joint author. II.–Title.
HF5667.A689   657'.45'0151952   80-26352
ISBN 0-13-039156-5

Editorial/production supervision by Alice Erdman
Cover design by 20/20 Services, Inc.
Manufacturing Buyer: Ray Keating

Printed in the United States of America

10 9 8 7 6 5 4 3 2 1

Prentice-Hall International, Inc., *London*
Prentice-Hall of Australia Pty. Limited, *Sydney*
Prentice-Hall of Canada, Ltd., *Toronto*
Prentice-Hall of India Private Limited, *New Delhi*
Prentice-Hall of Japan, Inc., *Tokyo*
Prentice-Hall of Southeast Asia Pte. Ltd., *Singapore*
Whitehall Books Limited, *Wellington, New Zealand*

contents

8

9

10

11

preface

OBJECTIVES

In writing the text the following six objectives were emphasized.

1. *Provide an introduction to statistical sampling for use in auditing.* The overriding consideration in writing the book is that it is intended for readers who have limited experience in statistical methods. Anyone with a background in auditing should be able to understand the text material, even if his or her background in statistics is lacking.

2. *Emphasize the readability of the material.* The book should be understandable and readable even for those with weak backgrounds in statistics. Naturally, for a statistics book to be useful, there must be sufficient technical material to enable the user to properly apply statistical methods.

3. *Provide enough information to enable auditors to apply statistical methods.* It is important that any student using this text should be provided sufficient information to actually do an entire statistical application correctly from beginning to end. In meeting this objective, comprehensive examples have been provided for applying statistical methodology to auditing.

4. *Identify the most common audit areas where each statistical method could most likely be applied.* A large number of alternative statistical methods can be applied to any given audit situation, but users of statistical methods must be able to determine which method is the most appropriate for a given situation. The text provides guidelines to help users with this decision process.

5. *Identify the most common difficulties auditors are likely to encounter in using statistical methods.* A major problem facing users of statistical methods for audit purposes is the potential for misusing the statistics. There is also the danger of using a method more costly than necessary to achieve the desired results. In each chapter where a statistical method is outlined, difficulties and concerns the auditor should have are addressed.

6. *Provide sufficient problem material to give users an opportunity to practice the statistical method.* It is difficult to develop an understanding of statistical methods without actually practicing their use through problem materials. Extensive problems are provided at varying levels of complexity to permit such practice. Solutions are available in a separate Solutions Manual.

BACKGROUND NEEDED

An understanding of basic auditing concepts is more important for using this book than an understanding of basic statistics. It is difficult to properly apply statistical methods to auditing until the reader has a good understanding of the objectives of the audit process. That understanding should be developed before the technical material in this book is used. Our experience in teaching this subject is that basic statistics courses are helpful but not essential.

INTENDED AUDIENCE

This text is potentially useful in four ways.

1. *As a supplement to the basic auditing course.* Instructors frequently want to spend more time on statistical methods in auditing than is practical with most auditing textbooks. Portions of the text could be conveniently used as a part of such a course.

2. *As a supplement or significant part of a second course in auditing at either the graduate or undergraduate level.* Such courses are becoming increasingly common in auditing education. The material in this text could be a major part of such a course.

3. *As primary text material for continuing education of auditors in statistical methods.* The material in this book is practical and applicable to actual audit situations. It could be used for a series of short courses in statistical methods in auditing, or for a longer, more intensive course.

4. *As a reference book for the use of statistical sampling in practice.* Practitioners will find the book useful as reference material when they plan to use statistical sampling in a specific audit area. It provides guidance on how to use statistical methods, as well as the best methods to apply in varying audit situations and potential problems to avoid.

ORGANIZATION

The first two chapters are the introduction and the use of random selection. The remainder of the book emphasizes various types and proper use of statistical methods available to auditors. Chapter topics and a brief introduction to each chapter follow.

Chapter	Topic	Brief Discussion
1	Introduction	The introductory chapter provides background information about the auditing process. For a student of auditing with a good understanding of auditing concepts, this chapter can be covered quickly. No statistical sampling material is found in this chapter.
2	Random Selection	This chapter, which deals with the problems of selecting samples from populations, should be covered before any subsequent chapters because the concepts and methods apply to all other text materials. It includes random number tables, systematic selection and computer terminals.
3	Attributes Sampling	In covering the appropriate uses and benefits of attributes sampling, emphasis is given to the methodology for using attributes, the decisions that must be made, and the audit implications of the results.
4	Variables Sampling	This chapter on variables sampling is important for the concepts it contains rather than for specific applications. The information it presents on variables sampling helps to provide a foundation for subsequent chapters.
5	Difference Estimation	Difference estimation is the first variables sampling technique covered because of its frequent use in practice and ease of understanding in an auditing context. The emphasis is to insure that readers know how to use difference estimation properly, the shortcomings of the method, and its strengths. The chapter includes a comprehensive illustration of a typical application in practice and situations where difference estimation is most likely to be used.
6	Ratio Estimation	This chapter parallels the previous one and demonstrates the similarities and differences between ratio and difference estimation. Use of the major Chapter 5 illustration shows that results are frequently similar for ratio and difference estimation.
7	Mean-per-Unit Estimation	This chapter shows where mean-per-unit is most likely to be applied in audit situations while demonstrating its proper use. Throughout the chapter it is shown that unstratified mean-per-unit estimation is used in relatively few audit situations.
8	Stratified Sampling	This chapter emphasizes stratified mean-per-unit sampling methodology, but also includes stratified ratio and difference estimation. The benefits of stratification are demonstrated and problems in determining strata and sample size for each stratum are shown. The ideal use of stratified sampling requires the use of a computer, but some benefits may be realized without a computer. Again, the benefits and problems of stratification as well as the likely situations where stratified sampling are applicable are shown.
9	Dollar Unit Sampling	This statistical method is presented in a simple understandable manner. It is related to both attributes and variables sampling covered earlier in the text. The benefits of using dollar unit sampling as well as its problems are covered. The most likely uses of dollar unit sampling are also shown.

Chapter	Topic	Brief Discussion
10	Use of Statistical Techniques in Analytical Tests	This chapter introduces some more advanced statistical methods for evaluating whether financial statements appear reasonable, based upon analytical test results. The chapter includes a discussion of linear regression analysis and an introduction to the concepts of Markov chain processes and discriminant analysis. The chapter is intended more as an introduction to the potential for more advanced statistical methods than an application that most practitioners could use without further study.
11	Strategy Development in the Use of Statistical Sampling	The last chapter summarizes the previous chapters, emphasizing the decisions that auditors must make, how those decisions are made, and the implications of those decisions. A summary examines the appropriate uses of the various statistical methods, when they should be used, and the advantages and disadvantages of each statistical method. This chapter should be especially useful to the reader who has studied the text material, understands the basic statistical concepts, and is now attempting to determine which statistical method to use.

PROBLEM MATERIALS

Extensive problem materials are included for each chapter. Some of the problems deal with basic statistical concepts. Others deal with the decisions that auditors make in applying statistical methods. Simple and complex problems deal with statistical calculations, the methodology of statistical sampling, and making audit decisions based on the results of the statistical applications.

The materials were developed by the authors, selected from CPA examination problems, and provided by several CPA firms. The material provided by the CPA firms, for the most part, was taken from continuing education seminars. Some materials were modified.

ACKNOWLEDGMENTS

We gratefully acknowledge the financial support provided by the Price Waterhouse Foundation for a graduate assistantship, typing, editing, and proofreading.

We are indebted to the American Institute of Certified Public Accountants, Inc., for permission to use copyright © materials from *Uniform CPA Examination Questions and Answers* which have been adapted for use in this text, and for permission to quote from *Statements on Auditing Standards*. Problem materials supplied by Price Waterhouse & Co., Ernst & Whinney, and Touche, Ross & Co. are very much appreciated.

Two reviewers of the completed text material also made significant contributions to the text: Professor Bart Ward, University of Oklahoma, and Price Waterhouse Professor William L. Felix, Jr., of the University of Washington.

The assistance of Richard L. Hartwick, a Ph.D. candidate at Michigan State University, in writing and reviewing certain solutions materials and in reviewing the entire text, was invaluable. We also appreciate the help of Ellen Foxman and Patti Bills for extensive editing and typing in the preparation of the manuscript.

We would also like to especially acknowledge Professor John Neter of the University of Georgia for the encouragement and assistance he has given us in our study of statistical sampling in auditing over the years.

Finally, the continuing encouragement and support of our families contributed in large measure to the completion of this book.

1

audit methodology

INTRODUCTION

The objective of most audits by independent auditors is to determine whether or not the financial statements of the auditor's client conform to generally accepted accounting principles. Deciding on the amount of evidence necessary to satisfy this objective is one of the most challenging problems the auditor faces. Chapter 1 identifies the major considerations affecting the evidence decision and summarizes the methodology competent practitioners follow.

THE AUDITOR'S RESPONSIBILITY

The third standard of fieldwork sets forth in general terms the requirements for evidence accumulation: "Sufficient competent evidential matter is to be obtained through inspection, observation, inquiry and confirmation to afford a reasonable basis for an opinion regarding the financial statements under examination."[1]

---

[1]*Codification of Statements on Auditing Standards*, Para. 330.01.

The key phrase in the standard is "a reasonable basis." The profession and the courts have both clearly indicated that auditors are not guarantors or insurers of the accuracy of the statements. Auditors would have to accumulate far more evidence than they now do if they were responsible for ascertaining the correctness of the financial statements with complete certainty. In addition, the costs of audits would be unacceptable if this were done.

Thus, the position the profession has taken is that the auditor's responsibility is limited to performing the audit investigation and reporting the results *in accordance with generally accepted auditing standards*. This includes the concepts of *reasonable assurance* and *materiality* that constitute the term "a reasonable basis" in the standard cited above.

Following this standard, the auditor will gather enough evidence to support the judgment that there is a relatively high probability that no material errors exist in the financial statements. In this regard, "errors" may be due to misrepresentation by management or employee fraud (these are termed "irregularities" in the professional literature), or to unintentional mistakes and omissions.

OVERALL LEVEL OF ASSURANCE

A critical judgment in every audit is how high the level of assurance to be attained must be. The *overall level of assurance* is the subjectively determined certainty that the auditor has of the fair presentation of the financial statements after the audit is completed. The higher the level of certainty attained, the more confident is the auditor that the financial statements contain no material misstatements or omissions. One hundred percent assurance would be certainty, and zero assurance would be complete uncertainty.

The higher the level of assurance the auditor demands, the more evidence he or she must obtain, since the auditor achieves assurance by gathering evidence. Of course, the quality of the evidence is a factor here, too. Since the greater the amount of evidence, the greater the cost, the basic audit decision of the proper level of assurance boils down to a cost–benefit equation. The important question is, at what point does the additional cost of acquiring more evidence exceed the benefit obtained from the additional information?

There is a close relationship between confidence level, as it is used in statistical sampling, and overall level of assurance, but they are also different. Confidence level in statistical sampling in an audit context, as discussed in subsequent chapters, deals with the probability of the absence of material errors for *one specific audit test*. Overall level of assurance deals with the probability of the absence of material errors in the overall financial statements after all audit tests, statistical and non-statistical, have been combined.

It is not possible to quantify the *overall* level of assurance achieved in an audit. It is practical to obtain a measure of the assurance for some individual audit procedures by using statistical sampling techniques; however, there is no objective measurement method for many types of audit tests. Because of this, auditors at present have no means of objectively combining levels of assurance. Therefore, the idea of a reasonable level of assurance is subjective, is determined by the auditor's professional judgment, and is expressed in terms of high levels, reasonable levels, or even low levels of assurance in some circumstances.

Effect of Different Circumstances on Level of Assurance

In order to achieve consistent performance in the profession, it would be desirable for the overall level of assurance attained by all auditors on all audits to be approximately the same. Nevertheless, there are two situations in which the auditor will generally alter the desired level of assurance based on his appraisal of the circumstances. These are as follows:

1. *The degree to which external users rely upon the statements.* When external users place heavy reliance upon the financial statements, it is appropriate that the auditor's overall level of assurance be increased. When the statements are extensively relied upon, a great social harm could result if a significant error were to remain undetected in the financial statements. The cost of additional evidence can be more easily justified when the loss to users from material errors is substantial. Several factors are good indicators of the degree to which statements are relied upon by external users. These include client size as measured by total assets or revenues, the degree to which the stock is widely distributed, and the nature and amount of the client's liabilities.

2. *The likelihood of the client's filing bankruptcy subsequent to the audit.* If a client is forced to file bankruptcy or even just suffers a significant loss subsequent to the completion of the audit, there is a much greater chance of the auditor being required to defend the quality of the audit than if the client were under no financial strain. There is a natural tendency for those who lose money in a bankruptcy or because of a stock price reversal to file suit against the auditor. This can result from the honest belief that the auditor failed to conduct an adequate audit, or from the users' desire to recover part of their loss regardless of the adequacy of the audit work.

In those situations where the auditor believes the chance of bankruptcy or loss is high, the overall level of assurance should be increased. If a subsequent challenge does occur, the auditor will then be in a much better position to successfully defend the audit results. The total audit evidence and the audit costs will increase in this circumstance, but this is justifiable because of the additional risk of lawsuits that the auditor faces.

It is difficult for an auditor to predict a bankruptcy before it occurs, but certain factors are good indicators of an increased probability of bankruptcy. They include the liquidity position of the client, profit or losses in previous years, the degree to which the client has financed growth through debt, and the competence and integrity of management.

EXPECTATION OF MATERIAL ERRORS

In addition to deciding on the overall level of assurance, it is also necessary for the auditor to assess the likelihood of material errors in the statements. A prudent auditor spends more time looking for errors in areas where they are apt to exist than where they probably do not.

Certain factors in the engagement should be used to predict material errors. It is the auditor's responsibility to *identify* the factors in a given audit affecting the expectation of errors, *evaluate* the significance of each, and *modify* the evidence to take each significant factor into account. Due to the lack of a precise measurement system, the effect of each factor must be evaluated subjectively. The most important factors the auditor should keep in mind throughout the engagement are identified and briefly discussed in this section.

System of Internal Control

The client's system of internal control greatly affects the auditor's expectation of errors and therefore the evidence the auditor accumulates. A thorough evaluation of the system must be completed before the audit can be regarded as adequate, and the results of this evaluation will aid the auditor in determining what evidence is to be accumulated throughout the audit. If the auditor believes the client's controls are sufficient to provide reasonable assurance that there are likely to be no material errors in the records, it is possible to keep the evidence accumulation fairly low. On the other hand, if the auditor believes the controls are so weak as to significantly increase the expectation of errors, it will be necessary to expand the audit tests accordingly to determine whether material errors actually exist. Internal control is such an important factor in evidence accumulation that it is discussed separately and integrated into subsequent chapters.

Materiality

The concept of materiality as it relates to auditing is simply that the auditor should concentrate on the financial statement information that is important and put less emphasis on the less significant accounts and transactions. This attitude is justified because auditors are concerned that the financial statements be reasonably stated, not necessarily correct to the penny. For example, in most cases, if the verification of a small supplies account is limited to a brief review and the primary audit emphasis is placed on verifying accounts receivable and inventory, the auditor will have a higher overall level of assurance than if an equal amount of time were devoted to each of these accounts. Similarly, it is usually better to emphasize the verification of larger transactions and subsidiary balances rather than to test without regard to items' size.

Population Size

Population size is closely related to materiality, but it is of sufficient importance to be considered as a separate factor. In general, it is reasonable to expect more errors to exist in a large population than in a small one, unless there are compensating factors. Therefore, the population size has traditionally been an important determinant of the auditor's sample size. The advent of statistical sampling in auditing has changed auditors' attitudes about the importance of population size. The population size affects the sample size when statistical sampling is used, but only to a certain point; as we shall see later on, a doubling of the population, for example, might have little effect on the number of items in the sample.

Makeup of the Population

The individual items making up the total of a population also frequently affect the auditor's expectation of a material error being included. For example, most auditors would be more concerned about the possibility of a material misstatement in a population of accounts receivable containing a small number of large customer balances than if there were a large number of small accounts. To compensate for the greater possibility of a significant error, a larger percentage of the accounts with bigger customer balances would normally be confirmed, and a different type of confirmation would be used. The nature and the source of individual transactions within a total balance also affect the audit tests. Transactions with affiliated companies, amounts due from officers, cash disbursements made payable to cash, and accounts receivable outstanding for several months are examples of situations requiring greater investigation because there is usually a higher likelihood of errors than in more typical transactions.

Initial versus Repeat Engagement

Evidence accumulation when the audit is being performed for a new client is different from that for one that has been an audit client in previous years. There are three primary reasons for this:

1. *On an initial engagement, it is necessary to verify the details making up those balance sheet accounts that are of a permanent nature, such as fixed assets, patents, and retained earnings.*

2. *It is necessary to verify the beginning balances in the balance sheet accounts on an initial engagement.* This step is necessary even if comparative financial statements are

not issued, because the accuracy of the current year's income statement is dependent on the accuracy of the beginning balances in the balance sheet accounts.

3. *The auditor is less familiar with the client's operations in an initial audit.* The lack of knowledge about a client's operations includes such considerations as unfamiliarity with the system of internal control, absence of reliable historical ratios and balances with which to compare the current year's results, and nonexistence of previous years' audit evidence and conclusions as a basis for developing a current year's audit program.

Results of the Current and Previous Audits

An auditor would be considered negligent if the results of the preceding year's examination were ignored during the development of the current year's audit program. If the auditor found a significant number of errors in the preceding year in an audit area such as inventory pricing, extensive testing would have to be done in the current audit as a means of determining whether the deficiency in the client's system had been corrected. On the other hand, if no errors have been found for the past several years in tests of an audit area, the auditor is justified in reducing the audit tests, provided that the internal control review indicates that the system has not deteriorated.

If, during the current year audit, the auditor finds errors leading to the conclusion that the total population being tested may be improperly stated, he must ultimately determine whether this conclusion is true. Before the tests are completed, the auditor must either (1) ascertain by additional testing that the original sample was not representative of an essentially satisfactory population, or (2) take corrective action regarding the population.

Other Factors

Several other factors also affect the expectation of errors. Following are some of the important situations in which the auditor can expect a high probability of errors:

1. *The transaction is an unusual one for the client.* Unusual transactions are more likely to be incorrectly recorded by the client than routine transactions, because the client lacks experience in recording them. Therefore, transactions that occur with relative infrequency for a particular client should be carefully scrutinized by the auditor. Examples include fire losses, major property acquisitions, disposals of assets, and lease agreements.

2. *The account being verified contains transactions or information that require considerable accounting judgment to record properly.* Transactions for major repairs or partial replacement of assets are examples of this type of situation. It is common for inexperienced accountants to record these transactions as repairs when company policy dictates that they should be recorded as assets, or vice versa.

3. *The asset being verified is highly susceptible to defalcation.* The auditor should be concerned about the risk of possible defalcation in situations where it is relatively

easy to convert company assets to personal use. Such is the case when currency or highly marketable inventory is not closely controlled.

4. *There is some motivation for the client to misstate the financial statements.* In many situations, management may believe that it would be advantageous to misstate the financial statements. For example, if management receives a percentage of total profits as a bonus, there may be a tendency to overstate net income.

5. *The client lacks basic integrity.* When management is dominated by a few individuals who lack the integrity to obey the law, the likelihood of significantly misrepresented financial statements is greatly increased.

The major difference between the factors affecting the overall level of assurance and those affecting the auditor's expectation of errors is the more *specific nature* of the latter. Evaluating the factors affecting the proper assurance has the effect of requiring higher or lower levels of overall assurance; by implication, additional or less evidence is needed in *all* audit areas. For example, the widespread distribution of client ownership implies the need for increased evidence in most facets of the audit, because a higher level of overall assurance is desired. The factors affecting the expectation of errors, on the other hand, guide the auditor toward emphasizing particular parts of the audit. For example, if there were numerous errors in the confirmation of accounts receivable in the preceding year's audit, accounts receivable should ordinarily be heavily emphasized in the current year.

OVERVIEW OF THE AUDIT PROCESS

Audits should be planned and executed as efficiently as possible to maximize the likelihood of uncovering all material errors and to minimize cost. It is useful to think of an audit as *an integrated process* in which the information gained early in the engagement is used throughout the entire audit and there is no duplication of effort. The overview of the audit process described in Figure 1-1 and discussed below is meant to achieve these goals.

Obtain a General Understanding of the Client

It is not possible to conduct an adequate audit without an understanding of the client's business and the factors affecting the auditor's level of assurance and expectation of errors. There are several steps and types of information in this category:

1. *Obtain background information for the audit.* Background information enables the auditor to better understand the peculiarities of the client's industry and business. The following are several means of obtaining this information:

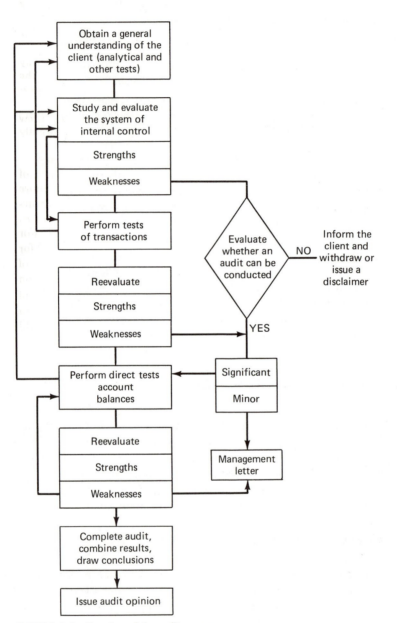

FIGURE 1-1 Overview of the audit process

- Obtain a letter of engagement detailing restrictions and client assistance.
- Read AICPA industry audit guides and industry textbooks and magazines.
- Review the permanent working papers file for general information and company policies.
- Tour the client's facilities.
- Investigate the results of previous audits.

2. *Perform analytical tests.* Analytical tests include the review of the records for unusual items, and calculations and comparison by the auditor of ratios and trends in the client's records. The ratios should include industry ratios and percentages to help in understanding the client's industry and business, indicate impending financial difficulty, and identify potential errors in the statements. Analytical tests of internal data are also useful. They include comparison of budgets with actual operating results, comparison of total or detail of an account balance with prior years, and the computation of ratios and percentage relationships for comparison with previous years.

3. *Obtain information concerning the client's legal obligations.* The legal commitments of the client, including such items as government regulations, the corporate charter and bylaws, corporate minutes, and contracts of all types, must be understood before it is possible to evaluate whether the financial statements are fairly stated.

4. *Evaluate the possibility of management involvement in fraud.* In recent years there has been an increasing incidence of involvement by management in fraudulent activities, including the massive theft of company assets and the issuance of intentionally misleading financial statements. A well-known example is the Equity Funding fraud. An evaluation of the environmental factors affecting the predictability of these frauds is useful in helping the auditor decide upon the proper evidence to accumulate. Following are a number of factors that increase the opportunity for management fraud:

- The integrity of management is questionable.
- The management is dominated by one or a few individuals.
- The accounting and financial functions appear to be understaffed, resulting in constant crisis conditions.
- The company seems to need, but lacks, an adequate internal audit staff.
- The company follows the practice of using different auditors for major subsidiaries or branches.
- The auditor must make numerous significant adjusting entries as a part of the audit.
- Heavy reliance is placed on computers without adequate internal controls.

Study and Evaluate the System of Internal Control

One of the most widely accepted concepts in the theory and practice of auditing is the importance of the client's accounting system, with its attendant internal controls, in generating reliable financial information. If the auditor is convinced the client has an excellent system, which includes controls for providing reliable data and for safeguarding assets and records, the amount of audit evidence to be accumulated can be significantly less than if the system is not adequate. On the other hand, in some instances, the controls may be so inadequate as to preclude conducting an effective audit.

The first step in the study and evaluation of the client's system of internal control is to *determine how it operates*. This is done by means of the auditor's review of organizational charts and procedural manuals, by discussions with client personnel, and by completing internal control questionnaires and flowcharts.

The second step is to make a *preliminary evaluation* of whether the system has been designed to effectively achieve the objectives of good control, including the prevention and/or timely detection and correction of errors. This evaluation involves identifying specific controls providing substance to the system that the auditor may be willing to rely upon to reduce certain audit tests, and identifying areas of the system where errors are more likely to occur owing to the absence of controls. This process is referred to by auditors as *identifying the strengths and weaknesses of the system*.

When the controls are so inadequate that it cannot reasonably be determined whether the statements are fairly presented, the auditor should withdraw from the engagement or issue a disclaimer. The client should be informed of all weaknesses discovered in the study of the system by the use of a *management letter* whenever an audit is performed.

Perform Tests of Transactions

The examination of underlying documentation and the performance of mechanical accuracy tests constitute the *testing of individual transactions*. The primary purpose of tests of transactions is to determine that the client's controls, which the auditor tends to rely upon to reduce other audit tests, have been complied with.

It is also often appropriate to test transactions when there are apparent weaknesses in the system. For example, if supporting documentation for purchase transactions is inadequate, the auditor may examine vendors' invoices, receiving reports, and other documents to be sure there are no material invalid transactions. This is referred to as a *substantive test of transactions* and has the objective of searching for monetary errors that affect the account. In virtually all tests of transactions, some substantive testing is performed simultaneously with compliance testing (termed *dual-purpose tests*).

The lines indicating an upward flow of information on the left side of Figure 1-1 are included to show that the auditor is constantly obtaining additional information about the client and the existing system of internal control. New information is obtained and used from the beginning to the end of the engagement.

Reevaluation

When the tests of transactions have been completed, the results must be carefully analyzed to determine whether the system is operating as effectively as the auditor originally believed. Those controls that are operating satisfactorily can be relied upon, and as a result, the direct tests of account balances can be reduced. For those controls where the system is not operating effectively, the auditor cannot rely upon the system but must act as if the control did not exist and increase other tests accordingly.

Similarly, if significant substantive tests of transactions have been performed, the results will influence the extent of direct tests of the account balances affected. If no monetary errors are found in the transactions, a reduced expectation of errors in the related account balances will result. This will allow the auditor to reduce the extent of direct tests pertaining to the types of errors tested. If errors are found in the transactions tested, additional tests of account balances will result unless the errors are clearly not significant.

Perform Direct Tests of Account Balances

The ending balances in the balance sheet and income statement accounts are verified by physical observation, documentation, and other types of evidence. Examples include the confirmation of accounts and notes receivable, the physical observation of inventory, and the examination of vendors' statements for accounts payable. These tests of ending balances are essential to the conduct of the audit because, for the most part, the evidence is obtained from a source independent of the client, and thus is considered to be of high quality.

There is a close relationship between the general review of the client's circumstances, the results of the evaluation and tests of the system of internal control, and the direct tests of the financial statement account balances. If the auditor has achieved a reasonable level of assurance about the fair presentation of the financial statements through the general review of internal control and tests of its effectiveness, the direct tests can be significantly reduced. In all instances, however, some tests of the financial statement accounts are necessary.

Reevaluation

The results of the direct tests of account balances also provide additional information about the system. If significant errors are found, it may be necessary to rechallenge the quality of internal controls and to perform additional tests to determine whether the financial statements are fairly presented. This step highlights the interrelationship of the different parts of the audit. The auditor's opinion about the client's organization and system of internal control is constantly revised as more information is obtained. At the completion of the engagement, the auditor should have an excellent understanding of the client's system and the business in general.

Complete the Audit, Combine the Results of All the Tests, and Draw Conclusions

In addition to direct tests of the financial statement account balances, the auditor must carry out such procedures as testing for material subsequent events and reviewing the working papers.

After the auditor has completed all the procedures, it is necessary to combine the information obtained in such a manner as to reach an *overall* conclusion as to whether the financial statements are fairly presented. This is a highly subjective process that relies heavily upon the auditor's professional judgment.

Issue an Audit Opinion

After sufficient evidence has been accumulated to satisfy the auditor as to whether the financial statements are fairly presented, an audit opinion is given. The auditor can never be completely certain about the statements, but a satisfactory level of assurance considering the risk factors in the audit must be reached. If the auditor is satisfied that the statements are fairly presented, the standard short-form report can be issued. Otherwise, a qualified, disclaimer, or adverse opinion must be given.

AUDITOR'S EVIDENCE DECISIONS

There are four ways the auditor can change the evidence accumulated in an engagement: through the audit procedures selected, the size of audit samples, the timing of the tests, and the particular items selected for testing. Each of these should be carefully decided upon for a particular engagement to achieve the desired level of assurance after consideration of the factors discussed in this chapter. Each of these four decisions is discussed briefly below.

Appropriate Audit Procedures

There are some procedures for each audit area that will almost always be used. These are the *minimum audit procedures*. If many actual audit programs of highly regarded CPA firms for many different clients were examined, those audit procedures common to all of them would be the minimum audit program. Neither the AICPA nor any other group serving more than one firm has ever specified a set of minimum audit procedures for each audit area. It is the responsibility of every firm to decide for itself its minimum standard of performance.

The minimum audit program is insufficient for most audits. The auditor must perform other audit procedures beyond these to take into account unusual situations in the engagement. Professional judgment comes into play in recognizing such situations and modifying the procedures accordingly. The factors of interest to the auditor in making this judgment include all those previously discussed in this chapter. For example, a weakness in internal control may result in procedures beyond those normally done.

Also, in most circumstances, the auditor will have a variety of procedures to choose from in achieving a particular objective. The choice will be governed by the relative quality of the evidence the procedure offers, balanced against the practical considerations of performing the procedure, including the costs involved.

A Proper Sample Size

Sample size should vary depending upon the same circumstances in the audit that affect the adequacy and selection of audit procedures. In most cases, the same factors that determine whether additional audit procedures should be used will have a major influence on the actual sample size. For example, an inadequacy in the system of internal control requires an increase in the number of audit procedures; it is also likely to cause a need for an increased sample size for some tests.

For most audits, determining the proper sample size is a more difficult decision than selecting the proper audit procedures, because most of the procedures are apt to be a part of the minimum audit program. In such situations, it is only necessary to decide whether to add one or two more procedures. It would be rare, even in those audit areas where the minimum audit program is not extensive, to add more than four or five. On the other hand, in selecting the proper sample size, the variation can be anywhere from a small number to all the items in the population. Since population size for different clients can vary in certain audit areas—such as cash disbursements and inventory—from a few dozen to hundreds of thousands, the sample size decision is indeed difficult. The problem is further complicated by the fact that a minimum sample size has not been well defined by either the organized profession or individual practitioners.

Wherever it is applicable, the use of statistical sampling is desirable in helping the auditor select the appropriate sample size. Statistical sampling techniques do not change the basic sample size decision, but they do help formalize the auditor's judgment. This will become apparent later when the use of statistical sampling is discussed in detail.

The Timing of the Procedures

The decision as to when to perform audit procedures is less difficult and less important than the decisions about proper audit procedures and sample size. Nevertheless, timing cannot be ignored. For a better understanding of the audit timing decision, it is necessary to be familiar with the time framework in which the auditor operates.

Certain audit procedures are usually done *as close to the balance sheet date as practical*. These are primarily tests of the most important current assets, such as the physical count of cash, securities, and inventory, and the confirmation of accounts receivable. The reason for testing these types of assets near year-end is their relatively fast turnover. If the assets are not tested at that time, it is often difficult to verify them at a later date. When the client's system of internal control is considered reliable, it is common to perform the tests somewhat earlier or later than the balance sheet date.

The tests of transactions of the client's system of internal control should be done *for the entire period under audit* wherever practicable, and they should be done before the direct tests of balances. This is because the results of the tests of transactions are a major determinant of the remaining audit evidence needed to reach a conclusion about the fair presentation of the financial statements.

The timing of audit tests other than tests of transactions and certain direct tests of current assets depends upon when the client has the records and documents prepared. After the end of the client's fiscal year, such *accounting tasks* as the pricing of inventory, computation of depreciation, and adjustment of prepaid expenses must be completed before the financial statements are ready for audit. It typically takes several weeks before the client's financial records are sufficiently complete to perform many of the necessary audit tests.

The Items Selected for Testing

The most important considerations in selecting the sample items from a population are (1) obtaining a representative sample of the entire population, and (2) emphasizing those items most likely to be in error. These can both be accomplished by taking a larger portion of certain types of items and, at the same time, making sure that some of each type of item is included. For example, in confirming accounts receivable, the auditor is likely to want to test the large balances and the balances that have been outstanding for a long period of time more extensively than the small and current balances. If the combined total of all the small balances is material, a representative sample of these accounts should also be selected.

SUGGESTED READINGS AND REFERENCES

AICPA, *Codification of Statements on Auditing Standards*. Chicago: Commerce Clearing House, Inc.:

  Section 320— The Auditor's Study and Evaluation of Internal Control
  Section 320A—Relationship of Statistical Sampling to Generally Accepted Auditing Standards
  Section 320B—Precision and Reliability for Statistical Sampling in Auditing
  Section 330— Evidential Matter

ARENS, ALVIN A., and JAMES K. LOEBBECKE, *Auditing: An Integrated Approach*, 2nd ed. Englewood Cliffs, N.J.: Prentice-Hall, 1980.

ELLIOTT, ROBERT K., and JOHN R. ROGERS, "Relating Statistical Sampling to Audit Objectives," *Journal of Accountancy*, July 1972, pp. 46–55.

ROBERTS, DONALD M., "A Statistical Interpretation of SAP No. 54," *Journal of Accountancy*, March 1974, pp. 47–53.

TAYLOR, ROBERT G., "Error Analysis in Audit Tests," *Journal of Accountancy*, May 1974, pp. 78, 80–82.

REVIEW QUESTIONS

1-1. Distinguish between the terms *errors* and *irregularities* as used in the professional literature. What is the difference in the auditor's responsibility for the discovery of errors as compared to irregularities?

1-2. Describe what is meant by an overall level of assurance. Explain why each of the following statements is true:
  a. A CPA firm should attempt to achieve the same overall level of assurance for all audit clients with approximately the same circumstances.
  b. A CPA firm should increase the overall level of assurance for audit clients where external users rely heavily upon the statements.
  c. A CPA firm should increase the overall level of assurance for audit clients where there is a reasonably high likelihood of a client's filing bankruptcy.
  d. Different CPA firms should attempt to achieve reasonably uniform overall levels of assurance for clients with similar circumstances.

1-3. State the two categories of circumstances that determine the overall level of assurance and list the factors that the auditor can use to indicate the degree to which each category exists.

1-4. When an auditor issues an unqualified opinion, it is the same for a publicly held company and a small, closely held firm. What justification is there for providing lower levels of assurance for closely held companies than for listed companies if the audit report is the same? Justify it from the point of view of auditors and users of financial statements.

1-5. Auditors have not been successful in measuring the levels of assurance achieved in different audits. How is it possible to think in terms of obtaining increased or decreased levels of assurance without a precise means of measuring the level achieved?

1-6. Explain the logic that results in the conclusion that the auditor should accumulate more audit evidence when there is a high expectation of errors than when there is a low expectation.

1-7. List the factors affecting the auditor's expectation of error and explain why each factor should affect the evidence needed to achieve a given level of assurance.

1-8. Explain the relationship between the factors affecting the expectation of error, the desired overall level of assurance, and the accumulation of audit evidence.

1-9. Assume that the client's internal controls over the recording and classifying of permanent asset additions are considered weak because the person responsible for recording new acquisitions has inadequate technical training and limited experience in accounting. How would this situation affect the evidence you should accumulate in auditing permanent assets as compared with another audit where the controls are excellent? Be as specific as possible.

1-10. Each of the following questions concerns the concept of materiality in auditing:
   a. What criteria should the auditor use in deciding whether an estimated error in inventory, based on a sample, is sufficiently material to require an adjustment to the financial statements?
   b. What criteria should the auditor use in deciding whether an account balance is sufficiently immaterial to justify performing minimal tests rather than extensive audit procedures? Using your criteria, state the conditions when extensive audit procedures are required for cash in the bank, federal income taxes payable, petty cash, and unexpired insurance.
   c. Assume the auditor has decided to perform no detailed tests of factory supplies on hand in the audit of a manufacturing company. List the overall reasonableness tests the auditor should use.

1-11. How would the conduct of an audit of a medium-sized company be affected by the company being a small part of a large conglomerate, as compared with it being a separate entity?

1-12. List and describe the major ways the auditor obtains an understanding of a client and its business. How does the auditor's understanding of the client and its business affect the conduct of the audit?

1-13. Your client, Harper Company, has a contractual commitment as a part of a bond indenture to maintain a current ratio of 2.0. If the ratio falls below that level on the balance sheet date, the entire bond becomes payable immediately. In the current year, the client's financial statements show that the ratio has dropped from 2.6 to 2.05 over the past year. How should this situation affect your audit plan?

1-14. Explain why the auditor must study and evaluate the system of internal control and test its effectiveness as a part of the ordinary audit.

1-15. Explain what is meant by a dual-purpose test. Give an example of one.

1-16. State the relationship between the preliminary evaluation of an internal control system and tests of compliance.

1-17. State the relationship between analytical tests, tests of transactions, and direct tests of balances.

1-18. Identify the four ways the auditor can change evidence in a particular engagement. For each of the four, state a circumstance that may affect the decision.

DISCUSSION QUESTIONS AND PROBLEMS

1-19. (AICPA adapted) Frequently, questions have been raised regarding the responsibility of the independent auditor for the discovery of fraud (including defalcations and other similar irregularities), and concerning the proper course of conduct for the independent auditor when an examination discloses specific circumstances arousing suspicion as to the existence of fraud.

REQUIRED :

a. What are (1) the function and (2) the responsibilities of the independent auditor in the examination of financial statements? Discuss fully, but in this part do not include fraud in the discussion.

b. What are the responsibilities of the independent auditor for the detection of fraud? Discuss fully.

c. What is the independent auditor's proper course of conduct when an examination discloses specific circumstances arousing suspicion as to the existence of fraud?

1-20. You are auditing sales and cash receipts transactions and the related accounts receivable balance for two different companies, each with a balance of $3,000,000. The companies are identical except for the differences specified in situations *a* through *f* below. Each situation is to be considered independently.

Situation	*Company A*	*Company B*
a. Internal control	Excellent controls over sales, cash receipts, and accounts receivable	Weak controls over sales and cash receipts
b. Ownership	Closely held company	Publicly held company
c. Materiality	Total current assets equal $15,000,000	Total current assets equal $4,000,000
d. First-year versus subsequent-year audit	First-year audit of company	Fifth-year audit of company
e. Financial health of company	Client is highly profitable and has no problems meeting its financial obligations	Client is losing money and having difficulty paying its bills
f. Composition of accounts receivable	A small number of large accounts and many small accounts	Many accounts of nearly the same size

REQUIRED:

For each situation, state the effect of the factor under consideration on negative versus positive confirmation, sample size, time of confirmations, and the particular sample items to select for the confirmation of accounts receivable. Give reasons for your answer. State all assumptions you consider appropriate.

1-21. (AICPA adapted) The concept of materiality is important to the CPA in examination of financial statements and expression of opinion upon these statements.

REQUIRED:

Discuss the following:
a. How are materiality (and immateriality) related to the proper presentation of financial statements?
b. In what ways will consideration of materiality affect the CPA in:
   (1) Developing an audit program?
   (2) Performing auditing procedures?
c. What factors and measures should the CPA consider in assessing the materiality of an exception to financial statement presentation?
d. How will the materiality of a CPA's exceptions to financial statements influence the type of opinion he or she expresses? (The relationship of materiality to *each type* of auditor's opinion should be considered in your answer.)

1-22. The last section of Chapter 1 discussed the four evidence decisions that must be made on every audit. These are:
1. Appropriate audit procedures
2. Proper sample size
3. Timing of the procedures
4. Particular items selected for testing
The following questions refer to these and related decisions.

REQUIRED:

a. In addition to the four evidence decisions above, name six decisions other than evidence decisions the auditor must make on a typical audit engagement.
b. For the audit of the client's physical count of inventory, state how each of the four evidence decisions might change depending on the circumstances. Also state the circumstances that are most likely to affect the decision. Organize your answer as follows:

Broad category of evidence decision	*Specific ways to modify evidence decision for audit of physical count*	*Factors affecting the decision*

1-23. Included in the AICPA *Statements on Auditing Standards* in the section on internal control (Section 320B.35) is the following formula:

$$S = 1 - \frac{(1 - R)}{(1 - C)}$$

where:

S = reliability level for substantive tests
R = combined reliability level desired
C = reliance assigned to internal accounting control and other relevant factors

For purposes of this problem, assume the following:
1. 1 minus reliability equals risk.
2. Substantive tests are the same as direct tests of balances. (This is an invalid assumption for most audits.)
3. Internal control reliance and other relevant factors are the same as tests of transactions and analytical tests. (This is an invalid assumption for most audits.)

REQUIRED:

a. Explain what the formula means in terms of overall level of assurance, tests of transactions, analytical tests, and direct tests of balances.
b. Which of the factors in the formula is equivalent to the overall level of assurance? Restate the formula so that it emphasizes the overall level of assurance, assuming that all other factors are known.
c. Assume that the auditor has decided that an overall level of assurance of 99% is appropriate for a given audit. Explain what a 99% overall level of assurance means. What factors would affect the decision to use a 99% assurance level?
d. Assume the auditor has performed analytical tests, evaluated the system of internal control, and tested the system of internal control. The level of reliability gained from these tests is 40%. Given the overall level of assurance of 99% in part *c*, what is the appropriate risk the auditor should be willing to take that direct tests of balances will fail to uncover material errors?

1-24. In the audit of the Worldwide Wholesale Company, you performed extensive ratio and trend analysis. No material exceptions were discovered except for the following:
1. Commission expense as a percentage of sales has stayed constant for several years but has increased significantly in the current year. Commission rates have not changed.
2. The rate of inventory turnover has steadily decreased for four years.
3. Inventory as a percentage of current assets has steadily increased for four years.
4. The number of days' sales in accounts receivable has steadily increased for three years.

5. Allowance for uncollectible accounts as a percentage of accounts receivable has steadily decreased for three years.
6. The absolute amount of depreciation expense and the ratio of depreciation expense to gross fixed assets is significantly smaller than in the preceding year.

REQUIRED:

a. Evaluate the potential significance of each of the factors above for the fair presentation of financial statements.
b. State the follow-up procedures you would use to determine the possibility of material errors.

2

sampling methods

INTRODUCTION

A decision about which items to select from a population of accounting data must be made regardless of whether or not the auditor is using statistical methods. For a sample of 20, for example, the auditor may decide to select the first ten and the last ten population items, the largest 20 items, or a random sample. The way the sample items are selected should be based on a consideration of the alternative sample selection methods available and a reasoned conclusion as to the best alternative.

This chapter includes a study of the sampling methods most commonly used in auditing and presents the circumstances in which each is appropriate. Do not be concerned about the source of any sample size used in the examples. Sample size for different types of audit tests is studied in subsequent chapters.

SAMPLING OBJECTIVES

The selection of sample items should be made only after the auditor establishes specific objectives. Several possible objectives are considered at this point:

1. *An amount of total dollar errors in the population must not be exceeded.* Frequently the auditor is concerned only that the balance in an account is not overstated or understated by a material amount. The amount of the actual population error is not relevant as long as it does not exceed the auditor's specified materiality.

2. *A measure of the amount of dollar errors is desired.* It is usually important to combine the amount of errors uncovered in each audit area that were not considered material enough to adjust individually, to determine their aggregate effect on such totals as current assets, working capital, and net earnings. The only practical way to combine the errors is to first obtain a fairly accurate estimate of the error in each account balance. Another case requiring a measure of the amount of error is one in which the auditor intends to propose a specific adjustment to an account balance.

3. *The rate of error must not exceed a certain amount.* When the system of internal control is being tested, the frequency of compliance deviations (rate of error) is a major consideration in measuring the system's effectiveness. It is common to specify a maximum error rate in the population that the auditor will permit before regarding the controls as unreliable. For example, the auditor may state in a particular situation that it is unnecessary to analyze certain expense accounts if account classification has been approved by the controller for at least 97 percent of all cash disbursement transactions (a maximum error rate of 3 percent).

4. *A measure of the rate of error is desired.* There are some instances where it is insufficient to establish that the rate of error does not exceed a specified amount. An example is where the auditor will perform almost no expense account analysis if the compliance procedure error rate for the account classification is less than 2 percent, will perform some analysis if the error rate is between 2 and 5 percent, and will perform extensive analysis if it exceeds 5 percent.

5. *The auditor desires to affect the future behavior of client personnel.* The psychological effect of an audit on the client's personnel is often not recognized by auditors. When personnel believe they can predict which time period, transaction, or amount the auditor will test, it is likely to affect their performance. For example, the auditor whose primary concern is with large transactions or amounts should leave the impression that it is primarily large dollar items that will be tested. Many times it is desirable to have client personnel believe that all items have an equal chance of selection, in order to encourage care in recording all transactions and amounts.

REPRESENTATIVE SAMPLE

Regardless of the auditor's sampling objectives, the foremost consideration in selecting sample items is to reach the same conclusion about the population on the basis of the sample as would be reached if complete knowledge of the population were obtained.

The primary concern, therefore, is that the sample be *representative* of the entire population in terms of the characteristics of audit interest. The sample characteristics need not be exactly the same as those in the population, but they should be approximately the same to be representative. For example, if the population contains material errors but the sample is almost error-free, the sample is not representative. An improper audit decision is likely when this occurs.

There are some situations in which a representative sample is unnecessary. Auditors frequently examine those population items that are most likely to contain errors. If the error rate or dollar errors are not significant in those, it is usually reasonable to conclude that the overall error rate or total error in dollars is also not material.

JUDGMENTAL SELECTION METHODS

A judgmentally selected sample is the selection of the sample items on the basis of sound reasoning by the auditor. Testing all repairs and maintenance expense items in excess of $1,000 is an example of judgmental selection.

The use of judgmental selection is widespread even by auditors who are strong advocates of statistical methods. There are parts of every audit where statistical methods either are not applicable, are insufficient, or are more costly than is justifiable.

The three most important methods of judgmental selection are *intentional bias, block sampling,* and *haphazard.*

Intentional Bias

Intentional bias is the selection of each item in the sample based on some judgmental criteria established by the auditor. Three general categories are common:

1. *Items most likely to contain errors.* Frequently, auditors are able to identify which population items are most likely to be in error, should errors exist. Examples are receivables outstanding for a long time, purchases from and sales to officers and affiliated companies, unusually large or complex transactions, and miscellaneous credits to cash in bank. These kinds of items can be efficiently investigated by the auditor and the results applied to the population on a judgmental basis.

2. *Items containing population characteristics.* The auditor may be able to describe the various types and sources of items that constitute the population and design the sample to be representative by selecting one or more items of each type. For example, a sample of disbursements might include some from each month, each bank account or location, and each major type of purchase.

3. *Large dollar coverage.* A sample can often be selected that covers such a large portion of total population dollars (as in the example of repairs and maintenance expense items) that the risk of drawing an improper conclusion by not examining small items is not a concern.

Block Sampling

A block sample is the selection of several items in sequence. Once the first item in the block is selected, the remainder of the block is chosen automatically. One example of a block sample is the selection of a *sequence* of 100 sales transactions from the sales journal for the third week of March. A total sample of 100 could also be selected by taking five blocks of 20 items each, ten blocks of ten, or 50 blocks of two.

It is ordinarily acceptable to use block samples only if a reasonable number of blocks is used. If few blocks are used, the probability of obtaining a non-representative sample is too great, considering the possibility of such things as employee turnover, changes in the accounting system, and the seasonal nature of many businesses.

Haphazard

When the auditor goes through a population and selects items for the sample without regard to their size, source, or other distinguishing characteristics, he is attempting to select without bias. This is called a haphazard sample.

The most serious shortcoming of haphazard sampling is the difficulty of remaining completely unbiased in the selection. Because of the auditor's training and "cultural bias," certain population items are more likely than others to be included in the sample.

Although haphazard and block sampling do not appear to be as reasoned as intentional bias sampling, they are often useful as audit tools and should not be automatically discarded. In many situations, the cost of more complex selection methods outweighs the benefits obtained from using them. For example, assume that the auditor wants to trace credits from the accounts receivable subsidiary ledger to the cash receipts journal and other authorized sources as a test for fictitious credits in the subsidiary records. A haphazard or block approach is simpler and less costly than other selection methods in this situation and would be employed by many auditors.

A serious problem whenever judgmental selection is used is the increased likelihood of the client being able to predict which items will be selected. There is a tendency for auditors to use the same selection approach and to include the same biases every year. It is difficult for auditors to avoid following predictable patterns.

STATISTICAL SELECTION METHODS

It is improper and a serious breach of due care to use *statistical measurement techniques* if the sample is selected by any of the judgmental approaches described above. Only valid statistical selection methods are acceptable when the auditor intends to evaluate a population statistically.

The most commonly used valid statistical selection method is a *random sample*. A random sample is defined as one in which every possible combination of elements (items) in the population has an equal chance of constituting the sample. The only way the auditor can be confident he has obtained a random sample is by adopting a formal methodology that is designed to accomplish this. Three methods of random selection are discussed in this book: *random number tables, computer terminals,* and *systematic sampling*. Each of these methods is used in audit practice.

Requirements of Random Selection

The selection of a random sample involves four important requirements. These apply equally to tests of transactions and account balance testing and to each of the three methods of random selection. The requirements are as follows:

1. *The population of interest must be defined.* The population is the set of data about which the auditor wishes to generalize. It is important that the population be defined consistently with the audit objectives. For instance, assume that the auditor decides to test for the possibility of invalid sales. Owing to the nature of the system of internal control, he decides to test the system for the entire year. It is inappropriate to take a random sample of items from only a few months to test for this objective, because the population of interest is the recorded sales for the entire year.

2. *The sampling unit must be defined.* A *sampling unit,* or *element,* is an individual item in the population. All sampling units sum to the population total. An example of a sampling unit is the individual sales invoice for a population of sales invoices, or an individual customer balance for a list of accounts receivable. Naturally, the sampling unit selected must be consistent with the objective of the test. It makes no sense to select shipping documents as the sampling unit if the objective is to test for the validity of recorded sales.

3. *Every possible combination of sampling units must have an equal probability of constituting the sample.* There are two aspects of this requirement. The first is the possibility of a sampling unit having no opportunity of being included. This can happen if some of the sampling units are inadvertently or intentionally excluded from the population. As an illustration, if the auditor is tracing from a file of unnumbered shipping documents as a test of unbilled shipments, it is not possible to determine whether all shipping documents have been included in the file. In fact, the missing documents may be the ones most likely to be in error. The auditor can avoid the problem of omitted sampling units by defining the sampling unit as a prenumbered document, a recorded line item in a journal, or a line item on a listing where the total equals a population control total.

The second aspect is the adoption of a proper methodology to ensure equal probability. The careful use of one of the three acceptable random sampling methods is meant to accomplish this.

4. *Once an item is selected, it must be pursued to a conclusion and included in the compilation of results.* It is inappropriate to discard a randomly selected population item and replace it with another one. Similarly, it is necessary to perform the appropriate audit tests on each item in the sample to determine whether any sample items con-

tain exceptions. When there are exceptions, the nature of each discrepancy must be investigated and included as a part of the generalization from the sample to the population.

Random Number Tables

A *random number table* is a listing of independent random digits conveniently arranged in tabular form to facilitate the selection of random numbers with multiple digits. An example of such a table, taken from the Interstate Commerce Commission "Table of 105,000 Random Decimal Digits," appears as Figure 2-1. This table has numbered lines and columns, with five digits in

| | | | | Columns | | | | |
Item	(1)	(2)	(3)	(4)	(5)	(6)	(7)	(8)
1000	37039	97547	64673	31546	99314	66854	97855	99965
1001	25145	84834	23009	51584	66754	77785	52357	25532
1002	98433	54725	18864	65866	76918	78825	58210	76835
1003	97965	68548	81545	82933	93545	85959	63282	61454
1004	78049	67830	14624	17563	25697	07734	48243	94318
1005	50203	25658	91478	08509	23308	48130	65047	77873
1006	40059	67825	18934	64998	49807	71126	77818	56893
1007	84350	67241	54031	34535	04093	35062	58163	14205
1008	30954	51637	91500	48722	60988	60029	60873	37423
1009	86723	36464	98305	08009	00666	29255	18514	49158
1010	50188	22554	86160	92250	14021	65859	16237	72296
1011	50014	00463	13906	35936	71761	95755	87002	71667
1012	66023	21428	14742	94874	23308	58533	26507	11208
1013	04458	61862	63119	09541	01715	87901	91260	03079
1014	57510	36314	30452	09712	37714	95482	30507	68475
1015	43373	58939	95848	28288	60341	52174	11879	18115
1016	61500	12763	64433	02268	57905	72347	49498	21871
1017	78938	71312	99705	71546	42274	23915	38405	18779
1018	64257	93218	35793	43671	64055	88729	11168	60260
1019	56864	21554	70445	24841	04779	56774	96129	73594
1020	35314	29631	06937	54545	04470	75463	77112	77126
1021	40704	48823	65963	39359	12717	56201	22811	24863
1022	07318	44623	02843	33299	59872	86774	06926	12672
1023	94550	23299	45557	07923	75126	00808	01312	46689
1024	34348	81191	21027	77087	10909	03676	97723	34469
1025	92277	57115	50789	68111	75305	53289	39751	45760
1026	56093	58302	52236	64756	50273	61566	61962	93280
1027	16623	17849	96701	94971	94758	08845	32260	59823
1028	50848	93982	66451	32143	05441	10399	17775	74169
1029	48006	58200	58367	66577	68583	21108	41361	20732
1030	56640	27890	28825	96509	21363	53657	60119	75385

FIGURE 2-1 Random number table

each column, as a convenience in reading the tables and documenting the portion of the table used.

The proper use of random number tables is important to ensure the selection of an unbiased sample. Five major steps are involved in the use of the tables:

1. *Establish a numbering system for the population.* Before a set of random numbers can be selected from the table, each item in the population must be identified with a *unique number.* This is usually not a problem, because many of the populations from which the auditor wants a random sample consist of prenumbered documents. When prenumbered records are not used, some type of numbering system must be developed. In rare instances, the entire population may have to be renumbered, but ordinarily a simple approach can be devised to meet the objective. An illustration is the selection of a random sample of accounts receivable for confirmation from a trial balance that contains forty pages with up to 50 lines per page. The sampling unit can be defined as a line on the listing with an outstanding balance. The combination of page numbers and line numbers provides a unique identifying number for every line in the population.

2. *Establish correspondence between the random number table and the population.* Once the numbering system has been established for the population, correspondence is established by deciding upon the *number of digits* to use in the random number table and their *association with the population numbering system.* For example, assume that the auditor is selecting a sample of 100 duplicate sales invoices from a file of prenumbered sales invoices beginning with document number 3272 and ending with 8825. Since the invoices carry four-digit numbers, it is necessary to use four digits in the random number table. If the first four digits of each five-digit set are used and the starting point in the random number table in Figure 2-1 is item 1000, column 1, the first invoice for inclusion in the sample is 3703. The next three numbers are *outside the range* of the population and are *discarded.* The next sample item is invoice 7804, and so forth.

3. *Establish a route for using the table.* The route defines which digits the auditor uses in a column and the method of reading the table. For a three-digit number, it is acceptable to use the first three digits, the middle three, or the last three. It is also acceptable to select numbers by reading vertically down columns or horizontally along rows. The route is an *arbitrary decision*, but it needs to be *established in advance* and *followed consistently.*

4. *Select a starting point.* Selecting a random starting point in the table is necessary only to eliminate the predictability of the sample. The client who has a copy of the random number tables that will be used and knows the starting point can determine which items the auditor will be testing. It is acceptable to pick a starting point by simply making a "blind stab" into the table with a pencil. The number the pencil falls on is the first item included in the sample and the place from which the established route begins.

5. *Put into sequential order.* Auditors usually find it more convenient to perform audit tests in the order in which they occur in journals and lists rather than in random order. An easy way to put them in sequential order is by use of a *grid.* An example of a three-digit grid is shown in Figure 2-2. The numbers for the grid are thirty random numbers selected from a population numbered between 1 and 620. The starting point is item 1005, column 3 in Figure 2-1. The last three digits are used and the route is down the page.

	00	10	20	30	40	50	60	70	80	90
000	9		27	31					87	
100		111 119			143		160			
200				236		250	268		288	299
300	305					359	367			
400				433	445	451 452		478		
500	500 509			535	541 545 546	557	563		584	
600										

FIGURE 2-2 Grid for putting random numbers in sequence

Special Considerations

A major problem in the use of random number tables occurs when there are a large number of *discards*. Discards increase the time it takes to select the sample and enhance the likelihood of making errors in using the table. Certain shortcuts can be used to reduce the discards, but care must be taken to avoid unequal probability of selection. An example is the selection of a random sample from a population of prenumbered shipping documents numbered from 14067 to 16859. If a five-digit number is used in the tables, only about three numbers out of 100 are usable ($[16,859 - 14,067] \div 100,000 = 0.28$). The discards can be greatly reduced by ignoring the first digit, which is common to all population items, and using a four-digit number in the table. The discards can be further reduced by carefully redefining the way the first digit in the four-digit random number is used. For example, 1 through 3 could be defined to produce a first digit *4*, 4 through 6 to produce a first digit *5*, and 7 through 9 to produce a first digit *6*. The digit *0* in the first column is a discard. Thus, the random number 7426 from the table would be shipping document number 16426 in the population. This method reduces the discards to only about 10 percent, but it is fairly complicated and difficult to use.

Regardless of the method used in selecting a random sample, it is necessary to have *proper documentation*. This is beneficial as a means of rechecking and reviewing the selection of the numbers, expanding the sample if additional items are desired, and defending the methodology if the quality of the audit is questioned. *Minimum documentation* would include sufficient information in the working papers to permit the reproduction of the numbers at a later date. This includes the name and page number of the table, the correspondence between the population and the table used, the route, the starting point, and the sample size. Many auditors simply include in the working papers a copy of the table they used, with the random numbers identified.

In the selection of a random sample, there is a distinction between replacement and nonreplacement sampling. In *replacement sampling*, an element in the population can be included in the sample more than once if the random number corresponding to that element is selected from the table more than once; whereas in *nonreplacement sampling*, an element can be included only once. If the random number corresponding to an element is selected more than once in nonreplacement sampling, it is simply treated as a discard the second time. For example, in the selection for the grid in Figure 2-2, the number 546 came up twice; it was discarded the second time. Although both selection approaches are consistent with sound statistical theory, auditors rarely use replacement sampling.

Computer Terminals

Most CPA firms now rent computers or have access to computer time-sharing programs that include programs for the selection of random numbers. The advantages of this approach over random number tables are *time saving, reduced likelihood of auditor error* in selecting the numbers, and *automatic documentation.*

In using computer terminals, it is still necessary for each population element to have a *unique identification number,* and *correspondence* must be established between the population numbers and the random numbers generated by the computer. There is no need for concern about discards in establishing correspondence, because the computer can eliminate most types of discards.

For a typical computer program, it is necessary to input the smallest and largest numbers in the population sequence, the quantity of random numbers desired and, in some cases, a random number to start the program. In addition, the auditor usually has the option of getting the list of random numbers in *selection order, in ascending numerical sequence,* or both. The input and output from a computer terminal are illustrated in Figure 2-3. In this illustration, the auditor is selecting a sample of 30 shipping documents from the same prenumbered population sequence illustrated in the preceding section, where the document numbers ranged from 14067 to 16859.

```
_RUN <TRC900> SAMGEN

THIS PROGRAM GENERATES UP TO 1,000 SINGLE
    OR SETTED RANDOM NUMBERS.

FILE OPTION-YES OR NO? NO
QUIK OPTION-YES OR NO? NO

        ******** D A T A   I N P U T ********

(1) INPUT THE QUANTITY OF RANDOM NUMBERS         (9) PRINT SELECTION-INPUT 1 FOR NUMERICAL
    TO BE GENERATED? 30                              ORDER, 2 FOR SELECTION ORDER OR 3 FOR BOTH? 3
(2) ARE THE NUMBERS FORMATTED INTO SETS-YES OR NO? NO
(6) INPUT THE QUANTITY OF DIGITS IN THE LARGEST  (10) DO YOU WANT TO CHANGE ANY INPUTS-YES OR NO? NO
    NUMBER? 5
(7) INPUT THE NUMBER OF RANGES OF VALUES              *****INPUT COMPLETE-DATA CHECK WILL BEGIN*****
    TO BE GENERATED (MAX=50)? 1
(8) FOR EACH OF THE    1 RANGES INPUT THE        (11) DO YOU WANT A LISTING OF RANGES SELECTED BEFORE
    LOWER (L) AND UPPER (U) LIMITS. SEPARATE SETS,     DATA CHECK CONTINUES-YES OR NO? NO
    IF ANY, WITH A HYPHEN (-).
                                                 (12) TOTAL COUNTED ITEMS =   2493
    RANGE                                             REASONABLE-YES OR NO? YES
    -----
      1 - 'L? 14067                                   ************DATA CHECK COMPLETE************
          U? 16559                                    ****RANDOM NUMBER GENERATION WILL BEGIN****

                                                          ****GENERATION COMPLETE****


                                                 RANDOM NUMBERS-NUMERICAL ORDER
                                                 ------------------------------

                                                 SEQUENCE
                                                 SELECTED    RANDOM NUMBERS
RANDOM NUMBERS-SELECTION ORDER                   --------    --------------
------------------------------                      14        14090
16258                                               30        14134
15472                                               17        14199
16159                                               21        14224
15223                                               11        14249
15390                                               18        14273
15470                                                9        14297
15592                                               25        14431
14916                                               23        14682
14297                                               19        14775
15063                                                8        14916
14249                                               10        15063
16241                                               15        15100
15701                                                4        15223
14090                                               22        15308
15100                                                5        15390
16473                                                6        15470
14199                                                2        15472
14273                                                7        15592
14775                                               20        15608
15608                                               29        15674
14224                                               13        15701
15308                                               24        15742
14682                                               28        15900
15742                                               26        16017
14431                                                3        16159
16017                                               27        16225
16225                                               12        16241
15900                                                1        16258
15674                                               16        16473
14134

        ***SORTING***                                     ****RUN FINISHED****

                                                 ANOTHER RUN-YES OR NO ? NO
```

FIGURE 2-3 Random selection by use of a computer terminal

Arens and Loebbecke, *Auditing: An Integrated Approach*, 2nd ed. (Englewood Cliffs, N.J.: Prentice-Hall, Inc., 1980), p. 331.

Systematic Selection

In systematic selection, the auditor calculates an *interval* and then methodically selects the items for the sample based on the size of the interval. The interval is determined by dividing the population size by the number of sample items desired. For example, if a population of sales invoices ranges from 652 to 3151 and the desired sample size is 125, the interval is 20 ([3151 − 652] ÷ 125). The auditor must now select a random number between 0 and 19 to determine the starting point for the sample. If the randomly selected number is 9, the first item in the sample is invoice number

661 (652 + 9). The remaining 124 items are 681 (661 + 20), 701 (681 + 20), and so on to the last item (3141).

The advantage of systematic sampling is its *ease of use*. In most populations, a systematic sample can be drawn quickly, the approach automatically puts the numbers in sequential order, and documentation is easy.

A major problem with the use of systematic sampling is the possibility of *bias*. Because of the way in which systematic samples are selected, once the first item in the sample is selected, all other items are chosen automatically. This causes no problem if the characteristic of interest, such as a compliance error, is distributed randomly throughout the population; however, in many cases it is not. If compliance errors occurred at a certain time of the month or with certain types of documents, a systematic sample would have a higher likelihood of failing to obtain a representative sample than would the two methods previously discussed. This shortcoming is sufficiently serious that some CPA firms do not permit the use of systematic sampling. Other firms require a careful examination of the way the population is listed to evaluate the possibility of a systematic error. In the opinion of the authors, *the use of systematic sampling is not advisable* unless the two other approaches discussed in this section are impractical.

A means of reducing the potential bias in systematic sampling is to use multiple starts. This is done by multiplying the interval by an *arbitrary constant* to arrive at a new interval. For example, if the arbitrary constant is 4, the new interval for the previous example is 80 (20 × 4). The same number of *random starts* must be selected as the arbitrary constant. In the example, there are four random starts, so four random numbers between 0 and 79 are selected to determine the starting point for the sample. If the randomly selected numbers are 0, 21, 46, and 64, the first four invoices selected are 652 (652 + 0), 673 (652 + 21), 698, and 716. The next four invoices are 732 (652 + 80), 753 (673 + 80), 778, and 796. This procedure is continued until all 125 sample items are selected.

The larger the arbitrary constant used, the closer systematic sampling with multiple starts approximates simple random sampling. For example, if a multiple of 125 were used in the preceding example, it would actually be a random sample of 125 items.

Stratified Selection

In many situations, an auditor will prefer not to obtain a simple (unrestricted) random sample. Typically, this occurs when certain segments or types of elements of the population differ significantly from the others with respect to the characteristic of audit interest. As an example, in the confirmation of accounts receivable, the auditor normally expects larger errors in accounts with large balances than in those with small balances. If there is a wide range of values in the accounts, it is inappropriate to select a random sample of the entire population without some consideration of the relative size of the items. This is accomplished through *stratification*: dividing the population into subpopulations or strata, and selecting a separate random sample from each stratum.

The most important aspect of stratification is deciding *the number of strata* needed and the *characteristics* that determine the elements to be included in each stratum. In the stratification design, each element in the population must be included in only one stratum, and all elements must appear in some stratum.

After the auditor has decided on the desirable number of strata, population items for each stratum, and sample size for each stratum, the random selection of items for each stratum is similar to unrestricted random selection. No problems arise when the population items for each stratum can be separated and sequentially numbered. Each stratum can be treated as a separate population and the procedures previously described can be followed. However, typically it is less costly to select the sample by leaving population items for different strata co-mingled. To illustrate, consider a population of accounts receivable of 940 receivables with a book value of $230,000. The auditor has decided to use three strata. The first has 20 items with a total book value of $60,000 (receivables over $2,000); the second, 100 items with a total book value of $80,000 (receivables between $500 and $2,000); and the third, 820 items with a total book value of $90,000 (receivables under $500). Sample sizes of 20, 40, and 50 are to be selected from the first, second, and third strata respectively. The receivables listing is 20 pages with a maximum of 50 lines per page. Since all receivables from stratum 1 are being selected, they can be identified on the listing without random selection. A three-digit random sample on the basis of page number and line number can be used for the other strata. A discard is defined as a blank line or a line with a receivable over $2,000. The randomly selected receivables are put into stratum 2 or 3 as they are chosen. The 50 receivables in stratum 3 are likely to be selected first because the population size is much larger. After the 50 receivables in that stratum have been selected, balances under $500 are also considered discards until all 40 stratum 2 items have been selected.

Dollar Unit Sampling

There are some situations in which an auditor wants to select sample items such that the likelihood of any given item being included in the sample is directly proportional to its *recorded dollar amount*. A recorded account receivable of $2,000 would have a likelihood of being selected 20 times greater than that of a $100 receivable. This sample selection method is referred to as dollar unit sampling, or sampling with probabilities proportional to size. In effect, dollar unit sampling defines the sampling unit as being each individual population dollar, as contrasted to each physical unit comprising the population, which is the sampling unit under the methods discussed above.

The advantage of dollar unit sampling is the automatic emphasis put on larger items. This selection method is usually used in conjunction with a particular set of statistical measurement techniques; these are studied in Chapter 9.

Several alternative selection methods are available for dollar unit samples. An illustration of an accounts receivable population including cumulative totals is provided below to demonstrate these methods.

Population Item	Recorded Amount	Cumulative Total	Population Item	Recorded Amount	Cumulative Total
1	$ 357	$ 357	7	$1,425	$4,530
2	1,281	1,638	8	278	4,808
3	60	1,698	9	942	5,750
4	573	2,271	10	826	6,576
5	691	2,962	11	404	6,980
6	143	3,105	12	396	7,376

1. *Random Number Table—Cumulative Amounts.* Assume that the auditor wants to select a random sample of four accounts for confirmation using dollar unit sampling. Since the sampling unit is defined as an individual dollar, the population size is 7376 and four digits are needed on a random number table. Using the first four digits on the random number table, Figure 2-1, with a starting point of line 1002, column 4, the usable random numbers representing random dollars are 6586, 1756, 850, and 6499. The population physical unit items that contain these random dollars are determined by reference to the cumulative total column. They are items 11 (containing dollars 6,577 through 6,980), 4 (1,699–2,271), 2 (358–1,638) and 10 (5,751–6,576). These will be audited and the result for each physical unit will be applied to the random dollar it contains.

The statistical methods used to evaluate dollar unit samples permit the inclusion of a population physical unit in the sample more than once. For example, in the previous example, if the random numbers had been 6586, 1756, 856, and 6599, the sample items would be 11, 4, 2, and 11. Confirmations would be sent for population items 2, 4, and 11, but item 11 would be treated as two sample items statistically and the sample total would be four items.

2. *Random Number Table—Noncumulative.* A disadvantage of the method of random number table with cumulative amounts is the time needed to accumulate subtotals for *each* population item. An alternative approach that results in the same random numbers is to put the random numbers in sequential order and locate the population items by trial and error with the use of an adding machine. The random numbers from the previous example in sequential order are 850, 1756, 6499, and 6586. An adding-machine tape identifying the four random sample items is shown in Figure 2-4. It intentionally shows where the auditor's estimates were occasionally inaccurate and resulted in unnecessary subtraction and subtotals.

When there are several pages of population items and large gaps between some pairs of random numbers, it is acceptable to locate single items by adding in an entire

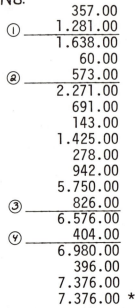

Sample
Item No.

```
                   *
              357.00
    ①      1.281.00
           1.638.00
              60.00
    ②        573.00
           2.271.00
             691.00
             143.00
           1.425.00
             278.00
             942.00
           5.750.00
    ③        826.00
           6.576.00
    ④        404.00
           6.980.00
             396.00
           7.376.00
           7.376.00  *
```

FIGURE 2-4 Dollar unit sample— non-cumulative approach

page total rather than adding every item on the page. Once the auditor gets skillful at selecting without accumulation, most dollar unit samples can be quickly attained.

3. *Systematic Sampling.* The selection procedures followed for systematic sampling of dollar unit samples are closely related to those for random selection. As with random selection, the sampling unit is an individual dollar and the population is the recorded total. An interval is determined the same way as for any systematic plan, by dividing the population size by the desired sample size. In the previous example, the interval is 1844 (7376 ÷ 4). A starting point between 0 and 1843 is randomly selected by the use of a random table (assume it is 921), and the interval is added. The random numbers are therefore 921, 2765 (921 + 1844), 4609, and 6453. The population items are 2, 5, 8, and 10.

An alternative approach resulting in the same sample items is to insert the *starting point* (921) in an adding machine as a negative number. Recorded population amounts are sequentially added into the total on a trial-and-error basis until a positive subtotal is recorded. The population item that caused the subtotal to be positive is the first item included in the sample. Next the *interval* (1844) is deducted from the total, and the adding of recorded amounts continues until the subtotal is again positive. This process is repeated until all random numbers are selected. An adding-machine tape indicating the four random numbers is shown in Figure 2-5.

Systematic sampling for dollar unit sampling has the same potential bias as previously discussed, but the likelihood is somewhat less because random dollars are being selected rather than random physical units. It is unlikely that a company will intentionally or unintentionally arrange population items in a manner that affects the randomness of the distribution of the errors among different dollars. Some CPA firms use systematic sampling extensively for dollar unit samples.

Sample
Item No.
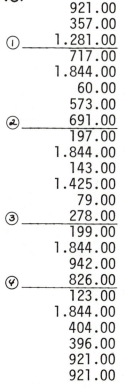

921.00
357.00
① 1.281.00
717.00
1.844.00
60.00
573.00
② 691.00
197.00
1.844.00
143.00
1.425.00
79.00
③ 278.00
199.00
1.844.00
942.00
④ 826.00
123.00
1.844.00
404.00
396.00
921.00
921.00

FIGURE 2-5 Dollar unit sample—systematic selection

4. *Computer Techniques.* Computer time-sharing programs can easily be used to generate and order random numbers for use in the first two methods discussed. Also, many CPA firms have special computer programs that select dollar unit samples when the population data are in machine-readable form.

Problems with Dollar Unit Selection. Population items having a zero recorded balance have no chance of being selected with dollar unit sampling even though they may be misstated. Similarly, small balances that are significantly understated have little chance of being included in the sample. This problem can be overcome by doing specific audit tests for zero and small balances if the auditor is concerned about them.

Another problem is the inability to include negative balances, such as credit balances in accounts receivable, in a dollar unit sample. It is possible to ignore negative balances for dollar unit sampling and test those amounts by some other means. An alternative is to treat them as positive balances and add them to the total being tested; however, this complicates the evaluation process.

	(1)	(2)	(3)	(4)	(5)	(6)	(7)
1	10480	15011	01536	02011	81647	91646	69179
2	22368	46573	25595	85393	30995	89198	27982
3	24130	48360	22527	97265	76393	64809	15179
4	42167	93093	06243	61680	07856	16376	39440
5	37570	39975	81837	16656	06121	91782	60468
6	77921	06907	11008	42751	27756	53498	18602
7	99562	72905	56420	69994	98872	31016	71194
8	96301	91977	05463	07972	18876	20922	94595
9	89579	14342	63661	10281	17453	18103	57740
10	85475	36857	53342	53988	53060	59533	38867
11	28918	69578	88231	33276	70997	79936	56865
12	63553	40961	48235	03427	49626	69445	18663
13	09429	93969	52636	92737	88974	33488	36320
14	10365	61129	87529	85689	48237	52267	67689
15	07119	97336	71048	08178	77233	13916	47564
16	51085	12765	51821	51259	77452	16308	60756
17	02368	21382	52404	60268	89368	19885	55322
18	01011	54092	33362	94904	31273	04146	18594
19	52162	53916	46369	58586	23216	14513	83149
20	07056	97628	33787	09998	42698	06691	76988
21	48663	91245	85828	14346	09172	30168	90229
22	54164	58492	22421	74103	47070	25306	76468
23	32639	32363	05597	24200	13363	38005	94342
24	29334	27001	87637	87308	58731	00256	45834
25	02488	33062	28834	07351	19731	92420	60952
26	81525	72295	04839	95423	24878	82651	66566
27	29676	20591	68086	26432	46901	20849	89768
28	00742	57392	39064	66432	84673	44027	32832
29	05366	04213	25669	26122	44407	44048	37937
30	91921	26418	64117	94305	26766	25940	39972
31	00582	04711	87917	77341	42206	35126	74087
32	00725	69884	62797	56170	86324	88072	76222
33	69011	65795	95876	55293	18988	27354	26575
34	25976	57948	29888	88604	67917	48708	18912
35	09763	83473	73577	12908	30883	18317	28290
36	91567	42595	27958	30134	04024	86385	29880
37	17955	56349	90999	49127	20044	59931	06115
38	46503	18584	18845	49618	02304	51038	20655
39	92157	89634	94824	78171	84610	82834	09922
40	14577	62765	35605	81263	39667	47358	56873
41	98427	07523	33362	64270	01638	92477	66969
42	34914	63976	88720	82765	34476	17032	87589
43	70060	28277	39475	46473	23219	53416	94970
44	53976	54914	06990	67245	68350	82948	11398
45	76072	29515	40980	07591	58745	25774	22987
46	90725	52210	83974	29992	65831	38857	50490
47	64364	67412	33339	31926	14883	24413	59744
48	08962	00358	31662	25388	61642	34072	81249
49	95012	68379	93526	70765	10592	04542	76463
50	15664	10493	20492	38391	91132	21999	59516

FIGURE 2-6 Random numbers

Note: *This is a reproduction of the Interstate Commerce Commission Bureau of Transport Economics and Statistics Table of 105,000 Random Decimal Digits.*

	(1)	(2)	(3)	(4)	(5)	(6)	(7)
51	16408	81899	04153	53381	79401	21438	83035
52	18629	81953	05520	91962	04739	13092	97662
53	73115	35101	47498	87637	99016	71060	88824
54	57491	16703	23167	49323	45021	33132	12544
55	30405	83946	23792	14422	15059	45799	22716
56	16631	35006	85900	98275	32388	52390	16815
57	96773	20206	42559	78985	05300	22164	24369
58	38935	64202	14349	82674	66523	44133	00697
59	31624	76384	17403	53363	44167	64486	64758
60	78919	19474	23632	27889	47914	02584	37680
61	03931	33309	57047	74211	63445	17361	62825
62	74426	33278	43972	10119	89917	15665	52872
63	09066	00903	20795	95452	92648	45454	09552
64	42238	12426	87025	14267	20979	04508	64535
65	16153	08002	26504	41744	81959	65642	74240
66	21457	40742	29820	96783	29400	21840	15035
67	21581	57802	02050	89728	17937	37621	47075
68	55612	78095	83197	33732	05810	24813	86902
69	44657	66999	99324	51281	84463	60563	79312
70	91340	84979	46949	81973	37949	61023	43997
71	91227	21199	31935	27022	84067	05462	36216
72	50001	38140	66321	19924	72163	09538	12151
73	65390	05224	72958	28609	81406	39147	25549
74	27504	96131	83944	41575	10573	08619	64482
75	37169	94851	39117	89632	00959	16487	65536
76	11508	70225	51111	38351	19444	66499	71945
77	37449	30362	06694	54690	04052	53115	62757
78	46515	70331	85922	38329	57015	15765	97161
79	30986	81223	42416	58353	21532	30502	32305
80	63798	64995	46583	09785	44160	78128	83991
81	82486	84846	99254	67632	43218	50076	21361
82	21885	32906	92431	09060	64297	51674	64126
83	60336	98782	07408	53458	13564	59089	26445
84	43937	46891	24010	25560	86355	33941	25786
85	97656	63175	89303	16275	07100	92063	21942
86	03299	01221	05418	38982	55758	92237	26759
87	79626	06486	03574	17668	07785	76020	79924
88	85636	68335	47539	03129	65651	11977	02510
89	18039	14367	61337	06177	12143	46609	32989
90	08362	15656	60627	36478	65648	16764	53412
91	79556	29068	04142	16268	15387	12856	66227
92	92608	82674	27072	32534	17075	27698	98204
93	23982	25835	40055	67006	12293	02753	14827
94	09915	96306	05908	97901	28395	14186	00821
95	59037	33300	26695	62247	69927	76123	50842
96	42488	78077	69882	61657	34136	79180	97526
97	46764	86273	63003	93017	31204	36692	40202
98	03237	45430	55417	63282	90816	17349	88298
99	86591	81482	52667	61582	14972	90053	89534
100	38534	01715	94964	87288	65680	43772	39560

FIGURE 2-6   (Cont'd)

	(1)	(2)	(3)	(4)	(5)	(6)	(7)
101	13284	16834	74151	92027	24670	36665	00770
102	21224	00370	30420	03883	94648	89428	41583
103	99052	47887	81085	64933	66279	80432	65793
104	00199	50993	98603	38452	87890	94624	69721
105	60578	06483	28733	37867	07936	98710	98539
106	91240	18312	17441	90929	18163	69201	31211
107	97458	14229	12063	59611	32249	90466	33216
108	35249	38646	34475	72417	60514	69257	12489
109	38980	46600	11759	11900	46743	27860	77940
110	10750	52745	38749	87365	58959	53731	89295
111	36247	27850	73958	20673	37800	63835	71051
112	70994	66986	99744	72438	01174	42159	11392
113	99638	94702	11463	18148	81386	80431	90628
114	72055	15774	43857	99805	10419	76939	25993
115	24038	65541	85788	55835	38835	59399	13790
116	74976	14631	35908	28221	39470	91548	12854
117	35553	71628	70189	26436	63407	91178	90348
118	35676	12797	51434	82976	42010	26344	92920
119	74815	67523	72985	23183	02446	63594	98924
120	45246	88048	65173	50989	91060	89894	36036
121	76509	47069	86378	41797	11910	49672	88575
122	19689	90332	04315	21358	97248	11188	39062
123	42751	35318	97513	61537	54955	08159	00337
124	11946	22681	45045	13964	57517	59419	58045
125	96518	48688	20996	11090	48396	57177	83867
126	35726	58643	76869	84622	39098	36083	72505
127	39737	42750	48968	70536	84864	64952	38404
128	97025	66492	56177	04049	80312	48028	26408
129	62814	08075	09788	56350	76787	51591	54509
130	25578	22950	15227	83291	41737	79599	96191
131	68763	69576	88991	49662	46704	63362	56625
132	17900	00813	64361	60725	88974	61005	99709
133	71944	60227	63551	71109	05624	43836	58254
134	54684	93691	85132	64399	29182	44324	14491
135	25946	27623	11258	65204	52832	50880	22273
136	01353	39318	44961	44972	91766	90262	56073
137	99083	88191	27662	99113	57174	35571	99884
138	52021	45406	37945	75234	24327	86978	22644
139	78755	47744	43776	83098	03225	14281	83637
140	25282	69106	59180	16257	22810	43609	12224
141	11959	94202	02743	86847	79725	51811	12998
142	11644	13792	98190	01424	30078	28197	55583
143	06307	97912	68110	59812	95448	43244	31262
144	76285	75714	89585	99296	52640	46518	55486
145	55322	07598	39600	60866	63007	20007	66819
146	78017	90928	90220	92503	83375	26986	74399
147	44768	43342	20696	26331	43140	69744	82928
148	25100	19336	14605	86603	51680	97678	24261
149	83612	46623	62876	85197	07824	91392	58317
150	41347	81666	82961	60413	71020	83658	02419
151	38128	51178	75096	13609	16110	73533	42564
152	60950	00455	73254	96067	50717	13878	03216
153	90524	17320	29832	96118	75792	25326	22940
154	49897	18278	67160	39408	97056	43517	84426
155	18494	99209	81060	19488	65596	59787	47939

FIGURE 2-6 (Cont'd)

	(1)	(2)	(3)	(4)	(5)	(6)	(7)
156	65373	72984	30171	37741	70203	94094	87261
157	40653	12843	04213	70925	95360	55774	76439
158	51638	22238	56344	44587	83231	50317	74541
159	69742	99303	62578	83575	30337	07488	51941
160	58012	74072	67488	74580	47992	69482	58624
161	18348	19855	42887	08279	43206	47077	42637
162	59614	09193	58064	29086	44385	45740	70752
163	75688	28630	39210	52897	62748	72658	98059
164	13941	77802	69101	70061	35460	34576	15412
165	96656	86420	96475	86458	54463	96419	55417
166	03363	82042	15942	14549	38324	87094	19069
167	70366	08390	69155	25496	13240	57407	91407
168	47870	36605	12927	16043	53257	93796	52721
169	79504	77606	22761	30518	28373	73898	30550
170	46967	74841	50923	15339	37755	98995	40162
171	14558	50769	35444	59030	87516	48193	02945
172	12440	25057	01132	38611	28135	68089	10954
173	32293	29938	68653	10497	98919	46587	77701
174	10640	21875	72462	77981	56550	55999	87310
175	47615	23169	39571	56972	20628	21788	51736
176	16948	11128	71624	72754	49084	96303	27830
177	21258	61092	66634	70335	92448	17354	83432
178	15072	48853	15178	30730	47481	48490	41436
179	99154	57412	09858	65671	70655	71479	63520
180	08759	61089	23706	32994	35426	36666	63988
181	67323	57839	61114	62112	47547	58023	64630
182	09255	13986	84834	20764	72206	89393	34548
183	36304	74712	00374	10107	85061	69228	81969
184	15884	67429	86612	47367	10242	44880	12060
185	18745	32031	35303	08134	33925	03004	59929
186	72934	40086	88292	65728	38300	42323	64068
187	17626	02944	20910	57662	80181	38579	24580
188	27117	61399	50967	41399	81636	16663	15634
189	93995	18678	90012	63645	85701	85269	62263
190	67392	89421	09623	80725	62620	84162	87368
191	04910	12261	37566	80016	21245	69377	50420
192	81453	20283	79929	59839	23875	13245	46808
193	19480	75790	48539	23703	15537	48885	02861
194	21456	13162	74608	81011	55512	07481	93551
195	89406	20912	46189	76376	25538	87212	20748
196	09866	17414	55977	16419	01101	69343	13305
197	86541	24681	23421	13521	28000	94917	07423
198	10414	96941	06205	72222	57167	83902	07460
199	49942	06683	41479	58982	56288	42853	92196
200	23995	68882	42291	23374	24299	27024	67460
201	78994	36244	02673	25475	84953	61793	50243
202	04909	58485	70686	93930	34880	73059	06823
203	46582	73570	33004	51795	86477	46736	60460
204	29242	89792	88634	60285	07190	07795	27011
205	68104	81339	97090	20601	78940	20228	22803
206	17156	02182	82504	19880	93747	80910	78260
207	50711	94789	07171	02103	99057	98775	37997
208	39449	52409	75095	77720	39729	03205	09313
209	75629	82729	76916	72657	58992	32756	01154
210	01020	55151	36132	51971	32155	60735	64867

FIGURE 2-6 (Cont'd)

	(1)	(2)	(3)	(4)	(5)	(6)	(7)
211	08337	89989	24260	08618	66798	25889	52860
212	76829	47229	19706	30094	69430	92399	98749
213	39708	30641	21267	56501	95182	72442	21445
214	89836	55817	56747	75195	06818	83043	47403
215	25903	61370	66081	54076	67442	52964	23823
216	71345	03422	01015	68025	19703	77313	04555
217	61454	92263	14647	08473	34124	10740	40839
218	80376	08909	30470	40200	46558	61742	11643
219	45144	54373	05505	90074	24783	86299	20900
220	12191	88527	58852	51175	11534	87218	04876
221	62936	59120	73957	35969	21598	47287	39394
222	31588	96798	43668	12611	01714	77266	55079
223	20787	96048	84726	17512	39450	43618	30629
224	45603	00745	84635	43079	52724	14262	05750
225	31606	64782	34027	56734	09365	20008	93559
226	10452	33074	76718	99556	16026	00013	78411
227	37016	64633	67301	50949	91298	74968	73631
228	66725	97865	25409	37498	00816	99262	14471
229	07380	74438	82120	17890	40963	55757	13492
230	71621	57688	58256	47702	74724	89419	08025
231	03466	13263	23917	20417	11315	52805	33072
232	12692	32931	97387	34822	53775	91674	76549
233	52192	30941	44998	17833	94563	23062	95725
234	56691	72529	66063	73570	86860	68125	40436
235	74952	43041	58869	15677	78598	43520	97521
236	18752	43693	32867	53017	22661	39610	03796
237	61691	04944	43111	28325	82319	65589	66048
238	49197	63948	38947	60207	70667	39843	60607
239	19436	87291	71684	74859	76501	93456	95714
240	39143	64893	14606	13543	09621	68301	69817
241	82244	67549	76491	09761	74494	91307	64222
242	55847	56155	42878	23708	97999	40131	52360
243	94095	95970	07826	25991	37584	56966	68623
244	11751	69469	25521	44097	07511	88976	30122
245	69902	08995	27821	11758	64989	61902	32121
246	21850	25352	25556	92161	23592	43294	10479
247	75850	56992	25165	55906	62339	88958	91717
248	29648	22086	42581	85677	20251	39641	65786
249	82740	28443	42734	25518	82827	35825	90288
250	36842	42092	52075	83926	42875	71500	69216
251	89429	26726	15563	94972	78739	04419	60523
252	43427	25412	25587	21276	44426	17369	29010
253	58575	81958	51846	02676	67781	95137	88430
254	61888	71246	24246	23487	78639	92006	63846
255	73891	47025	40937	71907	26827	98865	38882
256	40938	73894	40854	15997	95033	31736	31736
257	98053	43567	17292	86908	71364	06089	92394
258	59774	29138	46993	39836	99596	59050	25419
259	09765	07548	63043	59782	81449	13652	94420
260	38991	64502	24770	29209	82909	66610	84418
261	25622	27100	56128	62145	82388	45197	97609
262	31864	72120	66231	82306	91784	33177	17681
263	81171	75639	60863	49562	28845	81581	10249
264	69874	52803	28544	51569	56090	44558	42095
265	27848	51107	05761	02159	53911	01952	59273

FIGURE 2-6 (Cont'd)

	(1)	(2)	(3)	(4)	(5)	(6)	(7)
266	69407	69736	75375	31488	67528	84234	76462
267	29418	03091	06364	13151	40663	43633	87954
268	38222	31231	79415	44558	62490	26936	49628
269	94720	83796	93251	03568	62484	29140	14152
270	45275	16852	02284	41361	73733	61486	33189
271	97260	09552	82626	42915	45847	87401	13339
272	01990	65259	60684	78175	43825	45211	86287
273	24633	42314	81192	50253	67516	59076	92006
274	98071	52677	74920	74461	52266	26967	68284
275	34101	79442	88403	48541	13010	16596	72001
276	77186	93967	85918	66403	73837	73445	86663
277	83114	05481	48335	51396	60823	22680	50459
278	59988	49944	41038	99977	16348	41119	51548
279	11852	42254	82304	05388	75165	20179	94198
280	59992	87922	56299	01700	07003	97507	69260
281	42116	86593	22828	41422	18176	03250	06079
282	39663	61401	21471	42702	70588	53144	27087
283	53542	72009	96296	68908	58657	87117	21483
284	25996	76108	98476	36397	89457	19577	65877
285	91106	26450	14451	50328	29084	32332	08635
286	37133	88924	27845	13024	90687	23726	11212
287	13982	25736	10087	16762	02564	27250	79316
288	26663	36187	81688	25005	46677	75851	73938
289	62572	08275	16313	24936	81680	53829	40412
290	65925	95455	08383	24643	72962	08172	37824
291	97978	74676	08942	48919	51592	71196	48534
292	01914	42524	67820	47985	91773	10383	89514
293	68565	44811	39238	70394	78555	33539	56310
294	54370	31672	03893	32423	54092	69375	63308
295	79954	89601	23881	46951	69084	33477	87968
296	58479	01059	44229	56975	06785	80930	26443
297	38114	70330	42157	86699	46212	74692	92603
298	29766	83452	66202	02485	72704	97821	70614
299	31771	70640	34779	41831	33456	53194	19602
300	77522	87188	83577	99067	83835	48662	31503
301	64670	10396	82981	58320	71478	08143	48294
302	25771	02205	73984	28436	88192	11470	11775
303	27551	13537	54984	89406	88326	33993	92324
304	91224	22417	44820	26189	57541	87558	45835
305	75179	64320	71523	67868	38883	09674	27645
306	64654	91085	65818	03313	39273	46384	66677
307	98059	81123	67832	04102	66188	78200	67466
308	38765	63585	18810	95805	11414	58096	00295
309	01921	03564	71754	10213	80383	13473	94128
310	16211	93671	27704	66778	96307	06732	63750
311	70232	86076	61527	56123	48514	53935	86784
312	22332	94265	67627	85815	00394	75271	98385
313	81333	45965	64171	84367	15052	37965	03122
314	39333	47453	66174	04546	10594	64271	61026
315	29195	20825	50878	80273	26285	90070	79586
316	74420	64037	06960	25109	08821	60143	34485
317	22763	16508	24866	13177	07464	51730	65802
318	72919	54618	40616	33287	51274	78491	53604
319	92385	42402	15922	90033	21555	31647	22288
320	85431	19857	97246	46118	71222	82744	67892

FIGURE 2-6   (Cont'd)

	(1)	(2)	(3)	(4)	(5)	(6)	(7)
321	40778	12451	14921	51464	45331	75822	46859
322	88903	46592	60637	65231	08778	86813	47819
323	29830	34899	85457	19548	83355	52479	77801
324	22832	47422	08073	10107	46772	92299	42975
325	75159	14809	11930	83531	51239	86298	72661
326	99390	08217	56276	09263	82685	30451	25742
327	68622	80897	08902	10867	91379	30068	84289
328	92393	95901	41179	72129	72502	91097	09488
329	53122	66033	38229	51879	29925	45574	53938
330	43251	11941	86631	93264	53433	70281	55000
331	16613	24901	34866	75002	55163	68300	20070
332	12010	60852	92603	70393	17989	95755	14672
333	85528	97879	27814	08219	02908	71582	31439
334	32590	55079	33556	83169	92087	77939	53792
335	92934	30650	16449	15805	61551	38689	59179
336	80614	10150	09389	61892	79477	14522	40270
337	62398	12034	90764	52872	22285	50592	42505
338	02222	46811	05145	67916	15184	02636	59078
339	08690	31785	61664	61322	24149	21471	23328
340	61187	73897	66168	12885	73191	89432	65414
341	12324	61149	85643	64999	63738	46671	25408
342	47635	42279	98620	70677	52386	50904	97403
343	70965	00390	08878	15373	70276	71889	86953
344	58764	15262	96814	54548	00042	19721	78869
345	07429	05609	31207	50254	68389	07714	92268
346	15665	28659	54952	53217	76898	88931	25786
347	64208	53232	99459	43605	04553	48451	68154
348	17952	73276	52567	48489	64264	24220	55498
349	60531	43217	39999	38615	97195	76928	87688
350	76692	39999	43254	68110	88053	88727	14187
351	06433	80674	24520	18222	10610	05794	37515
352	39298	47829	72648	37414	75755	04717	29899
353	89884	59651	67533	68123	17730	95862	08034
354	61512	32155	51906	61662	64130	16688	37275
355	99653	47635	12506	88535	36553	23757	34209
356	95913	11085	13772	76638	48423	25018	99041
357	55864	44004	13122	44115	01601	50541	00147
358	35334	82410	91601	40617	72876	33967	73830
359	57729	88646	76487	11622	96297	24160	09903
360	86648	89317	63677	70119	94739	25875	38829
361	30574	06039	07967	32422	76791	39725	53711
362	81307	13114	83580	79974	45929	85113	72268
363	02410	96385	79007	54939	21410	86980	91772
364	18969	87444	52233	62319	08598	09066	95288
365	87863	80514	66860	62297	80198	19347	73234
366	68397	10538	15438	62311	72844	60203	46412
367	28529	45247	58729	10854	99058	18260	38765
368	44285	09452	15867	70418	57012	72122	36634
369	86299	22510	33571	23309	57040	29285	67870
370	84842	05748	90894	61658	15001	94055	36308
371	56970	10799	52098	04184	54967	72938	56834
372	83125	85077	60490	44369	66130	72936	69848
373	55503	21383	02464	26141	68779	66388	75242
374	47019	06683	33203	29608	54553	25971	69573
375	84828	61152	79526	29554	84580	37859	28504

FIGURE 2-6 (Cont'd)

SUGGESTED READINGS AND REFERENCES

ARKIN, HERBERT, *Handbook of Sampling for Auditing and Accounting*. New York: McGraw-Hill, 1974.

IJIRI, YUJI, and ROBERT S. KAPLAN, "The Four Objectives of Sampling in Auditing—Representative, Corrective, Protective, and Preventive," *Management Accounting*, December 1970, pp. 42–44.

RANDELL, BOYD, and PAUL FRISHKOFT, "An Examination of the Status of Probability Sampling in the Courts," H. Stettler, ed., Auditing Symposium III, University of Kansas, 1977, pp. 93–102.

VANASSE, ROBERT W., *Statistical Sampling for Auditing and Accounting Decisions: A Simulation*. New York: McGraw-Hill, 1976.

REVIEW QUESTIONS

2-1. Identify five possible sampling objectives the auditor might have in selecting sample items. For each objective, give an example for which the objective is likely to be appropriate.

2-2. State what is meant by a representative sample, and explain its importance in sampling audit populations.

2-3. Distinguish between judgmental and statistical selection methods. Discuss when each method is appropriate.

2-4. Identify general circumstances in which it may be desirable to select sample items with intentional bias.

2-5. Explain what is meant by block sampling, and describe how an auditor could obtain five blocks of 20 sales invoices from a sales journal.

2-6. Under what circumstances is it appropriate to use statistical measurement techniques with judgmental selection methods?

2-7. Compared with judgmental selection, what is the major advantage of random selection?

2-8. Define what is meant by random selection. What are three methods of random selection?

2-9. List the four requirements of random selection, and explain why each is important.

2-10. Explain what is meant by a random number table. Describe how an auditor would select 35 random numbers from a population of 1,750 items by using a random number table.

2-11. Explain the difference between sampling with replacement and sampling without replacement. Which method do auditors usually follow? Why?

2-12. List the five major steps needed to use a random number table. Explain how each step would be performed to select 15 accounts for confirmation from a listing of eight pages of accounts receivable with exactly 36 accounts receivable outstanding per page.

2-13. Describe what each of the following terms means in relation to random selection: *sequential ordering with a grid; discards; documentation.*

2-14. What are the advantages of computer terminals compared to random number tables for selecting random numbers? Identify the information that must be entered in the terminal in order to select the numbers.

2-15. Describe systematic sampling. What are the first four invoice numbers in the sample if a sample of 75 sales invoices is to be selected from a population with invoice numbers ranging from 16,297 to 21,411? Assume a random starting point of 46.

2-16. Explain how potential bias can result from using systematic sampling. How can the auditor reduce the likelihood of this potential bias?

2-17. Why do auditors use stratified sampling? Explain the similarities of and differences between stratified and unstratified random selection using tables.

2-18. Explain what is meant by dollar unit sampling and the difference between dollar unit and physical unit sampling. What are the advantages and problems with dollar unit sampling?

2-19. Explain the difference, for dollar unit sampling, between random number table with cumulative amounts, random selection noncumulative, and systematic sampling.

DISCUSSION QUESTIONS AND PROBLEMS

2-20. The following apply to statistical sampling. Choose the most appropriate response.

    a. Which of the following best describes the distinguishing feature of statistical sampling?

        i. It requires the examination of a smaller number of supporting documents.

        ii. It provides a means for measuring mathematically the degree of uncertainty that results from examining only part of a population.

        iii. It reduces the problems associated with the auditor's judgment concerning materiality.

        iv. It is evaluated in terms of two parameters: statistical mean and random selection.

    b. Which of the following is an advantage of systematic sampling over random number sampling?

        i. It provides a stronger basis for statistical conclusions.

        ii. It enables the auditor to use the more efficient sampling-with-replacement tables.

iii. There may be correlation between the location of items in the population, the feature of sampling interest, and the sampling interval.

iv. It does not require establishment of correspondence between random numbers and items in the population.

c. In performing a review of his client's cash disbursements, a CPA uses systematic sampling with a random start. The primary disadvantage of systematic sampling is that population items:

i. Must be reordered in a systematic pattern before the sample can be drawn.

ii. May occur in a systematic pattern, thus negating the randomness of the sample.

iii. May occur twice in the sample.

iv. Must be replaced in the population after sampling to permit valid statistical inference.

2-21. In each of the following independent problems, design an unbiased random sampling plan using the random number table in Figure 2-1. The plan should include defining the sampling unit, establishing a numbering system for the population, and establishing a correspondence between the random number table and the population. After the plan has been designed, select the first five sample items from the random number table for each problem. Use a starting point of item 1009, column 1, for each problem. Read down the table using the left-most digits in the column. When you reach the last item in a column, start at the top of the next column.

a. Prenumbered sales invoices in a sales journal where the lowest invoice number is 1 and the highest is 6211.

b. Prenumbered bills of lading where the lowest document number is 21926 and the highest is 28511.

c. Accounts receivable on 10 pages with 60 lines per page. Each line has a customer name and an amount receivable, except the last page, which has only 36 full lines.

d. Prenumbered invoices in a sales journal where each month starts over with number 1. (Invoices for each month are designated by the month and document number.) There are a maximum of 20 pages per month with a total of 185 pages for the year. All pages have 75 invoices, except for the last page for each month.

2-22. In each of the following independent problems, design a systematic sampling plan with one start. The plan should include defining the sampling unit, establishing a numbering system for the population, and establishing a correspondence between the random number table and the population in order to arrive at a starting point. The sample should be designed to select 50 items from the population. After the plan has been designed, select the first five sample items for each problem. As a starting point, use Figure 2-1, item 1003, column 2, for each problem. If that number results in a discard, read down the table to arrive at a starting point, using the left-most digits in the column.

a. Prenumbered sales invoices in a sales journal, where the lowest invoice number is 1 and the highest is 6211.

    b. Prenumbered bills of lading, where the lowest document number is 21926 and the highest is 28511.

    c. Accounts receivable, on ten pages with 60 lines per page. Each line has a customer name and an amount receivable, except the last page, which has only 36 full lines.

    d. Prenumbered invoices in a sales journal, where each month starts over with number 1. (Invoices for each month are designated by the month and document number.) There are a maximum of 20 pages per month, with a total of 185 pages for the year. All pages have 75 invoices, except for the last page of each month.

2-23. Charles White, CPA, has decided to use random selection in the audit of sales. The sales transactions are numbered from 1 to 3150. They are listed 35 to a page in the sales journal. The sample size for the audit test is 70.

    a. Describe five different methods for selecting a random sample of sales transactions.

    b. Which method would you prefer in this situation? Explain your answer.

2-24. Lenter Supply Company is a medium-sized distributor of wholesale hardware supplies in the central Ohio area. It has been a client of yours for several years and has instituted an excellent system for the control of sales at your recommendation. In providing control over shipments, the client has prenumbered "warehouse removal slips" that are used for every sale. It is company policy never to remove goods from the warehouse without an authorized warehouse removal slip. After shipment, two copies of the warehouse removal slip are sent to billing for preparation of a sales invoice. One copy is stapled to the duplicate copy of a prenumbered sales invoice, and the other copy is filed numerically. In some cases, more than one warehouse removal slip is used for billing one sales invoice. The lowest-number warehouse removal slip used for the year is 14682 and the highest is 37521. The lowest sales invoice number is 47821 and the highest is 68507.

    In the audit of sales, one of the major concerns is the effectiveness of the system in making sure all shipments are billed. The auditor has decided to use random selection in the current year for all audit tests where it is considered practical.

REQUIRED:

    a. State an effective audit procedure for testing whether shipments have been billed. What is the appropriate sampling unit for the audit procedure?

    b. Design a random selection plan for selecting the sample from the population using the random number table. Select the first ten sample items from the table in Figure 2-1. Use a starting point of item 1013, column 3.

    c. Design a random selection plan for selecting the sample from the population, using systematic sampling with one start. Select the first ten sample items from the table. Assume a sample size of 100 items and a starting point of item 1015, column 1, in Figure 2-1.

    d. Design a random selection plan for selecting the sample from the population, using systematic sampling with four starts. Assume a sample size of 100 items and a starting point of item 1020, column 3, in Figure 2-1. Select the first three sample items that result from each start.

e. Assume that it is also considered desirable to test the validity of recorded sales in the audit of Lenter Supply Company. Would it be appropriate to use the random sample selected in part *b* to test the validity of sales? Explain.

2-25. You plan to select a random sample of 100 vouchers from a voucher register. Each voucher is identified by a month and voucher number. Vouchers start with the number 1 each month. The largest voucher number for each month is as follows:

Month	Largest voucher number	Month	Largest voucher number
January	437	July	401
February	217	August	385
March	348	September	289
April	420	October	190
May	398	November	262
June	472	December	395

REQUIRED:

a. Establish a numbering system for the population and a correspondence between the population and random number tables. Select a starting point of item 1026, column 2, in the random number table, Figure 2-1. Select the first ten items in the sample using non-replacement sampling.

b. Explain why there is a large percent of discards. How could the number of discards be reduced?

c. Set up a systematic sampling plan using one start to select the systematic sample. Assume that the random number for the start is 18. Select the first ten items in the sample.

d. Set up a systematic sampling plan using five multiple starts to select the sample of 100 items. Assume that the five random numbers for the starts are 26, 37, 81, 14, and 06. Select all the random numbers for the first random start (all 20 numbers resulting from the random start of 26).

e. An enterprising young senior has recommended the following approach: Select a random sample of eight items between 1 and 472 (472 is the largest voucher number). If, for example, the number is 237, select voucher 237 for each month except February and October. Ten sample items result from the first number. A maximum of 96 numbers will result from the eight random numbers, but there will be a certain number of discards. Additional sample items beyond the first eight should be selected until a total of 100 vouchers has been selected. The senior concludes triumphantly, "The method of selection I have recommended is both random and efficient. That's the best of all worlds!" Evaluate the approach suggested by the enterprising senior.

2-26. The Bengton Manufacturing Company maintains one cash disbursement journal, but for purposes of relations with local banks, two different bank accounts are used. Internal controls are the same for both. The sequencing of checks used in the current year is as follows:

East Side State Bank	2621 to 4852
West Side National Bank	6261 to 9452

REQUIRED:

a. Set up a sampling plan using random number tables to obtain a random sample. Keep the plan as simple as possible.
b. Set up a sampling plan using random number tables, assuming that the East Side State Bank sequencing is 12,621 to 14,852, and the West Side National Bank is as stated previously.
c. Set up a sample plan using random number tables, assuming that the East Side State Bank sequence is 12,621 to 14,852, and the West Side National Bank is 10,261 to 13,452.

2-27. The following sales procedures were encountered during the regular annual audit of Marvel Wholesale Distributing Company.

Customer orders are received by the sales order department. A clerk computes the dollar amount of the order and sends it to the credit department for approval. Credit approval is stamped on the order and returned to the sales order department. An invoice is prepared in two copies, and the order is filed in the customer order file.

The customer copy of the invoice is sent to the billing department and held in the pending file awaiting notification that the order was shipped.

The shipping copy of the invoice is routed through the warehouse and the shipping department as authority for the respective department to release and ship the merchandise. Shipping department personnel pack the order and prepare a three-copy bill of lading: the original copy is mailed to the customer, the second copy is sent with the shipment, and the other is filed in sequence in the bill of lading file. The invoice shipping copy is sent to the billing department.

The billing clerk matches the received shipping copy with the customer copy from the pending file. Both copies of the invoice are priced, extended, and footed. The customer copy is then mailed directly to the customer, and the shipping copy is sent to the accounts receivable clerk.

The accounts receivable clerk enters the invoice data in a sales journal, posts the customer's account in the subsidiary customer accounts ledger, and files the shipping copy in the sales invoice file. The invoices are numbered and filed in sequence.

REQUIRED:

a. In order to gather audit evidence concerning the proper credit approval of sales, the appropriate sampling unit for the selection of transaction documents would be from the population represented by the:
(1) Customer order file

(2) Bill of lading file

(3) Subsidiary customer accounts ledger

(4) Sales invoice file

b. In order to determine whether the system of internal control operates effectively to minimize errors of failure to post invoices to the customer accounts ledger, the appropriate sampling unit for the selection of transactions would be from the population represented by the:

(1) Customer order file

(2) Bill of lading file

(3) Subsidiary customer accounts ledger

(4) Sales invoice file

c. In order to determine whether the system of internal control operates effectively to minimize errors of failure to invoice a shipment, the appropriate sampling unit for the selection of transactions would be from the population represented by the:

(1) Customer order file

(2) Bill of lading file

(3) Subsidiary customer accounts ledger

(4) Sales invoice file

d. In order to gather audit evidence that uncollected items in customer accounts represented valid trade receivables, the appropriate sampling unit for the selection of transactions would be from the population represented by the:

(1) Customer order file

(2) Bill of lading file

(3) Subsidiary customer accounts ledger

(4) Sales invoice file

2-28. You are doing price tests of raw materials inventory for the Merties Manufacturing Company using statistical sampling. Your sampling plan calls for a random sample of 125 part numbers. Since you are using FIFO inventory valuation, it is essential that you obtain a random sample of part numbers. Part numbers include a variety of alphabetical prefixes and a large range of numbers. For example, part number AC 467 is followed by ACX 46738.

Inventory is included on inventory pages in part number order, by location. There are approximately 4,000 different part numbers in two locations. There are between 40 and 50 part numbers on each page. The reason for fewer than 50 part numbers on a page is that occasionally the description of the part takes up two lines. There are 94 pages. Included in the raw-materials inventory are 200 lines with finished goods. These items have been clearly identified by the client and are being tested separately by the auditor.

Neither pages nor lines are numbered. Approximately 80 of the pages include inventory for location 1. Approximately 25 percent of the items included in the listing of location 2's inventory are of the same description as those in location 1. The remaining 75 percent part numbers are included only in location 2.

REQUIRED:

a. Why would systematic sampling be difficult to use for obtaining a random sample in this situation?
b. Establish a numbering system for the population and a correspondence between the random number table and the population.
c. Describe in detail a method you can use to obtain the random sample of 125 raw materials part numbers. The method must be unbiased and reasonably efficient. Keep in mind that there are unnumbered pages and lines, missing lines, some part numbers listed in two different places, and finished goods included with the raw materials. Your description should include the appropriate sampling unit, method of reading the table, and definition of discards.

2-29. Jack Ronson, CPA, is confirming accounts receivable for Regional Book Wholesale Company. He has decided to use stratified estimation. The basis for stratification and the population sample information are as follows:

Stratum	Population size	Sample size
1	80	80
2	369	50
3	950	60
4	4,694	80
Total	6,093	270

REQUIRED:

a. Assume the client has provided Ronson with a listing of accounts receivable in which all receivables for each stratum are grouped together. In addition, the receivables for a given stratum are numbered from 1 to the last population item for that stratum. (E.g., stratum 3 receivables are listed separately and numbered from 1 to 950.) Describe how the random sample for each stratum could be efficiently obtained using a random number table. Also, describe how the sample could be selected using systematic sampling.
b. Now assume the client has still provided Ronson with a listing of accounts receivable in which all receivables for each stratum are still grouped together. However, the individual receivables are not numbered. These are listed on unnumbered pages with unnumbered lines. Describe how the random sample could be efficiently selected using a random number table.
c. Now assume the client has listed the receivables in alphabetical order. They are not separated, and lines are not numbered. Describe how the random sample for each stratum could be reasonably efficiently obtained using random number tables. Neither you nor the client is to redo the listing.

2-30. The cash disbursement journal for Jones Electric includes checks listed in sequential order. The checks for the year begin with 2167 and end with 8573. A sample of 75 canceled checks is desired. The sampling unit for the random selection has been defined as the canceled check.

REQUIRED:

a. Select the first 25 random numbers using the random number table in Figure 2-1. Assume a starting point of item 1011, column 3, and use the four leftmost digits in the table. Read downward in the table. Start at the top of the next column when the bottom of a column is reached.

b. Set up a random number grid and record the random numbers in part *a* on the grid. What is the purpose of the grid?

c. Explain why there must be certain documentation of the random number selection. What is the proper documentation of the random sample for the auditor's working papers?

2-31. The payroll journal for Robinson Furniture Company includes 2,628 payroll checks for the year ended June 30. The first check number is 26,437 and the last one is 29,064. The checks are recorded sequentially, and the sample unit is defined as the check number. The auditor has decided to use systematic sampling to select a random sample of 120 checks.

REQUIRED:

a. Select the first ten check numbers to be included in the random sample. Assume a random starting point of 8.

b. What are the advantages and problems with the use of the approach in part *a*?

c. Assume the decision is made to use four multiple starts. The random numbers for each start are selected from the first two usable digits in the random number table (the starting point is item 1002, column 7, Figure 2-1). Select all numbers for the first start and the first three numbers for the other three starts.

d. What are the advantages and problems associated with using systematic sampling with multiple starts?

2-32. This problem requires the availability of a computer or computer terminal that is programmed to select random numbers.

REQUIRED:

a. Use the computer or terminal to select a sample of 75 canceled checks from a cash disbursement journal. The checks for the year begin with 2167 and end with 8573. The computer listing should include the numbers in both random and sequential order.

b. Explain the advantages and disadvantages of obtaining the random numbers by use of a computer, compared to a random number table.

c. What is the appropriate documentation for the auditor's working papers when random numbers are selected by use of a computer?

2-33. Roger Starr, CPA, has decided to use dollar unit sampling to select a random sample of 120 items from a voucher register. The voucher register has 194 pages, with 60 items per page. The total in the voucher register is $6,952,326.

REQUIRED:

a. What is the sampling unit? Explain how a random sample of 120 items would be selected using a random number table.

b. Explain how you would identify physical audit units containing the random dollars selected without computer assistance, assuming there are no cumulative totals.

c. Assume one population item in the voucher register was recorded at $67,468. Would that item be included in the sample? Could it be included in the sample twice?

d. Assume the client failed to record four vouchers in the voucher register. What is the likelihood of uncovering at least one of the unrecorded transactions in the dollar unit sample?

e. Assume Roger decided to use systematic rather than the random number table. What is the interval?

2-34. The following is the entire extended inventory for Jake's Bookbinding Company. The population is smaller than would ordinarily be used for statistical sampling, but an entire population is useful to show how to select samples by dollar unit sampling.

Population item	Recorded amount	Population item	Recorded amount
1	$ 1,410	21	$4,865
2	9,130	22	770
3	660	23	2,305
4	3,355	24	2,665
5	5,725	25	1,000
6	8,210	26	6,225
7	580	27	3,675
8	44,110	28	6,250
9	825	29	1,890
10	1,155	30	27,705
11	2,270	31	935
12	50	32	5,595
13	5,785	33	930
14	940	34	4,045
15	1,820	35	9,480
16	3,380	36	360
17	530	37	1,145
18	955	38	6,400
19	4,490	39	100
20	17,140	40	8,435
			$207,295

REQUIRED:

a. Select a random sample (nonreplacement) of ten items using the random number table in Figure 2-1. Define the sampling unit as a physical unit (population item). Use a starting point of item 1011, column 4, the first two digits.

b. Select a random sample of ten items using systematic sampling. Define the sampling unit as a physical unit and use a random starting point of 4.

c. Select a random sample of ten items using dollar unit sampling from the random number table in Figure 2-1. Use a starting point of item 1000, column 1. Take the first digit in the column to the right of the one being used to get six digits. Use only odd columns for the first five digits. Identify the physical units associated with the random numbers.

d. Select a random sample of ten items using systematic dollar unit sampling. Use a starting point of 1857. Identify the physical units associated with the random numbers.

e. Which sample items will always be included in the systematic dollar unit sample regardless of the starting point? Will that also be true of random number table dollar unit sampling?

f. Rank the four methods in terms of ease of selection in this case.

g. Why would an auditor use dollar unit sampling?

3

attributes sampling

INTRODUCTION

Attributes sampling is used to estimate the *proportion* of items in a population containing a characteristic or attribute of interest. This proportion is called the *occurrence rate* and is the ratio of the items containing the specific attribute to the total number of population items. It is generally expressed as a percentage. Auditors are usually interested in the occurrence of errors in populations and refer to the occurrence rate as an error rate. An error may be a compliance deviation or a monetary error, depending on the nature of the audit test.

Assume, for example, that the auditor wants to determine the percentage of duplicate sales invoices that do not have shipping documents attached. There is an actual but unknown percentage of unattached shipping documents. The error rate in the sample is used to statistically estimate the population error rate. The estimate is expressed as an *interval estimate* of the population error rate and is a statement of probability that the interval does contain the actual population error rate. The auditor might conclude, for example, that the percentage of unattached invoices is between 1 and 4 at a 95 percent confidence level.

The definition of what constitutes an error occurrence must be clearly stated for attributes sampling before statistical measurement is possible.

Every sample item tested must be classified as an error or a non-error. For example, would a missing shipping document for a sale of $1.27 be considered an error? The auditor must make such decisions based on audit judgment. This decision is preferably made before the testing starts, to ensure that the auditor is adequately prepared to evaluate his findings.

Although attributes sampling is used in direct tests of balances, its most common use is in testing transactions. In fact, the statistical sampling methods used in testing transactions are almost exclusively attributes sampling methods with simple random samples of either physical units or dollar units. This chapter discusses attributes sampling with simple random samples of physical units. Attributes sampling with dollar units is discussed in Chapter 9, along with the other methods used to evaluate dollar unit samples.

In order to understand properly the application of attributes sampling, therefore, it is important to understand clearly the nature of tests of transactions.

TESTS OF TRANSACTIONS

Nature of Tests of Transactions

Tests of transactions provide audit evidence concerning the *recording of individual transactions* in the client's books of original entry and their summarization in journals, subsidiary ledgers, and the general ledger. The primary audit procedures used for tests of transactions are examination of supporting documentation for transactions, performance of mechanical accuracy tests (footing, extending, and tracing totals), and observation of employees' activities.

Tests of transactions are performed for a given client in several audit areas, depending on the nature of the client's books and records. Usually, a separate test of transactions is performed for each of the books of original entry, since these contain the major types of transactions of the company and are a part of its primary accounting systems. Typical transactions areas in which tests are conducted are sales, cash receipts, purchases of goods and services, cash disbursements, payroll, and the general journal.

Purpose of Tests of Transactions

Auditors perform tests of transactions to determine the effectiveness of the client's accounting system and internal controls. Direct tests of balances and related audit costs can be reduced when the auditor has tested the system and concluded that it is reliable.

Two types of tests of transactions need to be distinguished: *compliance tests* and *substantive tests*.

Compliance Tests. These tests are audit procedures designed to verify whether the client's internal accounting controls are being applied in the manner described to the auditor and intended by the client's management. If, after the tests, the client's controls appear to be operating effectively, the auditor is justified in placing reliance upon the system and thereby reducing the substantive tests. Compliance tests are concerned primarily with three aspects of the client's controls:

1. *The frequency with which the necessary control procedures were performed.* Before controls can be relied upon to reduce substantive testing, the prescribed procedures in the system must be consistently complied with. An example of a compliance test is the examination of a sample of duplicate sales invoices to determine whether each one has been initialed for the approval of credit.

2. *The quality of the performance of the control procedures.* Even when a control procedure has been performed, it may not have been done properly. Quality of performance of a procedure can be tested by, for example, discussing with the credit manager the criteria used in deciding when credit sales should be approved and examining the details of approval documents for exceptions.

3. *The person performing the procedures.* The person responsible for a control procedure must be independent of incompatible functions if the control is to be effective. This is accomplished by segregation of duties—for example, between the handling of cash receipts and the recording of the transactions in the cash receipts journal and subsidiary accounts receivable ledger. Initials on documents can be inspected to determine who performed such procedures.

The client's control procedures can be conveniently divided into two types: those that leave a visual indication of having been performed (an *audit trail*), and those that do not. Examples of the former are the initials of an employee verifying the price and extensions on sales invoices, an internal auditor's initial indicating he has reviewed a bank reconciliation, and the signature of an authorized employee approving credit. Where no audit trail is available, the most likely control is the segregation of duties. An example is the opening of mail and the prelisting of cash receipts by an employee who does not prepare the cash receipts records.

When the auditor plans to rely upon a control that leaves an audit trail, it is usually tested for compliance by examining underlying documentation. For example, if the assistant credit manager approves sales returns and allowances, the auditor should discuss with that person the criteria used to grant credit memos, in order to determine if they are consistent with company policy, and then test a sample of returns and allowances for missing approvals.

In testing compliance for the segregation of duties, documents and records are usually not available for the auditor's examination. In those instances, it is necessary to make inquiries of personnel and observe the procedures as they are being performed to evaluate compliance. For example, a compliance test of the segregation of duties between the custody of cash and the recording of cash receipts can be made by asking each person to describe his or her duties. During the audit, the auditor should also observe who receives and deposits cash and who prepares cash receipts journal records.

Substantive Tests. A substantive test is a procedure designed to *test for dollar errors* directly affecting the fair presentation of financial statement balances. Such errors (often termed *monetary errors*) are a clear indication of the misstatement of the accounts. The only question the auditor must resolve is whether the errors are sufficiently material to require adjustment or disclosure. Examples of substantive tests of transactions are the comparison of a duplicate sales invoice with a shipping document to determine whether the quantity shipped equals the quantity billed and the footing of a duplicate sales invoice for accuracy.

Relationship between Compliance and Substantive Tests

For better understanding of the nature of compliance and substantive tests, an examination of their difference is useful. Compliance tests differ from substantive tests in that an error in a compliance test is only an indication of the *likelihood* of errors affecting the dollar value of the financial statements. Compliance errors are material only if they occur with sufficient frequency to cause the auditor to believe there may be material dollar errors in the statements. Substantive tests should then be performed to determine whether *dollar errors have actually occurred.* As an illustration, assume that the client's system requires an independent clerk to verify the quantity, price, and extension of each sales invoice, and then to initial the duplicate invoice to indicate performance. A compliance audit procedure would be to examine a sample of duplicate sales invoices for the initials of the person who verified the quantitative data. If there are a significant number of documents without a signature, the auditor should follow this up with substantive tests. This can be done by extending the test of the duplicate sales invoices to include verifying prices, extensions, and footings, or by increasing the sample size for the confirmation of accounts receivable. Of course, the actual invoices may be correct even though the compliance procedure is not operating effectively. This will be the result if the person originally preparing the sales invoices did a conscientious and competent job.

When Not to Perform Compliance Tests

There are two circumstances in which the auditor may decide not to perform compliance tests on a particular control in the system. The first occurs when the auditor concludes that the *control procedure is not effective*;

for example, because a person performing internal verification is incompetent or not independent. The justification for not testing is that there is no reason to test a control the auditor considers too ineffective to rely upon. The second case occurs when the *audit cost required to test for compliance is greater than the cost saving from reduced substantive tests* that would result from relying upon the client's controls. An example is the tests of sales invoices discussed in the preceding paragraph. The auditor could simply ignore the initials of the person who had verified the calculations and act as if no internal verification had taken place. Naturally, substantive tests would have to be increased accordingly.

Even if the auditor's compliance tests yield good results, some substantive tests are necessary, although they need not always be substantive tests of transactions. It would be inappropriate, for example, to limit the testing of duplicate sales invoices to examining the initials of a person who has performed internal verification. The presence of the initials is some evidence of clerical accuracy, but additional assurance is needed. Even if a control procedure exists, errors are still possible if the procedure is performed improperly. The audit procedures, sample size, selection of the items for testing, and timing of substantive tests can be modified and reduced by compliance tests, but they cannot be eliminated.

Both compliance and substantive tests of transactions are used for most audits. It is common to do both types simultaneously using attributes sampling methods. The methodology for doing this is illustrated in the remainder of this chapter.

SAMPLING DISTRIBUTION

Assume a population of sales invoices of which 5 percent have no shipping document attached. If the auditor takes a random sample of 50 invoices, how many will have missing shipping documents? The sample might contain no errors, or it might contain six or seven. The *probability* of each possible number of errors that would exist in the sample forms the *sampling distribution*.

The sampling distribution for the described sampled population is shown in Figure 3-1, where it can be seen that, with a sample of 50 items from a population with a population error rate of 5 percent, the likelihood of obtaining a sample with at least one error is 92.3 percent $(1 - .077)$.

There is a unique sampling distribution for each population error rate and sample size, which is mathematically determined. The distribution for a sample size of 100 from a population with a 5 percent error rate is different from the previous one, as is the distribution for a sample of 60 from a population with a 3 percent error rate.

In actual audit situations, the auditor does not take repeated samples

Number of errors	Percent of errors	Probability	Cumulative probability
0	0%	.0769	.0769
1	2%	.2025	.2794
2	4%	.2611	.5405
3	6%	.2199	.7604
4	8%	.1360	.8964
5	10%	.0656	.9620
6	12%	.0260	.9880
7	14%	.0120	1.0000

FIGURE 3-1 Probability of each error rate for a sample of 50 items from a population with a known 5% error rate

from known populations. He takes one sample from an unknown population and gets a specific number of errors in that sample. However, knowledge about sampling distributions enables the auditor to make statistical statements about the population. For example, with a sample of 50 sales invoices selected to test for attached shipping documents and a finding of one exception, the auditor could examine the previous probability table and know that there is a 20.25 percent probability that the sample came from a population with a 5 percent error rate, and a 79.75 percent $(1 - .2025)$ probability that the sample was taken from a population having some other error rate. Since it is similarly possible to calculate the probability distributions for other population error rates, these can be examined in the aggregate to draw more specific statistical conclusions about the unknown population being sampled.

NATURE OF ATTRIBUTES ESTIMATES

Assume that an auditor takes a random sample of 200 sales invoices from a population of 10,000 to determine if the quantities and descriptions on the related shipping documents are the same as on the invoices. The auditor carefully compares the documents and finds eight exceptions in the sample. What is the error rate in the population? Is it 4 percent? The auditor will never know the true population error rate, but can be fairly certain there are more or less than exactly 400 errors. Fortunately, the exact percentage is not that important. Usually the auditor is primarily concerned about whether the population error rate exceeds a certain upper percentage, such as 5 percent. If the population error rate appears to be more than the upper percentage set before the testing is done, some additional audit work is needed; otherwise, no more testing is necessary.

The statistical upper limit of the population error rate based on the sample results is referred to as the *computed upper precision limit* (CUPL) and is determined using a *one-sided attributes estimate*. The probability that the true population error rate does not exceed the computed upper precision limit is called the *confidence level*, or, alternatively, the *reliability level*. After the audit tests are completed for attributes sampling, the statistical result is stated as a computed upper precision limit at a particular confidence level. For example, an auditor might conclude that the computed upper precision limit of the comparison of quantities and descriptions on sales invoices to shipping documents is 6 percent at a 95 percent confidence level. An explanation of the meaning of that conclusion follows later.

Use of Tables

Auditors use statistical tables to determine the statistical results of attributes sampling in audit tests as a way of saving time. Tables are readily available and simple to use. The only difficulty is the occasional lack of availability of tables presenting the information in exactly the form the auditor wants it. Usually, this problem can be overcome.

The computed upper precision limit can be determined using tables with the following steps:

1. Select the attributes table for the desired confidence level.
2. Locate the actual number of sample items in the far left column and read to the right.
3. Locate the actual *sample occurrence rate* for the sample in the "occurrence rate" column and read downward.
4. Locate the intersection of steps 2 and 3. The result is the computed upper precision limit *in percent* at the confidence level stated for the table.

By the use of Figure 3-2, it can be seen that the computed upper precision limit at a 90 percent confidence level for the previous example is 6.4 percent (eight exceptions from a sample of 200). The result means the auditor can state with a 90 percent confidence level that the true population error rate does not exceed 6.4 percent. Stated another way, it means there is a 10 percent statistical risk (100% − 90%) that the true population error rate exceeds 6.4 percent. Does this result indicate that if 100 percent of the population were tested, the true error rate would be 6.4 percent? No, the true error rate is unknown, but there is only a 10 percent chance of its being more than 6.4 percent. There is a 90 percent chance of its being 6.4 percent or less.

Another useful way of looking at the statistical results is by a combination of the *point estimate of the error rate* and the *computed precision interval*. The point estimate of the population error rate is the same as the sample error rate; in this case, 4 percent. The computed precision interval is 2.4 percent (6.4% − 4%). It represents a statistical measure of the inability to accurately

Occurrence Rate

Sample Size	0.0	.5	1.0	2.0	3.0	4.0	5.0	6.0	7.0	8.0	9.0	10.0	12.0	14.0	16.0	18.0	20.0	25.0	30.0	40.0	50.0
50	4.5			7.6		10.3		12.9		15.4		17.8	20.1	22.7	24.7	27.2	29.1		39.8	50.0	59.9
100	2.3		3.8	5.2	6.6	7.8	9.1	10.3	11.7	12.7	14.0	15.0	17.3	19.6	21.7	24.0	26.1	31.4	36.6	46.9	56.8
150	1.5			4.4		6.9		9.3		11.6		13.9	16.1	18.4	20.5	22.7	24.8		35.2	45.5	55.4
200	1.1	1.9	2.6	4.0	5.2	6.4	7.6	8.8	10.0	11.0	12.2	13.3	15.5	17.7	19.8	22.0	24.0	29.3	34.5	44.4	54.4
250	.9			3.7		6.1		8.4		10.7		12.9	15.1	17.2	19.3	21.5	23.6		33.7	43.7	53.7
300	.8		2.2	3.5	4.7	5.9	7.0	8.2	9.3	10.4	11.5	12.6	14.7	16.9	19.0	21.1	23.2	28.2	33.2	43.2	53.2
350	.7			3.3		5.7		8.0		10.2		12.3	14.5	16.7	18.8	20.9	22.8		32.8	42.8	52.8
400	.6	1.3	2.0	3.2	4.4	5.6	6.7	7.8	8.9	10.0	11.1	12.2	14.3	16.5	18.5	20.5	22.5	27.5	32.5	42.5	52.5
450	.5			3.1		5.5		7.7		9.9		12.0	14.2	16.3	18.3	20.3	22.3		32.3	42.3	52.2
500	.5		1.8	3.1	4.2	5.4	6.5	7.6	8.7	9.8	10.9	11.9	14.1	16.1	18.1	20.1	22.1	27.1	32.1	42.1	52.0
550	.4			3.0		5.3		7.5		9.7		11.8	13.9	15.9	17.9	19.9	21.9		31.9	41.9	51.9
600	.4	1.1	1.7	2.9	4.1	5.2	6.3	7.4	8.5	9.6	10.7	11.6	13.7	15.7	17.7	19.7	21.7	26.7	31.7	41.7	51.7
650	.4			2.9		5.2		7.4		9.5		11.5	13.6	15.6	17.6	19.6	21.6		31.6	41.6	51.6
700	.3		1.7	2.9	4.0	5.1	6.2	7.3	8.4	9.5	10.5	11.4	13.5	15.5	17.5	19.5	21.5	26.5	31.5	41.5	51.5
750	.3			2.8		5.1		7.3		9.4		11.3	13.4	15.4	17.4	19.4	21.4		31.4	41.4	51.4
800	.3	1.0	1.6	2.8	3.9	5.0	6.1	7.2	8.3	9.3	10.3	11.3	13.3	15.3	17.3	19.3	21.3	26.3	31.3	41.3	51.3
850	.3			2.8		5.0		7.2		9.2		11.2	13.2	15.3	17.3	19.3	21.3		31.3	41.3	51.3
900	.3		1.6	2.7	3.9	5.0	6.0	7.1	8.2	9.1	10.2	11.2	13.2	15.2	17.2	19.2	21.2	26.2	31.2	41.2	51.2
950	.2			2.7		4.9		7.1		9.1		11.1	13.1	15.1	17.1	19.1	21.1		31.1	41.1	51.1
1000	.2	.9	1.5	2.7	3.8	4.9	6.0	7.1	8.1	9.1	10.1	11.1	13.1	15.1	17.1	19.1	21.1	26.1	31.1	41.1	51.1
1500	.2		1.4	2.5	3.6	4.7	5.7	6.7	7.7	8.7	9.7	10.7	12.7	14.7	16.7	18.7	20.7	25.7	30.7	40.7	50.7
2000	.1	.8	1.3	2.5	3.5	4.5	5.5	6.5	7.5	8.5	9.5	10.5	12.5	14.5	16.5	18.5	20.5	25.5	30.5	40.6	50.6
2500	.1		1.3	2.4	3.4	4.4	5.4	6.4	7.4	8.4	9.4	10.4	12.4	14.4	16.4	18.4	20.4	25.4	30.4	40.4	50.4
3000	.1	.7	1.3	2.4	3.4	4.4	5.4	6.4	7.4	8.4	9.4	10.4	12.4	14.4	16.4	18.4	20.4	25.4	30.4	40.4	50.4
4000	.1	.7	1.2	2.3	3.3	4.3	5.3	6.3	7.3	8.3	9.3	10.3	12.3	14.3	16.3	18.3	20.3	25.3	30.3	40.3	50.3
5000	.0	.7	1.2	2.3	3.2	4.2	5.2	6.2	7.2	8.2	9.2	10.2	12.2	14.2	16.2	18.2	20.2	25.2	30.2	40.2	50.2

FIGURE 3-2 One-sided upper precision limits for confidence level of 90.0 percent

Arens and Loebbecke, *Auditing: An Integrated Approach*, 2nd ed. (Englewood Cliffs, N.J.: Prentice-Hall, Inc., 1980), p. 336. Reprinted with permission.

measure the population error rate owing to the restriction of the test to a sample. The combination of the two is the "worst likely error rate," which is called the computed upper precision limit, at the confidence level specified.

Interpolation. Interpolation of the tables may be necessary for two reasons: either the actual sample size or the percentage of errors in the sample may be different from those in the tables. Interpolation on a straight-line basis is satisfactory. For example, if there were eight errors from a sample of 150 (5.33 percent), the computed upper precision limit at a 90 percent confidence level would be calculated as 8.5 percent $\left[6.9 + \frac{5.33 - 4.0}{6.0 - 4.0}(9.3 - 6.9) \right]$. The interpolation is taking place between an upper precision limit of 9.3 percent from the table for a 6 percent error rate and 6.9 percent for a 4 percent error rate.

Effect of Population Size. In the preceding discussion, the size of the population was ignored in determining the computed upper precision limit. It may seem strange to some readers, but statistical theory proves that in most types of populations where attributes sampling applies, the population size is only a minor consideration in determining statistical results. This is because representativeness is ensured by the random selection process. Once an adequate sample size is obtained that includes a good cross-section of items, additional items are not needed regardless of population size.

The tables used by most auditors, including the tables in this text, are based upon infinite population sizes. It is possible to take the population size into account in determining the computed upper precision limit by making an adjustment called the *finite correction factor*. The calculation is as follows:

$$\text{Revised CUPL} = \text{Sample error rate} + \left(\text{Computed precision interval}\sqrt{\frac{N - n}{N}}\right)$$

where N = population size, and n = actual sample size. If the population size in the previous example had been 1,000, the revised CUPL would be 6.2 percent $\left(4\% + 2.4\%\sqrt{\frac{1{,}000 - 200}{1{,}000}}\right)$. The reduction of the CUPL is ordinarily not worth the effort to calculate unless the sample size is at least equal to 10 percent of the population.

Effect of a Change in the Factors. At this point, the reader should be able to see the effect of changing the four factors making up the computed upper precision limit, assuming the other factors are held constant. The following shows the effect of increasing each of the four factors:

Type of change	Effect on the CUPL
1. Increase the confidence level.	Increase
2. Increase the sample size.	Decrease
3. Increase the number of errors.	Increase
4. Increase the population size.	Minor increase

Determining the Initial Sample Size

Factors Affecting Sample Size. Determining the sample size for an audit test involves the same concepts as determining the computed upper precision limit. Four factors determine the initial sample size of attributes samples: the *population size*, the *desired upper precision limit*, the *desired confidence level*, and an *advance estimate of the population error rate*.

The population size is not a major factor for the reasons just discussed. The initial sample size is called initial because the errors in the actual sample must be evaluated before it is possible to decide whether the sample is sufficiently large to achieve the audit objectives.

The desired upper precision limit is specified by the auditor. It answers the question, What is the largest computed upper precision limit the auditor is willing to allow? If the auditor could have a computed upper precision limit of 6 percent and be satisfied with the statistical results, the desired upper precision limit should be set at 6 percent.

The desired confidence level can be looked at in the same manner as the desired upper precision limit. Assume the auditor wants to be 95 percent certain that the true population error rate is not over 6 percent. The desired confidence level is therefore 95 percent.

In determining the advance estimate of the population error rate, it is common to use the *results of the preceding year's audit* as information to help make this estimate. If last year's results are not available or if they are considered unreliable, the auditor can take a small *preliminary sample* of the current year's population for this purpose. Most auditors consider a preliminary sample impractical. Instead, an advance estimate is often based on internal control evaluation and discussions with management. It is not critical that the estimates be absolutely correct, because the current year's sample error rate is ultimately used to estimate the population characteristics.

Use of Tables. When the three major factors affecting sample size have been determined, it is possible to compute an initial sample size by using tables based on the binomial distribution in the same manner as for evaluating results. These tables may be the same ones used for evaluating results, or they may have changes in form for convenience of use. It should be kept in mind that these are "one-sided tables," which means that they represent the *upper* precision limit only for the given confidence level.

In using the tables to compute the initial sample size, three steps are required:

1. Select the table corresponding to the desired confidence level.
2. Locate the expected (advance estimate) occurrence rate at the top of the table.
3. Read down the table in that column to the line that contains the desired upper precision limit. The left-hand column for that line contains the initial sample size to use. Interpolation for values not in the table is valid.

To illustrate the use of the table, assume an auditor is willing to rely upon the system of credit approval if the rate of missing credit approvals in the population (desired upper precision limit) does not exceed 6 percent at a 95 percent confidence level. On the basis of past experience, the sample error rate has been about 4 percent. Using the 95 percent confidence level in Figure 3-3, the initial sample size is determined to be 400. (Read down the 4 percent column until 6 percent is reached.)

Finite Correction Factor. The finite correction factor is applied to determining sample size as follows:

$$n = \frac{n'}{1 + \dfrac{n'}{N}}$$

where:

n' = sample size before considering the effect of the population size
N = population size
n = revised sample size after considering the effect of the population size

As an example, assume the size of the population of sales orders in the previous problem to be 2,000. The revised sample size is computed as follows:

$$n = \frac{400}{1 + 400/2{,}000} = 333$$

If the population is 20,000 rather than 2,000, the revised sample size is 392, which is not significantly lower than the 400 shown in the table.

Is this a large enough sample size for this audit? It is not possible to answer that question until after the tests have been performed. If the actual error rate in the sample turns out to be somewhat over 4 percent but less than 6 percent, the auditor will be unsure of the adequacy of the controls. This will become apparent as we proceed.

Occurrence Rate

Sample Size	0.0	.5	1.0	2.0	3.0	4.0	5.0	6.0	7.0	8.0	9.0	10.0	12.0	14.0	16.0	18.0	20.0	25.0	30.0	40.0	50.0
50	5.8			9.1		12.1		14.8		17.4		19.9	22.3	25.1	27.0	29.6	31.6		42.4	52.6	62.4
100	3.0		4.7	6.2	7.6	8.9	10.2	11.5	13.0	14.0	15.4	16.4	18.7	21.2	23.3	25.6	27.7	33.1	38.4	48.7	56.6
150	2.0			5.1		7.7		10.2		12.6		15.0	17.3	19.6	21.7	24.0	26.1		36.7	47.0	56.8
200	1.5		3.1	4.5	5.8	7.1	8.3	9.5	10.8	11.9	13.1	14.2	16.4	18.7	20.9	23.1	25.2	30.5	35.7	45.7	55.6
250	1.2	2.4		4.2		6.7		9.1		11.4		13.7	15.9	18.1	20.3	22.4	24.6		34.8	44.8	54.7
300	1.0		2.6	3.9	5.2	6.4	7.6	8.8	10.0	11.1	12.2	13.3	15.5	17.7	19.8	22.0	24.1	29.1	34.1	44.1	54.1
350	.9			3.7		6.2		8.5		10.8		13.0	15.2	17.4	19.5	21.7	23.6		33.6	43.6	53.6
400	.7	1.6	2.3	3.6	4.8	6.0	7.2	8.3	9.5	10.6	11.7	12.8	15.0	17.2	19.2	21.2	23.2	28.2	33.2	43.2	53.2
450	.7			3.5		5.9		8.2		10.4		12.6	14.8	16.8	18.9	20.9	22.9		32.9	42.9	52.9
500	.6		2.1	3.4	4.6	5.8	6.9	8.0	9.2	10.3	11.4	12.5	14.6	16.7	18.6	20.7	22.6	27.6	32.6	42.6	52.6
550	.5			3.3		5.7		7.9		10.1		12.3	14.4	16.4	18.4	20.4	22.4		32.4	42.4	52.4
600	.5	1.3	2.0	3.2	4.4	5.6	6.7	7.8	9.0	10.0	11.2	12.2	14.2	16.2	18.2	20.2	22.2	27.2	32.2	42.2	52.2
650	.5			3.2		5.5		7.7		10.0		12.1	14.1	16.1	18.1	20.1	22.1		32.1	42.1	52.1
700	.4		1.9	3.1	4.3	5.4	6.6	7.7	8.8	9.9	10.8	11.9	13.9	15.9	17.9	19.9	21.9	26.9	31.9	41.9	51.9
750	.4			3.1		5.4		7.6		9.8		11.8	13.8	15.8	17.8	19.8	21.8		31.8	41.8	51.8
800	.4	1.1	1.8	3.0	4.2	5.3	6.4	7.5	8.7	9.7	10.7	11.7	13.7	15.7	17.7	19.7	21.7	26.7	31.7	41.7	51.7
850	.4			3.0		5.3		7.5		9.6		11.6	13.6	15.6	17.6	19.6	21.6		31.6	41.6	51.6
900	.3		1.7	3.0	4.1	5.2	6.3	7.5	8.5	9.5	10.5	11.5	13.5	15.5	17.5	19.5	21.5	26.5	31.5	41.5	51.5
950	.3			2.9		5.2		7.4		9.4		11.4	13.4	15.5	17.4	19.5	21.4		31.5	41.5	51.5
1000	.3	1.0	1.7	2.9	4.0	5.2	6.3	7.4	8.4	9.4	10.4	11.4	13.4	15.4	17.4	19.4	21.4	26.4	31.4	41.4	51.4
1500	.2		1.5	2.7	3.8	4.9	5.9	6.9	7.9	8.9	9.9	10.9	12.9	14.9	16.9	18.9	20.9	25.9	30.9	40.9	50.9
2000	.1	.8	1.4	2.6	3.7	4.7	5.7	6.7	7.7	8.7	9.7	10.7	12.7	14.7	16.7	18.7	20.7	25.7	30.7	40.7	50.7
2500	.1		1.4	2.6	3.6	4.6	5.6	6.6	7.6	8.6	9.6	10.6	12.6	14.6	16.6	18.6	20.6	25.6	30.6	40.6	50.6
3000	.1	.8	1.4	2.5	3.5	4.5	5.5	6.5	7.5	8.5	9.5	10.5	12.5	14.5	16.5	18.5	20.5	25.5	30.5	40.5	50.5
4000	.1	.7	1.3	2.4	3.4	4.4	5.4	6.4	7.4	8.4	9.4	10.4	12.4	14.4	16.4	18.4	20.4	25.4	30.4	40.4	50.4
5000	.1	.7	1.3	2.3	3.3	4.3	5.3	6.3	7.3	8.3	9.3	10.3	12.3	14.3	16.3	18.3	20.3	25.3	30.3	40.3	50.3

FIGURE 3-3 One-sided upper precision limits for confidence level of 95.0 percent

Arens and Loebbecke, *Auditing: An Integrated Approach*, 2nd ed. (Englewood Cliffs, N.J.: Prentice-Hall, Inc., 1980), p. 337. Reprinted with permission.

Effect of a Change in the Factors. The following table illustrates the effect on sample size of increasing each of the four factors. A decrease of any of the factors will have the opposite effect.

Type of change	Effect on preliminary sample size
1. Increase the desired confidence level.	Increase
2. Increase the desired upper precision limit.	Decrease
3. Increase the estimate of the population error rate.	Increase
4. Increase the population size.	Increase (slight)

APPLICATION OF ATTRIBUTES SAMPLING

Now that the underlying concepts of attributes sampling have been examined, it is desirable to study in more detail how the method can be applied to auditing.

Generally, more than one attributes sampling application is used for a given audit, and often a single use includes applying several audit procedures simultaneously in a given audit area. The most common audit areas where attributes sampling is used are acquisition of goods and services, cash disbursements, payroll, sales, and cash receipts. The discussion that follows uses the acquisition of goods and services (purchases) as the frame of reference for illustrating the use of attributes sampling.

It is assumed throughout the illustration that the auditor has evaluated the system of internal control and has already decided upon the necessary audit procedures for purchases for Holly Manufacturing Company. Holly Mfg. uses a prenumbered voucher system. A voucher for a particular transaction includes a vendor's invoice, a receiving report, and a purchase order whenever these are applicable. The audit procedures for purchases are as follows:

1. Test foot and crossfoot the voucher register and trace the balances to the general ledger.
2. Review the journals and general ledger for unusual transactions and amounts.
3. Review the accounts payable subsidiary ledger for miscellaneous debits and credits.
4. Select vouchers from the voucher register, and for each voucher, do the following to the extent applicable:

   a. Examine voucher file for inclusion of vendor's invoice, receiving report, and purchase order to the extent each is applicable.

   b. Evaluate the transaction by examining supporting documentation to determine if it is a valid business transaction conducted at arm's length.

   c. Examine vendor's invoice for approval by an authorized official (i.e., up to $5,000, S. Weber; $5,000 and over, K. Stair).

   d. Examine vendor's invoice for an initial indicating internal verification of unit prices, quantities, and clerical accuracy.

   e. Trace from vendor's invoice to related purchase order and compare vendor's name, quantity, unit price, and description. Examine authorization by purchasing department. Examine other evidence of authorization and propriety of purchase for non-inventory items.

   f. Trace from vendor's invoice to related receiving report and compare vendor's name, quantity, and description. Examine other evidence of receipt of goods or services for non-inventory items.

   g. Compute total cost by extending prices and quantities and footing the totals.

   h. Compare vendor name, amount, date, and account classification recorded in the purchase journal to the vendor's invoice.

   i. Evaluate the reasonableness of the account classification by examining the description of the goods and services on the vendor's invoice and comparing it to the chart of accounts.

   j. Trace from the voucher register to related accounts payable subsidiary ledger and compare amount, date, and voucher number.

   k. Trace from the voucher register to related perpetual inventory records and compare quantity, unit cost, date, and voucher number.

   l. Examine vendor's invoice, receiving report, and purchase order for entry of voucher number and date to prevent their reuse.

5. Account for a sequence of receiving reports in the accounting department's receiving report file, and examine each one to be sure there is a voucher number.

The following steps provide an outline of the methodology for using attributes sampling in tests of transactions. Each step will be studied separately in the discussion that follows.

1. State the objectives of the audit test.
2. Define the population.
3. Define the sampling unit.
4. Define the attributes of interest.
5. Specify the desired upper precision limit.
6. Specify the desired confidence level.
7. Estimate the population error rate.
8. Determine the initial sample size.
9. Randomly select the sample.
10. Perform the audit procedures.
11. Determine the computed upper precision limit.
12. Decide on the acceptability of the population.

State the Objectives of the Audit Test

The overall objectives of the test must be stated in terms of the particular audit area being tested. Generally, the overall objective of tests of transactions is to test the controls in a particular cycle. In the test of purchases, the overall objective is usually to test the reliability of controls over acquisition of goods and services.

Define the Population

The population represents the body of data about which the auditor wishes to generalize. The auditor can define the population to include whatever data are desired, but must *randomly sample from the entire population* as it has been defined and may *generalize only about that population from which samples have been taken.* For example, in performing tests of recorded purchase transactions, the auditor generally defines the population as all vouchers for the year. If random samples are chosen from only one month's transactions, it is invalid to draw statistical conclusions about the invoices for the entire year. It is important that the auditor carefully define the population in advance for consistency with the objectives of the audit tests. Furthermore, in some cases it may be necessary to define more than one population for a given set of audit objectives. For example, if the auditor intends to trace from receiving reports to vendors' invoices to test for unrecorded purchases, and from vendors' invoices to receiving reports to test validity, there are two populations (receiving reports and vendors' invoices, respectively).

Define the Sampling Unit

There are two major considerations in defining the sampling unit. First, all sampling units, as defined, must constitute the population defined. The definition of the population and the planned audit procedures thus dictate the appropriate sampling unit. For example, if the auditor wants to determine how frequently the client fails to receive goods that have been ordered, the sampling unit will probably be defined as the purchase order.

Second, where alternatives exist, the sampling unit will be defined as the alternative that is the easiest to obtain and apply the audit procedures to, in view of the sample selection methods available. For example, if the audit objective is to determine whether the proper quantity of goods described on the purchase order is received and billed by the vendor, it is possible to define the sampling unit as the purchase order, the receiving report, or the vendor's invoice. If purchase orders are entered in a journal and the other alternatives are only in source document form, definition of purchase orders as the sampling unit would be preferable, since journals generally facilitate sampling correspondence (that is, using page number, line number).

Define the Attributes of Interest

The auditor must carefully define the attributes being tested whenever attributes sampling is used. Unless a precise statement of what constitutes the attribute is made in advance, the staff person who performs the audit procedure will have no guidelines for identifying exceptions.

The attributes should include all the procedures in the audit program the auditor wants to test using attributes sampling, but frequently some procedures are combined. The decision about which attributes to combine and which to keep separate is the most important aspect of defining the attributes. If all possible types of attributes—such as vendor name, date, unit cost, and quantity—are separated for each procedure, the large number of attributes makes the problem unmanageable. On the other hand, if all the procedures are combined into one or two attributes, greatly dissimilar errors are evaluated together. A reasonable compromise is needed somewhere in between.

The attributes used for Holly Mfg. are shown in Figure 3-4. The attributes were taken directly from the audit procedures described in step 4 of the audit program for Holly (attribute 7 is a combination of steps 4g and 4h). Notice that the attributes are defined as positive statements, as compared to

---

Client: *Holly Manufacturing Co.*   Year ended *12–31–8X*

Attribute code	Description
1	Voucher file includes a vendor's invoice, receiving report, and purchase order when applicable.
2	The purchase appears to be a valid business transaction conducted at arm's length.
3	Vendor's invoice is approved by authorized official (up to $5,000, S. Weber; $5,000 and over, K. Stair).
4	Initial is on invoice indicating internal verification of unit price, quantity, and clerical accuracy.
5	Vendor's invoice has same vendor's name, quantity, description, and unit price as the purchase order; the purchase order is properly approved. (Non-inventory items are properly approved and are reasonable.)
6	Vendor's invoice has same vendor's name, quantity, and description as the receiving report. (Other evidence exists for the receipt of goods and services for which no receiving report is prepared.)
7	Total cost on the vendor's invoice has been correctly extended and footed; it is recorded at the proper amount and date in the purchase journal.
8	Account classification is reasonable.
9	The purchase is recorded in the accounts payable subsidiary ledger to the correct vendor, and at the correct date and amount.
10	The purchase is recorded in the inventory subsidiary ledger to the correct inventory item and at the correct date, quantity and unit cost.
11	Vendors' invoices, receiving reports, and purchase orders are canceled to avoid reuse.

FIGURE 3-4 Attributes sampling—description of attributes

audit procedures, which are stated as instructions. It is also notable that attributes sampling is not applicable for audit procedures 1, 2, and 3. It is possible to use attributes sampling for procedure 5, but a separate application is needed because the sampling unit is a receiving report rather than a voucher.

Each of the eleven attributes for Holly is verified for every item randomly selected for the sample relating to that attribute. When the item selection does not meet the attribute description, it is an exception for that attribute. For example, if there is no indication of internal verification for a particular vendor's invoice, attribute 4 is in error even if the price (attribute 5) and clerical records (attribute 7) are correct.

There may be situations in which an attribute is not applicable for a sample item. The monthly payment on a lease is an example. Attribute 1 (supporting documentation) is defined broadly enough to be applicable to all sample items, but attribute 10 (trace to inventory perpetuals) is applicable only to inventory purchases. When a sample item is not applicable for an attribute, it should be considered a discard for that attribute. The result is frequently a smaller sample size for some attributes unless additional items are selected.

Specify the Desired Upper Precision Limit

Establishing the *desired* upper precision limit requires the auditor to make a professional judgment. It represents the error rate the auditor will permit in the population and still be willing to rely upon the controls in the system. The suitable upper precision limit is a question of *materiality* and is therefore affected by the *definition of the attribute* and the *importance of the attribute*. It is common to use a different desired upper precision limit for different attributes. A classification error for Holly (attribute 8) is usually more important for purchases than the failure to internally verify prices, extensions, and footings (attribute 4). Therefore, a smaller desired upper precision limit is likely for the classification attribute. The desired upper precision limits for Holly are shown in Figure 3-5.

It is unusual for auditors to use desired upper precision limits larger than 10 percent or smaller than 2 percent. When population error rates exceed 10 percent, the control is usually meaningless anyway. Testing for such high error rates must be questioned from an audit logic standpoint. For precision limits of less than 2 percent, the required sample sizes are so large that auditors are reluctant to incur the high cost. The attribute would have to be critically important to use a desired upper limit of less than 2 percent. The most common desired upper limits for tests of transactions are between 3 and 7 percent.

Client: _Holly Mfg. Co._ Date: _12-31-8x_

Audit Area: _Test of Transactions—Purchases_

Define the Objective: _Examine vouchers and related documents to determine_
if the system is functioning as intended and as described in the
audit program.

Define the Population Precisely: _Vouchers for the period 1-1-8x to 12-31-8x. First_
voucher number = 3689; last voucher number = 9452.

Define the Sampling Unit, Organization of Population Items, and Random Selection Procedures: _Voucher number_
recorded in the voucher register sequentially; random number table

Description of Attributes	Planned Audit				Actual Results			
	Expected Error Rate	Upper Prec. Rate	Confidence Level	Sample Size	Sample Size	Number of Errors	Sample Error Rate	CUPL
1. Voucher file includes proper supporting documents.	1	5	90	80				
2. Transactions are reasonable for client.	0	3	95	100				
3. Vendor's invoice properly approved.	1	4	95	160				
4. Initials indicating internal verification	2	6	90	90				
5. Approved purchase order corresponds to vendor's invoice.	1	6	90	70				
6. Receiving report corresponds to vendor's invoice.	1	4	95	160				
7. Invoice is mechanically accurate and correctly entered in purchase journal.	0	3	95	100				
8. Account classification is reasonable.	1	4	95	160				
9. Purchase correctly posted to accounts payable subsidiary record.	0	4	95	80				
10. Purchase correctly posted to perpetual inventory record.	1	5	90	80				
11. Documents are canceled.	1	4	95	160				

FIGURE 3-5 Attributes sampling data sheet—partial

Specify the Desired Confidence Level

Choosing the appropriate confidence level in a particular situation is an important decision requiring the auditor's best judgment. Since the confidence level is a measure of the level of audit assurance the auditor desires, the important considerations affecting its choice are the *degree to which the auditor wishes to rely upon the system* and the *overall level of assurance appropriate for the engagement.* If the auditor plans to rely heavily upon the system as a basis for reducing substantive tests, a high level of assurance is desirable. Similarly, if the auditor feels the exposure to legal liability is great, it is desirable to set high confidence levels to minimize the likelihood that the true error rates will be greater than the computed results for all tests. Where significant reliance on controls is planned, there is general consensus in the profession that confidence levels used for tests of transactions should range from *90 to 95 percent.*

The auditor can also establish different confidence level requirements for different attributes of a particular audit test. This is illustrated in Figure 3-5. There is a lower confidence level for attributes 1, 4, 5, and 10 than for all the others. This indicates an intention to put heavier reliance on accounts payable controls than inventory controls for direct tests of balances.

Estimate the Population Error Rate

The advance estimate of the population error rate is used only for determining the initial sample size. This does not imply that it is unimportant. Assume that the auditor sets the desired confidence level at 95 percent, the desired upper precision limit at 5 percent, and the estimated error rate at 4 percent. The required sample size is determined from Figure 3-3 to be over 1,000 items. Assume that a 1 percent estimated error rate is more appropriate. The table indicates that a sample size of 100 is large enough.

It should be noted that the difference between the expected error rate and the desired upper precision limit ("precision") has a drastic effect on sample size. The larger that difference, the smaller the required sample size. The reason for this is that a larger difference indicates the need for a less precise estimate.

Determine the Initial Sample Size

The sample size for each attribute can be determined by the use of tables, as previously shown. The desired upper precision limit, the desired confidence level, and the advance estimate of the population error rate must be known for each attribute to determine the number of items to select. The required information and sample sizes are shown for Holly Manufacturing Company in Figure 3-5. The finite correction factor was not used for Holly, because less than 10 percent of the population items are tested.

Randomly Select the Sample

After computing the initial sample size for the attributes sampling application, the auditor must choose the particular elements in the population to be included in the sample. It is essential that the selection be random whenever statistical sampling is used. This can be done by the use of random number tables, computers, or systematic sampling, as previously discussed.

The random selection for Holly is straightforward except for the need for different sample sizes for several different attributes. One possibility is to select a random sample of 160 items and test the required number of items for each attribute (80 for attribute 1, 100 for attribute 2, and so on). One difficulty in this approach is the requirement that the testing be performed in random order to ensure a random sample for each attribute. An alternative approach, which was followed for Holly, is to increase to 100 items the sample size for all attributes except 3, 6, 8, and 11. Those four items would have a sample of 160 items. Now a random sample of 100 items can be selected for all attributes and an additional sample of 60 for the remaining four attributes.

The random sample must be properly documented. The documentation for the selection of the first 50 numbers is illustrated in Figure 3-6.

Perform the Audit Procedures

The audit procedures are performed in the same manner in statistical sampling as in judgmental sampling. The auditor examines each item in the sample to determine whether it is consistent with the definition of the attribute, and maintains a record of all the errors found.

In performing the audit procedures, it is essential that the auditor avoid *nonsampling errors*. A nonsampling error occurs when the auditor fails to recognize the existence of an actual error in the sample items. This can result from many causes, including lack of understanding of the objectives of the test, fatigue or boredom, carelessness, and client deception by using fictitious documents or records. Nonsampling errors have the effect of understating the population error rate because of the omission of actual errors in the sample. For example, if the actual number of exceptions in a sample of 200 items is nine, but the auditor unintentionally overlooks four of them because his mind wanders, a serious nonsampling error has occurred. Because of the auditor's failure to follow due care, an unacceptable population may be accepted.

Holly Manufacturing Company
Random Sample for Testing Purposes

1036	77339	64605	4 82583	18 85011	00955	50 84348
1087	61714	57933	5 37342	26000	33 93611	93346
1088	15232	48027	15832	19 62924	11509	End 95853
1089	41447	34275	10779	20 83515	34 63899	30932
1090	23244	43524	16382	21 36340	35 73581	76780
1091	53460	83542	25224	22 70378	36 49604	14609
1092	53442	16897	6 61578	05032	37 81825	76822
1093	55543	19096	04130	23104	38 60534	44842
1094	18185	63329	02340	23 63111	39 41768	74409
1095	02372	45690	7 38595	23121	40 73818	74454
1096	51715	35492	8 61371	24 87132	41 81585	55439
1097	24717	16785	9 42786	25 86585	21858	39489
1098	78002	32604	10 87295	26 93702	99438	68184
1099	35995	08275	11 62405	27 43313	03249	74135
1100	29152	86922	31508	28 42703	42 59638	31226
	Start					
1101	84192	90150	02904	26835	17174	42301
1102	21791	24764	12 53674	30093	43 45134	24073
1103	63501	05040	13 71881	17759	44 91881	69614
1104	07149	1 69285	14 55481	24889	45 67061	06631
1105	59443	98962	15 74778	29 96920	46 65620	36794
1106	39059	2 58021	28485	30 43052	99001	44400
1107	73176	3 58913	22638	31 69769	21102	72292
1108	11851	09065	96033	02752	47 58232	56504
1109	37515	25668	16 55785	32 66463	48 52758	67588
1110	45324	00016	17 46818	04373	49 75360	87519

Population = 3689 to 9452.
Correspondence — First 4 digits in table.
Route — Read down to end of column; start at top of the next column.
Sample size — 50, represented by sequential numbers 1 to 50.

FIGURE 3-6 Random sample for testing purchases

Arens and Loebbecke, *Auditing: An Integrated Approach*, 2nd ed. (Englewood Cliffs, N.J.: Prentice-Hall, Inc., 1980), p. 355. Reprinted with permission.

A related consideration is the identification of types of *errors not defined as attributes* during planning. These must never be overlooked just because they were not expected. Unexpected errors usually result in the auditor's revising his initial definition of attributes of interest, and may even necessitate a revision of the planned sample size.

It is necessary to document the audit tests to aid in summarizing the results and in providing information for review. It is common to use a worksheet for documentation. Some auditors prefer to use a worksheet containing a listing of all the elements in the sample; others prefer to limit the documentation to identifying the errors. This latter approach is followed in the example.

At the completion of the testing, the errors are tabulated to determine sample size after consideration of not-applicables and the number of errors in the sample for each attribute. This enables the auditor to compute the sample error rate and determine the computed upper precision limit from the tables. This information is summarized in Figures 3-7 and 3-8.

Determine the Computed Upper Precision Limit

After completing tests of the sample, the auditor is in a position to generalize about the population. It would be wrong to conclude that the population error rate is exactly the same as the sample error rate; the odds of this being the case are just too low. Instead, the auditor must compute the upper precision limit for the population error rate at the confidence level desired, based on the actual sample results. This is easily accomplished by using the attributes sampling tables previously discussed. To find the computed upper precision limit, it is necessary to know the number of errors that were found in the sample, the actual sample size, and the desired confidence level.

The computed upper precision limits for each attribute in the Holly Mfg. Co. example are shown in Figure 3-8. It can be seen that sample size, confidence level, and number of exceptions each affect the computed upper precision limit.

It is also necessary to examine the nature and causes of the errors found in order to understand their implications about the proper functioning of the accounting system. For example, if all the errors in the tests of account classification of vendors' invoices occurred while the person normally responsible for performing the tests was on vacation, this would affect the auditor's evaluation of the system and the subsequent investigation. An illustration of error analysis for Holly Mfg. is included in Figure 3-9.

Decide on the Acceptability of the Population

It is important to distinguish between the desired upper precision limit and confidence level that were *chosen by the auditor* before the tests were performed and the computed upper precision limit and confidence level that *resulted from the sample*. The first set represents the *standards that were deemed necessary* by the auditor, and the second set is the *result that is objectively computed* on the basis of the sample.

Before the population can be considered acceptable, the computed upper precision limit determined on the basis of the actual sample results must be

Identity of Item Selected	Attribute Present										
Voucher No.	1	2	3	4	5	6	7	8	9	10	11
3699										X	
3859				X							
3990				X							
4071			X	X							
4270										X	
4331										X	
4513				X							
4859				X							
5367								X			
5578	X										
5802								X			
5823										X	
5963										X	
6157			X	X							
6229				X							
6311										X	
7536				X							
8351										X	
8517				X							
8713										X	
9364							X				
9370										X	
9445				X							
No. Errors..	1	0	2	10	0	0	1	2	0	9	0
Sample Size	100	100	160	100	100	160	100	160	100	50	160

FIGURE 3-7 Documentation of sample items for attributes

Client: _Holly Mfg. Co._   Date: _12-31-8x_

Audit Area: _Test of Transactions—Purchases_

Define the Objective: _Examine vouchers and related documents to determine if the system is functioning as intended and as described in the audit program._

Define the Population Precisely: _Vouchers for the period 1-1-8x to 12-31-8x. First voucher number = 3689; last voucher number = 9452._

Define the Sampling Unit, Organization of Population Items, and Random Selection Procedures: _Voucher number, recorded in the voucher register sequentially; random number table_

Description of Attributes	Planned Audit				Actual Results			
	Expected Error Rate	Upper Prec. Rate	Confidence Level	Sample Size	Sample Size	Number of Errors	Sample Error Rate	CUPL
1. Voucher file includes proper supporting documents.	1	5	90	80	100	1	1%	3.3%
2. Transactions are reasonable for client	0	3	95	100	100	0	0	3
3. Vendor's invoice properly approved.	1	4	95	160	160	2	1.3	4
4. Initials indicating internal verification	2	6	90	90	100	10	10	15
5. Approved purchase order corresponds to vendor's invoice	1	6	90	70	100	0	0	2.3
6. Receiving report corresponds to vendor's invoice.	1	4	95	160	160	0	0	2
7. Invoice is mechanically accurate and correctly entered in purchase journal	0	3	95	100	100	1	1	4.7
8. Account classification is reasonable.	1	4	95	160	160	2	1.3	4
9. Purchase correctly posted to accounts payable subsidiary record.	0	4	95	80	100	0	0	3
10. Purchase correctly posted to perpetual inventory record.	1	5	90	80	50	9	18	27.2
11. Documents are canceled.	1	4	95	160	160	0	0	1.9

FIGURE 3-8 Completed attributes sampling data sheet

HOLLY MANUFACTURING COMPANY
Analysis of Errors (Partial)

Attribute	Number of Exceptions	Nature of Exceptions	Effect of this Audit and Other Comments
1	1	Purchase order is missing. Examined copy in purchasing dept. files.	—
2	0	—	—
3	2	No signature was present on vendor's invoice in both cases. All documents were complete; however, no indication of internal verification on either document —see 4.	A certain number of invoices are expected to lack signatures. At this level, found no breakdown in controls is considered to have occurred
4	10	No indication of internal verification. None of these vouchers contained any other types of errors or monetary errors.	Level of exceptions very high. Even though none of these had monetary errors, control is significantly lessened by this exception rate. We will: a) Increase planned extent of vouching of property, additions and other charges arising from disbursements b) Include items in management letter.

FIGURE 3-9 Analysis of errors (partial)

less than or equal to the desired upper precision limit when both are based upon the desired confidence level. In the Holly Manufacturing Company example, only attributes 4, 7, and 10 have a significantly larger computed upper precision limit than the desired limit. In this case, the control being tested can be relied upon to reduce the direct tests of balances as planned for all but three attributes. Careful analysis of the cause of errors may still indicate the possibility of a significant problem in a particular aspect of the controls not previously considered. The error analysis does not indicate a serious problem for any of the acceptable attributes in the Holly case.

Action When Computed Result Exceeds That Desired. When the computed upper precision limit fails to meet the planned requirements, it is necessary to take specific action. Four courses of action can be followed:

1. *Revise the upper precision limit or confidence level desired.* Ordinarily this action should not be taken. It should be followed only when the auditor has concluded that the original specifications were too conservative. The relaxing of either the upper precision limit or the confidence level may be difficult to defend if the auditor is ever subject to review by a court or a commission. If these requirements are changed, it should be on the basis of well-thought-out reasons. For example, a reduction of the confidence level for an attribute may be acceptable when the auditor finds a second control to rely on partially. A lower confidence level for the original control is then justified.

2. *Expand the sample size.* An increase in the sample size has the effect of decreasing the computed upper precision limit if the actual sample error rate does not increase. This can be demonstrated with Figures 3-2 and 3-3 by keeping the sample error rate constant and observing the decrease in the computed upper precision limit for increases in sample size.

The decision of whether to increase the sample size until the computed upper precision limit is less than the desired upper precision limit must be made on the basis of the cost versus the benefits. If the sample is not expanded, it is necessary to perform additional substantive tests because of the unacceptability of the controls. The cost of the additional compliance testing must be compared with the cost of the additional substantive tests. Of course, there is always a chance that an expanded attributes sample will continue to produce unacceptable results and additional substantive tests will still be necessary. Another examination of Figures 3-2 and 3-3 will demonstrate that when the sample error rate is close to the desired upper precision limit, a large sample size is needed to satisfy the statistical requirements.

It is obvious from examining the results in Figure 3-8 for Holly that it would be imprudent to increase the sample size for attributes 4 or 10. Given the sample error rate, it is unlikely that the computed upper limit will ever be less than that desired. It may be practical to increase the sample size in attribute 7 to obtain a satisfactory result. Using Figure 3-3, it can be seen that a computed upper precision limit of 3 percent, with one error in the sample, can be obtained with a sample of about 160. Naturally, if the auditor increases the sample size and finds more errors, the results would still be unsatisfactory. The auditor must evaluate how important it is to meet the desired upper precision limit.

3. *Alter the substantive procedures.* Instead of expanding the sample in order to rely upon the controls, it is acceptable to perform additional substantive proce-

dures. This alternative is followed in Holly for attributes 4, 7, and 10, as illustrated in Figure 3-9. There is an increase in testing of extensions, footings, and pricing, on a judgmental basis, owing to the lack of internal verification of vendors' invoices. The perpetual inventory records will not be relied upon at all for the physical observation and price tests of inventory.

4. *Write a management letter.* Writing a management letter is not a disposition of the current year audit problem. However this action is desirable, in combination with one of the other three actions, regardless of the nature of the errors, to help management take corrective action for subsequent years. Inclusion in the management letter is suggested for attribute 4 in Figure 3-9.

In some instances, it may be acceptable to limit the action to writing a management letter when the computed precision limit exceeds the required limit. This occurs if the auditor has no intention of relying on the control being tested or has already carried out sufficient substantive tests as part of tests of transactions.

SUGGESTED READINGS AND REFERENCES

CARMICHAEL, D. R., "Tests of Transactions—Statistical and Otherwise," *Journal of Accountancy*, February 1968, pp. 36–40.

WARREN, CARL S., "Interpreting and Evaluating Attributes Sampling," *The Internal Auditor*, July–August 1975, pp. 45–56.

REVIEW QUESTIONS

3-1. Define what is meant by tests of transactions. What is the purpose of performing tests of transactions?

3-2. Describe what is meant by compliance and substantive tests of transactions. What is the relationship between them?

3-3. There are two types of control procedures—those that leave an audit trail and those that do not. Which of these two types can be tested for compliance by using attributes sampling? How is the other type tested for compliance?

3-4. What is meant by a sampling distribution? Why are sampling distributions important in attributes sampling?

3-5. Define the term confidence level. What is the relationship between the confidence level the auditor selects and the intended reliance on the client's system of internal control?

3-6. An auditor selects a sample size of 100 items from a population of 10,000 items. How large should the sample size be, all other things being equal, if the population were 10,000,000 items? Explain your conclusion.

3-7. What is the relevance of the advance estimate of the population error rate in attributes sampling? How can it be determined?

3-8. What is meant by nonsampling errors, and why are they important? How can they be minimized?

3-9. Distinguish between the computed upper precision limit and the sample error rate. How is each determined?

3-10. What is the relationship between a tests of transactions audit program and the attributes of interest for a given audit area?

3-11. Distinguish between the desired upper precision limit and the computed upper precision limit. How is each determined?

3-12. Assuming that all other factors remain constant, state the relationship between the following:

a. Confidence level and sample size
b. Population size and sample size
c. Desired upper precision limit and sample size
d. Expected error rate and sample size

3-13. Assume that the auditor has selected 100 sales invoices from a population of 10,000 to test for an indication of internal verification of pricing and extensions. Determine the upper precision limit of the error at a 95 percent confidence level if three exceptions existed in the sample. Explain the meaning of the statistical results in auditing terms.

3-14. When the computed upper precision limit exceeds the desired upper precision limit, what courses of action are available to the auditor? Under what circumstances should each of these courses of action be followed?

3-15. Distinguish between random selection and statistical measurement. State the circumstances under which one can be used without the other.

DISCUSSION QUESTIONS AND PROBLEMS

3-16. The following multiple-choice questions about attributes sampling and related issues were taken from recent CPA examinations:

a. There are many kinds of statistical estimates that an auditor may find useful, but basically, every accounting estimate is either of a quantity or of an error rate. The statistical terms that roughly correspond to "quantities" and "error rate" respectively are:
   (i) Attributes and variables
   (ii) Variables and attributes
   (iii) Constants and attributes
   (iv) Constants and variables

b. The purpose of tests for compliance is to provide reasonable assurance that the accounting control procedures are being applied as prescribed. The sampling method that is *most* useful when testing for compliance is:
   (i) Judgmental sampling
   (ii) Attributes sampling
   (iii) Unrestricted random sampling with replacement
   (iv) Stratified random sampling

c. An example of sampling for attributes would be estimating the:
   (i) Quantity of specific inventory items

     (ii) Probability of losing a patent infringement case

     (iii) Percentage of overdue accounts receivable

     (iv) Dollar value of accounts receivable

d. The auditor's failure to recognize an error in an amount or an error in an internal control data processing procedure is described as a:

     (i) Statistical error

     (ii) Sampling error

     (iii) Standard error of the mean

     (iv) Nonsampling error

e. For a large population of cash disbursement transactions, Janet Smith, CPA, is testing compliance with internal control by using attributes sampling techniques. Anticipating an occurrence rate of 3 percent, she finds from a table that the required sample size is 400, with a desired upper precision limit of 5 percent and a reliability of 95 percent. If Smith anticipates an occurrence rate of only 2 percent but wants to maintain the same desired upper precision limit and reliability, the sample size would be closest to:

     (i) 200

     (ii) 400

     (iii) 533

     (iv) 800

f. When using statistical sampling for tests of compliance, an auditor's evaluation of compliance would include a statistical conclusion concerning whether:

     (i) Procedural deviations in the population were within an acceptable range

     (ii) Monetary precision is in excess of a certain predetermined amount

     (iii) The population total is not in error by more than a fixed amount

     (iv) Population characteristics occur at least once in the population

g. Which of the following best describes what the auditor means by the rate of occurrence in an attributes sampling plan?

     (i) The number of errors that can reasonably be expected to be found in a population

     (ii) The frequency with which a certain characteristic occurs within a population

     (iii) The degree of confidence that the sample is representative of the population

     (iv) The dollar range within which the true population total can be expected to fall

h. To satisfy the auditing standard to make a proper study and evaluation of internal control, Harvey Jones, CPA, uses statistical sampling to test compliance with internal control procedures. Why does Jones use this statistical sampling technique?

     (i) It provides a means of measuring mathematically the degree of reliability that results from examining only part of the data.

     (ii) It reduces the use of judgment required of Jones, because the AICPA has established numerical criteria for this type of testing.

    (iii) It increases Jones's knowledge of the client's prescribed procedures and their limitations.

    (iv) It is specified by generally accepted auditing standards.

3-17. (AICPA adapted) The use of statistical sampling techniques in an examination of financial statements does not eliminate judgmental decisions.

REQUIRED:

    a. Identify and explain four areas where judgment may be exercised by a CPA in planning a statistical sampling test.

    b. Assume that a CPA's sample shows an unacceptable error rate. Describe the various actions the CPA may take based upon these findings.

    c. A nonstratified sample of 80 accounts payable vouchers is to be selected from a population of 3,200. The vouchers are numbered consecutively from 1 to 3,200 and are listed, 40 to a page, in the voucher register. Describe four different techniques for selecting a random sample of vouchers for review.

3-18. Davidson Supply Company is a medium-sized distributor of wholesale hardware supplies in the central Ohio area. It has been a client of yours for several years and has instituted an excellent system for the control of sales at your recommendation.

    In providing control over shipments, the client has prenumbered "warehouse removal slips" that are used for every sale. It is company policy never to remove goods from the warehouse without an authorized warehouse removal slip. After shipment, two copies of the slip are sent to billing for preparation of a sales invoice. One copy is stapled to the duplicate copy of a prenumbered sales invoice, and the other copy is filed numerically. In some cases, more than one warehouse removal slip is used for billing one sales invoice. The smallest warehouse removal slip number for the year is 35682, and the largest is 58521. The smallest sales invoice number is 47821 and the largest is 68507.

    In the audit of sales, one of the major concerns is the effectiveness of the system in making sure all shipments are billed. The auditor has decided to use attributes sampling in testing the system.

REQUIRED:

    a. State an effective audit procedure for testing whether shipments have been billed. What is the sampling unit for the audit procedure?

    b. Assuming that you expect no error in the sample but are willing to accept a maximum error rate of 3 percent at a 90 percent confidence level, what is the initial sample size for the audit test?

    c. Your supervisor suggests the possibility of performing other sales tests with the same sample as a means of efficiently using your audit time. List two other audit procedures that could conveniently be performed using the same sample, and state the purpose of each of the procedures.

    d. Is it desirable to test the validity of sales with the random sample you have designed in part *c*? Why?

3-19. (AICPA adapted) Mavis Stores had two billing clerks during the year. Snow worked three months and White worked nine months. As the auditor for Mavis

Stores, Jones, CPA, uses attributes sampling to test clerical accuracy for the entire year, but owing to the lack of internal verification, the system depends heavily upon the competence of the billing clerks. The quantity of bills per month is constant.

REQUIRED:

a. Jones decides to treat the billing by Snow and White as two separate populations. Discuss the advisability of this approach, considering the circumstances.

b. Jones decides to use the same confidence level, expected error rate, and desired upper precision limit for each population. Assuming Jones decides to select a sample of 200 to test Snow's work, approximately how large a sample is necessary to test White's?

3-20. The following questions concern the determination of the proper sample size in attributes sampling:

a. For each of the columns numbered 1 through 7, determine the initial sample size needed to satisfy the auditor's requirements from the appropriate table in Figures 3-2 and 3-3. Wherever the sample size is more than 10 percent of the population, adjust it with the finite correction factor.

	1	2	3	4	5	6	7
Confidence level	90%	95%	95%	95%	95%	95%	95%
Desired upper precision limit	6%	6%	4%	6%	8%	6%	5%
Estimated population error rate	3%	3%	3%	3%	3%	3%	0%
Population size	1,000	100,000	6,000	1,000	500	500	1,000,000

b. Using your understanding of the relationship between the factors above and sample size, state the effect on the initial sample (increase or decrease) of changing each of the following factors while the other three are held constant:

  (i) An increase in the confidence level
  (ii) An increase in the desired upper precision limit
  (iii) An increase in the estimated population error rate
  (iv) An increase in the population size

c. Compare your answers in part *b* with the results you determined in part *a*. Which of the four factors appears to have the greatest effect on the initial sample size? Which one appears to have the least effect?

d. Why is the sample size referred to as the initial sample size?

3-21. The following questions relate to determining the computed upper precision limit in attributes sampling.

a. For each of the columns numbered 1 through 8, determine the computed upper precision limit from the appropriate table in Figures 3-2 and 3-3. Wherever the sample size is more than 10 percent of the population, adjust the computed upper precision limit with the finite correction factor.

	1	2	3	4	5	6	7	8
Confidence level	90%	95%	95%	95%	95%	95%	95%	95%
Population size	5,000	5,000	5,000	50,000	500	900	5,000	500
Sample size	200	200	50	200	400	100	100	200
Number of error occurrences	4	4	1	4	8	10	0	4

b. Using your understanding of the relationship between the four factors above and the computed upper precision limit, state the effect on the computed upper precision limit (increase or decrease) of changing each of the following factors while the other three are held constant:
  (i) A decrease in the confidence level
  (ii) A decrease in the population size
  (iii) A decrease in the sample size
  (iv) A decrease in the number of occurrences in the sample
c. Compare your answers in part *b* with the results you determined in part *a*. Which of the four factors appears to have the greatest effect on the computed upper precision limit? Which one appears to have the least effect?
d. Why is it necessary to compare the computed upper precision limit with the desirable upper precision limit?

3-22. In performing tests of transactions of sales for the Oakland Hardware Company, Ben Frentz, CPA, is concerned with the internal verification of pricing, extensions, and footings of sales invoices and the accuracy of the actual calculations. In testing sales using attributes sampling, he uses separate attributes for the compliance test (the existence of internal verification) and the substantive test (the actual accuracy of the calculation). Since the internal control is considered excellent, Frentz uses a 90 percent confidence level, a zero estimated population error rate, and a 5 percent desired upper precision limit for both attributes; therefore, the initial sample size is 50 items.

In conducting the tests, the auditor finds three sample items where there is no indication of internal verification on the sales invoice, but no sales invoices tested in the sample have a financial error.

REQUIRED:

a. Determine the computed upper precision limit for both the attributes, assuming a population of 5,000 sales invoices.
b. Compare the computed upper precision limit with the desired upper precision limit.
c. Discuss the most desirable course of action the auditor should follow in deciding upon the effect of the computed upper precision limit's exceeding the desired upper precision limit.
d. Which type of error analysis is appropriate in this case?

3-23. For the audit of Carbald Supply Company, Carole Wever, CPA, is conducting a test of sales for nine months of the year ended 12/31/X7. Included among her audit procedures are the following:

Foot and crossfoot the sales journal and trace the balance to the general ledger.

Review all sales transactions for reasonableness.

Select a sample of recorded sales from the sales journal, and trace the customer names and amounts to duplicate sales invoices and the related shipping document.

Select a sample of shipping document numbers and perform the following tests:

  (i) Trace the shipping document to the related duplicate sales invoice.

 (ii) Examine the duplicate sales invoice to determine whether copies of the shipping document, shipping order, and customer order are attached.

(iii) Examine the shipping order for an authorized credit approval.

 (iv) Examine the duplicate sales invoice for an indication of internal verification of quantity, price, extensions, footings, and trace the balance to the subsidiary ledger.

  (v) Compare the price on the duplicate sales invoice with the approved price list and the quantity with the shipping document.

 (vi) Trace the balance on the duplicate sales invoice to the sales journal and subsidiary ledger for customer name, amount, and date.

REQUIRED:

a. For which of these procedures could attributes sampling be conveniently used?

b. Considering the audit procedures Wever has developed, what is the most appropriate sampling unit for conducting most of the attributes sampling tests?

c. Set up an attributes sampling data sheet similar to the one in Figure 3-5. For all compliance tests, assume an acceptable upper precision limit of 3.5 percent and an expected population error rate of 1 percent. For all substantive tests, use 2.5 percent for the upper precision limit and a zero expected population error rate. Use a 90 percent confidence level for all tests.

d. For the audit procedures not included in the attributes sampling test in part c, describe appropriate judgmental sampling procedures to determine the items to include in the sample.

3-24. You decided to use attributes sampling in your testing of Frederics Clothing's sales procedures for the year ended July 31, 198X. The client has a straightforward system that in previous years has yielded excellent results with conventional testing. Of course, the fact that July and August were the only two months ever tested could account for part of the excellent results. Recently, however, the gross margin for Frederics has somewhat declined. Although a cause has not yet been determined, there is concern that some shipments are unintentionally not being billed. For every duplicate invoice, a shipping document is attached. In addition, there is a separate file of prenumbered shipping documents filed in numerical order. There is a formal price list that can be deviated from only with an authorized signature from Bill Newshirt. George Sloppyslacks authorizes credit by initialing the sales document before shipment. There are 2,340 sales invoices for the year, beginning with invoice number 18721 and ending with 21060. There are 3,590 shipping documents, because some shipments are combined for billing. The shipping documents begin with 2893 and end with 6482.

REQUIRED:

a. Define the sampling unit to test for unbilled shipments. Why did you use that sampling unit?
b. Assume you decide to test for validity a sample of sales invoices.
   (i) Can you use the same random numbers?
   (ii) How many "attributes sampling data sheets" do you need—one or two?
   (iii) How many worksheets do you need—one or two?
   (iv) How can you organize this problem to minimize the effort and still do an adequate job?

3-25. In the preliminary work for a July 31, 198Y, audit, the auditor decided to test the operation of the accounts payable/cash disbursements system. Checks written between August 1, 198X, and April 30, 198Y, numbered 2,731. A sample of these checks and supporting documents was examined for propriety. For each canceled check there was a voucher jacket with supporting documents included. The voucher was assigned the check number as its identification number. The check was defined as the sampling unit. The attributes to be tested were:

—Receiving report included
—Invoice included
—A valid supplier
—Transaction consistent with firm policy
—Approval by authorized personnel
—Stamped that prices, extensions, and quantities were reviewed by the purchasing department

and other items not listed for this case. Judgmentally, the auditor decided to use a sample of 80.

The client assembled the specific checks and supporting documents. Columns on a worksheet were headed for each of the items to be examined. During the examination of each check and related documents, a tick mark was placed in the column as each item of audit interest was approved. After the 80th check and supporting documents had been examined, there were still a number of positions without tick marks. Efforts to clear the open positions were successful in every respect except one: The "Invoice included" column contained four blank spaces. The related columns, "Invoice approved" and "Reviewed by purchasing department," of course contained open spots on the same check numbers. Since there was only one basic error, invoice not attached, the auditor was in a dilemma. Did he have only one exception, or did he have four? A note in the working papers by the manager says the practice to which exceptions were taken "appears to be a normal practice, not an exception."

REQUIRED:

a. Should the auditor combine all errors into one overall error rate, or should the errors in each attribute be evaluated separately?
b. Evaluate the auditor's method of defining an error.
c. Did the auditor have one or four exceptions?
d. How can the auditor resolve the problem that a blank in one column can automatically result in a blank in other columns?
e. What are the implications (audit and statistical) of the manager's note in the final paragraph?
f. Is it acceptable to use statistical sampling when the auditor selects a random sample that includes only part of the year's population?
g. A sample size of 80 items was judgmentally determined. Is that acceptable? Discuss.

3-26. You are responsible for the 12/31/8X audit of Reynolds Jewelry Company, a medium-sized manufacturer of custom jewelry. This is the second year of the engagement, but the first year in which attributes sampling is to be used.

Engagement planning, including internal control evaluation, began on 9/15/8X. The internal control questionnaire and flowcharts have been updated. Weaknesses of internal control and control areas on which you intend to rely have been identified. In this case, you are to concern yourself only with acquisitions and payments and related balance sheet accounts.

The material internal control weaknesses in acquisitions and payments have been identified as follows.

(1) There are no subsidiary records for accounts payable. Transactions are first recorded when payment is made for an acquisition. Owing to a cash shortage, there are large numbers of unpaid invoices at any given time.
(2) Signed checks are returned to the accountant. The accountant reviews all checks before they are submitted to the president for his signature, and reviews all recorded disbursement transactions.
(3) The bank account is reconciled by the accountant.
(4) Documents are marked "paid" before they are signed by the owner. No date or check number is included on the documents.
(5) Checks are not recorded sequentially in the cash disbursements journal. This arises because checks are prepared at the time vendors' invoices and receiving reports are matched.

The significant controls the auditor plans to rely on are as follows:

Audit area	*Controls*
Inventory counts for raw materials and finished goods	Perpetual records are prepared when goods are received into shipping and when they are completed. There is a quarterly inventory of major items and an annual count of all inventory.
Inventory price tests	Raw materials perpetual records are maintained, including unit prices. Cost records are maintained for finished goods.
Expense analysis	The accountant reviews all transactions for account classification and indicates his agreement with the account number inserted by the bookkeeper by initialing the document.
Vouching of fixed asset additions	The accountant reviews all fixed assets and repair and maintenance transactions for proper valuation and account classification.

The acquisition and payment tests of transactions audit program was developed after considering:

(1) Normal audit objectives that are fulfilled by tests of transactions
(2) Weaknesses in the system that can most efficiently be tested by tests of transactions
(3) Controls the auditor intends to rely on that can most efficiently be tested by tests of transactions

The audit program, attributes sampling data sheet, error analysis schedule, and internal control memo are included in the following pages. The random selection and worksheet documentation are not a part of this case.

REQUIRED:

a. Evaluate the audit program, given the weaknesses in internal control and the controls the auditor intends to rely on.
b. Evaluate the completed attributes sampling data sheet for completeness and adequacy. Include in your evaluation the appropriateness of the defined objectives, sampling unit, and attributes being used. Also evaluate the confidence level and desirable upper precision limit used.
c. What is your opinion of testing the population for only 11 months? Support your conclusion.
d. Evaluate the need for an error analysis schedule. Evaluate the conclusions drawn on the schedule included.
e. Evaluate the need for an internal control memo. Evaluate the adequacy of the memo included.
f. To what degree do you believe the system can be relied on to reduce audit tests in those areas where reliance was intended?

Audit program—acquisitions and cash disbursements

Client *Reynolds Jewelry Company*   Balance sheet date *12/31/8X*

	Prep. by	Date	Comments
1. Review disbursement transactions for the year, looking for large, unusual, and related-party transactions.			
2. Do a proof of cash disbursements for a randomly selected month.			
3. For the same month as procedure 2, foot and crossfoot the cash disbursement journal and trace the totals to the general ledger.			
4. For six vendors selected by you, request president to have the bookkeeper prepare a listing of all payments for the year. Investigate any two transactions where the amounts are approximately the same to test for duplicate payments by examining vendors' invoices, receiving reports, and purchase orders.			
5. Account for three sequences of 100 check numbers in the cash disbursements journal, looking for duplicates as well as omissions.			
6. Select a random sample of disbursement transactions from the cash disbursements journal on the basis of page number and line number. a. Examine related canceled check for payee, amount, date, signature, and endorsement. b. Trace to the vendor's invoice and examine other supporting documents where appropriate. Evaluate whether the transaction is for company business. c. Examine purchase order for approval by president. d. Examine invoice for evidence of internal verification by accountant. e. Compare receiving report to the vendor's invoice and purchase order for quantity and description and recheck clerical accuracy. f. Compare amount on vendor's invoice with amount recorded in the cash disbursements journal. g. Examine description of acquisition on the vendor's invoice and evaluate the account classification by reference to the chart of accounts. h. Verify discounts taken where appropriate; maintain a record of the amount of discounts lost.			

7. Trace inventory transactions included in procedure 6 to perpetual inventory records for description, date, quantity, and unit cost.			
8. Trace selected entries in the perpetual records to related vendors' invoices for proper quantity, description and unit cost.			
9. Draw conclusions about the results of the acquisition and cash disbursements audit program.			

Note: *The rest of the Reynolds Jewelry Co. data can be found on pages 92–94.*

3-27. Grambing Manufacturing Co. is engaged in the manufacture of Product Xs—small, nonfunctional devices designed for the mass market. The company produces approximately 2,000 varieties of Xs, which it distributes direct to retail stores. Grambing has approximately 460 employees—350 in production and warehouse functions, 75 in sales and distribution, 15 in general adminiistration, and 20 in cost and general accounting.

The company has been a client for several years. Past experience indicates that it is well managed, efficient, and profitable. The system of internal control has been considered relatively strong.

The current audit period ends December 31. As on prior audits, preliminary work through September is to be performed. However, this year management has requested that the audit be completed by January 31. In prior years, timing was not as critical, so all substantive tests were performed as of the year-end.

Owing to this time requirement, accounts receivable and inventory will be verified as of October 31. Heavy reliance is to be placed on Grambing's system of internal control. Other items present no significant time problems and will be evaluated at year-end.

The plant is currently operating at full capacity to meet expanding business. Management is reluctant to take a complete physical inventory, which has required an inconvenient shutdown of production in prior years. Further, management feels that the perpetual records are extremely accurate, since they have been tested by periodic spot-check counts. There is no regular cycle inventory program.

You are in charge of the fieldwork for the Grambing audit. Because of the degree of reliance to be placed on internal controls, statistical methods are to be used wherever it makes audit sense to do so. Specifically, the sales and collection cycle is to be reviewed using attributes sampling and evaluation techniques.

At this point in the engagement, there has been a careful study and evaluation of internal control. The evaluation of internal control and the related attributes sampling data sheets are as shown on pages 95–97.

ATTRIBUTES SAMPLING DATA SHEET

Client: _Reynolds Jewelry Company_   By: _Phil Rollet_

Period Covered: _1-1-X to 12-31-8X_   Date: _1-16-8Y_

Define the Objective(s): _Test the effectiveness of the system of internal control for acquisitions and disbursements. Special emphasis is to be in testing the effectiveness of the perpetual records._

Population: Description _Checks recorded in the cash disbursements journal, not recorded sequentially._   Size _2352_

Sampling Unit _Check number_

Random Selection Procedures _Random number table_

Attributes Tested (Error Definition)	Required		Expected Error Rate	Planned Sample Size	Actual Results			
	Conf. Level	Accept. UPL			Sample Size	Occurrence No.	Rate	CUPL
1. Name, date and amount of cancelled check agree with cash disbursement journal, and the signature & endorsement appear reasonable.	95%	5	0	50	70	0	0	5%
2. All transactions appear to be for a valid business purpose.	95%	5	0	50	70	0	0	5%
3. The purchase orders have been approved by Chandler.	96%	8	2	50	70	2	2.9%	9%
4. There is evidence of internal verification by Ross.	90%	8	2	50	70	3	4.3%	12%
5. Quantities and description on vendors' invoice agree with purchase orders 2-3. Vendor's invoice is mechanically accurate.	95%	6	1	70	70	0	0	5%
6. The amount in the cash disbursements journal agrees with the vendor's invoice.	95%	6	1	70	70	0	0	5%
7. The account classification is reasonable.	95%	5	0	50	70	0	0	5%
8. Discounts were taken at the correct amount.	95%	9	3	50	43	8	18.6%	NC*
9. The quantities, date & unit cost were correctly recorded in the perpetual record.	95%	5	0	50	41	0	0	8
10.								

Intended use of Sampling Results: *Not calculated. Sample too small.

1. Effect on Audit Plan: _Reduce expense analysis. Price test inventory from perpetual records rather than vendors' invoices_

2. Effect on Opinion: _None._

3. Recommendation to Management: _① Removal of all purchase orders by Chandler. ② Internal verifications by Ross ③ Consider the cost of not taking discounts._

4. Other Action: _____

Whenever CUPL ⟩ AUPL there must be some action.

REYNOLDS JEWELRY COMPANY
Analysis of Errors
12 - 31 - 8X

Prepared by _P. R._

Date _1 - 18 - 8X_

(No.)	Attribute	Error Analysis	Effect on the Audit and Other Comments
3	Failure to approve purchase order	(1) Discussed with Chandler. He stated that on smaller items he does not look at them. Both items were for less than $35. (2) Examined nature of items & looked at supporting documentation to be sure they were valid transactions. Found no exceptions.	Audit tests not extended owing to immateriality of purchase orders and apparent policy in effect of not approving all small purchase orders.
4	Lack of internal verification	(1) Asked Ross why they had not been verified. She did not know why. (2) Recomputed clerical accuracy.	Examined purchase orders for Ross's approval on all purchase orders in audit procedure 4 in the audit program. — Management letter item.
8	Discounts were not taken	(1) Discussed with Hart why discounts not taken. Reason: due to cash shortage. (2) Determined that all exceptions were due to failure to take the discount. (3) Calculated an estimate of total discounts not taken for the year for discussion with Chandler: Eight discounts not taken — Total $ value of all $142.00 50 items in the sample — % .0067 Total disbursements for the year $2,675,800 Estimate of discounts lost $17,900	No effect — purpose was for a discussion with Chandler.

REYNOLDS JEWELRY COMPANY
Internal Control Memo
12 - 31 - 8X

Purpose of Audit Tests:

The purpose of the test of acquisitions and disbursements was to determine the effectiveness of internal control. We were especially concerned with the possibility of omitted or duplicate recording of checks and the payment of the same acquisition more than once. The account classification and the proper recording of unit costs on the perpetual records were considered important controls to reduce other audit tests. Tests of discounts taken and quantities on the perpetual records were done to help management improve its systems.

Work Performed and Sample Selection:

The audit program was designed after reviewing internal control and deciding which internal controls we intended to rely on. The audit program identifies the audit procedures we consider necessary. Sample sizes are indicated on the audit program except for procedures 6 & 7. Sample sizes for these two procedures are indicated on the attributes sampling data sheet.

Results of Audit Tests:

There were no errors found in the audit tests except as indicated on the attributes sampling data sheet and error analysis schedule. Except for those tests, the internal control system can be considered effective.

Due to the evaluation of internal control and results of the audit tests in acquisitions and disbursements, the following is recommended:

1. The ending cash balance to be verified by comparing the cancelled checks on the statement to the 11-30 bank reconciliation and the December cash disbursement journal. A cut-off bank statement is also important.
2. Substantial tests for out of period liabilities are needed, including confirmation of balances.
3. Expense analysis for transactions resulting from the cash disbursement journal can be reduced substantially, depending on the results of analytical tests.
4. Price tests of inventory can be made by reference to the perpetual records rather than examination of vendors' invoices.
5. Management to be informed of the items included on the error analysis schedule.

Conclusions:

Except as indicated in this memo and the error analysis schedule, the system of internal control for acquisitions and payments is considered effective.

Phil Rollet
1-18-8X

Objectives of good control and impact of poor control	*Key controls, weaknesses, and detailed compliance tests for this system*
Objective: Prevention of invoicing errors (pricing, quantities, extensions) *Impact of Poor Control:* Misstatement of sales, accounts receivable, gross profit, and inventory (through perpetual records)	*Key Control:* Independent checking of invoices *Tests:* Observe checking function Test invoices for accuracy *Weakness:* Bill of lading prepared from sales order controls quantity shipped, but is not matched against invoice. *Test:* Compare bill of lading to sales invoice.
Objective: To ensure that all goods shipped are billed *Impact of Poor Control:* Generally same as for invoicing errors, except errors would be one-sided; i.e., sales would be understated	*Weaknesses:* Numerical sequence of sales orders not accounted for (controlled). No follow-up on bills of lading to ensure a corresponding invoice. *Tests:* Account for numerical sequence of sales orders. Trace sales orders to corresponding bills of lading and sales invoices
Objective: To ensure that all sales invoices prepared are recorded *Impact of Poor Control:* Same as for invoicing errors	*Key Controls:* Sales are posted in the sales journal before invoices are sent to the A/R clerk who accounts for their numerical sequence. Control and detail of accounts receivable is balanced monthly. *Tests:* Observe A/R clerk. Test numerical sequence of invoices. Trace postings. Examine balancing.
Objective: To ensure that sales invoices are properly costed *Impact of Poor Control:* Misstatement of gross-profit-related data between physical inventories Creation of overages/shortages at time of physical inventory	*Key Controls:* Invoice costing is a regular part of the system, using sales invoices, cost of sales journal, and standard costs. *Tests:* Test-cost invoices. Trace postings to cost of sales journal.
Objective: To prevent the intentional misappropriation of cash proceeds *Impact of Poor Control:* Loss of assets Improper classification in accounts	*Key Controls:* Segregate cashier function from A/R function. Customers are sent statements monthly. *Weaknesses:* Cashier also prepares disbursements and reconciles bank account. The shipping clerk could easily collude with an outsider to order goods for which he would destroy the sales order. This would go unnoticed because numerical sequence of sales orders is not accounted for.

The treasurer reconciles the aged trial balance to the control account, handles mailing of monthly statements, and also initiates adjustments and approves credit. The A/R clerk could initiate a credit memo, although it would not be approved.

Tests: Observe segregation of cashier and A/R functions.

Trace postings to customers' accounts and examine support.

Investigate noncash entries to A/R.

Review A/R balancing.

Test numerical sequence of sales orders.

Trace bills of lading to corresponding sales order.

Attributes sampling—description of attributes

Client   *Grambing Manufacturing Co.*   Year-end   *12/31/19XX*

Attribute Code	Description
1	Invoice is properly priced.
2	Invoice is supported by and agrees with a bill of lading (evidencing shipment).
3	Each invoice is represented by and agrees with an entry to the sales journal.
4	Each invoice agrees with an entry in the accounts receivable ledger (to proper customer).
5	Numerical sequence of invoices is accounted for.
6	Invoice is properly costed.
7	Each invoice agrees with an entry in the cost of sales journal.
8	Invoice is properly extended.
9	Each item on the invoice is traceable to an entry in the finished goods inventory ledger.
10	Credit limit approval on shipments over $2,500 is indicated.
11	Numerical sequence of sales orders in billing department file is accounted for.
12	Each bill of lading is traceable to and agrees with an invoice.
13	Numerical sequence of bills of lading is accounted for.
14	Each bill of lading is traceable to and agrees with a sales order.
15	Entry to sales journal is supplied by and agrees with an invoice.

Attributes sampling—one-sided estimate tabulation of results

Client *Grambing Manufacturing Co.*   Year-end *12/31/19XX*

| | *Planned results* | | | | *Final results (2)* | | | |
Attri-bute code	Expected Occur-rence rate	Upper precision limit	Reli-ability	Sample size (1)	# of occur-rences (1)	Sample occur-rence rate	Reli-ability	Upper precision limit
1	2%	5%	95%					
2	1.5%	5%	95%					
3	0%	5%	95%					
4	1%	5%	95%					
5	0%	5%	95%					
6	3%	10%	95%					
7	0%	10%	95%					
8	1%	5%	95%					
9	0%	10%	95%					
10	0%	10%	95%					
11	0%	5%	95%					
12	1%	5%	95%					
13	0%	5%	95%					
14	1%	8%	95%					
15	2%	5%	95%					

(1) From Schedule S/S-1.
(2) Comment on any significant errors found that are not included in the listed attributes:

_____

_____

_____

_____

REQUIRED:

a. For each attribute tested, state:
   (i) Whether it is a compliance or substantive test
   (ii) The purpose(s) of each test (relate back to the internal control evaluation)
b. Evaluate the reliability and acceptable upper precision limit for each attribute.
c. Compute the required sample size for each attribute, given the expected occurrence rate, upper precision limit, and reliability specified.
d. Specify the appropriate sampling unit for each audit test. Keep in mind that a separate random sample is required for each sampling unit you specify. At the same time, it is improper to perform a test where the audit objectives are not met.

e. Determine the number of errors in each audit test by following the instructions in the case.

f. Complete the attributes sampling data sheet, given the errors you have identified in part *e.*

g. Write an internal control memorandum that includes:

　(i) The results of the attribute sampling tests

　(ii) The implications of the results of the tests with regard to the final audit program and scope of the audit.

ERROR DATA FOR PROBLEM REQUIREMENT

This section contains detailed listings of the results of four different possible samples arising from tests of the sales cycle. The samples are:

Document selected and examined	*Sample size up to*
Invoices	250
Sales orders	250
Bills of lading	250
Sales register entries	250

The error types included in each listing apply to the document chosen and *all* related documents and postings that could result from tracing from the selected document. For example, under sales orders, you will see an occurrence labeled *Price error on invoice.* This means that the invoice applicable to the sales order had a price error. You will also see an occurrence labeled *Wrong amt. to cust. acct.* This means that the invoice resulting from the selected sales order eventually ended with a posting error to the customer account.

Your use of these results depends on your audit strategy and scope, as follows:

1. The headings mean the indicated population was sampled from. They *do not* mean the documents were examined in conjunction with another test. Therefore, if your tests specify a selection of sales orders with an examination of the related bill of lading, you would use the list for *Sales Orders,* but not *Bills of Lading.* You would use the *Bills of Lading* list only if your tests specifically called for a random selection of bills of lading.

2. The occurrences are identified by *Sample Item No.* Evaluate only those occurrences with a sample item number equal to or less than the number of items you specified to be examined. For example, if you indicated that 100 sales orders are to be selected, ignore all sample item numbers greater than 100.

3. As indicated above, the error types apply to the document chosen and all related documents. *Do not* count an occurrence if your test did not indicate an examination of the secondary documents. For example, if your sales order test specified an examination of the related invoice through posting to the cost journal, you would consider occurrences to this point. If you did not specify a complete follow-through to customer account posting, you would not consider any customer account posting errors *in this test.*

The results of the tests are to be interpreted as follows:

1. The dollar amounts of any errors are to be considered both nonmaterial and ordinary.

2. The occurrences on the listings are only for those items that escaped internal control checks. For example, if an extension error is initially made, but then corrected by the checker, it is not on the listing as an error. If an account was misposted and subsequently corrected because of monthly balancing, it is not on the listing as an error.

Grambing Manufacturing Co.—results of tests

	Invoices		*Sales orders*
Sample item no.	*Occurrence*	*Sample item no.*	*Occurrence*
9	Price error on invoice	1	Price error on invoice
12	Exten. err. on invoice	3	Invoiced late
17	Price error on invoice	5	Price error on invoice
25	Inv. not located	11	Wrong cust. acct. post
30	Inv. costed wrong	22	Invoiced early
33	Bill of lading lost	23	Quan. diff. from bill lad.
46	Inv. costed wrong	27	Price error on invoice
48	Price error on invoice	33	Inv. costed wrong
49	Invoice voided	38	Inv. costed wrong
52	Inv. not costed	45	Price error on invoice
53	Wrong quan. on perp.	46	Invoiced late
54	Wrong cust. acct. post.	52	Inv. not costed
55	Cost posted wrong	53	Price error on invoice
59	Wrong cust. acct. post.	61	Price error on invoice
62	Cost posted wrong	64	Inv. costed wrong
64	Inv. not post. to perp.	76	Order voided
66	Quan. diff. from bill lad.	77	Price error on invoice
67	Quan. err. on invoice	79	Wrong cust. acct. post.
68	Price error on invoice	82	Wrong amt. to cust. acct.
73	Invoiced late	90	Price error on invoice
76	Quan. err. on invoice	96	Inv. costed wrong
77	Price error on invoice	100	Quan. err. on invoice
79	Price error on invoice	102	Price error on invoice
80	Quan. diff. from bill lad.	111	Inv. costed wrong
81	Wrong cust. acct. post.	117	Bill of lading lost
83	Inv. costed wrong	119	Quan. diff. from bill lad.
87	Inv. costed wrong	121	Price error in invoice
89	Wrong perp. rec. posted	128	Wrong amt. to cust. acct.
92	Price error on invoice	146	Exten. err. on invoice
98	Inv. not costed	155	Inv. costed wrong
100	Wrong quan. on perp.	173	Inv. costed wrong
122	Cost posted wrong	179	Price error on invoice
126	Wrong perp. rec. posted	187	Inv. not located
145	Inv. costed wrong	207	Wrong amt. to cust. acct.
146	Price error on invoice	213	Price error on invoice
147	Quan. err. on invoice	214	Invoiced late

150	Quan. diff. from bill lad.	219	Inv. not located
151	Bill of lading lost	225	Order lost
159	Invoice voided	226	Order voided
181	Quan. err. on invoice	228	Order lost
185	Quan. diff. from bill lad.	236	Inv. not post. to perp.
190	Price error on invoice	245	Exten. err. on invoice
193	Inv. not costed		
196	Exten. err. on invoice		
197	Inv. costed wrong		
199	Invoice voided		
209	Exten. err. on invoice		
216	Exten. err. on invoice		
218	Inv. costed wrong		
224	Quan. err. on invoice		
231	Invoiced early		
232	Invoiced late		
239	Inv. costed wrong		
241	Inv. not costed		
247	Price error on invoice		

Grambing Manufacturing Co. results of tests (cont.)

	Bills of lading		*Sales register*
Sample item no.	Occurrence	Sample item no.	Occurrence
9	No sales order	2	Inv. costed wrong
12	Price error on invoice	6	Inv. costed wrong
13	Order lost	7	Exten. err. on invoice
27	Inv. not post. to perp.	32	Exten. err. on invoice
31	Bill of lading lost	39	Cost posted wrong
33	Invoiced late	53	Price error on invoice
36	Exten. err. on invoice	67	Exten. err. on invoice
38	Inv. costed wrong	70	Inv. costed wrong
40	Wrong amt. to cust. acct.	72	Quan. diff. from bill lad.
49	Inv. costed wrong	73	Inv. costed wrong
52	No sales order	83	Inv. costed wrong
56	Inv. costed wrong	87	Inv. costed wrong
57	Inv. costed wrong	88	Inv. costed wrong
59	Exten. err. on invoice	90	Price error on invoice
61	Quan. diff. from bill lad.	94	Price error on invoice
64	Price error on invoice	103	Price error on invoice
66	Wrong quan. on perp.	109	Price error on invoice
67	Bill of lading lost	121	Wrong cust. acct. post.
70	Inv. costed wrong	135	Price error on invoice
75	Inv. costed wrong	137	Price error on invoice
87	Price error on invoice	141	Inv. costed wrong
91	Wrong quan. on perp.	146	Price error on invoice
98	Price error on invoice	151	Cost posted wrong
100	Inv. not located	159	Inv. costed wrong
105	No sales order	162	Inv. costed wrong
106	Price error on invoice	166	Price error on invoice
108	Exten. err. on invoice	169	Wrong cust. acct. post.
111	Invoiced late	176	Price error on invoice

114	Inv. costed wrong	185	Quan. err. on invoice
121	Wrong cust. acct. post.	189	Cost posted wrong
133	Invoiced late	212	Invoiced late
139	Price error on invoice	229	Price error on invoice
145	Inv. not costed	232	Inv. costed wrong
147	Cost posted wrong	240	Cost posted wrong
149	Wrong amt. to cust. acct.	250	Inv. costed wrong
154	Cost posted wrong		
155	Exten. err. on invoice		
159	No sales order		
161	Inv. not located		
172	Inv. costed wrong		
189	Price error on invoice		
195	Cost posted wrong		
197	Cost posted wrong		
206	Invoiced early		
208	Wrong quan. on perp.		
210	Bill of lading lost		
232	Inv. costed wrong		
237	Inv. not costed		
241	Price error on invoice		
247	Inv. not located		

4

an overview of
variables sampling
methods

INTRODUCTION AND CONCEPTS

Variables sampling methods are used to measure the value of an account balance or some other pertinent amount. For auditing purposes, the objective of variables sampling is almost always to estimate the *true dollar amount* of an account balance or some similar total. The computed result is stated in terms of *the dollar amount of the point estimate plus and minus the dollar amount of the precision interval at the confidence level desired*. It is common to calculate both *an upper and a lower limit* for variables estimates, because an account balance can be understated or overstated. As an example, assume that the auditor is confirming accounts receivable and computes the point estimate of the total balance as $1,470,000, with a $200,000 computed precision interval at a confidence level of 95 percent. This means the auditor estimates that, at a 95 percent confidence level, the true value of the accounts receivable is between $1,270,000 and $1,670,000 ($1,470,000 ± $200,000). At this early stage in the study of variables sampling, it is not possible for the reader to determine how these values are computed, but it is possible to observe that the results are stated in the same basic form as in attributes sampling.

Variables sampling is generally a more useful measurement device than attributes sampling for substantive tests, because auditors are generally more interested in the monetary amount of errors than in the frequency of errors.

As an illustration, assume that the auditor could use either attributes or variables sampling in confirming accounts receivable. If attributes sampling is used, the statistical conclusion is stated in terms of the percentage of the accounts receivable that are in error, regardless of the amount of the individual errors in the sample. In variables sampling, the auditor is measuring the correct dollar value of the accounts in the sample. Which of these is more useful? Variables sampling is, because the correct dollar value of total accounts receivable is of primary interest to the auditor. As a result, attributes sampling is normally applied to tests of transactions, and variables sampling is applied to direct tests of balances. The only time attributes sampling is used for direct tests of balances is when the cost of variables sampling is prohibitive or the method does not give useful results.

The introductory material in this section includes certain general concepts applicable to all variables sampling methods. Chapters 5 through 8 will deal with specific variables sampling methods.

POPULATION DISTRIBUTIONS

Populations that are audited using variables sampling methods are made up of various elements, the sum of which equals the population value. An example is a population of 20,000 accounts receivable for Wade Wholesale Co. that have recorded values ranging from $1 to $90, totaling $744,000. If these account balances are divided into nine intervals of $10 each, the *frequency distribution* in Figure 4-1 exists. This frequency distribution can be graphed showing the percent of accounts in each interval in the form of a *frequency histogram*, as in Figure 4-2.

The range of these intervals can be narrowed by making the intervals $1, or even 1 cent, instead of $10. The distribution of the elements where the

Class interval	*No. of accounts*	*Percent of accounts*
$ 0.01–$10	1,200	6%
10.01– 20	2,800	14
20.01– 30	5,800	29
30.01– 40	3,600	18
40.01– 50	1,800	9
50.01– 60	1,600	8
60.01– 70	1,400	7
70.01– 80	1,000	5
80.01– 90	800	4
Totals	20,000	100%

FIGURE 4-1 Frequency distribution

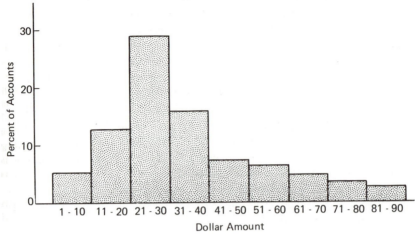

FIGURE 4-2 Frequency histogram

range of class intervals is extremely narrow, such as 1 cent, is called a *continuous population distribution curve*. For Wade's population of accounts receivable it would appear as in Figure 4-3.

The population distribution includes all the elements in the population; therefore, the area under the curve in Figure 4-3 represents 100 percent. By examining the distribution, one can see that the range of values is between about $0.01 and $90. The largest percent of accounts has a value of about $22.

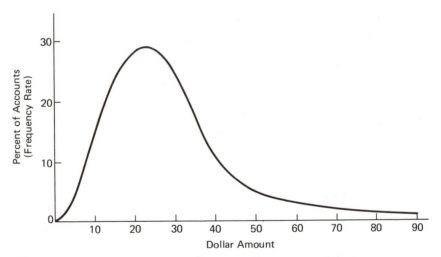

FIGURE 4-3 Continuous population distribution curve

Population Mean and Standard Deviation

Any population of data can be summarized in a variety of ways through the use of common statistical measures. The two most important for auditors are the mean and the standard deviation.

The *population mean* is the sum of the values of all population elements divided by the number of elements in the population. The mathematical expression is:

$$\bar{X} = \frac{\sum X_j}{N}$$

where:

$\bar{X}$ = population mean

$\sum$ = sum of

X_j = value of each individual population item

N = number of items in the population

The population mean for Wade's accounts receivable population is:

$$\bar{X} = \frac{\$744,000}{20,000} = \$37.20$$

There is a distinction between the population mode, median, and mean. The *mode* is the single amount appearing most frequently in the population. It is the highest point in the continuous population distribution curve. Individual values for the accounts receivable example are not shown, but the population distribution indicates the mode to be approximately $22. The *median* is the value of the element for which there are an equal number of items with values above and below it. The median for Wade's receivables is between $30 and $40, since there are 9,800 items below $30 and 6,600 above $40. It is likely to be approximately $31. The mean, median, and mode are shown for Wade in Figure 4-4.

The *population standard deviation* is a statistical measure of the *variability* of the values of the individual items in the population. The population standard deviation is mathematically described as:

$$\sigma = \sqrt{\frac{\sum (X_j - \bar{X})^2}{N}}$$

where:

σ = standard deviation.

If there is a large amount of variation in the values of the population items, the standard deviation is larger than when the variation is small. For

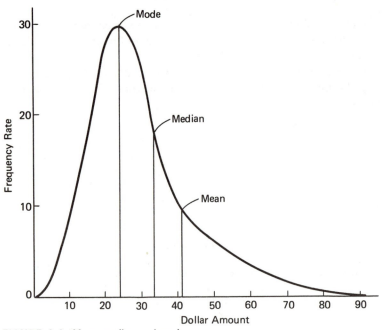

FIGURE 4-4 Mean, median, and mode

example, if the accounts receivable were distributed between values of $1 and $1,000 rather than $1 and $90, as in Wade's, the standard deviation would be much larger.

Nature of Accounting Populations

Population distributions can have different shapes, depending upon the makeup of the population being tested. Figure 4-5 shows a few.

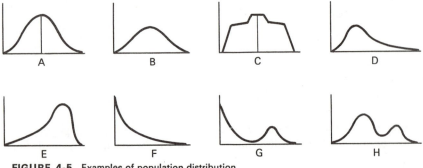

FIGURE 4-5 Examples of population distribution

Distributions A, B, and C are symmetrical curves. The mean, median, and mode are the same, and the left side of the distribution is equal to the right side. Distributions A and B are a special type of symmetrical distribution, called a *normal curve*. The two characteristics of a normal curve for a population are that (1) it must be symmetrical, and (2) known proportions of the population are contained within fixed distances from the arithmetic mean. These fixed portions are measured by the standard deviation. For example, approximately 68 percent of the population items of a normal curve must fall within *one* standard deviation on each side of the mean, and about 95 percent within *two* standard deviations on each side of the mean. This is shown graphically in Figure 4-6.

There is a difference between distributions A and B in Figure 4-5, even though they are both normal. On average, the values of population items are closer to the mean for A than for B. This means that the population standard deviation is smaller for A.

Distribution C is symmetrical, but not normal. It is apparent that condition 2 for normality has not been met.

Distributions D and E are referred to as *skewed distributions*. Distribution D has a large number of population items with small values and few items with large values. It is called a *positively skewed* or a *skewed-to-the-right* distribu-

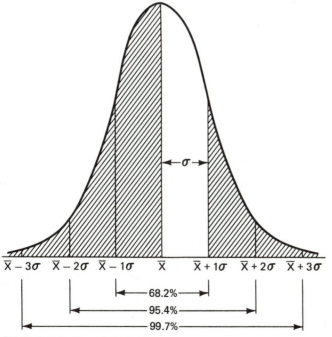

FIGURE 4-6 Normal distribution

tion. A large number of accounting populations are shaped somewhat like D. For example, it is not unusual to have a large number of accounts receivable with small balances and a few with large balances. The conditions for distribution E are the reverse of D. A distribution of this type is negatively skewed, or skewed to the left.

Distribution F indicates the existence of an exceptionally large number of small items in the population and some larger items. The same conditions exist for distribution G, except that there is also a reasonably large number of items with high values.

Distribution H appears to be a combination of two distributions. It is called a *bimodal distribution*.

Effects of Population Distributions on Auditing

Auditors are usually concerned about one or both of two characteristics of accounting populations—the *audited value* and the *errors* in the population. To illustrate, imagine the population of ten recorded inventory items as shown in Figure 4-7. The auditor, in this case, can look at the population as having an audited value of $2,106 or having an understatement error of $146. It will be shown later that different statistical methods are used when the auditor looks at the audited values and at the errors in the sample.

Inventory items	Recorded value	Audited value	Error
1	$ 14	$ 17	$— 3
2	26	31	— 5
3	31	26	5
4	93	93	0
5	114	100	14
6	225	262	— 37
7	230	230	0
8	275	306	— 31
9	350	350	0
10	602	691	— 89
Total	$1,960	$2,106	$—146
$\bar{X}$	$ 196.0	$ 210.6	$— 14.6
σ	$ 174	$ 198	$ 29

FIGURE 4-7 Illustrative population values

There is practically no research on the exact nature of accounting populations. This is because auditors rarely test every item in the population to determine the audited values or the population errors. However, there is reason to believe that the distribution of the *audited values* of many populations is shaped much like distribution D in Figure 4-5. Many accounting populations have a large number of fairly small values and some large values. There are many possible shapes for those skewed-to-the-right distributions. Some are highly skewed, whereas others may be fairly close to symmetrical.

The distribution of the *absolute value of errors* in many populations is believed to be like F and G in Figure 4-5. Frequently, accounting populations have a large number of items without error (error amount equals zero) and a smaller number of errors as the size of the individual error gets larger (distribution F). Notice that in distribution G, there would be a large number of small errors, but there also would be quite a few large errors. It is possible that the total dollar value of the combined large errors is considerably larger than the total of all small errors.

The form and distribution of the population are essential to auditors. These two considerations determine the appropriate statistical methods to use in a given audit situation and also affect sample size. The auditor who uses an improper statistical method can easily reach an incorrect audit conclusion or use a larger sample size than would have been necessary with an alternative method.

The problem of selecting an appropriate statistical method is complicated by three considerations. First, the auditor does not know the exact shape of the distribution either before or after the audit has been completed. The client's recorded values of individual transactions and balances are normally available, but the auditor is interested in the correct balance for each population element. If there are significant errors in a population, the auditor may erroneously conclude that the client's recorded distribution is the actual distribution. For example, if the auditor of the population shown in distribution G in Figure 4-5 is not aware of the hump in the right side of the distribution, it would be easy to draw wrong conclusions about the population.

Second, the auditor estimates the population's standard deviation on the basis of a sample. If the auditor's estimate of the standard deviation based on a sample is materially different from the actual standard deviation, the statistical estimate will not be a good measure of the actual population value.

Third, the auditor must know which statistical method to use in a given set of circumstances. Certain statistical methods are so likely to result in incorrect audit decisions in certain situations that it is improper to use those methods in those situations at all.

STATISTICAL METHODS

Several variables methods are applicable to auditing. These include unstratified difference, ratio, and mean-per-unit estimation; stratified sampling; and dollar unit sampling. Each of these is discussed in summary below and in detail in subsequent chapters.

Difference Estimation

Difference estimation is used to measure the estimated total error amount in a population when there is both a recorded value and an audited value for each item in the population (and in the sample). An example is to confirm a sample of accounts receivable and determine the difference (error) between the client's recorded amount and the amount the auditor considers correct for each selected account. The auditor makes an estimate of the population error based on the number of errors, average error size, and individual error size in the sample. The result is stated as a point estimate plus or minus a computed precision interval at a stated confidence level. Unstratified difference estimates are examined in Chapter 5.

Ratio Estimation

The *ratio estimate* is similar to the difference estimate in that both deal with the difference between the value of a population item as indicated by the client's records and the amount the auditor concludes is the correct balance. In the difference estimate, the auditor determines the point estimate of the error on the basis of the average error in the sample times the population size, and computes a precision interval on the basis of the value of the individual errors in the sample. The ratio estimate projects the point estimate of the population error on the basis of the *net ratio of error* in the sample times the recorded total dollar amount of the population. For example, assume that the auditor discovered twelve errors with a net overstatement of $226 in a random sample of 100 items from a population of 4,000 with a book value of $1,872,500. If the 100 sample items had a book value of $39,612, the point estimate of the population error is an overstatement of $10,673; that is, ($226 ÷ $39,612) × $1,872,500. The precision interval is calculated on the basis of the ratio of error of each individual sample item in much the same manner as for difference estimates. Unstratified ratio estimates are examined in Chapter 6.

Mean-per-Unit Estimation

In *mean-per-unit estimation*, the auditor concentrates on the *audited value* rather than the error amount of each item in the sample. Except for the definition of what is being measured, the mean-per-unit estimate is calculated in exactly the same manner as the difference estimate. The *point estimate* of the audited value is the mean audited value of each item in the sample times the population size. The *computed precision interval* is calculated on the basis of the audited value of the sample items, rather than the errors. When the auditor has computed the upper and lower confidence limits, a decision is made about the acceptability of the population by comparing these amounts with the recorded book value. Mean-per-unit estimation is studied in Chapter 7.

Stratification

Stratified sampling is an extension of variables sampling in which all the elements in the total population are divided into two or more subpopulations. Each subpopulation is then independently tested and statistically measured in the same manner as is used for the other variables sampling methods. After the results of the individual parts have been computed, they are combined into one overall population estimate in terms of a confidence interval.

Subdividing or stratifying a population is not unique to statistical sampling, of course. Auditors have traditionally emphasized certain types of items when they are testing a population. For example, in confirming accounts receivable, it has been customary to place more emphasis on large accounts than on small ones. The major difference is that in statistical stratified sampling, the approach is more objective and better defined than it is in most traditional stratification methods.

The purpose of stratified sampling is to *reduce the effect of skewness* in population distributions on samples and to reduce the overall standard deviation, thereby gaining efficiency. This is done by controlling the overall sample mix through sampling selectively from each stratum. It is very important to define the strata so their items are as homogeneous as possible. Stratification is commonly used with difference, ratio, and mean-per-unit estimation. Most auditing populations are skewed; therefore, wherever practicable, some stratification should be used. Stratified sampling is studied in Chapter 8.

Dollar Unit Sampling

Dollar unit samples are generally evaluated using attributes sampling or modified attributes sampling methods. However, under certain circumstances, they can be evaluated using mean per-unit estimation. This approach is discussed in Chapter 9.

SAMPLING DISTRIBUTIONS

Auditors do not know the mean value or the distribution of the populations they are testing in audit engagements. The population characteristics must be estimated from samples. In this section, we discuss *sampling distributions* which are essential to drawing conclusions about populations on the basis of samples using variables sampling methods.

Assume that, as an experiment, an auditor takes thousands of repeated samples of equal size from a population of accounting data having a mean value of $\bar{X}$. For each sample, the auditor calculates the mean value of the items in the sample, as follows:

$$\bar{x} = \frac{\sum x_j}{n}$$

where:

$\bar{x} = $ mean value of the sample items

$x_j = $ value of each individual sample item

$n = $ sample size

After the auditor calculates $\bar{x}$ for each sample, he plots them into a *frequency distribution*. The frequency distribution of the sample will probably be as in Figure 4-8. A distribution of the sample means such as this is *ordinarily normal*, having all the characteristics of the normal curve stated earlier if the sample size is sufficiently large. The curve is usually symmetrical, and the sample means fall within known portions of the sampling distribution around the mean, measured by the distance along the horizontal axis in terms of standard deviations. Further, the mean of the sample means (the midpoint of the sampling distribution) is equal to the population mean, and the standard deviation of the sampling distribution is equal to $\sigma/\sqrt{n}$, where σ is the population standard deviation and n is the sample size. Later in the chapter, in the section on reliability, a discussion of potential problems of normality of the distribution of sample means is discussed.

To illustrate these concepts, assume a population with a mean of \$40 and a standard deviation of \$15 ($\bar{X} = \$40$ and $\sigma = \$15$), from which we elect to take many random samples of 100 items each. The standard devia-

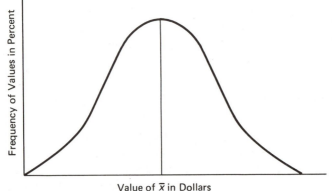

Value of $\bar{x}$ in Dollars

FIGURE 4-8 Frequency distribution of sample means

tion of our sampling distribution would be $1.50 ($\sigma/\sqrt{n} = 15/\sqrt{100} =$ $1.50). The reference to standard deviation of the population and to standard deviation of sampling distribution is often confusing. To avoid the confusion, the standard deviation of the distribution of the sample means is often called the *standard error of the mean* [symbol $SE(\bar{X})$]. With this information, the tabulation of the sampling distribution can be made, as reflected in Figure 4-9.

(1) No. of standard errors of the mean *(Confidence Coefficient)*	*(2)* Value $[(1) \times \$1.50]$	*(3)* Range around $\bar{X}$ $[\$40 \pm (2)]$	*(4)* Percent of sample means included in range
1	$1.50	$38.50–$41.50	68.2%
2	$3.00	$37.00–$43.00	95.4%
3	$4.50	$35.50–$44.50	99.7% (from table for normal curve—see Figure 4-6)

FIGURE 4-9 Calculated sampling distribution from a population with a known mean and standard deviation

To summarize, three things are important about the results of the experiment of taking a large number of samples from a known population.

1. The sample mean value ($\bar{x}$) with the highest frequency of occurrence is equal to the population mean ($\bar{X}$).
2. The shape of the frequency distribution of the sample means is that of a normal curve if the sample is reasonably large, *regardless of the distribution of the population.* A graphic representation of this conclusion is shown in Figure 4-10.
3. The percentage of sample means between any two values of the sampling distribution is measurable. The percentage can be calculated by (a) determining the number of standard errors of the mean between any two values, and (b) locating the percentage of sample means represented by reference to a table for normal curves. There is more discussion of this later.

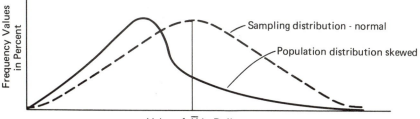

FIGURE 4-10 Sampling distribution for a population distribution

STATISTICAL INFERENCE

Naturally, an auditor sampling from a population in an actual audit situation does not know the population's characteristics, and there is ordinarily only one sample taken from the population. Even so, the *knowledge of sampling distributions* enables auditors to draw statistical conclusions (make statistical inferences) about the population. For example, assume that we take a sample from a population and calculate $\bar{x}$ as \$46 and $\sigma(\bar{x})$ as \$9 (the way to calculate each of these will be shown for each statistical method in subsequent chapters). Using the logic gained from the study of sampling distributions, we can now calculate a confidence interval of the population mean. It is:

$$\text{CI}_{\bar{X}} = \hat{X} \pm Z \cdot \text{SE}(\bar{X})$$

where:

$\text{CI}_{\bar{X}} =$ confidence interval for the population mean

$\hat{X} =$ point estimate of the population mean (from the sample)

$Z =$ confidence coefficient (1 = 68.2% confidence level; 2 = 95.4% confidence level; 3 = 99.7% confidence level)

$\text{SE}(\bar{X}) =$ estimate of the standard error of the mean (from the sample)

For the example:

$\text{CI}_{\bar{X}} = \$46 \pm 1\ (\$9) = \$46 \pm \$9$ at a 68.2% confidence level

$\text{CI}_{\bar{X}} = \$46 \pm 2\ (\$9) = \$46 \pm \$18$ at a 95.4% confidence level

$\text{CI}_{\bar{X}} = \$46 \pm 3\ (\$9) = \$46 \pm \$27$ at a 99.7% confidence level

The results can also be stated in terms of confidence limits. The upper confidence limit ($\text{UCL}_{\bar{X}}$) is $\hat{X} + Z\text{SE}(\bar{X})$ (\$46 + \$18 = \$64 at a 95.4% confidence level) and a lower confidence limit ($\text{LCL}_{\bar{X}}$) is $\hat{X} - Z\text{SE}(\bar{X})$ (\$46 − \$18 = \$28 at a 95.4% confidence level). Graphically, the results are as in Figure 4-11.

The conclusion about the confidence interval based on a sample from an unknown population can be stated in different ways, but care must be taken to avoid incorrect conclusions. In making statistical inferences, the auditor

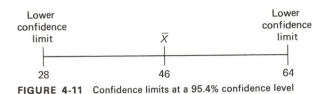

FIGURE 4-11 Confidence limits at a 95.4% confidence level

should remember that the true population value is always unknown. There is always a possibility that the sample is not representative of the true population value and the sample result is significantly different from the population value. The auditor can say, in the previous example, that the confidence interval for the true population mean value is $46 ± $18 at a 95.4 percent confidence level, or that the confidence limits are between $28 and $64 at a 95.4 percent confidence level. These statements are correct but are not an explanation of the result. A more meaningful statement is, "Assume an auditor took repeated samples of a certain size from a given population, and from each sample computed a confidence interval. Each confidence interval would be based on a somewhat different point estimate and have differing limits. However, the auditor would know that 95.4 percent of those confidence intervals would, in fact, contain the true, but unknown, population value. The auditor can also say that 4.6 percent of the intervals do not contain the true population value, where 2.3 percent will be above the value and 2.3 percent will be below it." In this sense it is proper, when the auditor takes one sample from one population, to state that there is a 95.4 percent probability that the true population mean value is between $28 and $64. Naturally, there is only one true but unknown population mean value, so in that sense, there can be no probability statement.

There is one incorrect conclusion reached by students so frequently that it is worth discussing. Assume again that the auditor has taken one sample from one population that resulted in a confidence interval of $28 to $64 at a 95.4 percent confidence level. If the auditor took a large number of samples from that population, would approximately 95 percent of the sample means be between $28 and $64? *The answer is, almost certainly, no.* The result would occur only if *the true population mean was* $46, a highly unlikely occurrence. If the true population mean was $40, which is about as likely as $46, about 95.4 percent of the repeated sample results would have means between $22 and $58 ($40 ± $18). If the true population mean was $60, 95.4 percent of the repeated samples would have means between $42 and $78 ($60 ± $18). Stated in reverse, the sample mean has no greater chance of exactly equaling the true but unknown population mean than has any other value in the confidence interval.

SELECTING AMONG ALTERNATIVE METHODS

Recent research has indicated that there is no *one* statistical sampling method that is adequate for all situations. Different methods suit different audit objectives, perform well or poorly under different population conditions, and are more or less practical in different circumstances. In addition,

auditors do not know in advance all the factors that determine which particular method performs best under the circumstances at hand. The problem
is anticipating the frequency, magnitude, and direction of the errors in the
population.

There are three important factors affecting the desirability of alternative
methods: *efficiency, sample selection and calculation costs,* and *reliability of the
estimator.*

Efficiency

The efficiency of an estimation method is a function of the sample size
required to satisfy the auditor that no material error exists for a population,
compared to an alternative estimation method. For example, if the sample
size needed to satisfy the auditor that inventory is not misstated by more
than $50,000 is smaller when a stratified difference estimate is used than for
an unstratified mean-per-unit estimate, the difference estimate is more
efficient. The most important factor that affects the efficiency of the estimate
is the population standard deviation. When the population standard deviation is small, the sample size needed to meet a given materiality requirement
is also smaller.

Sample Selection and Calculation Costs

However, stratifying a population in an optimal manner, selecting the
sample items, and calculating the statistical results can significantly increase
the cost of doing an audit test when done without computer assistance.
Typically, the sample size (efficiency) is a more important consideration
than sample selection and calculation costs, because the actual auditing of
the sample is usually relatively costly.

Reliability of the Estimator

The reliability of an estimator is a measure of how well the computed
confidence limits for a population conform to the results that should be
expected from a normal distribution. An example should help us understand
this idea. Assume that a researcher has a *known population* with a mean of
$150 and a population standard deviation of $70. The researcher knows that
if repeated samples of reasonable size are taken, approximately 95 percent of
the sample means should be between $130 and $170 [$150 \pm 2(70 \div \sqrt{50})$].
The researcher takes 1,000 samples of 50 items each and finds that 995
(99.5 percent) fall within the expected limits of $130 to $170. Since 950 such
items were expected, the researcher would conclude that the statistical method
was not a reliable estimator. If the researcher finds that 750 (75 percent)
of the samples fall within the range, the conclusion would also be that the
estimator was not reliable. The estimator is reliable only if the actual results

fall within the confidence limits approximately the same percentage of the time as the stated confidence level. Stating this conclusion in terms of a single sample from an unknown population: an estimate of a population using a statistical method is considered reliable when the *actual* probability that the confidence interval obtained contains the true population value is equal to the *nominal* probability (expected from the normal distribution).

It is important for auditors to use reasonably reliable estimators because this is the basis for controlling sampling risk. A judgment error could easily result if the statistical conclusion is that the auditor has a 95 percent confidence level that a population value is between two values, such as $45,000 and $55,000, when a reliable estimator would have concluded that it is actually between $35,000 and $65,000.

Determining the reliability of an estimator is difficult in practice because the auditor takes only one sample from an unknown population. The conclusion may be reached that a population is correctly stated when it actually is not, owing to the use of an unreliable estimator. Alternatively, the auditor may select a larger sample size than is necessary in order to reduce the effects of an unreliable estimator. Naturally, the larger sample is more costly.

The auditor must make a subjective evaluation of the reliability of the estimator chosen on the basis of the facts available before sampling begins. This is done by considering various factors that cause statistical evaluation methods to yield unreliable results for a given sample size. Recent research by John Neter and James K. Loebbecke has contributed greatly to helping auditors evaluate which estimates are most reliable. Their research concludes that there is no one most reliable estimator. The conclusion is also clear that when both cost and reliability are considered, there is certainly no one best statistical method for all audits.

The factors that the Neter and Loebbecke research indicates as having the greatest effect on the reliability of estimators are these:

1. *Skewness in the population of book values.* When a population is skewed, unstratified mean-per-unit estimation is often unreliable.
2. *Frequency (rate) of errors.* Difference and ratio estimation are likely to be unreliable estimators when there are few errors in the population.
3. *Direction of errors.* The reliability of the difference and ratio estimators is less when most errors are in one direction than when there are both overstatements and understatements in the population.
4. *Magnitude of errors.* The size of the errors affects the reliability of most estimators, especially when considered in conjunction with the frequency and direction of errors. For example, difference or ratio estimation is apt to be highly unreliable for populations with error rates of 1 or 2% that are all overstatements or understatements, and of relatively high magnitude.[1]

---

[1]Neter and Loebbecke, *Behavior of Major Statistical Estimators in Sampling Accounting Populations* (New York: AICPA, 1975).

The reliablity of an estimator is a more important consideration than efficiency or sample selection and calculation costs. It does no good and may cause harm to do an inexpensive test that is not reliable; a wrong audit decision could result. On the other hand, frequently the reliability of an estimator can be increased by increasing the sample size. Efficiency, sample selection and calculation costs, and reliability will be considered for each of the statistical methods as we proceed.

SUGGESTED READING AND REFERENCE

NETER, JOHN, WILLIAM WASSERMAN, and G. A. WHITMORE, *Applied Statistics.* New York: Allyn and Bacon, 1978.

REVIEW QUESTIONS

4-1. What is meant by the term *variables sampling*? Explain the objective of variables sampling.

4-2. Compare and differentiate what is being measured in variables sampling and attributes sampling. Under what circumstances would variables sampling be a more appropriate statistical method than attributes? When would attributes be more appropriate?

4-3. Define what is meant by a population distribution. What is the relevance of population distributions for variables sampling?

4-4. Distinguish among the following three terms: *frequency distribution, frequency histogram,* and *continuous population distribution curve.*

4-5. Define and distinguish among the following three terms: population *mean, mode,* and *median.* Calculate or determine the value of each term for the following population: 26, 71, 56, 3, 47, 865, 14, 3, 86, 111. Explain why the three values are dissimilar in this situation.

4-6. Explain what is meant by *population standard deviation.* Why is the size of the standard deviation in a given population important for variables sampling?

4-7. Evaluate the following statement: "Every population with individual values making up a total value has a population mean, population standard deviation, and population distribution. The population standard deviation is the most important of these three for using variables sampling."

4-8. Define what is meant by a normal population distribution. Why is a normal population distribution important in statistical sampling in auditing?

4-9. Distinguish among the following four types of population distributions: skewed to the right, bimodal, normal, and skewed to the left. Graph each type.

4-10. An auditor is verifying inventory costs by examining supporting documentation. Explain how the auditor would approach the audit differently depending on whether his interest was in the audited value of the inventory items or in the value of errors in the population.

4-11. Why are the shape and standard deviation of populations important to auditors planning to use variables sampling? Identify two factors that make it difficult for auditors to determine the shape and standard deviation of the population.

4-12. Distinguish among the following three variables sampling methods in terms of what the auditor is measuring: difference estimation, ratio estimation, and mean-per-unit estimation.

4-13. What is meant by stratified sampling in variables sampling? What is the purpose of using stratified as opposed to unstratified sampling?

4-14. What is meant by a *sampling distribution*? Distinguish between a sampling distribution and a population distribution.

4-15. Explain how it would be possible to determine a sampling distribution from a population in each of the following two ways: (1) repeated samples from a given population, or (2) mathematically. What information would have to be known to determine the sampling distribution mathematically?

4-16. Calculate the confidence limits of the population mean at a confidence level of 95% if one sample of 100 items resulted in a point estimate of the mean of $937 and a standard error of the mean of $126. What assumptions are necessary before the calculated confidence limits can be considered reliable? State the results of the calculation in words.

4-17. Evaluate each of the following conclusions for correctness if an auditor selected a random sample of 100 items from a population of 2,000 and, based upon accurate statistical calculations, determined that the confidence interval was $4,200 $\pm$ $1,500 at the 90% confidence level:

a. The confidence limits are between $2,700 and $5,700 at a 90% confidence level.

b. There is a 5% statistical risk that the true population value is more than $5,700.

c. If the auditor took a large number of additional samples, each with a sample size of 100 items, the point estimate would fall between $2,700 and $5,700 approximately 90% of the time.

4-18. The determination of a sampling distribution requires a population with a known mean, standard deviation, sample size, and knowledge of the population distribution. In practice, the auditor is usually certain of only the sample size. Why is it important to understand sampling distributions when most of the information to calculate them is not known in practice?

4-19. What is meant by the efficiency of an estimator as it is used in variables sampling? Why is efficiency an important factor in deciding on a variables method?

4-20. What is meant by the reliability of an estimator as it is used in variables sampling and nominal reliability? Why is actual reliability an important factor in deciding on a variables method?

4-21. Identify the four factors indicated by the Neter and Loebbecke research as having the greatest effect on the reliability of estimators.

DISCUSSION QUESTIONS AND PROBLEMS

4-22. The following items apply to statistical sampling. Choose the best response.

  a. There are many kinds of statistical estimates that an auditor may find useful, but basically, every accounting estimate is either of a quantity or of an error rate. The statistical terms that roughly correspond to "quantities" and "error rate," respectively, are:
  (i) Attributes and variables
  (ii) Variables and attributes
  (iii) Constants and attributes
  (iv) Constants and variables

  b. In connection with his review of charges to the plant maintenance account, Mr. Wilson is undecided whether to use probability sampling or judgment sampling. As compared to probability sampling, judgment sampling has the primary disadvantage of
  (i) Providing no known method for making statistical inferences about the population solely from the results of the sample
  (ii) Not allowing the auditor to select those accounts that he believes should be selected
  (iii) Requiring that a complete list of all the population elements be compiled
  (iv) Not permitting the auditor to know which types of items will be included in the sample before the actual selection is made

  c. In an examination of financial statements, a CPA would not find the use of statistical sampling techniques to be generally applicable if
  (i) The population of items were large
  (ii) Absolute precision of measurement were required
  (iii) None of the items were individually significant
  (iv) The population were not normally distributed

(AICPA adapted)

4-23. Each of the following applies to concepts used in variables sampling. Choose the best response.

  a. An important statistic to consider when using a statistical sampling audit plan is the population variability. The population variability is measured by the
  (i) Sample mean
  (ii) Standard deviation
  (iii) Standard error of the sample mean
  (iv) Estimated population total minus the actual population total

  b. The greater the variability of the items being sampled (as measured by population standard deviation), the
  (i) Greater the usefulness of a table of random numbers in selecting a sample
  (ii) Larger the sample size required to make reliable statements with a given precision

    (iii) Greater should be the level of confidence required when establishing the estimate

    (iv) More likely that an interval estimate made from sample data will be correct

c. The size of a statistical sample is influenced by the degree of variability in the value of the items being sampled. The standard deviation, a basic measure of variation, is the

    (i) Average of the absolute differences between the individual values and their mean

    (ii) Square root of the average of the absolute differences between the individual values and their mean

    (iii) Average of the squared differences between values and their mean

    (iv) Square root of the average of the squares of the differences between the individual values and their mean

d. A CPA specifies that a sample shall have a confidence level of 90%. The specified confidence level assures him of

    (i) A true estimate of the population characteristic being measured

    (ii) An estimate that is at least 90% correct

    (iii) A measured precision for his estimate

    (iv) How likely he can estimate the population characteristic being measured

4-24. The following frequency distribution is for the accounts receivable of Herman Rental Products:

Interval for the range of accounts receivable values	Number of accounts	Percent of accounts
0 to 25	20	2
25.01 to 50	50	5
50.01 to 75	80	8
75.01 to 100	120	12
100.01 to 125	150	15
125.01 to 150	160	16
150.01 to 175	150	15
175.01 to 200	120	12
200.01 to 225	80	8
225.01 to 250	50	5
250.01 to 275	20	2
	1,000	100

REQUIRED:

a. Prepare a frequency histogram for Herman Rental Products' accounts receivable.

b. Prepare a continuous population distribution curve for Herman Rental Products' accounts receivable.

c. Calculate the mean, approximate median, and most likely mode for the data. In general, explain when they are likely to be approximately the same.

d. Demonstrate whether or not the population distribution in part *b* is a normal distribution. Assume the standard deviation to be $45.

4-25. The following frequency distribution is the physical inventory of Wholesale Natural Foods, Inc., at the balance sheet date.

Interval for the range of inventory values	Number of inventory descriptions
0 to 50	126
50.01 to 100	215
100.01 to 200	273
200.01 to 500	172
500.01 to 1000	106
1000.01 to 2000	77
2000.01 to 5000	31
	1,000

REQUIRED:

a. Prepare a frequency histogram for Wholesale Natural Foods' inventory.
b. Prepare a continuous population distribution curve for Wholesale Natural Foods' inventory.
c. Calculate the mean, approximate median, and most likely mode for the data. Explain why they are not apt to be the same.
d. Assuming a population standard deviation of $680, demonstrate that the population in part *b* is not a normal distribution.
e. As an experiment, assume that the auditor took 1,000 different samples of 100 inventory descriptions. The standard error of the mean was calculated to be $68. Prepare a continuous sampling distribution curve for the population mean. Assume a normal curve.
f. Explain why it is justifiable to prepare a curve with a normal distribution in part *e* when the distribution in part *b* was skewed.

4-26. Below are seven population distributions and one sampling distribution:

1.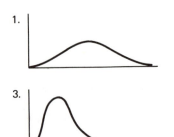

2.

3.

4.

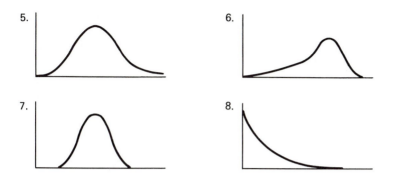

REQUIRED:

a. Identify all distributions that are symmetrical.
b. Identify all distributions that might be normal.
c. Identify all distributions that are skewed. Label each one as "skewed to the right" or "skewed to the left."
d. Identify the distribution that is bimodal.
e. Between distributions 5 and 7, which distribution is the sampling distribution? What characteristic made it identifiable?
f. Assume that you were drawing sampling distribution number 1 and you wanted it to look more like distribution 5. How could you make that happen?
g. Which distribution best represents a population of leases outstanding where the mean is $80,000, 5% of the balances are under $20,000, and 20% of the balances are over $150,000?
h. Which distribution best represents a population of errors in accounts payable where there are a large number of small errors and a few large errors?
i. Which distribution best represents a population of accounts receivable where the mean is $600, and where there are many small accounts including zero balances and some large balances?

4-27. The following are sampling distributions for difference estimation from two different populations. Both distributions have the same shape, and the horizontal and vertical axes have the same values and scales.

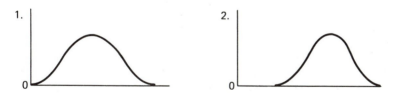

REQUIRED:

a. Which of the distributions has the larger mean?
b. Which of the distributions has the larger standard deviation?
c. Assume the mean for distribution 1 is 87. Determine the approximate

standard deviation for distribution 1 and complete the horizontal scale using 15 scale points on the axis.

d. Determine the approximate population mean and standard deviation for population 2. Assume that the left point of the distribution intersects the horizontal axis at scale point 5.

4-28. The following are four distributions that have different shapes, but the same values and scales on the horizontal axis:

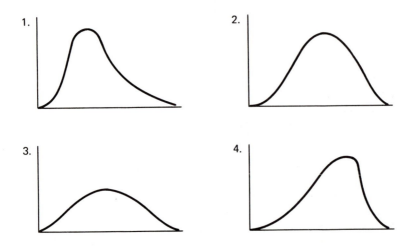

REQUIRED:

a. Assuming the distributions represent populations of data, explain how the sampling distribution for each population could have been determined.

b. Assuming the distributions are sampling distributions derived using difference estimation, which ones are likely to indicate difference estimation to be a reliable estimator? Explain your answer.

c. Continuing from part *b*, for which of the four distributions shown is difference estimation likely to be the least efficient estimator? Explain your answer.

d. Assuming again, as in part *a*, that the distributions represent population data, for which of the populations, where one sample is taken from the population, would there be a greater likelihood than the nominal probability of the population's being accepted as fairly stated, assuming that each of the populations is misstated by an amount slightly greater than the amount the auditor considers material? Explain your answer.

e. Explain how the auditor can determine whether difference estimation is a reliable estimator in a particular situation.

4-29. a. Calculate the confidence interval and confidence limits of the population mean for each of the following independent sample results from populations with unknown population characteristics:

Population	Point estimate of the population mean	Standard error of the mean	Confidence level
1	50	15	95
2	50	15	99.7
3	40	15	95
4	50	30	95

b. Assume you are using mean-per-unit estimation with population 3. Describe an example in auditing in which mean-per-unit could result in the figures shown. State in words the result of your calculations for population 3.

c. Assume you are using difference estimation with population 4. Describe an example in auditing in which difference estimation could result in the figures shown. State in words the result of your calculation for population 4.

d. Based on the results of your calculations in part *a* and your knowledge of statistics, state the effect on the upper and lower confidence limit of each of the following independent changes. (Increase, decrease, or cannot determine from information provided.)

	Effect on upper confidence limit	Effect on lower confidence limit
1. Increase the confidence level.		
2. Decrease the point estimate of the population.		
3. Increase the standard error of the mean.		
4. Increase the point estimate of the population mean and decrease the confidence level.		

e. Why would it be inappropriate to graph a sampling distribution for any of these four populations with the information given?

4-30. The following is a situation in which information about a population is needed.

A large CPA firm has in effect a staff evaluation system by which all assistants are ranked on a scale ranging from 0 to 100. (100 is considered perfect.) Each supervisor ranks all assistants under his or her supervision with one number on the scale for each of several criteria, including accuracy of work, relations with the client, innovation, and neatness. There is also a numerical overall evaluation. Each assistant in the firm gets ranked approximately 30 times per year. Experience has shown that a few supervisors give abnormally higher or lower evaluations of a given assistant than other supervisors do. The firm would like a simple but useful evaluation of assistants that minimizes the effect of the abnormal evaluations but provides sufficient information. The firm does not want to identify which personnel give the abnormal evaluations.

REQUIRED:

a. Evaluate the advantages and disadvantages of each of the following three methods of summarizing the information for each employee for the situation described: mode, mean, and median.

b. Make a specific recommendation as to a method to be followed for summarizing the results for each employee.

5

difference estimation without stratification

INTRODUCTION

There are two general situations in which the auditor is likely to use difference estimation:

- When the auditor believes *errors exist* in the balance being audited, but does not know if they are material. An example is the determination of whether a material error exists in the accounts receivable balance.
- When the auditor believes *material errors exist* in the balance being audited and uses difference estimation as a means of estimating the amount of the adjustment. A common example is the adjustment of inventory recorded at standard cost to an actual cost.

In statistical terms, the first situation requires the use of a *hypothesis test*, and the second requires an *interval estimate*. The basic concepts of difference estimation are the same for hypothesis tests and interval estimates. The distinction between the two comes in determining the sample size and using the computed results. Both a hypothesis test and an interval estimate can be done with the same sample.

Typical uses of difference estimation are in the confirmation of accounts receivable and price tests of inventory. For instance, the basis for making the calculations of the total client error in price tests of inventory is the *difference* between the client's recorded value for an inventory item and the correct value as determined by the auditor using appropriate audit tests.

An important characteristic of difference estimation is that it cannot be used unless there is both a recorded value and an audit value for each item in the sample.

This chapter covers the following topics regarding unstratified difference estimation:

1. Calculating statistical results from a sample
2. Using statistical results for decision making
3. Calculating sample size and making decisions using hypothesis tests
4. Calculating the required sample size for interval estimates
5. Efficiency, sample selection and calculation costs, and reliability
6. Appropriate uses of difference estimation

In practice, the auditor does these in almost a reverse order. First, it must be decided which statistical methods, such as difference estimation or dollar unit sampling, are applicable for the circumstances. Next, efficiency, sample selection and calculation costs, and reliability must be considered. At this point, the auditor usually selects the most appropriate statistical method. The sample size is then determined on the basis of available information. Next, the auditor performs the tests and calculates the results from the sample. Finally, audit adjustment decisions are made on the basis of the statistical results and other information. The order presented here is designed to make difference estimation more understandable for readers who are new to statistical methodology. The order that practitioners usually follow is used in subsequent illustrations.

CALCULATING STATISTICAL RESULTS
FROM A SAMPLE

The calculation of confidence limits is done in the same way for both hypothesis tests and interval estimates. It is in the determination of sample size and the use of the confidence limits that there are distinctions.

Regardless of the way the auditor obtains the sample size, it is appropriate to draw statistical conclusions if the sample is random. Let us illustrate the calculation of statistical results for difference estimation by assuming that the auditor has selected a random sample of 100 items for the positive confirmation of accounts receivable from a population of 4,000 accounts receivable with a total recorded book value of $848,271. The assumption throughout is that all confirmations were returned or that effective alternative procedures were carried out. Hence, the sample size is the number of positive confirmations mailed. The objective is to obtain an interval estimate of the total error amount at a given confidence level. The steps for calculating the confidence limits of this estimate are these:

- Select a random sample.
- Determine the value of each error in the sample.
- Compute the point estimate of total errors in the population.
- Compute an estimate of the population standard deviation.
- Compute the precision interval.
- Compute the confidence interval.
- Compute the confidence limits.

Select a Random Sample

The *sampling unit* is defined as the individual customer balance on the accounts receivable aged trial balance. The random sample is selected in the same manner as for attributes sampling, perhaps on the basis of page number and line number. The number of confirmations mailed is the sample size.

Determine the Value of Each Error in the Sample

For confirmations, the error is the *difference* between the confirmation response and the client's balance after reconciliation of all timing differences and customer errors. For example, if a customer returns a confirmation stating that the correct balance is $887.12, and the balance in the client's records is $997.12, the difference of $110 is an overstatement error if the auditor concludes that the client's records are incorrect. For *nonresponses*, the errors discovered by alternative procedures are treated identically to those discovered through confirmation. At the end of this step, each item in the sample has an error value, many of which are likely to be zero. The sample results for the illustration are shown in Figure 5-1.

---

100 accounts receivable are selected randomly from the aged trial balance containing 4,000 accounts.

75 accounts are confirmed by customers, and 25 accounts are verified by alternative procedures. After reconciling timing differences and customer errors, the following twelve items are determined to be client errors (understatements):

1.	$ 12.75	7.	(.87)
2.	(69.46)	8.	24.32
3.	85.28	9.	36.59
4.	100.00	10.	(102.16)
5.	(27.30)	11.	54.71
6.	41.06	12.	71.56

Sum = $226.48

FIGURE 5-1 Errors in the sample

Compute the Point Estimate of Total Errors in the Population

The *point estimate* is a direct extrapolation from the errors in the sample to the entire population. If the auditor sends 100 confirmations from a population of 4,000 accounts receivable and determines that the combined net amount of the errors in the sample is an overstatement of $226.48, the point estimate of the population error is an overstatement of $9,040. The calculation of this amount is shown in Figure 5-2.

$$\bar{e} = \frac{\sum e_j}{n}$$

$$\hat{E} = N \cdot \bar{e} \quad \text{or} \quad N \cdot \frac{\sum e_j}{n}$$

where:

$\bar{e}$ = average error in the sample
$\sum$ = sum of
e_j = an individual error in the sample
n = sample size
$\hat{E}$ = point estimate of the total error
N = population size
$\bar{e} = \frac{226.48}{100} = 2.26$
$\hat{E} = 4{,}000 \cdot 2.26 = \$9{,}040$

or

$$\hat{E} = 4{,}000 \cdot \frac{226.48}{100} = \$9{,}040$$

FIGURE 5-2 Point estimate of the total errors

It is unlikely, of course, for the actual but unknown error to be *exactly* the same as the point estimate. It is more realistic to estimate the error in terms of a *confidence interval determined by the point estimate plus and minus a computed precision interval*. For example, $9,040 ± $16,640 at a 95 percent confidence level would mean the auditor is 95 percent confident that the true error is between an understatement of $7,600 and an overstatement of $25,680. It should be apparent at this point that the calculation of the confidence interval is an essential part of variables sampling, and that the process used to develop it depends on the obtaining of a *representative sample*.

Compute an Estimate of the Population Standard Deviation

One of the important aspects of the confidence interval is the *population standard deviation*, which is, as previously stated, a statistical measure of the variability in the values of the individual items in the population. If there is a large amount of variation, the standard deviation will be large.

The standard deviation has a direct effect on the computed precision interval. As might be expected, the ability to predict the true total value of a population is better when there is a small rather than a large amount of variation in the individual values of the population.

A *reasonable estimate* of the value of the population standard deviation is computed by the use of a standard statistical formula applied to the sample. The amount of the standard deviation estimate is determined solely by the characteristics of the auditor's sample results and is not affected by professional judgment. The calculation of the standard deviation for the illustration is shown in Figure 5-3. This calculation is basically the same as for the standard deviation of a population, shown in Chapter 4. The form is altered to facilitate computation, and the denominator is slightly modified for statistical reasons.

$$\text{SD} = \sqrt{\frac{\sum e_j^2 - n(\bar{e})^2}{n-1}}$$

where:

SD = standard deviation (from the sample)
e_j = an individual error in the sample
n = sample size
$\bar{e} = \dfrac{\sum e_j}{n}$

	e_j	e_j^2 (rounded to nearest dollar)
1.	13	169
2.	(69)	4,761
3.	85	7,225
4.	100	10,000
5.	(27)	729
6.	41	1,681
7.	(1)	1
8.	24	576
9.	36	1,296
10.	(102)	10,404
11.	55	3,025
12.	72	5,184
	227	45,051

$$\text{SD} = \sqrt{\frac{45,051 - 100(2.27)^2}{99}}$$

$$\text{SD} = 21.2$$

FIGURE 5-3 Estimated standard deviation of the population errors

Compute the Precision Interval

The *precision interval* is a statistical measure of the inability to predict the true population error because the test is based on a sample rather than on the entire population. The formula and the ongoing example are shown in Figure 5-4.

$$\text{CPI} = \frac{N \cdot Z \cdot \text{SD}}{\sqrt{n}} \cdot \sqrt{\frac{N - n}{N}}$$

where:

$\text{CPI} =$ computed precision interval
$N =$ population size
$Z =$ confidence coefficient (two-sided) for the confidence level (CL), as follows:

CL	Z
99%	2.58
95%	1.96
90%	1.64
80%	1.28
60%	.84

$\text{SD} =$ estimated population standard deviation

$n =$ sample size

$\sqrt{\dfrac{N - n}{N}} =$ finite correction factor

$$\text{CPI at 95\% CL} = 4{,}000 \cdot 1.96 \cdot \frac{21.2}{\sqrt{100}} \sqrt{\frac{4{,}000 - 100}{4{,}000}}$$

$$= 4{,}000 \cdot 1.96 \cdot \frac{21.2}{10} \cdot .988$$

$$= 4{,}000 \cdot 1.96 \cdot 2.12 \cdot .988 = \$16{,}420$$

FIGURE 5-4 The computed precision interval for the estimate of the population of the errors at the desired confidence level

In order for the computed precision interval to be useful, it must be associated with a particular confidence level. A point estimate of the error of $9,040 plus or minus a computed precision of $16,420 at a confidence level of 95 percent has a completely different meaning from the same point estimate and computed precision at an 80 percent confidence level. (The computed precision for an 80 percent confidence level can be calculated by substituting 1.28 for 1.96 in the formula.)

Four factors directly affect the size of the computed precision interval. With the assumption that the auditor has already calculated a precision interval of $16,420, the four factors, and the effect of changing each, are as follows:

The Standard Deviation Calculated on the Basis of the Sample. When the standard deviation increases, the computed precision increases proportionately. For example, if the standard deviation is changed from $21.2 to $42.4, the computed precision of $16,420 increases to $32,840.

An increase in the computed precision interval as a result of an increase in the standard deviation is a reasonable conclusion, because a less precise measure of the population should be expected if the errors in the sample vary considerably. (The reader should recognize that an increase in the computed precision interval results in a less precise measure of the true population total value.)

The Population Size. An increase in the number of items in the population increases the computed precision interval somewhat more than proportionately. For example, if all the other factors remained constant, the computed precision interval of $16,420 in a population of 4,000 items would become $33,004 if the population were 8,000 items:

$$8,000 \cdot 1.96 \cdot \frac{21.2}{\sqrt{100}} \cdot \sqrt{\frac{8,000 - 100}{8,000}}$$

It will be recalled that in attributes sampling, the effect of the population size on the computed precision interval is small, but in variables sampling, a doubling of the population size results in approximately a doubling of the computed precision interval. The difference in the effect of the population size comes about because attributes sampling conclusions are stated in terms of a population *error rate*, whereas the difference estimate conclusions are stated in terms of the *total value* of the error. If the auditor was interested in the *total* number of errors for attributes rather than the error rate, the upper precision limit would be multiplied by the population size. Then the population size would be as important for attributes as it is for variables. Auditors usually prefer to measure in terms of error rates for attributes and total dollar amount of the error for difference estimation.

Owing to the effect of population size on the point estimate and the computed precision interval, a correct count of the total number of items in the population is essential for variables sampling.

The Sample Size. When the sample size is increased, the computed precision interval decreases if everything else stays constant. If every item in the population is tested, the computed precision interval becomes zero, because the inability to predict has been eliminated. For small samples, the computed precision interval is often too large to be useful.

The computed precision interval does not decrease proportionately with the increase in the sample size. In fact, to cut the computed precision interval in half, it is necessary to quadruple the sample size in most populations; this is because there is a square-root relationship. If the auditor desires to significantly reduce the computed precision interval, the additional sampling cost is normally very high.

The Confidence Level. The concept of the confidence level is the same for variables sampling as it is for attributes. It is a statement of the probability that the true population error value actually falls within the limits of the confidence interval. When the confidence level is small, the statistical calculations provide a computed confidence interval that is narrow; but of course, there is a high risk that the true error lies outside the resultant confidence interval.

Compute the Confidence Interval

The *confidence interval* is the combination of the point estimate and the precision interval. Combining the point estimate and the computed precision interval makes them more meaningful than either of them separately. The confidence interval is shown for the continuing example in Figure 5-5. The auditor can now state with a 95 percent confidence that the true value of the total population error is $9,040 \pm$ $16,420.

$$CI = \hat{E} \pm CPI$$

where:

CI = computed confidence interval
$\hat{E}$ = point estimate of the total error
CPI = computed precision interval at desired confidence level
CI = $9,040 $\pm$ $16,420

The auditor can state with a 95% statistical confidence level that the true value of the error is $9,040 $\pm$ $16,420.

FIGURE 5-5   The confidence interval at the desired confidence level

Compute the Confidence Limits

The *confidence limits* are the extreme points in the confidence interval. There is a computed upper confidence limit and a lower confidence limit. The calculation of the upper and lower limits is shown in Figure 5-6.

$$UCL = \hat{E} + CPI$$
$$LCL = \hat{E} - CPI$$

where:

UCL = computed upper confidence limit
LCL = computed lower confidence limit
$\hat{E}$ = point estimate of the total error
CPI = computed precision interval at desired confidence level
UCL = $9,040 + $16,420 = $25,460
LCL = $9,040 - $16,420 = $(7,380)

The auditor can state with a 95% statistical confidence level that the true value of the error is between an understatement of $7,380 and an overstatement of $25,460.

FIGURE 5-6   The confidence limits at the desired confidence level

The *computed lower confidence limit* (LCL) is a $7,380 understatement of accounts receivable, and the *computed upper confidence limit* (UCL) is a $25,460 overstatement. For this example, there is a 95 percent probability of the true error's being between an understatement of $7,380 and an overstatement of $25,460. Another way of stating the same thing is to say there is a 2.5 percent statistical risk that the true error is less than a $7,380 understatement and another 2.5 percent risk that it exceeds a $25,460 overstatement. In total, there is a 5 percent risk that the true value does not lie within the interval.

It is easy to calculate the confidence limits for different confidence levels by calculating a different precision interval using the confidence coefficient (Z) relating to each confidence level (see Figure 5-4). Figure 5-7 shows the

---

80% Confidence level
Confidence Coefficient = 1.28

10% risk↘   CPI = (4,000)(1.28)(2.12)(.988) = 10,724   ↙10% risk

| −1,684 | 9,040 | 19,764 |

95% Confidence level
Confidence Coefficient = 1.96

2½% risk↘   CPI = (4,000)(1.96)(2.12)(.988) = 16,420   ↙2½% risk

| −7,380 | 9,040 | 25,460 |

99% Confidence level
Confidence Coefficient = 2.58

½% risk↘   CPI = (4,000)(2.58)(2.12)(.988) = 21,616   ↙½% risk

| −12,576 | 9,040 | 30,656 |

FIGURE 5-7 Confidence limits for different confidence levels

confidence limits for three confidence levels. Observe that the upper limit at a 99 percent confidence level is much higher than at 80 percent, but there is only a 1/2 percent likelihood that the true error is greater than the upper limit, compared to a 10 percent likelihood for the 80 percent confidence level example. If the auditor wants both an increased confidence level and a lower upper confidence limit, an increased sample size is required.

USING STATISTICAL RESULTS
FOR DECISION MAKING—HYPOTHESIS TESTING

The auditor uses hypothesis testing in difference estimation to help decide whether or not an account balance is materially misstated. The hypothesis the auditor generally tests is that the account balance being tested is *not* materially misstated. The auditor either accepts this hypothesis or rejects it. If the hypothesis is accepted, the account balance is accepted and the test is complete. If the hypothesis is rejected, additional action is required. For example, the auditor may increase the sample size or make an audit adjustment.

Considerations for a Hypothesis Test

There are three important considerations for a hypothesis test: materiality, Beta risk (β), and Alpha risk (α).

Materiality. The auditor must first decide on the amount believed to be material for the audit test. For our purposes, materiality is the maximum amount of error the auditor will allow for an audit test without requiring an audit adjustment or additional work. It is a matter of professional judgment. The problem is complicated, because auditors must ultimately combine the results of various statistical and judgmental tests to decide whether the overall financial statements are fairly stated (that is, not materially misstated). For now, the only concern is about materiality for a specific audit test.

Beta risk. *Beta risk (β) is the statistical risk that the auditor has accepted a population that is actually materially misstated.* After an audit test is performed and statistical results are calculated, the auditor must *either* conclude that the population is not materially misstated *or* conclude that it is materially misstated. There can be a Beta risk only when the population has been *accepted* as not materially misstated. The Beta risk is a serious concern to the auditor because of the magnitude of potential legal implications of concluding that an account balance is fairly stated when it is in error by a material amount.

Alpha risk. *Alpha risk (α) is the statistical risk that the auditor has concluded the population is materially misstated when actually it is not.* There can be an Alpha risk only when the hypothesis that the book value was not materially misstated has been *rejected*. One possible action when the auditor does not accept a balance is to increase the sample size. If the account is actually free of material error, an increased sample size will usually lead the auditor to conclude that the balance is fairly stated. Low levels of Alpha risk are important when there is a high cost of increasing the sample size, or when increasing the sample size is not a practical alternative. Beta risk is always important to auditors.

Alpha and Beta risks are summarized in Figure 5-8. It seems apparent from Figure 5-8 that the auditor should attempt to minimize both the Alpha and Beta risks. This can be done only by increasing the sample size, sometimes to very high levels. Therefore, having reasonable Alpha and Beta risks is a more likely goal.

Actual audit decision	Actual state of the population	
	Materially misstated	*Not materially misstated*
Conclude that the population is materially misstated	Correct conclusion— no risk	Incorrect conclusion— risk of making equals α
Conclude that the population is not materially misstated	Incorrect conclusion— risk of making equals β	Correct conclusion— no risk

FIGURE 5-8 Risks in hypothesis testing

Decision Rule

In hypothesis testing, the auditor must prespecify a set of conditions that must exist before the hypothesis is accepted, using a formal decision rule. This decision rule assumes an equal concern for understatements and overstatements and requires the auditor to specify an exact amount that is material. The decision rule for difference estimation, as well as for other variables sampling methods, is:

If the two-sided confidence interval for the errors is completely within zero plus and minus the amount considered material, accept the hypothesis that the book value is not misstated by a material amount. *Otherwise, reject* the hypothesis that the book value is not misstated by a material amount.

The decision rule may be illustrated graphically as follows:

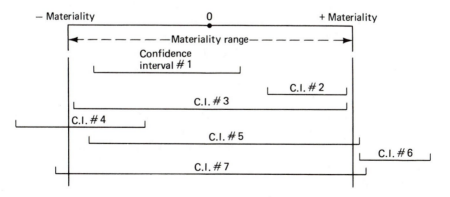

Here, the auditor should reach the following conclusions:

- For confidence intervals 1, 2, and 3 : These fall completely within the bounds of the materiality range. Therefore, the hypothesis that the population *is not* misstated by a material amount is accepted in each case.
- For confidence intervals 4, 5, 6, and 7 : These confidence limits do not fall entirely within the materiality range. Therefore, the hypothesis that the population *is not* misstated by a material amount is rejected in each case.

We will now return to the example discussed previously in which the auditor concluded that the confidence interval was $9,040 \pm $16,420 at a 95 percent confidence level. Assume that the auditor is willing to accept the population if the total error for this test does not exceed a $30,000 over- or understatement. Use of the decision rule is illustrated as follows:

Materiality	− $30,000	0	+ $30,000
range of			
error	− materiality		+ materiality
95% confidence	−$7,380	$9,040	$25,460
interval			

The entire confidence interval (both confidence limits) is within the materiality range of error; therefore, the hypothesis that the account is not materially misstated is accepted. If the materiality limit had been $25,000, the auditor would *not* accept the recorded book value.

Figure 5-9 shows why the hypothesis that the population is fairly stated is accepted. The distribution centered around the upper materiality amount assumes that the actual population error is equal to materiality ($30,000). A distribution based on the actual population sample size and estimated population standard deviation is shown. The auditor is asking the question, "What is the likelihood of obtaining a sample value of $9,040 from a population containing a $30,000 overstatement?" In this case, the likelihood is far below 2 1/2 percent. The same question is now asked for an understatement of $30,000. Similarly, by examining the left-hand distribution in Figure 5-9, we can see that the likelihood of obtaining the actual sample results from a population with an actual understatement error of $30,000 is extremely remote.

Why should we assume an error of exactly the amount of materiality? If we assume that the actual error is less than materiality, there would be no Beta risk, because the population should be accepted as not being materially misstated. If the population is misstated by more than $30,000, the Beta risk is smaller than at exactly $30,000. Therefore, an assumed population error exactly equal to materiality is the most conservative estimate of the risk of accepting a materially misstated population.

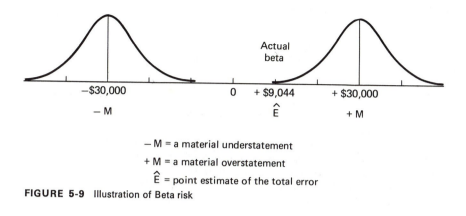

Actual
beta

-$30,000   0   + $9,044   + $30,000

— M $\hat{E}$ + M

— M = a material understatement

+ M = a material overstatement

$\hat{E}$ = point estimate of the total error

FIGURE 5-9 Illustration of Beta risk

CALCULATING SAMPLE SIZE— HYPOTHESIS TESTING

The calculation of the *preliminary estimate* of the sample size is studied, first considering only the Beta risk, and subsequently considering both the Beta and Alpha risks.

Beta Risk Only

The preliminary estimate of the sample size for difference estimates can be calculated by using the same basic formula as for computing the confidence interval. The formula $AE = E^* + \text{API}$ is used, where AE = acceptable error in the population, E^* = *estimated* point estimate of the population error, and API = acceptable precision interval. The acceptable precision interval is the same as the computed precision interval except that the standard deviation (SD*) is an advance estimate, based upon previous years' results or a preliminary sample rather than the standard deviation (SD) calculated on the basis of the errors actually discovered. Instead of using Z for the confidence coefficient, $Z(1 - 2\beta)$ is used. It has the same effect as using Z, but it shows that Beta risk is used rather than the confidence level. More will be said about that shortly. For convenience, the finite correction factor is ignored at this point. The auditor who desires to include it may employ the same adjustment of the sample size for population size that was used for attributes sampling. The formula as modified now becomes:

$$\text{API} = AE - E^*$$

$$\text{API} = \frac{N \cdot Z(1 - 2\beta) \cdot \text{SD}^*}{\sqrt{n}}$$

If we solve the formula for n, the preliminary estimate of the sample size is:

$$n = \left(\frac{N \cdot Z(1 - 2\beta) \cdot \text{SD*}}{\text{API}}\right)^2$$

where:

n = preliminary estimate of the sample size
N = population size
$Z(1 - 2\beta)$ = confidence coefficient for the Beta risk; e.g. a Beta risk of 5% has the same confidence coefficient as a confidence level of 90%
SD* = advance estimate of the standard deviation
AE = acceptable error in the population (materiality)
E^* = estimated point estimate of the population error

As an illustration, assume the auditor is willing to allow a total error in accounts receivable of $80,000 at a Beta risk of 5 percent and allows for a $30,000 point estimate of total errors. The population size is 4,000 items, and the population standard deviation of the errors in the preceding year's audit was $100. What is the appropriate sample size?

$$n = \left[\frac{4,000 \cdot 1.64 \cdot 100}{80,000 - 30,000}\right]^2 = (13.1)^2 = 172$$

Note that the confidence coefficient used for the Beta risk of 5 percent is the same as that used for an interval estimate with a confidence level of 90 percent (that is, 1.64). This is because in hypothesis testing, all confidence coefficients used are always *one-sided*, rather than the two-sided confidence coefficients used in interval estimation.

The intuitive reason for this can be seen by referring back to Figure 5-9. Following the decision rule established, if the book value is misstated by a material amount, it is going to be either overstated or understated, but not both. Therefore, only one tail of one of the possible sampling distributions around a material error is applicable to the decision made.

A one-sided confidence coefficient for a particular risk level can be determined where two-sided confidence coefficients are known, as follows:

One-sided confidence coefficient = The two-sided confidence coefficient for the reliability level corresponding to 1 − (2 × risk factor)

Thus, if the risk factor (Beta) is 5 percent, the one-sided confidence coefficient equals the two-sided confidence coefficient for a 90 percent reliability level $(1 - [2 \times .05] = .90$; confidence coefficient $= 1.64$). Similarly, if the risk is 10 percent, the confidence coefficient used would be that for a two-sided 80 percent reliability, or 1.28.

Will a sample size of 172 be large enough to meet the audit objectives? It is impossible to answer that question until the actual audit results are known. If the actual standard deviation exceeds $100 or the point estimate exceeds $30,000, the results are likely to be unacceptable.

An examination of the formula indicates the effect on sample size of independently changing each of the factors in the formula. The relationships are as follows:

Type of change	*Effect of factors on preliminary sample size*
1. Decrease the Beta risk. (Equivalent to an increase in confidence level.)	Increase
2. Decrease the acceptable precision interval.	Increase
3. Decrease the estimate of the population standard deviation.	Decrease
4. Decrease the population size.	Decrease

The results are consistent with the conclusions reached in Chapter 3 when the four factors that affect attributes sampling were individually changed.

Alpha Risk and Beta Risk

Now assume the auditor decides to sample a population of 10,000 accounts receivable that actually includes errors that net out to zero. The auditor defines materiality as $20,000, decides on a 5 percent Beta risk and expects a standard deviation of $15. The auditor therefore takes a sample of 152 items $[(10,000 \cdot 1.64 \cdot 15/20,000)^2]$.

The sampling distribution for samples of 152 items from this population can be shown because the population characteristics are known. The sampling distribution is shown below.

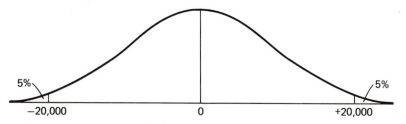

5%   5%

−20,000   0   +20,000

Now assume the auditor selects 152 items, tests each item, and finds net errors of zero and a population standard deviation of $15. The calculated confidence interval would be 0 ± $20,000 at a 90 percent confidence level $(0 \pm 10,000 \cdot 1.64 \cdot 15/\sqrt{152})$, and the auditor will correctly accept the population as being not materially misstated.

Notice, however, that many point estimates other than zero are not only possible, but highly likely, and that any of these would result in *rejecting the hypothesis that the population is not materially misstated* (a conclusion that would be incorrect). In this situation where precision and materiality are the same, the likelihood that the point estimate of the population will be anything other than the true value is equivalent to the Alpha risk. As can be seen, this likelihood, and therefore the Alpha risk, is extremely high—almost 100 percent. Another way of saying the same thing is that in this example, there is almost a 100 percent probability that the auditor will reject the hypothesis that the population is correctly stated within $20,000, even though the net error is actually zero.

The auditor can reduce the Alpha risk by increasing the sample size. For example, assume in the preceding case that a sample size of 300 had been taken. At a confidence level of 90 percent (relating to a 5 percent Beta risk), the computed precision interval is $14,203 ($10,000 \cdot 1.64 \cdot 15/\sqrt{300}$). Now the auditor will accept the population as being fairly stated if the point estimate of the errors is between $-$5,797 ($-$20,000 + $14,203) and $5,797 ($20,000 − $14,203). This is illustrated below.

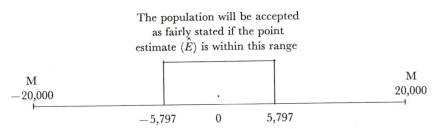

The population will be accepted
as fairly stated if the point
estimate ($\hat{E}$) is within this range

Naturally, in practice the auditor does not know whether the population is fairly stated. He takes a sample, performs the audit tests, and calculates a confidence interval. The population is accepted if the confidence interval falls entirely *within* the materiality limits, but there is still a risk that the population is materially misstated (Beta risk). The population is not accepted if either confidence limit is outside the materiality limits. When the population is not accepted, there is a risk that the population is not materially misstated (Alpha risk). When the latter result occurs, the auditor typically increases the sample size, performs some other audit procedures, and/or makes an audit adjustment.

The auditor can decide upon the desired Alpha risk before the sample size is calculated. The use of a small Alpha risk will increase the sample size somewhat, depending upon its size. The decision should be based upon the cost of increasing the sample size. For example, the auditor should use a higher Alpha risk if it is no more costly to sample 40 additional items after a population has been rejected than it would have been to test them as a part of the original sample. A low Alpha risk is appropriate if the cost of selecting and testing additional items is higher than the cost of testing them originally. The confirmation of accounts receivable is an example in which it is costly to send out another sample (requiring a low Alpha risk). The additional cost of testing inventory unit costs is not usually affected much by testing as a part of the original sample or testing at a later point (allowing a higher Alpha risk). Keep in mind that when the auditor uses a high Alpha risk and concludes that the population is fairly stated, the additional items that would have been required with a low Alpha risk do not have to be tested.

The calculation of planned sample size when both Alpha and Beta are considered is made by changing the auditor's acceptable precision interval (API). It is as follows:

$$\text{API*} = AE - E^* \cdot \frac{Z(1 - 2\beta)}{Z(1 - 2\beta) + Z(1 - \alpha)}$$

where:

$$\text{API*} = \text{acceptable precision interval, including Alpha and Beta risk}$$
$$AE = \text{acceptable error in the population}$$
$$E^* = \text{estimated point estimate of the population error}$$
$$Z(1 - 2\beta) = \text{confidence coefficient for } 1.0 - (2 \times \text{Beta risk})$$
$$Z(1 - \alpha) = \text{confidence coefficient for } 1.0 - \text{Alpha risk}$$

For example, assume a desired Beta risk of 5 percent, an Alpha risk of 20 percent, an allowable error of $80,000, and an expected error of $30,000. Then:

$$\text{API*} = \$80,000 - \$30,000 \cdot \frac{Z(1 - .10)}{Z(1 - .10) + Z(1 - .20)}$$

$$= \$50,000 \cdot \frac{1.64}{1.64 + 1.28} = \pm \$28,100$$

The required sample size can be calculated from the previously used formula:

$$n = \left(\frac{N \cdot Z(1 - 2\beta) \cdot \text{SD*}}{\text{API*}} \right)^2$$

The sample size for the data previously used is:

$$n = \left(\frac{4,000 \cdot 1.64 \cdot 100}{28,100} \right)^2 = (23.3)^2 = 543$$

The sample size with a Beta of 5 percent is 172. With both a Beta of 5 percent and an Alpha of 20 percent, the sample size is 543. The entire reason for the difference is the inclusion of Alpha risk in the calculation of API*. This is shown as follows:

$$n_1 = n_0 \cdot \left(\frac{Z(1 - 2\beta) + Z(1 - \alpha)}{Z(1 - 2\beta)} \right)^2$$

where:

n_1 = sample size including consideration of both Beta and Alpha
n_0 = sample size without Alpha
$Z(1 - 2\beta)$ = confidence coefficient for $1.0 - (2 \times$ Beta risk)
$Z(1 - \alpha)$ = confidence coefficient for $1.0 -$ Alpha risk

The result for the previous example, with a minor difference due to rounding, is:

$$n_1 = 172 \cdot \left(\frac{1.64 + 1.28}{1.64} \right)^2 = 543$$

CALCULATING SAMPLE SIZE FOR INTERVAL ESTIMATES

When the auditor uses interval estimation for difference estimation, the intent is not to evaluate whether a recorded account balance is fairly stated; it is to determine the dollar amount of errors in an account. For example, a common use of interval estimation is the adjustment needed to convert FIFO to LIFO for financial reporting and tax purposes. Similarly, it is common to use interval estimation to determine the total amount of discounts lost during a certain period.

When interval estimation is used to determine the amount of an adjustment, the adjustment equals the *calculated point estimate*. The precision interval is used to determine whether the adjustment is apt to be sufficiently accurate to meet the auditor's needs.

Determination of sample size for interval estimation requires the following factors:

Factor	*Comparison to hypothesis test*
1. Estimation of the standard deviation	Same as hypothesis test
2. Population size	Same as hypothesis test
3. Confidence level	Same concept as Beta risk except that it is two-sided.
4. Allowable error (materiality)	Same as hypothesis test (equals materiality)

Three factors in hypothesis tests are not used for interval estimates: Beta risk, Alpha risk, and expected error.

Beta and Alpha risks are risks of making a wrong decision. Since a decision is not being made in interval estimation, neither risk applies. The confidence level replaces these two risks.

There is no concern for the estimated point estimate in interval estimation because the intent is to adjust the recorded value by the actual point estimate. When the adjustment is planned, such as for estimating discounts lost, the auditor is providing information, not making a decision.

The sample size is calculated as follows:

$$n = \left(\frac{N \cdot Z \cdot \text{SD*}}{AE}\right)^2$$

where:

n = preliminary estimate of the sample size
N = population size
Z = confidence coefficient for the confidence level
SD* = advance estimate of the standard deviation
AE = acceptable error

For example, refer to the illustration on page 140, and assume an interval estimate rather than a hypothesis test. The confidence level is 90 percent $(1 - 2\beta)$, and everything else is the same as stated in that example.

$$n = \left(\frac{4,000 \cdot 1.64 \cdot 100}{80,000}\right)^2 = 67$$

The sample size of 67 compared to 172 results entirely from the estimated point estimate's not being in the formula.

Now assume that, based on the sample of 67 items, the following confidence interval was calculated at a 90 percent confidence level:

$12,200 ± $73,200 (see Figures 5-1 to 5-6 for formulas used to calculate confidence interval)

The auditor first determines whether the computed precision interval ($73,200) is less than the allowable error. Since it is, the recorded balance is adjusted by the amount of the point estimate ($12,200).

When the computed precision interval is larger than the allowable error, the sample size must be increased. The only reason for the computed precision interval being larger than the allowable error is a larger actual estimated population standard deviation than was expected.

Effect of Finite Correction Factor

The preceding discussion of determining sample size has ignored the finite correction factor. As in attributes sampling, adjustment for the finite correction factor has the effect of reducing the preliminary sample size somewhat when more than 10 percent of the total population is being tested. The calculation is applicable for both hypothesis testing and interval estimation. The calculation is as follows:

$$n = \frac{n'}{1 + \dfrac{n'}{N}}$$

where:

n' = preliminary sample size before considering the effect of finite correction factor

N = population size

n = required preliminary sample size after considering the effect of the finite correction factor

For example, assume that the preliminary sample size calculated with consideration of both Alpha and Beta risk is 400 items from a population of 2,000. The revised preliminary sample size is computed as follows:

$$n = \frac{400}{1 + 400/2,000} = 333$$

ILLUSTRATION OF THE USE OF DIFFERENCE ESTIMATION

Let us illustrate a common use of difference estimation. The purpose is to show the steps from beginning to end in the manner commonly followed in practice. A hypothesis test is used.

Background

The Marshall Wholesale Company records inventory at historical cost using FIFO. There are 2,700 inventory items included on 45 prenumbered pages, with 60 inventory items per page. The book value is $3,600,000. Previous experience shows that approximately 20 percent of the inventory items were incorrectly priced, but usually the misstatements were not significant. There were 25 errors in the previous year's inventory. The population standard deviation using difference estimation was $135, and the point estimate was $12,000. The auditor has decided on a Beta risk of 10 percent, an Alpha risk of 40 percent, and an acceptable error of $80,000.

Step 1. Decide on the objectives of the test. Determine if the dollar value of the error in costing raw materials inventory using a FIFO method is material (hypothesis test). If the error is considered material, the sample size will be increased or the book balance will be adjusted.

Step 2. Decide on the net total error that would be considered material for the price test of inventory. Based on prior years' earnings, anticipated current-year earnings, and the results of tests in other audit areas, a materiality limit of $80,000 is set.

Step 3. Decide on an acceptable Beta risk. Owing to the company's relatively high profitability, low risk of exposure to liability, and adequate internal controls over purchases, a Beta risk of 10 percent is used.

Step 4. Decide on an acceptable Alpha risk. An Alpha risk of 40 percent is selected because of the relatively low cost of taking a second sample if the hypothesis that the population is fairly stated is rejected.

Step 5. Decide on the sampling unit. Each type of raw material is listed on a printout and costed separately. The sampling unit is a line item that includes a raw material item on the inventory listing.

Step 6. Estimate the standard deviation and population error, and determine the population size. The standard deviation is estimated as $135 and the population error as $12,000. These were based on results of the prior year's inventory price tests, which had also been done using difference estimation. There are 2,700 raw material items.

Step 7. Calculate the acceptable precision interval, considering both the Alpha and Beta risk.

$$\text{API*} = AE - E* \cdot \frac{Z(1 - 2\beta)}{Z(1 - 2\beta) + Z(1 - \alpha)}$$

$$\text{API*} = 80{,}000 - 12{,}000 \cdot \frac{1.28}{1.28 + .84} = \$41{,}057$$

Step 8. Calculate the required sample size.

$$n = \left(\frac{N \cdot Z(1 - 2\beta) \cdot \text{SD*}}{\text{API*}} \right)^2$$

$$n = \left(\frac{2{,}700 \cdot 1.28 \cdot 135}{41{,}057} \right)^2 = (11.4)^2 = 130$$

Step 9. Select a random sample of 130 items and perform the audit tests. An error must be calculated for each sample item wherever the book value is different from the audit value. Great care must be taken in performing the tests. A small mistake by the auditor could significantly affect the statistical results.

The following 20 errors were found in the test of inventory items:

Sample item	Recorded value	Audit value	Error	Error squared
7	$ 2,611	$ 2,408	$ 203	$ 41,209
9	87	136	(49)	2,401
21	890	451	439	192,721
30	501	611	(110)	12,100
36	1,208	1,103	105	11,025
41	3,150	2,982	168	28,224
42	2,493	2,111	382	145,924
53	216	459	(243)	59,049
59	511	51	460	211,600
62	1,821	2,463	(642)	412,164
69	660	0	660	435,600
73	1,408	1,521	(113)	12,769
96	3,408	2,167	1,241	1,540,081
101	799	751	48	2,304
106	1,293	1,121	172	29,584
109	181	811	(630)	396,900
114	3,415	4,026	(611)	373,321
121	2,117	1,809	308	94,864
127	315	415	(100)	10,000
130	136	92	44	1,936
	$27,220	$25,488	$1,732	$4,013,776

Step 10. Calculate the point estimate.

$$\hat{E} = N \cdot \frac{\sum e_j}{n}$$

$$\hat{E} = 2,700 \cdot \frac{\$1,732}{130} = 2,700 \cdot 13.32 = \$35,972$$

Step 11. Calculate the estimated population standard deviation.

$$SD = \sqrt{\frac{\sum e_j^2 - n(\bar{e})^2}{n - 1}}$$

$$SD = \sqrt{\frac{4013776 - 130(13.32)^2}{(130 - 1)}}$$

$$SD = \sqrt{30,936} = \$175.9$$

Step 12. Calculate the precision interval at a two-sided confidence level equal to 1 minus Beta times 2.

$$\text{CPI} = \frac{N \cdot Z(1 - 2\beta) \cdot \text{SD}}{\sqrt{n}} \cdot \sqrt{\frac{N - n}{N}}$$

$$\text{CPI} = \frac{2{,}700 \cdot 1.28 \cdot 175.9}{\sqrt{130}} \cdot \sqrt{\frac{2{,}700 - 130}{2{,}700}}$$

$$\text{CPI} = \frac{607{,}910}{11.40} \cdot .98 = \$52{,}258$$

Step 13. Calculate the confidence limits.

$$\text{CL} = \$35{,}972 \pm \$52{,}258$$
$$\text{LCL} = -\$16{,}286$$
$$\text{UCL} = \$88{,}230$$

Step 14. Decide on the acceptability of the population.

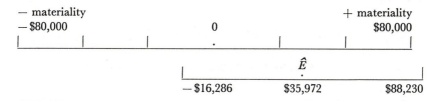

The upper confidence limit exceeds the upper materiality limit; therefore, the population cannot be considered acceptable. The auditor must now consider the options and discuss them with the client.

Option 1. Reduce the client's book value so that both confidence limits will be within the materiality range. Many possibilities exist, but three basic ones are presented here:

   a. Reduce the client's book value by $8,230 ($88,230 − $80,000). The point estimate of the error is thereby reduced to $27,742 ($35,972 − $8,230). The computed precision interval remains the same. The confidence interval is now $27,742 ± $52,258. The lower confidence limit is −$24,516 ($27,742 − $52,258) and the upper limit is $80,000 ($27,742 + $52,258).

   b. Reduce the client's book value by $63,714 ($80,000 − $16,286). This alternative reduces the point estimate to −$27,742 and results in a new confidence interval with a lower limit of −$80,000 and an upper limit of $24,516.

   c. Reduce the client's book value by $35,972, the amount of the point estimate of the total population error. This would result in a confidence interval with a lower limit of −$52,258 and an upper limit of +$52,258, the amount of computed precision. The population would be satisfactory after any of these adjusting entries.

Although all are acceptable, many auditors prefer c, adjusting by the point estimate, as it gives equal regard to both under- and overstatement errors. Both an upper and a lower confidence limit should be recalculated after any adjustment of the book value to make sure the entire confidence interval is within the materiality limits.

Option 2. Increase the sample size. Many times a client will not permit an adjustment for unknown errors. Management could justifiably argue that any of the alternative amounts in Option 1 almost certainly does not represent the actual errors and any other adjustment within the confidence interval is just as acceptable. Such a response is especially likely when a large Alpha risk is used. An appropriate response to the client is to inform him that a larger adjustment would be satisfactory, but the alternative to an adjustment to the book value is an increase in the sample size. This will require incurring an additional cost, which should be borne by the client.

The additional sample size can be calculated by starting at Step 7 and redoing Steps 7 and 8, using new information about E^* and a revised Alpha risk if appropriate.

(Step 7)

$$API^* = AE - E^* \cdot \frac{Z(1-2\beta)}{Z(1-2\beta) + Z(1-\alpha)}$$

$$API^* = 80,000 - 36,000 \cdot \frac{1.28}{1.28 + .84} = \$26,570$$

E^* is now \$36,000, because the actual point estimate was approximately that amount.

(Step 8)

$$n = \left(\frac{N \cdot Z(1-2\beta) \cdot SD^*}{API^*}\right)^2$$

$$n = \left(\frac{2,700 \cdot 1.28 \cdot 176}{26,570}\right)^2 = (22.9)^2 = 524$$

The auditor should test 394 additional sample items (524 less the 130 already tested) if the client will not accept the adjustment.

Even if the additional 394 items are selected, it does not mean the confidence limits will fall within the \$80,000 materiality limits. The sample may result in a higher standard deviation and/or a larger point estimate.

It is necessary to determine the errors in the additional sample of 394 items and combine them with the 20 errors from the first sample. (It would be improper to ignore the first sample results.) These errors would be scheduled the same way as was done in Step 9. The same calculations that were made in Steps 10 through 13 would be repeated, including all errors for all 524 sample items. If the results were still not within the \$80,000 materiality limits, the options would again be reviewed.

In situations such as this, known errors—those found in the actual sample—may be adjusted by the client. This would alter the point estimate and both confidence limits by the amount of the adjustment. In this case, the net amount of $1,732 would not be sufficient for the adjusted book value to be accepted for audit purposes.

EFFICIENCY, SAMPLE SELECTION AND CALCULATION COSTS, AND RELIABILITY

Efficiency

Unstratified difference estimation is likely always to result in smaller sample sizes than in unstratified mean-per-unit estimation. The reason is that the standard deviation of the errors is smaller than the standard deviation of the audit values. For example, the standard deviation of the errors for the example on page 148 is 175.9, whereas the standard deviation of the population, based upon the audited value of the 20 sample items with errors, is approximately 1,150. It was shown earlier that the standard deviation greatly affects the sample size.

Difference estimation is more efficient than ratio estimation in some cases and less efficient in others. Difference estimation is more efficient when the size of the errors in the population is *independent* of the size of the client's recorded values, whereas ratio estimation is more efficient when the size of the errors is directly related to the size of the recorded values. For example, assume that the client has 1,000 recorded sales transactions ranging in size from $10 to $2,000. If the size of the errors is larger for the larger population items than for the smaller ones, ratio estimation is a more efficient estimator. If the size of the errors has nothing to do with the size of the population items, difference estimation is more efficient. For many populations, there is some relationship, but not a particularly close one, between error size and the size of population items. In those cases, difference and ratio estimation are approximately equally efficient.

Sample Selection and Calculation Costs

The method and cost of selecting an unstratified random sample is the same for any of the three statistical methods, assuming an equal sample size. The cost of selecting an unstratified sample is considerably less than for a stratified sample, unless the accounting information is stored on a computer. The differences in sample selection and calculation costs for alternative methods are significant only when selection and calculation are done manually.

An important consideration that affects sample selection and calculation cost is the degree to which the computer is involved. There are three
possibilities:

1. *The accounting information being audited is in computer-readable form and the auditor
uses the computer for selecting samples and calculating statistical results.* The sample selection
and calculation costs of the alternative statistical methods are not relevant, because
they are approximately the same for all methods. Efficiency and reliability are then
the only considerations.

2. *The auditor has a computer terminal available for selecting sample items and making
statistical calculations.* (The information must be manually fed into the terminal.)
There is no significant difference in random selection costs for the three unstratified
random sampling methods, but sample selection for any of the stratified methods
may be considerably more costly because it is necessary to do the stratification
manually. Stratification costs will be covered in Chapter 8.

The statistical calculation costs for difference, ratio, and mean-per-unit estimation are similar when a terminal is used. The advantage of difference estimation is
that only the value of the errors must be entered into the system (for instance, there
may be only 15 errors in a sample of 100), whereas for mean-per-unit, every sample
item must be entered. Both the audit and book value of every sample item must be
entered for ratio estimation.

3. *The auditor must do all sample selection and calculations manually.* The sample
selection costs for the three unstratified methods will be approximately the same,
assuming equal sample sizes. Selecting sample items for stratified sampling is often
much more expensive than for unstratified, but the cost will not vary significantly
between alternative methods.

Calculation of statistical results is an important consideration when it must be
done manually. The least expensive method is difference estimation, because the
auditor restricts calculations to the errors. The biggest problem with ratio estimation
is the extensive calculations required. It is costly to make ratio estimate calculations,
and the large number of calculations increases the likelihood of nonsampling errors.

The calculation cost for mean-per-unit is also higher than for difference estimation, but less than for ratio estimation. Usually, however, mean-per-unit calculation costs are not too burdensome.

Reliability of the Estimator

Difference estimation is an unreliable estimator under certain conditions. The
circumstance in which difference estimation is most likely to result in
incorrect audit decisions based on the statistical results occurs when there is
a relatively small number of errors in a population containing errors that
are material in total.

A simple example illustrates how this could occur. Assume a population
of 3,000 items with only 30 errors, which are material when combined. If the
auditor takes a random sample of 50 items, there is a good chance (almost
50 percent) that he will find no errors in the sample, even though the
population is materially in error. If statistical results were calculated, the
auditor would erroneously conclude that the point estimate, standard

deviation, and confidence interval of the population are all zero at a 100 percent confidence level. Auditors have recognized for a long time that difference estimation cannot be used when there are no errors in the sample. For example, it is intuitively obvious that it would be improper to conclude that a population of 3,000 items is 100 percent error-free when there are no errors in a sample of 50 items.

In recent years, there has been some question as to the reliability of difference estimation where some errors in the sample are found. For example, if the auditor has found four small errors in a sample of 50 items, it would be possible to calculate a point estimate, standard deviation, and a confidence interval. Nevertheless, there is still a good chance that the estimator is unreliable if the sample came from a distribution of errors in a population such as that in Figure 5-10.

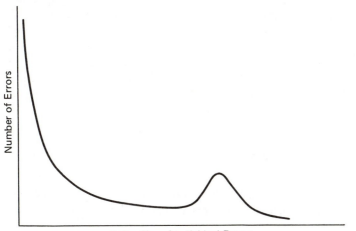

Dollar Size of Individual Errors

FIGURE 5-10 Distribution of errors in a hypothetical population. The combined errors are material.

The auditor would not know the larger errors existed unless one or more of the sample items included a large dollar error. He could thereby easily and erroneously conclude that a materially misstated population is fairly stated (Beta risk).

How likely is the distribution of errors in actual audit populations to be sufficiently similar to the distribution in Figure 5-10 to cause serious problems of reliability for difference estimation? Many practicing auditors believe there is a great enough likelihood to require extreme care in using unstratified difference estimation. The Neter and Loebbecke study supported existing reservations by showing the reliability of difference estimation in a number of circumstances. These are shown in Figure 5-11.

Study population	Sample size	Population error rate				
		1/2%	1%	5%	10%	30%
1	100	30.5	37.3	96.8	94.0	96.3
	200	40.0	53.0	99.2	93.5	93.7
2	100	31.2	41.8	82.3	97.2	95.5
	200	44.0	54.5	90.2	97.0	96.0
3	100	23.3	36.8	73.7	80.3	90.8
	200	42.3	57.0	82.3	87.7	92.2
4	100	21.2	30.0	58.2	62.0	74.8
	200	28.0	47.0	69.7	70.7	87.5

FIGURE 5-11   Percent of correct confidence intervals; nominal percent 95.4

In this study, 600 repeated samples were taken from four populations with different characteristics, for which the error rate was varied. Using the normal distribution, an expected proportion of the samples should provide confidence intervals that contain the true population error amount. As can be seen, only those samples for three populations where the error rate was quite high (boxed-in area) exhibited a reasonably acceptable level of reliability with difference estimation.

APPROPRIATE USES
OF DIFFERENCE ESTIMATION

The authors believe that unstratified difference estimation is the most desirable statistical method for auditors in many common audit circumstances. These circumstances are:

1. The population data are not in a computer-readable form.
2. The auditor does not have a computer terminal available to perform the required arithmetic to get the statistical results.
3. The auditor has evaluated the client's accounting system and reviewed the client's population data and has concluded that there is minimal likelihood of a small number of large errors that will, when combined with all other errors, be material.
4. The auditor expects a large number of small errors in the population that could in total be material. It is not possible to state the exact number of errors that should be found in the sample before difference estimation is acceptable. Arbitrarily, we recommend the larger of the following:
    a. At least 10 items in the sample are in error
    b. At least 10 percent of the sample items are in error up to a sample size of 300.
    c. For sample sizes exceeding 300, the number of errors should be at least 30 (300 × 10%) plus 5% of the sample size exceeding 300.

For example, assume the auditor has taken a sample of 80 inventory items for pricing. At least ten of the items would have to be in error before difference estimation could be used, if our arbitrary guidelines are followed. There would have to be twelve errors if the sample size had been 120 items. If the sample size were 500, there would have to be 40 errors before difference estimation could be used $[(300 \times .10) + (200 \times .05)]$. It is also assumed that the auditor is satisfied that there are not likely to be any large errors in the population.

Further, if all errors are in one direction or the differences are very large relative to their book values, we recommend these requirements be increased. If more than 75 percent of the errors are in one direction, it is recommended that the error rate be at least 50 percent.

It is possible, but perhaps unlikely, that even if conditions 1 and 2 do not exist, unstratified difference estimation *may* still be the best method. Since conditions 3 and 4 relate to reliability of the difference estimate, these conditions *must* exist.

ILLUSTRATIONS OF LIKELY APPLICATIONS OF DIFFERENCE ESTIMATION

At the end of Chapter 6 are several illustrations of situations in which either ratio or difference estimation may be a useful audit tool. A better understanding of difference estimation can be obtained by studying these illustrations at this point. The following illustrations are included:

- Price test of inventory
- Reliance on perpetual inventory records instead of a physical count
- LIFO conversion
- Accounts receivable confirmation
- Calculation of discounts lost
- Sales tests of transactions

For each of the illustrations, five aspects of using either difference or ratio estimation are discussed:

1. *Description.* The description includes a brief discussion of the circumstances in which the statistical test is likely to be used and the purpose for calculating the statistics.
2. *Sampling Unit.* There is a brief discussion of the most likely sampling unit for the test and alternatives in certain circumstances.
3. *Random Selection.* The purpose of this part is to describe random selection difficulties, if any are likely.
4. *Information needed to calculate statistics.* Only the information that is most difficult to determine is discussed under this part.
5. *Likely problems.* Problems frequently encountered in each illustration are discussed.

SUGGESTED READINGS AND REFERENCES

LOEBBECKE, JAMES K., and JOHN NETER, "Statistical Sampling in Confirming Accounts Receivable," *Journal of Accountancy*, June 1973, pp. 44–50.

NETER, JOHN, and JAMES K. LOEBBECKE, *Behavior of Major Statistical Estimators in Sampling Accounting Populations*. New York: AICPA, 1975.

REVIEW QUESTIONS

5-1. When is difference estimation a more useful statistical method than attributes? When is attributes more useful?

5-2. During a professional development program at a CPA firm, an audit manager was instructing several younger staff members on how to calculate confidence intervals in the accounts receivable area by using difference estimation. As part of the discussion, he explained the importance of the population size in calculating the point estimate of the total error and the precision interval for the population. He ended his talk by informing the group that a 20 percent error in counting the number of accounts in the population would probably result in a misleading statistical calculation.

At that point, one of the staff members raised his hand and said that these conclusions were inconsistent with what he had learned about using attributes sampling. He said a statistics professor had explained to him when he was in college that the finite correction factor, which is affected by the population size, could frequently be ignored in variables sampling.

REQUIRED:

a. Explain why the population size is far more important for making variables sampling calculations than it is for attributes sampling.
b. Explain how the population size affects the statistical results in variables sampling in more ways than only by the finite correction factor.

5-3. An audit partner is developing an office training program to familiarize his professional staff with difference estimation applicable to the audit of dollar-value balances. He wishes to demonstrate the relationship of sample sizes to population size and variability and the auditor's specifications as to precision and confidence level. The partner prepared the table below to show comparative population characteristics and audit specifications of two populations. In items (i) through (v) below, you are to indicate for the specific case from the table, the required sample size to be selected from population 1 relative to the sample from population 2. Your answer choice should be selected from the following responses:
  (i) Larger than the required sample size from population 2
  (ii) Equal to the required sample size from population 2

(iii) Smaller than the required sample size from population 2
(iv) Indeterminate relative to the required sample size from population 2
  a. In case 1, the required sample size from population 1 is _____ .
  b. In case 2, the required sample size from population 1 is _____ .
  c. In case 3, the required sample size from population 1 is _____ .
  d. In case 4, the required sample size from population 1 is _____ .
  e. In case 5, the required sample size from population 1 is _____ .

	Characteristics of population 1 relative to population 2		*Audit specifications as to a sample from population 1 relative to a sample from population 2*	
	Size	*Variability*	*Acceptable precision interval*	*Specified confidence level*
Case 1	Equal	Equal	Equal	Higher
Case 2	Equal	Larger	Wider	Equal
Case 3	Larger	Equal	Narrower	Lower
Case 4	Smaller	Smaller	Equal	Lower
Case 5	Larger	Equal	Equal	Higher

5-4. In testing the cash discounts on vendors' invoices, the auditor did not expect to find any errors in the sample and therefore used attributes sampling techniques. Based upon the statistical requirements for the test, a sample size of 120 items was randomly selected and carefully tested. Much to the auditor's surprise, there were 15 sample items on which the client had failed to take the discount even though company policy clearly indicated one should have been taken. At this point, the auditor decided to switch to variables estimation to measure the amount of the lost discounts. The 15 items in the sample on which the client had failed to take the discount are summarized as follows:

Invoice amount	*Discount*
$120.00	2%
$87.50	1%
$510.00	3%
$1,715.00	2%
$13.60	1%
$327.00	2%
$5,235.00	1%
$175.00	2%
$13,025.00	$\frac{1}{2}$%
$695.00	1%
$1,000.00	$2\frac{1}{2}$%
$960.00	5%
$501.00	2%
$2,620.00	2%
$270.00	1%

Required:

a. Is it acceptable to change to variables estimation at this point? Explain.

b. If variables estimation is used, explain how the auditor should proceed. State in words the meaning of the confidence limits the auditor will calculate in this case.

c. Calculate the confidence interval for total discounts that the client failed to take based on the 15 items in the sample, assuming that the total population size was 4,850. Use a 90% confidence level.

5-5. An audit client has decided to determine the ending valuation of inventories by physically counting and costing only a sample of their total inventory. There are no perpetual records. Explain why difference estimation would not be an appropriate statistical method in these circumstances.

5-6. Distinguish between a hypothesis test and an interval estimate. When is each used?

5-7. What is meant by the point estimate of the total errors for difference estimation? Calculate the point estimate when there are the following client errors in a sample of 120 items from a population of 3,000 (understatements are in parentheses): 48.12, 56.11, 97.16, (41.14), 13.06, 191.67, (84.91), 1.56.

5-8. Using difference estimation, an auditor took a random sample of 100 inventory items from a large population to test for proper pricing. Several of the inventory items were in error, but the combined net amount of the sample error was not material. In addition, a review of the individual errors indicated that no error was by itself material. As a result, the auditor did not investigate the errors or make a statistical evaluation. Explain why this practice is improper.

5-9. Distinguish between the point estimate of the total errors and the true value of the errors in the population. How can each be determined?

5-10. What is meant by the population standard deviation? Calculate the estimate of the population standard deviation based on the sample errors in question 5-7.

5-11. What is meant by the precision interval? What are the four factors that affect the size of the computed interval? Calculate the precision interval, at a confidence level of 90%, for the errors in question 5-7.

5-12. Distinguish between the terms *confidence interval* and *confidence limits*. Describe how each is calculated. Calculate both for the error information in question 5-7.

5-13. Distinguish between the following terms: *confidence level, confidence limits, confidence interval,* and *computed precision interval*. For the statistical statement, "The population value of the errors is $50,000 ± $16,000 with a reliability of 90 percent," calculate or identify the value for each of the four terms.

5-14. In reviewing the results of a difference estimation calculation, an in-charge auditor, Roger Murphy, concluded that the confidence limits were larger than he could accept. In examining the details of the calculation, he determined that the point estimate of the population was nearly zero, but the standard deviation was large. He decided that there must be an error in the calculation, since it was impossible to get a small point estimate and a large standard deviation. His assistant, Lannell Tigg, expressed a different viewpoint. She stated that the problem was simply the failure to take a sufficiently large sample size. Tigg ended her explanation by informing Murphy that an increase in the sample size would automatically reduce the population standard deviation and thereby reduce the confidence limits.

REQUIRED:

a. Explain how it is possible to have a small point estimate in the population and a large standard deviation when difference estimation is used.

b. Was Tigg's explanation of the way to reduce the population standard deviation correct? Discuss.

5-15. What is meant by materiality for hypothesis testing using difference estimation? Explain how the auditor decides what is material and the effect of the decision on the required sample size.

5-16. Define what is meant by Alpha and Beta risk for hypothesis testing, and distinguish between the two risks. Explain the advantages and disadvantages of a small Beta risk. Do the same for Alpha risk.

5-17. Distinguish between confidence level and Beta risk. Also distinguish between confidence level and Alpha risk.

5-18. State the decision rule using hypothesis testing for difference estimation. Assume the confidence interval at a 95% confidence level is $25,000 ± $15,000 and a materiality limit of $45,000. What is the decision in that circumstance?

5-19. What options does the auditor have when the decision rule rejects the population as not acceptable? State the circumstances for which each option is preferable.

5-20. Two auditors follow different approaches in determining sample size for unstratified difference estimation. The first auditor always selects a sample size of 75 items. He then calculates the confidence limits and compares them to materiality. If the population is rejected, he carefully goes through the options you identified in 5-19 and selects the best option considering the circumstances. The second auditor determines the proper preliminary estimate of the sample size by the use of a formula. If the population is rejected, he goes through a process identical to that of the first auditor. Are both methods correct? Which method is preferable? Explain your answers.

5-21. Assume that the preliminary estimate of the sample size for hypothesis testing is determined by using only Beta risk. What problem is the auditor apt to encounter when the sample results are evaluated? Under what circumstances is that problem likely to be serious?

5-22. The following formula is to determine the preliminary estimate of the sample size for difference estimation considering only Beta risk:

$$n = \left(\frac{N \cdot Z(1 - 2\beta) \cdot SD^*}{AE - E^*} \right)^2$$

Define each of the terms affecting sample size and state the effect on the preliminary estimate of changing each factor independently.

5-23. Explain how the inclusion of Alpha risk affects the calculation of the preliminary estimate of the sample size. Explain the circumstances in which it is desirable to include or exclude Alpha risk in determining sample size.

5-24. How do determining a sample size for hypothesis testing and for interval estimation differ? Explain the reason for the difference.

5-25. Assume you are using interval estimation for the purpose of making an adjusting entry. What would you do if materiality were $20,000 and the calculated confidence interval were $8,000 ± $16,000 at a 95% confidence level? Would your answer be different if the confidence interval were $8,000 ± $23,000?

5-26. Explain what is meant by *efficiency* as the term is used in difference estimation. Under what circumstances is difference estimation apt to be more efficient than unstratified mean-per-unit?

5-27. Explain what is meant by the reliability of difference estimation. Under what circumstances is difference estimation likely to be reliable, and when is it likely to be unreliable?

5-28. Assume that the auditor is in a situation in which the unstratified difference estimate is an unreliable estimator. How will she know the estimator is unreliable in that situation? What can the auditor do if she knows the estimator is unreliable?

5-29. Under what circumstances is unstratified difference estimation a desirable statistical method for auditors?

DISCUSSION QUESTIONS AND PROBLEMS

5-30. The following apply to difference estimation variables sampling. Choose the best response.
  a. The auditor's failure to recognize an error in an amount or an error in an internal control data-processing procedure is described as a:
     (i) Statistical error
     (ii) Sampling error
     (iii) Standard error of the mean
     (iv) Nonsampling error
  b. An auditor makes separate compliance and substantive tests in the accounts payable area, which has good internal control. If the auditor uses statistical sampling for both these tests, the confidence level established for the substantive test is normally:
     (i) The same as that for tests of compliance
     (ii) Greater than that for tests of compliance
     (iii) Less than that for tests of compliance
     (iv) Totally independent of that for tests of compliance
  c. How should an auditor determine the precision required in establishing a statistical sampling plan?
     (i) By the materiality of an allowable margin of error the auditor is willing to accept

    (ii) By the amount of reliance the auditor will place on the results of the sample

    (iii) By reliance on a table of random numbers

    (iv) By the amount of risk the auditor is willing to take that material errors will occur in the accounting process

5-31. a. Using difference estimation, calculate the preliminary sample size for *a* to *e* from the information provided. Apply the finite correction factor when it is appropriate.

	a	*b*	*c*	*d*	*e*
Population size	5,000	10,000	5,000	10,000	5,000
Alpha risk	20%	49%	20%	25%	5%
Beta risk	5%	5%	$\frac{1}{2}$%	10%	5%
Allowable error	50,000	80,000	50,000	80,000	50,000
Estimated standard deviation	100	150	100	150	100
Estimated point estimate	20,000	30,000	20,000	30,000	20,000

    b. In general, what is the effect on the preliminary sample size (increase, decrease, no effect, or cannot determine without additional information) of each of the following independent changes, assuming the other components of sample size are held constant?

	Effect on preliminary sample size
1. Increase Beta risk.	
2. Increase Alpha risk.	
3. Increase estimated point estimate.	
4. Increase population size.	
5. Increase Alpha risk and decrease Beta risk.	
6. Increase allowable error and increase estimated standard deviation.	

5-32. a. Calculate the preliminary sample size using difference estimation for *a* to *e* from the information provided. Apply the finite correction factor when it is appropriate.

	a	*b*	*c*	*d*	*e*
Population size	5,000	10,000	5,000	10,000	5,000
Required confidence level	90%	90%	99%	80%	90%
Allowable error	50,000	80,000	50,000	80,000	50,000
Estimated standard deviation	100	150	100	150	100

b. In general, what is the effect on the preliminary sample size (increase, decrease, no effect, or cannot determine without additional information) for each of the following independent changes, assuming the other components of sample size are held constant?

	Effect on preliminary sample size
1. Increase confidence level.	
2. Increase estimated point estimate.	
3. Increase allowable error.	
4. Increase confidence level and population size.	
5. Increase population size and allowable error.	

c. Explain why each of your answers in 5-31.*a* is the same as or different from the answer 5-32.*a*.

5-33. The following are five different sets of sample information from a population of 5,000 accounts receivable with a book value of $4,600,000. (In each situation, the net book value of the items in the sample exceeds the audit value.)

Situation	Sample size	Total net error in the sample	Population standard deviation estimated from the sample	Desired confidence level
1	100	1,000	25	95%
2	200	2,000	25	95%
3	200	2,000	50	95%
4	200	2,000	25	90%
5	200	1,000	25	95%

REQUIRED:

a. Using difference estimation, calculate the point estimate of the errors in the population, the computed precision interval, and the confidence limits for each of the five situations.

b. In general for a given population, state the effect on the computed upper confidence limit for each of the following (increase, decrease, no effect, or cannot determine from the information given):
   (i) An increase in the sample size (the average error in the sample, population standard deviation, and confidence level remain constant).
   (ii) An increase in the average error in the sample (the sample size, population standard deviation, and confidence level remain constant).
   (iii) An increase in the population standard deviation (the sample size, average error in the sample, and confidence level remain constant).

(iv) An increase in the confidence level (the sample size, average error in the sample, and population standard deviation remain constant.)

(v) An increase in the sample size and population standard deviation (the average error in the sample and confidence level remain constant).

(vi) An increase in the confidence level and the population standard deviation (the average error in the sample and sample size remain constant).

5-34. In confirming accounts receivable with a recorded value of $6,250,000 for the Blessman Wholesale Drug Company, Gerald Bloomstad, CPA, has decided that if the total error in the account exceeds $60,000, he will consider the error material. He believes the point estimate of the error will approximate $20,000. He has decided to use unrestricted random sampling for difference estimation, and he believes a Beta risk of 5% and an Alpha risk of 20% are appropriate, considering the circumstances of the engagement. Although Bloomstad does not know the standard deviation, he decides to estimate it a little bit high to make sure he does not undersample. The standard deviation is estimated at $22. There are 14,300 total accounts receivable in the trial balance.

REQUIRED:

a. Calculate the number of accounts receivable Bloomstad should confirm.

b. Assuming only 100 confirmation responses are received in the first and second requests, what should the auditor do at this point?

c. What would the sample size in part *a* have been if the estimated standard deviation were $32 instead of $22?

d. What would the sample size in part *a* have been if the allowable error were $80,000 and the expected point estimate were $20,000?

e. What would the sample size in part *a* have been if the allowable error were $90,000 and the expected point estimate were $50,000? Explain the relationship between your answers in *a* and *e*.

5-35. a. Calculate confidence limits for *a* to *e* using difference estimation from the information provided:

	a	b	c	d	e
Population size	2,000	2,000	5,000	5,000	1,000
Beta risk	5%	10%	10%	10%	$\frac{1}{2}$%
Alpha risk	20%	100%	20%	40%	20%
Sum of sample errors (net)	320	320	1,750	1,750	250
Standard deviation	17	17	30	40	50
Sample size	100	100	400	400	50
Allowable error	13,000	9,000	30,000	35,000	15,000

b. In general, what is the effect on the upper confidence limit (increase, decrease, no effect, or cannot determine without additional information) of each of the following independent changes, assuming the other components are held constant?

	Effect on upper confidence limit
1. Increase Beta risk.	
2. Increase population size.	
3. Increase standard deviation.	
4. Increase Alpha risk.	
5. Increase allowable error and decrease the sum of the sample errors.	
6. Add two more sample errors, one for $450 and one for ($450).	

    c. Determine whether the population value is acceptable as stated for each confidence limit calculated in *a*.

5-36. a. Using difference estimation, calculate confidence limits for *a* to *e* from the information provided.

	a	b	c	d	e
Population size	2,000	2,000	5,000	5,000	1,000
Confidence level	90%	80%	80%	80%	99%
Sum of sample errors (net)	320	320	1,750	1,750	250
Standard deviation	17	17	30	40	50
Sample size	100	100	400	400	50
Materiality	13,000	9,000	30,000	35,000	15,000

    b. In general, what is the effect on the upper confidence limits (increase, decrease, no effect, or cannot determine without additional information) of each of the following independent changes, assuming the other components are held constant?

	Effect on upper confidence limit
1. Increase confidence level.	
2. Increase sample size.	
3. Increase standard deviation.	
4. Increase population size.	
5. Increase allowable error and decrease the sum of the sample errors.	
6. Add two more sample errors, one for $450 and one for ($450)	

    c. Compare your answers in *a* to those given in part 5-35.*a*.

    d. Determine the appropriate adjustment entry for each of *a* to *e* in part *a*. Where an entry would be inappropriate, write "none."

5-37. For each of the following populations, the auditor has established an acceptable precision interval as a part of using difference estimation and has calculated actual statistical results after conducting the audit tests:

Population	Allowable error at the same Beta risk as the computed precision interval	Point estimate of the population error (understated book value in parentheses)	Computed precision interval
1	$25,000	$ 6,000	$16,000
2	25,000	0	24,000
3	25,000	(14,000)	18,000
4	25,000	21,000	10,000
5	25,000	(12,000)	11,000

REQUIRED:

a. Determine which of the calculated results satisfy the acceptable precision interval the auditor set before the sample was selected.
b. For any result in part *a* that does not satisfy the acceptable precision interval, state the minimum adjustment in the client's book value, if any, that will make the sample result satisfactory.
c. What options does the auditor have for any sample result that does not satisfy the acceptable precision interval established by the auditor?

5-38. An auditor is using difference estimation for the confirmation of accounts receivable in the audit of Lafferty Hardware Supply. A random sample of 100 positive confirmations has been sent to customers. Second requests have been mailed to all no-responses. Alternate procedures have been done for all confirmations not received.

After all responses have been received and alternate procedures performed, follow-up procedures are used to determine the value of each error in the sample. Difference estimation is then used to calculate the confidence interval.

REQUIRED:

a. Why is difference estimation apt to be a better statistical method than attributes in this situation?
b. Define what is meant by a nonsampling error. Why might nonsampling errors be a serious problem in the circumstances described in the case?
c. Evaluate the following statement: "The calculation of the confidence interval for hypothesis testing and interval estimation is identical. The difference between the two methods is the use of the results."
d. Describe how the auditor would use the calculated confidence interval for a hypothesis test.
e. Explain the circumstances in which an adjusting journal entry would be necessary and appropriate when a hypothesis test has been used.
f. Under what circumstances would unstratified difference estimation be an appropriate statistical method for the confirmation of accounts receivable?

5-39. Marjorie Jorgensen, CPA, is verifying the accuracy of outstanding accounts payable for Marygold Hardware, a large, single-location, retail hardware store. There are 650 vendors listed on the outstanding accounts payable list. She has eliminated from the population 40 vendors that have large ending balances and will audit them separately from the planned test for this problem. (There are now 610 vendors.)

She plans to do one of three tests for each item in the sample: examine a vendor's statement in the client's hands, obtain a confirmation when no statement is on hand, or perform an extensive search for invoices when neither of the first two is obtained. There are no accounts payable subsidiary records available, and a large number of errors are expected. Marjorie has obtained facts or made audit judgments as follows:

Alpha risk	20%	Beta risk	10%
Allowable error	$ 45,000	Expected error	$20,000
Recorded book value	$600,000	Estimated standard deviation	$ 280

a. Under what circumstances is it desirable to use unstratified difference estimation in the circumstances described? Under what circumstances would it be undesirable?

b. Calculate the required sample size for the audit tests of accounts payable, assuming Alpha risk is ignored.

c. Assume the auditor selects exactly the sample size calculated in part *b*. The point estimate calculated from the sample results is $21,000, and the estimated population standard deviation is 267. Is the population fairly stated as defined by the decision rule? Explain what causes the result to be acceptable or unacceptable.

d. Calculate the required sample size for the audit tests of accounts payable, assuming Alpha risk is considered.

e. Explain the reason for the large increase of the sample size resulting from including Alpha risk in determining sample size.

f. Fred Lehne calculates the required sample size using the formula without consideration of Alpha risk. After the sample size is determined, he increases the sample size 25%. Fred believes this does the same thing as using Alpha risk without having to bother with making the calculation. Is this approach appropriate? Evaluate its desirability.

5-40. Roybuilt Machines has computerized its fixed-asset records during the past year. The company feels that the conversion was completed with only minor errors in recording useful lives and depreciation methods, but, based on past experience, you are not so sure. When Roybuilt Machines converted its inventory system two years ago, almost 25% of the items were incorrectly priced. You have satisfied yourself as to the fixed-asset costs by means by other tests, and want to apply difference estimation sampling to test the depreciation expense for the year.

The following data are available or have been developed by you:

Depreciation expense for the year	$635,400
Population size—number of depreciable assets (N)	3,000
Materiality	$ 15,000
Required confidence level:	
Beta risk	5%
Alpha risk	100%

You have no prior experience with the fixed-assets data file, so you select a preliminary sample of 50 items in order to estimate the standard deviation. The results are as follows (understatements are in parentheses):

Item no.	Difference
1	$(45)
2	83
3	124
4	(90)
5	27
Total	$ 99

For the other 45 items in the sample, there are no differences.

REQUIRED:

a. What is the sample size necessary to achieve your audit objectives?
b. Is it valid to include the 50 items from the preliminary sample in your final sample analysis?
c. Ignoring your answers to part *a*, assume that you select 150 additional items and the following differences between book and audited values are identified. (Understatements are in parentheses.)

Item no.	Difference	Difference^2
1	$ (80)	$ 6,400
2	190	36,100
3	42	1,764
4	95	9,025
5	(60)	3,600
6	135	18,225
7	(33)	1,089
8	(12)	144
9	91	8,281
10	(115)	13,225
11	(72)	5,184
12	127	16,129
Total	$ 308	$119,166

Calculate the confidence interval at the required confidence level based on your sample (i.e., total sample of 200 items).

d. What audit conclusion would you reach based on this analysis? Would an adjusting entry be necessary? If so, for what amount?

5-41. You are using difference estimation in the costing of inventory as part of the audit of the Rubber Products and Supply Company. The following data are available or have been developed by you:

Population book value	$648,050
Population size (N)	2,000
Materiality	$ 16,000
Estimated point estimate	$ 4,000
Required confidence level: Beta risk	5%
Estimated standard deviation (based on data contained in last year's work papers)	$30

REQUIRED:

a. What is the sample size necessary to achieve your audit objectives?

b. What would be the necessary sample size if the allowable error had been $10,000 and everything else the same as in the original data?

c. Why did the change in the allowable error have such a large effect on sample size?

d. What would be the necessary sample size if the population size had been 4,000 and everything else the same as in the original data?

e. Why is the effect of the change in d the same as the effect of the change in b?

f. Without regard to your answer to part a above, assume that a sample of 60 items is selected and the following differences between book and audited values are identified. (Understatements are in parentheses.)

Item no.	Difference
1	$ 19
2	11
3	(19)
4	40
5	90
6	38
7	(90)
8	70
9	(85)
Total	$ 74

For each of the other 51 items in the sample, there was no difference between the book and audited values.

Calculate the achieved confidence interval at the required confidence level based on this sample.

g. Given that the actual sample size in part *f* was smaller than the required sample size in part *a*, explain why the confidence limits still fall within the materiality limits.

5-42. For a number of years, the accounts receivable confirmation process at John's Printing Company has been more time-consuming than is considered desirable. Typically, about 20% of the 500 active accounts were sent positive confirmations. About 70% of these were returned either initially or after a second request, but these represented only about 40% of the dollar amount. The problem was that larger customers had as many as 100 invoices listed on their statements, and they were simply unwilling to take the time to check the detail. Considerable time had to be spent following up on these items.

In an attempt to combat this problem, you have decided to redefine the population of accounts receivable this year. Specifically, you have defined the population of accounts receivable as the 4,000 individual invoices listed by the open invoice system. The total book value of accounts receivable (open invoices) is $875,350. You feel an error of $25,000 would be material. The internal control system and prior-year results are such that you set Beta risk at 10%. The cost of selecting and sending out an additional sample of confirmations would be high, so you want an Alpha risk of only 10%.

Based on prior years' work and this year's tests of invoices for other purposes, you estimate the standard deviation of the population of errors at $17. Your advance estimate of the point estimate of the population error is $4,000.

a. What is the sample size necessary to achieve your audit objectives?
b. Ignoring your answer to part *a*, assume that you select a sample of 80 invoice amounts. Confirmations are mailed, and 80% are returned either initially or after a second request. Alternative procedures are used to evaluate the remaining invoices in the sample. Based on these confirmations and tests, the following errors are noted:

Item no.	Difference
1	$ (70)
2	40
3	134
4	12
5	(93)
6	(8)
7	78
8	74
9	(51)
10	40
Total	$ 156

Calculate the confidence interval at the required confidence level based on the sample results.

c. Graph the materiality requirements and the confidence limits calculated in part *b*. What is the appropriate audit conclusion about the population?

d. Explain the conclusion in *c*, given the actual sample size compared to the planned sample size, the actual standard deviation compared to the expected standard deviation, and the actual point estimate compared to the expected point estimate.

5-43. Your client, Dowlray Motor Co., is a small, one-plant operation that manufactures only motors for large boats, but in numerous shapes and models. The company, following the lead of the larger firms in the industry, several years ago converted from FIFO to LIFO for its raw-materials, work-in-process, and finished-goods inventories.

Your responsibility is to compute the LIFO valuation to be used for valuing the raw-materials portion of the inventory. Since the company is largely an assembler of parts acquired from other manufacturers, the raw materials consist of easily identifiable, completed parts, well organized in the company's single warehouse.

You determine there are 14,326 items listed in the client's FIFO inventory listing, with unit costs ranging from a few cents to just under $1,000. The book value of the raw-materials inventory was $4,560,640 at the balance sheet date.

You are satisfied, based on normal audit tests not involving statistical methods, that the book value of inventory at FIFO is fairly stated.

You have been instructed to first determine the difference between the recorded and LIFO values for each sample item. The estimated total adjustment is calculated by multiplying the population size by the average value of the difference. The inventory valuation for financial statement purposes is determined by subtracting the estimated total adjustment from the recorded value. Your firm has decided that the inventory value should not be misstated by more than $120,000 at a confidence level of 95%.

You take a preliminary random sample of 100 items and calculate the LIFO valuation for each item. The following are the results of the sample:

Sum of the LIFO values	$31,467
Sum of the recorded values	$42,856
Sum of the squared difference between recorded and LIFO values	$2,675,420

REQUIRED:

a. Determine the LIFO inventory valuation at a 95% confidence level based on the sample size of 100 items.

b. Explain why it would not be appropriate to adjust the recorded value to LIFO by the amount of the estimated total adjustment.

c. Determine the appropriate total sample size for determining the estimated total adjustment.

d. Evaluate whether unstratified difference estimation is an appropriate statistical method in this situation.

5-44. Phil Mayberg is reviewing the work of an assistant who performed tests of transactions in sales using attributes sampling for the audit of Rogers Supply Company. The assistant found procedural errors in several different areas, but much to Phil's surprise, he also found a much larger number of monetary errors than expected. Two audit tests in particular were of concern to him. The information in the attributes sampling data sheet for those two tests are as follows:

Attribute code	Description
8	Price per sales invoice agrees to the authorized price listing in effect on the date of sale.
9	Sales invoices are accurately extended.

	Planned Results				*Final Results (2)*				
Attribute code	Expected occurrence rate	Upper precision limit	Reli-ability	Sample size	Sample size (1)	Number of occur-rences (1)	Sample occurrence rate	Reli-ability	Upper precision limit
8	2.0%	4.0%	90%	200	200	14	7%	90%	10.7%
9	1.0%	3.0%	90%	170	200	15	7.5%	90%	11.3%

Phil concludes because of the attributes test results that there is a reasonable likelihood that the financial statements are misstated. The first step he takes is to determine the nature and amount of each of the 29 errors. The following is the result of the analysis of the errors:

Description of Errors	Number of occurrences	Amount of each error
Price errors:		
Price taken from out-of-date price list	3	46.20, (81.11), 8.41
Pricing clerk used "approximate" price	6	3.84, 19.20, 15.00, 35.50, 29.11, 1.50
Wrong price used (item confused with an item of similar name)	5	49.50, (11.25), (18.35), 12.75, 26.00
	14	
Extension errors:		
Misplaced decimal	2	90.00, 63.00
Extended unit price into total column (rather than unit price × quantity)	3	(1200.00), (300.00), (600.00)
Partial shipments extended at full quantities		
On initial shipment invoice	5	30.00, 170.00, 15.00, 550.00, 320.00
On subsequent shipment invoice	5	240.00, 89.00, 65.00, 1700.00, 13.00
	15	

There were no invoices on which both types of errors occurred (i.e., the 29 errors occurred on 29 invoices).

Phil determines from the attributes sampling tests that there are 18,652 sales invoices. The recorded value on the general ledger is $14,625,405. He decides that he would be unwilling to accept the recorded sales amount if it were misstated by more than $200,000. He wants no more than a 10% risk of accepting the recorded value if it is materially misstated.

REQUIRED:

a. Evaluate the appropriateness of using difference estimation in this set of circumstances.
b. Calculate the estimated value of the combined pricing and extension errors in total sales, assuming that the purpose is to evaluate whether the recorded value is materially misstated.
c. What is the appropriate conclusion as to whether sales is materially misstated? Give reasons for your answer.
d. What should Phil do at this point?

5-45. You are doing the audit of Maylo Supply Company. You plan to check quantities, prices, and extensions on a selected random sample of inventory tags, and to evaluate your results by using difference estimation. You will have to foot the client's inventory listing, because this method depends on having a known book value.

A brief summary of the procedures Maylo is following in counting its physical inventory follows:

(1) The general manager and the warehouse foreman supervise the inventory taking.
(2) Two-man teams perform the counts, using two-part inventory tags.
(3) The general manager and the foreman place the tags, prenumbered, on the inventory items.
(4) One member of the two-man team counts each item and the other verifies it. They mark each portion of the tag with the agreed-upon quantity.
(5) After counting is completed, the general manager and the foreman remove the upper part of each tag and assure themselves that all items were counted and that counts appear reasonable. If appropriate, recounts are made. The lower portion is sent to the accounting department for pricing.
(6) On receiving the inventory tags, the client's accounting department prepares a list showing the tag number, identification data, quantity, and unit price. These sheets are extended, footed, and totaled to determine the total inventory value.

In prior years, your firm observed the inventory and tested compilation and pricing in several separate steps. Various minor errors were always found. These errors have always been considered immaterial, in part because they were often offsetting. About 5% of the inventory items were usually tested.

This year, in terms of your overall audit objectives, you believe that a misstatement of $4,000 in the client's book amount of $86,857 of inventory would represent a material error. The audit tests are considered highly important, and expansion of sample size would be difficult.

To assist in determining an appropriate sample size, you analyze last year's results. Last year's sample of 50 tags, not randomly chosen, showed eight differences in quantities, three differences in pricing, and none in extensions. (The calculated standard deviation of these 50 items was 16.0.) Realizing the twin dangers that last year's sample was not random and that such a small number of observed differences might lead to a poor estimate of the standard deviation, you wish to be certain that you select a sample large enough to provide an adequate number of differences for reliable and usable results.

You determine in advance that the client has 868 inventory items this year. These are not identified by inventory codes, but each item will correspond with an inventory tag prenumbered from 1 to 868.

REQUIRED:

a. Determine an appropriate sample size, assuming a Beta risk of 10% and an Alpha risk of 20%.

b. Ignoring your answer in *a*, assume you have selected a sample of 100 items randomly. For each of the sample items, appropriate audit tests are performed to make sure the physical count is correct, pricing is accurate in accordance with company policy and prior years, and the extensions of unit price and quantity are correct. The results have been summarized as follows:

Inventory tag number	Audited value	Book value	Difference	Difference^2
6	$100	$100	$—	$—
42	85	85	—	—
46	120	120	—	—
51	420	450	30	900
55	18	18	—	—
56	10	10	—	—
⋮	⋮	⋮	⋮	⋮
851	25	· 25	—	—
854	152	150	(2)	4
857	85	85	—	—
862	76	86	10	100
Totals	$8,456	$8,723	$268	$8,488

There were eighteen differences, making up the net difference of $268. The recorded total of the client's inventory sheets is $86,857.

Express the results of the audit tests in terms of confidence intervals, using a Beta risk of 10%.

c. What should you conclude about the inventory?

6

ratio estimation

INTRODUCTION

Ratio estimation is used for the same reasons as difference estimation—to measure the estimated total error in a population for either hypothesis testing or interval estimation. In fact, ratio and difference estimation are so similar that a good understanding of difference estimation should make the study of ratio estimation relatively simple. As was done for difference estimation, this chapter first presents a brief discussion of the calculation of confidence limits. A specific example is shown later in the chapter to illustrate the use of ratio estimation, including calculation of sample size as well as statistical results. To encourage a comparison of the two methods, there will be frequent reference to difference estimation throughout the chapter.

The organization of Chapter 6 is as follows:

1. Calculation of statistical results for ratio estimation
2. Efficiency, sample selection and calculation costs, and reliability
3. Calculation of required sample size and statistical results, and the use of the results
4. Appropriate uses of ratio estimation
5. Illustrations of likely applications of difference or ratio estimation

CALCULATION OF STATISTICAL RESULTS

After the auditor has selected a random sample, the point estimate and the confidence limits of the total errors must be calculated. This is done in a way similar to difference estimation.

Point Estimate

The point estimate is calculated by first taking the ratio of the error values in the sample to the recorded values in the sample. Next, this ratio is multiplied by the client's book value to arrive at a point estimate. The formula is shown in Figure 6-1.

$$\hat{E} = Y \cdot r$$

where:

$\hat{E} =$ point estimate of the total error
$Y =$ total recorded value of the population
$r = \dfrac{\sum e_j}{\sum y_j}$
$e_j =$ an individual error in the sample (when the recorded value is less than audited value, e_j is a minus)
$y_j =$ the recorded value of an individual item in the sample

---

FIGURE 6-1 Point estimate of the total errors

For example, assume a population of 6,000 items with a book value of $3,000,000. The auditor took a sample of 200 items for a price test and found net overstatement errors of $7,320 in the sample. The 200 items had a recorded value of $68,500. The point estimate of the total error in the population is therefore $320,580 ($7,320/$68,500 × $3,000,000). The point estimate of the total errors using difference estimation would have been $219,600 ($7,320/200 × 6,000).

Using two alternative methods for calculating the point estimate for the same population in this example resulted in a big difference ($320,580 compared to $219,600). The ratio estimation point estimate is based on the *percent of error in the sample*, whereas the difference estimation point estimate is based on the *average amount of error in the sample*, independent of the recorded value of the sample items.

Confidence Interval

The confidence interval is determined for ratio estimation in exactly the same way as for difference estimation. The formula is shown in Figure 6-2.

$$\text{CI} = \hat{E} \pm \text{CPI}$$

where:

CI = computed confidence interval
$\hat{E}$ = point estimate of the total error
CPI = computed precision interval at desired CL

FIGURE 6-2 The confidence interval at the desired confidence level (CL)

Computed Precision Interval

The calculation of the computed precision interval is shown in Figure 6-3. A comparison of this formula to the one for difference estimation in Figure 5-4 shows that they are identical.

$$\text{CPI} = \frac{N \cdot Z \cdot \text{SD}}{\sqrt{n}} \cdot \sqrt{\frac{N-n}{N}}$$

where:

CPI = computed precision interval
N = population size
Z = confidence coefficient (two-sided) for CL desired
SD = estimated population standard deviation
n = sample size
$\sqrt{\dfrac{N-n}{N}}$ = finite correction factor

FIGURE 6-3 The computed precision interval at the desired confidence level

Standard Deviation

The calculation of the estimated population standard deviation is shown in Figure 6-4. It can be seen by comparing the calculation to the one in Figure 5-3 for difference estimation that they are calculated differently.

$$\text{SD} = \sqrt{\frac{\sum e_j^2 + r^2 \sum y_j^2 - 2r \sum e_j y_j}{n-1}}$$

where:

SD = standard deviation
e_j = an individual error in the sample
y_j = the recorded value of an individual item in the sample
$r = \dfrac{\sum e_j}{\sum y_j}$ (when the summation of the recorded values is less than the summation of the audited values, $\sum e_j$ is a minus)
n = sample size

FIGURE 6-4 Estimated standard deviation of the population errors

Calculation of the estimate of the population standard deviation is one of the major distinctions between ratio and difference estimation. The size of the population standard deviation for difference estimates is determined by the number of errors in the population and the *size of each of the individual errors*. The value of the client's recorded book value has nothing to do with the standard deviation for difference estimates. The size of the population standard deviation for ratio estimation is determined by the number of errors and the *size of each of the individual errors relative to the client's recorded book value*. A simple example of two populations of six items each, shown below, will illustrate this difference.

	Population 1		
Population item	*Book value of item*	*Error in item*	*Ratio of error to book value*
1	$ 862	$ 50	5.8%
2	421	50	11.9%
3	57	50	87.7%
4	916	50	54.6%
5	211	50	23.7%
6	533	50	9.4%
Total	$3,000	$300	10.0%

	Population 2		
Population item	*Book value of item*	*Error in item*	*Ratio of error to book value*
1	$ 862	$ 86.20	10%
2	421	42.10	10%
3	57	5.70	10%
4	916	91.60	10%
5	211	21.10	10%
6	533	53.30	10%
Total	$3,000	$300.00	10%

The standard deviation of Population 1 using difference estimation is zero, because all errors are the same size. There is a reasonably large standard deviation of 31.4 for Population 2 using difference estimation, owing to the dispersion of the errors. (*Note*: The denominator for calculating the standard deviation is n when $n = N$.) The situation is reversed for ratio estimation. The standard deviation is zero for Population 2, because all errors are of exactly the same size relative to the book value, whereas the standard deviation for Population 1 is 31.4 using ratio estimation.

Few, if any, populations can be characterized in such an extreme as the illustration. However, when the size of errors is closely related to the size of the population items, the ratio estimate results in smaller standard deviations than difference estimation.

Some computer programs automatically calculate the standard deviation and other statistics for both ratio and difference estimation. Practitioners who use such programs frequently find that neither method uniformly results in a smaller standard deviation. Typically, both standard deviations are reasonably close together, but exceptions occur.

In summary, the calculation of the confidence interval for ratio and difference estimation differs only in the calculation of the point estimate and estimated population standard deviation.

Alternative Form of Ratio Calculation

In the ratio calculation presented above, the numerator was the error amount and the denominator was the book value amount. An alternative often followed by auditors is to use the audited amount as the numerator. This ratio is then used to estimate the total audited amount of the population. The estimate can be subtracted from the total population book value to obtain an estimate of the total population error amount.

When this alternative is used,

$$r = \frac{\sum x_j}{\sum y_j}$$

where:

$x_j =$ the audited value of an individual item in the sample, and

$$SD = \sqrt{\frac{\sum x_j^2 + r^2 \sum y_j^2 - 2r \sum x_j y_j}{n - 1}}$$

All other aspects of calculating the confidence interval will be the same. The standard deviation will be the same amount for a given set of data using either form of calculation.

EFFICIENCY, SAMPLE SELECTION
AND CALCULATION COSTS, AND RELIABILITY

Efficiency

Ratio estimation is likely always to result in smaller sample sizes than unstratified mean-per-unit estimation. The reason is that the standard deviation of the errors as determined by ratio estimation is usually much smaller than the standard deviation for the audited values. It has been shown in previous chapters that a smaller standard deviation results in a smaller sample size. The same conclusion was reached in comparing difference and mean-per-unit estimation.

The efficiency of ratio estimation compared to difference estimation depends on the standard deviation of the population for the two methods. The statistical method that has the smallest standard deviation for a particular population will be more efficient for that population. The reason is that the two statistical formulas are identical except for calculating the standard deviation. A smaller standard deviation results in a smaller sample size, which is the definition of efficiency.

The population standard deviation for ratio estimation is smaller than for difference estimation when there is a high correlation between the size of individual errors and the population items being audited (for instance, larger population items tend to have larger errors than smaller population items). The ratio estimation standard deviation is larger when there is a low correlation. In many accounting populations, the population standard deviation does not differ significantly between the two methods. There are, however, exceptions of which the auditor should always be aware. A common way to make sure there is no significant difference in the two methods is to calculate the standard deviation for both.

Sample Selection and Calculation Costs

The costs of selecting the sample and calculating the statistical results depend on the extent to which computer facilities are available. When the client's data are in computer readable form and the auditor uses the computer to calculate statistical results, sample selection and calculation costs can be relatively minor.

It is somewhat more costly to calculate statistical results for ratio than for difference estimation, even when a computer is used. Only the items in error have to be entered into the computer for difference estimation, whereas for ratio estimation, every audited value and the related client error must be entered.

It is also more costly to calculate statistical results for ratio than for difference estimation when all calculations are manual; more calculations are needed for ratio estimation. Calculation costs are generally not a major factor in deciding between ratio and difference estimation, however, because there is usually no great difference in cost between the methods unless the sample size is very large.

Reliability of the Estimator

Like difference estimation, ratio estimation is an unreliable estimator of the total population errors under some conditions. The most likely case is the same as for difference estimation—when the population contains a small number of errors that are material in total.

The actual and nominal reliabilities determined from the Neter and Loebbecke study for ratio estimation are shown in Figure 6-5. It can be

					Actual (two-sided) reliability			
					Difference estimation		Ratio estimation	
Study pop.	Error rate	Size of errors	Direction of errors	Skewness of book values	Sample size of 100	Sample size of 200	Sample size of 100	Sample size of 200
1	1%	small	both	very high	37.3%	53.0%	36.2%	52.0%
2	1%	large	both	moderate	41.8%	54.5%	41.7%	55.0%
3	1%	moderate	over	high	36.8%	57.0%	35.2%	57.0%
4	1%	large	over	moderate	30.0%	47.0%	31.0%	47.3%
5	5%	small	both	very high	96.8%	99.2%	94.3%	97.2%
6	5%	large	both	moderate	82.3%	90.2%	82.2%	89.2%
7	5%	moderate	over	high	73.7%	82.3%	72.8%	81.8%
8	5%	large	over	moderate	58.2%	69.7%	59.3%	70.2%
9	10%	small	both	very high	94.0%	93.5%	91.5%	92.7%
10	10%	large	both	moderate	97.2%	97.0%	96.5%	96.5%
11	10%	moderate	over	high	80.3%	87.7%	79.5%	86.3%
12	10%	large	over	moderate	62.0%	70.7%	63.3%	71.2%
13	30%	small	both	very high	96.3%	93.7%	92.8%	91.3%
14	30%	large	both	moderate	95.5%	96.0%	94.2%	94.3%
15	30%	moderate	over	high	90.8%	92.2%	86.2%	91.3%
16	30%	large	over	moderate	74.8%	87.5%	76.0%	87.5%

Note: *An actual reliability of 95.4% is ideal. An actual reliability less than 95.4% means that the actual Beta risk is greater than 2.3%. A low actual reliability is undesirable.*

FIGURE 6-5 Comparison of actual to nominal 95.4% confidence coefficient under varying circumstances, ratio and difference estimation

seen, by comparing actual reliability for ratio and difference estimation, that the conclusions about reliability are almost the same. The reliability of ratio estimation is low when the frequency of errors in the population is less than 10 percent and when all the errors are in one direction.

Calculating Required Sample Size
and Statistical Results

The steps used for applying ratio estimation parallel the ones followed to illustrate difference estimation in the preceding chapter. The intent is to encourage comparison of the two methods. The frame of reference for the discussion is the same population of raw materials used in the difference estimation illustration on page 146.

Step 1. Decide on the objectives of the test. The objective is identical to that used for difference estimation: to determine if the dollar value of the error in costing raw-materials inventory using a FIFO method is material. If the error is considered material, the sample size will be increased or the book balance will be adjusted.

Step 2. Decide on the net total error that would be considered material for the price test of inventory. The amount is identical to that used for difference estimation: Based on prior years' earnings, anticipated current-year earnings, and the result of tests in other audit areas, a materiality limit of $80,000 is set.

Step 3. Decide on an acceptable Beta risk. The percent is identical to that used for difference estimation: Owing to the company's relatively high profitability, low risk of exposure to liability, and adequate internal controls over purchases, a Beta risk of 10 percent is used.

Step 4. Decide on an acceptable Alpha risk. The percent is identical to that used for difference estimation: An Alpha risk of 40 percent is selected because of the relatively low cost of taking a second sample if the hypothesis that the population is fairly stated is rejected.

Step 5. Decide on the sampling unit. The definition is identical to that used for difference estimation. Each type of raw material is listed on a printout and costed separately. The sampling unit is a line item that includes a raw-material item on the inventory listing.

Step 6. Estimate the standard deviation and the amount of error in the population, and determine the population size and total book value. The advance estimate of the standard deviation for both ratio and difference estimation is determined by testing a small preliminary sample from the population or by examining the working papers of the prior year. The latter approach should only be used when the auditor believes the results of audit tests will be similar to those of the prior year. There is no reason to believe the standard deviation will be different for ratio and difference estimation. Therefore, $135 is used.

The estimated error in the population can also be determined from the same preliminary sample used to estimate the standard deviation or from prior years' working papers. An easy way to obtain the estimated error on the basis of prior years is to calculate the ratio of the net errors in the previous year to that year's book value and multiply it by the current-year book value. The population error is again estimated at $12,000.

The population size is determined the same way as for difference estimation. There are 2,700 raw-materials items. The total book value is determined from the raw-materials inventory summary to be $3,600,000.

Step 7. Calculate the acceptable precision interval, considering both the Alpha and Beta risk. The calculation is identical to that used for difference estimation. See page 147.

$$\text{API*} = AE - E* \cdot \frac{Z(1 - 2\beta)}{Z(1 - 2\beta) + Z(1 - \alpha)}$$

$$\text{API*} = 80,000 - 12,000 \cdot \frac{1.28}{1.28 + .84} = \$41,057$$

Step 8. Calculate the required sample size.

$$n = \left(\frac{N \cdot Z(1 - 2\beta) \cdot \text{SD*}}{\text{API*}}\right)^2$$

$$n = \left(\frac{2,700 \cdot 1.28 \cdot 135}{41,057}\right)^2 = (11.4)^2$$

$$n = 130$$

A few words of explanation about the sample size are appropriate at this point. First compare the formulas for ratio and difference estimation:

Ratio estimation formula for sample size	Difference estimation formula for sample size
$n = \left(\dfrac{N \cdot Z(1 - 2\beta) \cdot \text{SD*}}{\text{API*}}\right)^2$	$n = \left(\dfrac{N \cdot Z(1 - 2\beta) \cdot \text{SD*}}{\text{API*}}\right)^2$

The following should be noted:

1. The basic formula is identical for both.
2. The estimate of the standard deviation (SD*) could be different for each method. The method of calculating each of the two standard deviations is different. Therefore, the estimate could be higher or lower for ratio estimation.
3. The acceptable precision interval (API*) could be different for each method. Both are calculated from API* = AE − E*. Allowable error (AE) should be the same for either method, but the estimate of the error (E*) could vary, because they are calculated differently.

Step 9. Select a random sample of 130 items and perform the audit tests. An error amount is determined for each sample item in exactly the same manner as for difference estimation. The 130 sample items are assumed to be identical to the ones selected for difference estimation, and the same 20 errors found. These are shown in Figure 6-6.

Sample item in error	y_j Recorded value	x_j Audit value	e_j Error	e_j^2 Error squared	y_j^2 Recorded value squared	$e_j y_j$ × Error recorded value
7	$2,611	$2,408	$+203	$41,209	$6,817,321	$+530,033
9	87	136	(49)	2,401	7,569	(4,263)
21	890	451	+439	192,721	792,100	+390,710
30	501	611	(110)	12,100	251,001	(55,110)
36	1,208	1,103	+105	11,025	1,459,264	+126,840
41	3,150	2,982	+168	28,224	9,922,500	+529,200
42	2,493	2,111	+382	145,924	6,215,049	+952,326
53	216	459	(243)	59,049	46,656	(52,488)
59	511	51	+460	211,600	261,121	+235,060
62	1,821	2,463	(642)	412,164	3,316,041	(1,169,082)
69	660	0	+660	435,600	435,600	+435,600
73	1,408	1,521	(113)	12,769	1,982,464	(159,104)
96	3,408	2,167	+1,241	1,540,081	11,614,464	+4,229,328
101	799	751	+48	2,304	638,401	+38,352
106	1,293	1,121	+172	29,584	1,671,849	+222,396
109	181	811	(630)	396,900	32,761	(114,030)
114	3,415	4,026	(611)	373,321	11,662,225	(2,086,565)
121	2,117	1,809	+308	94,864	4,481,689	+652,036
127	315	415	(100)	10,000	99,225	(31,500)
130	136	92	+44	1,936	18,496	+5,984
Subtotal	27,220	25,488	1,732	4,013,776	61,725,796	4,675,723
Summation of 110 sample items not in error	150,372	150,372	0	0	255,827,185	0
Totals	$177,592	$175,860	$1,732	$4,013,776	$317,552,981	$4,675,723

FIGURE 6-6 Sample results and calculations of the sample of the raw-materials inventory (Sample Size = 130)

A major difference between difference and ratio estimation is the need in ratio estimation to maintain a careful record of the recorded value of each sample item that is not in error. There are 110 (130−20) of these for the sample. The sum of these 110 items (details are not shown in Figure 6-6) is $150,372. Thus, the total book value of all sample items is $177,592.

Step 10. Calculate the point estimate. (See Figure 6-1.)

$$\hat{E} = Y \cdot r$$

$$r = \frac{1,732}{177,592} = .0098$$

$$\hat{E} = \$3,600,000 \cdot .0098 = \$35,280$$

Step 11. Calculate the estimated population standard deviation. (See Figure 6-4.)

$$SD = \sqrt{\frac{\sum e_j^2 + r^2 \sum y_j^2 - 2r \sum e_j y_j}{n-1}}$$

$$= \sqrt{\frac{4,013,776 + (.0098)^2(317,552,981) - 2(.0098)(4,675,723)}{130-1}}$$

$$= \sqrt{\frac{4,013,776 + 30,498 - 91,644}{129}} = \sqrt{30,641} = \$175.0$$

A few comments follow about the standard deviation for ratio as compared to difference estimation.

1. $\sum e_j^2$ and $n-1$ are always identical for the two statistical methods for a given sample result.
2. The difference in the standard deviation is caused by the factor $r^2 \sum y_j^2 - 2r \sum e_j y_j$ for ratio estimation compared to the factor $n(\bar{e})^2$ for difference estimation.

If the combined net error $(\sum e_j)$ is zero, the standard deviations for the two methods are identical, because both these factors are zero. When there are a reasonably large number of overstatements and understatements and the net error is small relative to the book value, the standard deviations will be approximately equal. ($\sum e_j^2$ will be relatively large, and r and e will be small: therefore, the standard deviations are about equal.)

On the other hand, when $\sum e_j$ is large, $\sum e_j^2$ is less dominant in the standard deviation computation, and there is potential for greater differences between the standard deviations of the two methods. If there are a large number of errors that are of approximately equal size and all in one direction, $n(\bar{e})^2$ is almost as large as $\sum e_j^2$. The standard deviation of the difference estimate is therefore small. If there are a large number of errors where the error as a percent of the book value is nearly constant and primarily in one direction, $r^2 \sum y_j^2 - 2r \sum e_j y_j$ is negative and almost as large as $\sum e_j^2$. The standard deviation of the ratio estimate is therefore small.

Step 12. Calculate the precision interval at a two-sided confidence level equal to 1 minus Beta times 2. (See Figure 6-3.)

$$CPI = \frac{N \cdot Z(1-2\beta) \cdot SD}{\sqrt{n}} \cdot \sqrt{\frac{N-n}{N}}$$

$$CPI = \frac{2,700 \cdot 1.28 \cdot 175.0}{\sqrt{130}} \cdot \sqrt{\frac{2,700-130}{2,700}}$$

$$CPI = \frac{604,800}{11.40} \cdot .98 = \$51,992$$

The only difference between the CPI for difference and for ratio estimation is the standard deviation calculated in Step 11.

Step 13. Calculate the confidence limits.

$$\text{UCL} = \hat{E} + \text{CPI}$$

$$\text{LCL} = \hat{E} - \text{CPI}$$

$$\text{UCL} = \$35,280 + \$51,992 = \$87,272$$

$$\text{LCL} = \$35,280 - \$51,992 = -\$16,712$$

The amount of the difference in the upper confidence limits between ratio and difference estimation for the illustration is as follows:

Amount of difference			
UCL — Difference estimation		$88,230	
UCL — Ratio estimation		87,272	
Difference			$958
Cause of difference			
Point estimate difference			
Difference estimation		$35,972	
Ratio estimation		35,280	
			$692
Computed precision interval difference			
Difference estimation		$52,258	
Ratio estimation		51,992	
			266
			$958

Step 14. Decide on the acceptability of the population. The same decision methodology followed for difference estimation is repeated for ratio estimation.

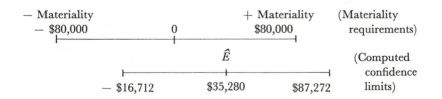

Since the upper confidence limit falls outside the upper bound of the materiality range, the auditor will conclude that the total recorded book amount may be substantially in error. In other words, the hypothesis is rejected. In doing this, the auditor has a 40 percent chance of being wrong (the Alpha risk). The auditor will pursue the options discussed in Chapter 5.

Had both confidence limits been within the materiality limits, the book value would have been accepted at a Beta risk of 10 percent, and additional work or an adjustment would not be considered necessary. Note, however, that this presumes that two estimates using different evaluation methods—one leading to an accept decision (for example, ratio) and one leading to a reject decision (for example, difference)—would be obtained from the same sample. Auditors will often simultaneously evaluate samples on both a difference and a ratio basis and use the result giving the best precision (CPI), for the reason that that estimator indicates the least variability in the population data and is therefore based on the more representative sample. Other auditors may disagree with this, feeling that the more conservative approach of using the least precise estimator is preferable because it will ensure that the desired Beta risk is always met. At this point in the development of audit sampling, this appears to be a matter of individual judgment and preference.

Effect on the Required Sample Size of Changing Various Factors

It is important to know the effect on the required sample size of changing each of the factors in the formula. It has already been shown that six factors determine the required sample size for both ratio and difference estimation: estimated population standard deviation, Beta risk, Alpha risk, acceptable error in the population, estimated point estimate of the population error, and population size.

The effect of independently changing each of these six factors while the other five factors are held constant is shown below.

Factors being changed while others are held constant	Nature of change	Effect of change on required sample size	Comments
1. Estimated population standard deviation	Increase	Increase	An increase in the number or size of individual errors usually increases the standard deviation. Keep in mind that the standard deviations for ratio and difference estimation are not likely to be the same.

Factors being changed while others are held constant	Nature of change	Effect of change on required sample size	Comments
2. Beta risk	Increase	Decrease	An increase of Beta risk from 5% to 15% decreases the confidence level from 90% to 70%.
3. Alpha risk	Increase	Decrease	α doesn't alter confidence level, but does alter precision $\div$ materiality.
4. Acceptable error in the population	Increase	Decrease	See 5.
5. Estimated point estimate of the population error	Increase	Increase	The acceptable total error (4) less the estimated point estimate is more important than either 4 or 5 considered separately. An increase in 4 minus 5 decreases the required sample size.
6. Population size	Increase	Increase	The population size has a significant effect on sample size in variables sampling. The size of the population has only a minor effect through the finite correction factor, but it significantly affects sample size in the other part of the formula.

APPROPRIATE USES OF RATIO ESTIMATION

The authors believe that unstratified ratio estimation is the most desirable statistical method for auditors in a number of circumstances. These circumstances are:

1. The population data are not in a computer-readable form.
2. The auditor has evaluated the client's accounting system and reviewed the client's population data and has concluded that there is minimal likelihood of a small number of large errors that will, when combined with all other errors, be material.
3. The auditor expects a large number of small errors in the population that could in total be material. It is not possible to state the exact number of errors that should be found in the sample before ratio estimation is acceptable. Arbitrarily, we recommend the larger of the following:
   a. At least 10 items in the sample are in error
   b. At least 10% of the sample items are in error up to a sample size of 300.
   c. For sample size exceeding 300, the number of errors should be at least 30 (300 × 10%) plus 5% of the sample size exceeding 300. In addition, no more than 75% of the errors should be in one direction unless the error rate is at least 50%.
4. There is likely to be a fairly close relationship between the size of errors in the sample and the size of the recorded values in the population. (Large sample

errors will tend to be found in large population items rather than in small population items).

When all four conditions exist, unstratified ratio estimation is likely to be the best statistical method. Even if condition 1 does not exist, unstratified ratio estimation *may* be the best method. Condition 4 is the characteristic that will indicate whether ratio or difference estimation is preferable.

ILLUSTRATIONS OF LIKELY APPLICATIONS OF DIFFERENCE OR RATIO ESTIMATION

There are a great many situations where either ratio or difference estimation may be a useful audit tool. Several examples will illustrate the applicability of these methods. The auditor should not automatically assume that unstratified ratio or difference estimation should be used whenever a situation exists similar to the ones described in the following pages. There may be an insufficient number of differences to justify using either of these methods, stratification may be necessary, or an alternate statistical method may be less costly.

For each of the illustrations, the aspects discussed are:

1. *Description.* The description includes a brief discussion of the circumstances in which the statistical test is likely to be used and the purpose of calculating the statistical results.
2. *Sampling Unit.* There is a brief discussion of the most likely sampling unit for the test and alternatives in certain circumstances.
3. *Random Selection.* The purpose of this part is to describe random selection difficulties, if any are likely.
4. *Information needed to calculate statistics.* Only the information that is most difficult to determine is discussed in this part.
5. *Likely problems.* The problems commonly encountered in each illustration are discussed.

Price Test of Inventory

Description. Difference and ratio estimation are commonly applied to inventory price tests because populations are often large, errors in inventory pricing are frequent on many audits, and often it is easy to do the statistical test.

A typical test occurs where there is a listing of inventory items including description, quantity, and price, which has been set by clearly established criteria, such as FIFO. The objective may be to adjust the population for an estimate of the population errors (estimation test), or to evaluate whether the amount of error in the population is material (hypothesis test).

One example of an estimation test occurs when the client uses a standard cost system during the year and asks the auditor to adjust the balance to reflect historical cost at the balance sheet date. A hypothesis test is more likely if the auditor believes the inventory is probably already priced correctly.

Sampling Unit. Ideally the sampling unit would be the *inventory description*, such as a part number. It is typically easier, however, to determine the population size and randomly select sample items when the sampling unit is defined as the line item rather than the inventory description. However, the use of the line item can easily result in a serious measurement error, because most inventory pricing methods require consideration of all items for each inventory description before the price can be correctly determined. For example, if part number 2106 is listed in three different places on an inventory listing, it is necessary to verify the prices of the combined quantity in all three places when FIFO or LIFO valuation is used. Naturally, no problem exists if all like inventory items are included on the same line in the listing. In this case, the line item can be used as the sampling unit.

Random Selection. It is frequently more time-consuming to obtain a random sample for inventory price tests than for many other audit tests, even when a computer terminal can be used. When the sampling unit is defined as inventory items, it is necessary to establish a numbering system for all inventory items, select the inventory items, and locate them on the inventory listing. Random selection is much easier when the sampling unit is the line item. The page and line number are the usual basis for determining the sample items.

Information Needed to Calculate Statistics. The population size and individual exceptions in the sample are the two most difficult things to determine.

When items are not prenumbered, it is often necessary to count every item in the population to obtain the population size. An accurate count is important because, as shown earlier, a 10 percent error in the count results in an almost equal error in the statistical calculations.

Determining the exceptions is the most difficult part of the price test. The auditor must know the criteria for determining the correct price of each inventory item. He must also determine the total cost of the entire quantity of the sample element being tested in order to determine the amount of the error.

Likely Problems. There are several common problems encountered in inventory price tests using difference or ratio estimation:

1. The lack of a sufficient number of errors in the sample to permit a reliable estimate of the population. The only solution to this problem is to use a dif-

ferent estimation method, such as mean-per-unit estimation. Great care should be taken to avoid this problem, because the lack of reliability of the estimate will not be apparent from the calculated results. Lack of reliability of the estimator is the one problem the auditor is most likely to overlook.

2. The audit cost of testing an individual sample item for certain inventory items. Some inventory items, particularly manufactured work-in-process and finished goods, are costly to verify as precisely as required by difference or ratio estimation. The auditor must estimate the cost to get a statistical measure of the error in the population and compare that cost to the importance of a statistical measure. Naturally, the cost and usefulness of nonstatistical alternatives of verifying a balance must also be considered.

3. The difficulty of obtaining a precise measure of cost for certain inventory items. It is difficult and sometimes important to get a precise measure of cost for such things as obsolete or damaged inventory. A clearly established company policy, such as 50% valuation for all inventory items over one year old and zero valuation for all those over three years old, facilitates the accurate measurement of confidence intervals. When company policies are not available or appropriate, it may be necessary to measure the historical cost statistically and subsequently make a subjective evaluation of the obsolescence.

4. Random selection and calculation costs. There may be some difficulty of the type previously described in random selection, and the cost of calculation for ratio estimation may be higher in some cases. The availability of a computer terminal solves most of these problems.

Reliance on Perpetual Inventory Records Instead of a Physical Count

Description. When a client has adequate perpetual inventory records, it may be acceptable for the client to take the annual physical count at a date other than the balance sheet date, count only certain parts of the inventory, or in some cases take no count at all. It may be unnecessary to compare the perpetual records to the actual physical count on the balance sheet date when the interim physical is close to the balance sheet date. If the interim physical takes place a long time before the balance sheet date, and in the other two cases described, a sample of inventory items near the balance sheet date should be compared to the perpetual record. Naturally, some of the inventory might not be included on perpetual records. This part of inventory would be tested by a complete physical inventory at the balance sheet date if it is material.

The objective of the test may be to evaluate whether there is a material difference between the perpetual records and the actual inventory on hand (hypothesis test), or to determine the amount to adjust for a difference that is believed to be material (estimation test).

Sampling Unit. The most likely sampling unit is the actual perpetual inventory record, which should be identical to the inventory description, such as a part number. There may be types of inventory for which there are no perpetual records, and the auditor should become aware of these through discussions with management and tests of the perpetual as a part of the vouching of purchases.

Random Selection. Assuming the client prepares a listing of the inventory quantity for each inventory description at the balance sheet date, it should be easy to obtain a random sample by selecting line numbers and page numbers. When there is no listing, it is necessary to use existing perpetual record numbers or assign numbers to the records.

Information Needed to Calculate Statistics. The population size, the amount of each sample item (where ratio estimation is used), and individual exceptions in the sample are the only information needed to calculate the statistical results. Determining the population size should not be difficult if there is a listing of inventory or a sequential numbering of the records. The amount of each sample item is evident from the items themselves.

The amount of an exception is the difference between the recorded inventory on the perpetuals and the actual physical count times the actual cost of the inventory. It may be necessary to use standard unit cost or even last year's actual inventory cost as a reasonable estimate of the actual cost of an inventory item if the current actual cost is not readily available at the date of the comparison. It is also necessary to calculate the client's recorded dollar value for each inventory item in the sample if ratio estimation is used.

It is common to combine tests of perpetual records and the price tests of inventory described in the preceding section. Assume the client has each inventory item as stated on its perpetual records already priced. The difference between the actual count at the audited price and the client's recorded value for an inventory item is a difference that incorporates both the test of the accuracy of the quantities on the perpetuals and the inventory price test.

Likely Problems. The most common problems for the test of perpetual records are:

1. The existence of more than one inventory location, each of which has separate physical controls and perpetual records. It is probably necessary to test each, or at least several, of the locations. An unstratified sample may then be inappropriate.
2. Inventory items of sufficiently different values to require the use of stratified sampling. It would be improper to use unstratified sampling when there is a high likelihood of a small number of large errors.
3. The need for the perpetual records to be updated as of the date of the physical count. Unless great care is used in adjusting for sales and purchase transactions near the date the sample of inventory is counted, the statistical results can be misleading.

4. The lack of a sufficient number of differences in the sample to permit a reliable estimate of the population. Generally, this is not a problem. There is less likelihood of a small number of errors in comparing perpetuals to actual counts than in most other audit areas, because most perpetual records are not completely accurate.

5. Random selection and calculation costs. The cost of selecting a sample and calculating the statistical results is similar to the previous example. Therefore, the discussion is not repeated here.

LIFO Conversion

Description. Many companies maintain their detailed inventory records on a FIFO basis for purposes of pricing inventory and working-capital management and control, but report on a LIFO basis for financial and tax purposes. In order to do this, these companies are required to compute an amount to convert total inventories from one basis (FIFO) to the other (LIFO). This is termed the *LIFO conversion.*

It is essential that the LIFO conversion be carried out in accordance with Internal Revenue Service regulations in order to be acceptable for tax purposes. These regulations permit the use of statistical sampling to estimate the conversion amount, although the IRS can require a 100 percent determination, if it wishes, in any given situation. There are several elements in the conversion. These elements and related IRS requirements are as follows:

LIFO conversion element	*IRS requirements*

LIFO index:
    Numerator—FIFO value
        of inventory
    Denominator—LIFO value
        of inventory
	The LIFO index is determined statistically and is used to determine the adjustment to LIFO for the year.

Statistical accuracy of estimate:
    Precision
    Reliability
	The IRS has not as yet issued regulations specifying these values for LIFO conversion. However, based on regulations in other areas, such as deferred credit sales, and experience, an estimate made at 95% reliability with precision of $\pm 2\%$ would be acceptable.

LIFO conversions are an extremely common use of ratio estimation. They serve both the client in computing the amount and the auditors in judging the fairness of the amount shown on the financial statements.

Sampling Unit. The sampling unit is the individual inventory item. This is complicated where there are multiple locations, and in such cases, the sampling unit can be either:

1. The individual inventory item collectively at all locations, or
2. The individual inventory item at each location.

The choice will depend on the relative ease of visiting locations and obtaining inventory quantity and price data. Usually, alternative approaches will be evaluated in advance, and the least costly one that meets both audit and tax objectives will be followed.

Random Selection. The method of selecting the random sample of inventory items for a LIFO conversion will be subject to the same considerations as for the other inventory tests considered above.

Information Needed to Calculate Statistics. The information needed to calculate the LIFO index is the population size (number of inventory items), the FIFO value of each sample item, and the LIFO value of each sample item. The FIFO and LIFO values are the quantity of the sample item times the respective FIFO and LIFO prices, not just the prices alone.

The FIFO value is easy to obtain, as that is the amount maintained by the company's regular inventory system. The LIFO value must usually be obtained by reference to detailed records, such as purchasing documents. The total of the FIFO values for the sample is divided by the total of the LIFO values to obtain the index. A confidence interval about the index is determined by computing a precision amount in accordance with the formulas for ratio estimation (using FIFO as e_j and LIFO as y_j), and converting the results into a ratio, as follows:

1. Divide the point estimate of the index into the total inventory FIFO amount to obtain a point estimate of the total LIFO inventory amount.
2. Divide the computed precision amount by the point estimate of the total LIFO inventory amount to express it as a decimal fraction.
3. Multiply the decimal fraction by 100 to express it as a percent.

Likely Problems. The major problems in LIFO conversions relate to multiple locations and a possible lack of good planning information to determine sample size. It is generally important to:

1. Meet IRS requirements.
2. Visit many locations.
3. Minimize costs.
4. Avoid revisiting locations for expanded samples.

These requirements mean that sample size and allocation among locations must be very carefully planned. If a good estimate of the standard deviation is not available, good planning is difficult. To provide these data, pilot samples are often taken from selected locations at a date prior to the valuation date. Stratification may also be used effectively.

Accounts Receivable Confirmation

Description. The measurement of the amount of error in *gross accounts receivable*, on the basis of the confirmation results, is a common application of difference or ratio estimation. It is not usually practical to measure the likelihood that an individual receivable will be uncollectible; therefore, difference or ratio estimation is usually limited to measuring the error in gross accounts receivable, not net. The objective is usually to test whether the balance is fairly stated rather than to estimate the amount of error.

Owing to the potential for nonsampling error, more care must be exercised in statistical measurement of confirmation results than in most other applications of statistical sampling. There are three serious concerns: the need to use positive confirmations, the problem of nonresponse, and the possibility of inaccurate confirmations.

Statistical measurement of error amounts is appropriate only when *positive confirmations* are used. Negative confirmations are meant to inform the auditor of exceptions to the confirmations, but recent empirical evidence indicates that many recipients of confirmations do not inform the CPA of differences between the client's and customers' balances. The existence of errors that are not measured in the statistical calculations because the auditor believes the accounts confirmed are correct could materially affect the confidence interval.

Should the sample size used for calculating the confidence interval when positive confirmations are sent be the sample sent or the sample received? Assuming the auditor has carefully followed the requirements of Statements on Auditing Standards (AU331.08) including the follow-up of nonresponses with second requests and alternative procedures, the sample size should be the number of confirmations sent.

Recent empirical studies have concluded that positive confirmations are more likely to provide the auditor with correct information than are negatives. However, even for positive confirmations, customers frequently sign confirmations and return them to the auditor when the balance on the confirmations and the customer's recorded balances disagree. The difficulty for the auditor is that it is hard to determine whether the customer has responded correctly or incorrectly. There are four things the auditor can do to reduce the incidence of incorrect information from confirmations. First, the auditor can assess the likelihood that the customers respond correctly on the basis of empirical evidence from previous years' results or results of other, similar circumstances. Positive confirmations should be statistically measured only when the auditor believes they are highly reliable. Second, the auditor can perform alternative procedures for all confirmations mailed, even those received back on first or second requests. The effect is to increase the reliability of the responses. Third, it is possible to use "fill in the amount of the balance due" confirmations. The use of that type of confirmation may reduce the response rate and increase the audit cost, but the reliability should be higher. Fourth, it may be possible to confirm individual sales transactions receivable from customers rather than the entire receivable balance. This has the advantage of concentrating on a small part of the total receivable from a customer and is likely to reduce errors by respondents. It may, however, be costly to get a listing of sales invoices receivable, and also, this confirmation procedure tests only for validity and valuation of individual invoices and ignores invoices that have not been recorded by the client.

Sampling Unit. The customer is the most likely sampling unit, but the individual invoice will be used in those cases where the auditor plans to confirm individual invoices rather than balances.

A more serious problem than the sampling unit is the related problem of deciding on the population to test. It is important to decide if some types of accounts, such as credit balances and zero balances, are to be included or excluded from the population. It may also be decided to exclude altogether smaller balances or accounts from certain branches.

Random Selection. It should not be difficult to obtain a random sample if the sampling unit and population have been carefully defined. The most likely approach is to select line numbers on pages.

Information Needed to Calculate Statistics. After the problems discussed earlier have been resolved, the only difficult part of applying ratio or difference estimation to accounts receivable is determining the amount of the error for each confirmation. It is essential to reconcile each difference reported by the customer to determine the amount of client error. A difference, for example, can be due to client or customer recording lags. It is also necessary to distinguish between errors in gross receivables and those in net receivables. For example, are disputed amounts and confirmation requests returned by the post office errors in gross receivables?

Likely Problems. The major problems apt to be encountered in using ratio and difference estimation for accounts receivable confirmation have been discussed on preceding pages. They are listed below without further discussion:

1. The need to use only positive confirmations.
2. Likelihood of nonresponse.

3. Possibility of nonsampling errors owing to customer responses.
4. The need to measure the error carefully.
5. Receivables of sufficiently different values to require the use of stratified sampling. When there are a small number of large accounts receivable included in total receivables, it is usually necessary to stratify.
6. Lack of a sufficient number of errors in the sample to permit a reliable estimate of the population. An alternative statistical method, such as mean-per-unit or dollar unit sampling, may be appropriate if the auditor expects few exceptions.
7. Setting the Alpha risk. Alpha risk is more important for confirmations than for many other tests, because there is a long time lag between the mailing of the confirmations and the calculation of the statistical results. If the population is not accepted, the cost of sending more confirmations may be high. Therefore, the auditor wants a low risk of rejecting a population that is actually fairly stated. The result of the desire for a low Alpha risk for confirmations is frequently a large sample size.

Calculation of Discounts Lost

Description. Informing a client of the total discounts lost by not paying vendors before expiration of the discount period is often a useful client service. The determination of the amount of discounts lost in the sample is ordinarily done as a part of tests of acquisition transactions. The statistical measure is also done as a part of acquisition transactions testing. The objective of the test is to estimate the total discounts for the year that were not taken but could have been if timely disbursements had been made. Using ratio estimation, the amount of lost discount is the numerator value, and the total amount of the sample item (that is, total amount of the acquisition) is the denominator.

It is also easy to calculate the total of the discounts available to the client as a part of the same audit tests. It may be useful for the client to know the value of both the total discounts available and the total discounts lost.

Sampling Unit. The most convenient sampling unit for determining discounts lost is the same one used for testing purchase transactions. Frequently, the unit is individual transactions in the purchase journal, but it may well be checks recorded in the cash disbursements journal. The sampling unit depends primarily on the purpose of the test of transactions and type of journals used.

It may seem desirable to define the sampling unit as any acquisition transaction where there is an available discount, but in most cases, this is not practical. If that sampling unit were used, it would be necessary to determine the total population of acquisition transactions where there is an available discount. It would be impractical to determine both the number of these transactions (for difference estimation) and the total dollar value of all such transactions (for ratio estimation) in most systems.

Random Selection. The audit tests for discounts lost are done as a part of tests of transactions. The random sample is selected in the manner described in Chapter 3.

Information Needed to Calculate Statistics. The only information needed to calculate the total discounts is the population size, the total amount of each sample item (where ratio estimation is used), and the amount of discount lost for each sample item. The population size is easy to determine in any system that has prenumbered documents or where items are recorded in a journal; the total amount of each sample item is evident on its face; and the amount of discount lost for each sample item is calculated as a part of tests of transactions. For a transaction where no discounts were available, the item is one sample item with a discount lost of zero. The same is true when the client has taken the available discount.

A separate statistical test must be made if the auditor also calculates the total discounts available, but the population size and sample size are the same as for calculating discounts lost. When the client has taken no discounts in the sample items, the statistical results are identical for both tests.

Likely Problems. There are three problems the auditor is apt to have in measuring discounts lost:

1. *There are an insufficient number of discounts and discounts lost to permit a reliable difference or ratio estimate.* The auditor should be extremely careful in making an estimate when the estimate is believed to be unreliable. On the other hand, the auditor is not making an audit decision on the basis of the statistical conclusion. It is acceptable to inform the client of the statistical estimate as long as the lack of reliability is clearly communicated. Management can then decide whether it wants to study the problem further.

2. *The confidence interval of the estimate may be so wide that its usefulness is questionable.* When there is an unreasonably wide confidence interval, the auditor must decide whether to increase the sample size or inform the client of the *potential* problem. Again, the problem is far less serious than when an audit decision must be made. Usually, management should be informed of the facts and permitted to decide what it would prefer to have done.

3. *Calculation costs.* Calculating the statistical results is not difficult, but it does take some time. The auditor must evaluate the cost and benefit to the client.

Sales Tests of Transactions

Description. Tests of transactions are ordinarily thought of as areas where attributes sampling or dollar unit sampling is used, but there may be some instances where ratio or difference estimation is appropriate.

The most likely use of ratio or difference estimation for sales tests of transactions is the situation in which the auditor finds a large number of monetary errors in the sample items. Examples include the incorrect transfer of quantity or description from the shipping document to the sales invoice, the use of the wrong unit selling price, freight or handling charge errors, quantity discount errors, and errors in recording sales invoices in the journals or subsidiary ledgers. After monetary errors are found in an attributes sampling application, it is acceptable to use the same sample results to calculate an estimate of error amount using ratio or difference estimation. Sometimes, if frequent monetary errors are expected, the auditor may plan the sales tests using difference or ratio estimation from the beginning. The objective of the statistical measurement is to determine whether the error is material or to estimate the amount of the total error.

Sampling Unit. The most likely sampling unit is the same one used for an attributes sampling test of the sales transactions. It would depend on the overall objective of the sales transaction audit tests. Typically, the sampling unit would be the sales invoice, but it could also be the shipping document or a line item in the sales journal.

Random Selection. The audit tests for monetary errors in sales transactions are usually done as a part of tests of transactions. The random sample is selected in the manner described in Chapter 3.

Information Needed to Calculate Statistics. The only information needed to calculate the total dollar amount of error in sales is the population size, the amount of error in sales for each sample item, and the amount of each sample item (where ratio estimation is used). The population size is rarely difficult to determine and is especially easy to find out when there are prenumbered invoices. The amount of the error in each sample item can be determined if the auditor is competent and careful. The amount of each sample item is readily evident.

The auditor must decide whether it is desirable to combine different types of errors affecting sales transactions or keep them separate. For example, it seems logical to combine extension, footing, and pricing errors. It may not be quite as reasonable to combine a pricing error with the erroneous granting of a discount to a customer that had paid its account after the discount period. The auditor must decide which errors to combine and which ones to keep separate based on the objectives of the audit tests.

Likely Problems. The major problems the auditor is apt to face are these:

1. *The lack of a sufficient number of errors in the sample to permit a reliable estimate of the population.* The auditor may decide an estimate of the error is unnecessary when there are few sample errors. When there are a few large errors, an alternative statistical method such as mean-per-unit or dollar unit sampling may be appropriate. However, dollar unit sampling requires advance planning, because it differs from a simple random sample. It is essential for the auditor to determine the cause of the breakdown in the system of internal control that permitted the errors found.

2. *The auditor believes there may be some large dollar errors in the population even though the sample errors are small.* Stratification of the population is desirable in this case; also, it may be improper to make statistical inferences with the actual sample results if no large errors are found and the auditor still has reason to believe large (and unlocated) errors exist.

SUGGESTED READINGS AND REFERENCES

AKRESH, ABRAHAM D., "Use of the Ratio Estimate Statistical Sampling—A Case Study," *New York CPA*, March 1971, pp. 221–224.

RESTALL, LAWRENCE J., and PETER J. CZAKOWSKI, "Computation of LIFO Index: A Statistical Approach," *Management Accounting*, September 1969, pp. 43–48.

REVIEW QUESTIONS

6-1. Reexamine all review questions for Chapter 5. Wherever the words *difference estimation* are used, substitute *ratio estimation*, except where the question refers to a specific formula or requires a calculation.

6-2. Distinguish among attributes sampling, difference estimation, and ratio estimation. Which two sampling methods are similar?

6-3. What is meant by the point estimate of the total errors for ratio estimation? Calculate the point estimate when there are the following client errors in a sample of 120 items from a population of 3,000.

The recorded value of all 120 items in the sample was $5,820. The sum of the recorded value of all sample items squared is $482,270. The total population value was $162,560. Compare your answer to the one for question 5-7, where the same errors were used to determine a point estimate for difference estimation.

Book value	Error
$ 95.02	$48.12
143.50	56.11
213.16	97.16
15.10	(41.14)
45.00	13.06
191.67	191.67
27.20	(84.91)
38.53	1.56
$769.18	$281.63

6-4. Distinguish between the methods of calculating the population point estimate for ratio and for difference estimation. Give one specific example of an audit test in which you believe ratio estimation is likely to result in a more efficient estimate of the population error. Provide another example in which difference estimation is likely to result in a more efficient estimate.

6-5. What is meant by the population standard deviation for ratio estimation? Calculate the estimate of the population standard deviation based on the sample results in question 6-3. Compare your answer to the one for question 5-10 where the same errors were used to determine a standard deviation for difference estimation.

6-6. What is meant by the precision interval for ratio estimation? Calculate the precision interval for the errors in question 6-3 at a confidence level of 90%. Compare your answer to the one for question 5-11, where the same errors were used to determine the precision interval for difference estimation.

6-7. Calculate the confidence interval and confidence limits for the errors in question 6-3 using ratio estimation. Compare your answer to the one for question 5-12 where the same errors were used to determine the confidence interval and confidence limits for difference estimation.

6-8. When difference estimation is used for calculating confidence intervals in a hypothesis test, the auditor must know the population size, sample size, value of each individual error in the sample, and Beta risk. It is also necessary to square each error and sum the total. Which of this information is also needed for ratio estimation? Identify additional information required to calculate a ratio estimation confidence limit.

6-9. Compare the formula to calculate the computed precision interval for ratio estimation (Figure 6-3) to the one for difference estimation (Figure 5-4). In what way are they different?

6-10. The formula to determine sample size for both ratio and difference estimation is:

$$ n = \left(\frac{N \cdot Z(1 - 2\beta) \cdot \text{SD*}}{\text{API*}} \right)^2 $$

Define each term in the formula. Explain the two causes for possible differences in the required sample size in a given audit situation for ratio estimation as compared to difference estimation.

6-11. Assuming all other factors are held constant, identify the effect (increase or decrease) on the required sample size for ratio estimation when each of the following four factors is independently increased: confidence level, population size, acceptable error in the population, and estimated population standard deviation.

6-12. Assuming all other factors are held constant, identify the effect (wider, narrower, or no effect) on the computed precision interval for ratio estimation when each of the following four factors is independently decreased: Beta risk, size of the individual errors in the sample, acceptable error in the population, and actual sample size.

6-13. Explain the difference between the confidence level and Beta risk as it is used in ratio estimation. When should each be used?

6-14. The confidence interval for an audit test where ratio estimation was used is $26,000 ± $40,000. The allowable error for the audit test was set at $60,000. Show graphically by the use of the proper decision rule that the population is not acceptable. Calculate the amount of the adjustment to the recorded balance that would be necessary for the population to be accepted as not materially misstated. Assuming an adjustment is not made, what other options does the auditor have?

6-15. An auditor uses ratio estimation to determine the value of the errors in accounts receivable. He concludes that the error value is from $(14,000) to $26,000 at a 90% reliability. State the results of the audit test in words. Identify the value in the example for the following terms: confidence level, point estimate of the errors, confidence interval, lower confidence limit, and precision interval.

6-16. Describe how ratio or difference estimation could be used for the confirmation of accounts receivable. Why is it necessary to use positive confirmations when a statistical estimate is to be made? Describe the most likely problems affecting the statistical results that will be encountered in confirming receivables.

6-17. An auditor has decided in a particular situation that the population characteristics needed to make either ratio or difference estimation a sufficiently reliable estimator for his purposes are present. Provide specific criteria that should be used in deciding whether to use ratio or difference estimation.

6-18. What is meant by the efficiency of an estimator? Under what circumstances is ratio estimation likely to be a more efficient estimator than mean-per-unit estimation?

6-19. Sample selection and calculation costs are factors to consider in deciding upon a statistical method. Which of these two costs is apt to be affected in deciding between ratio and difference estimation, and which cost is not apt to be affected? Explain your answer. Under what circumstances is the difference in the total sample selection and calculation cost apt to be insignificant?

6-20. What is meant by the reliability of an estimator? Describe the circumstances in which ratio estimation is likely to be a reliable estimator. When is it likely to be an unreliable estimator?

6-21. Describe the circumstances in which unstratified ratio estimation is a desirable statistical method for auditors compared to mean-per-unit estimation or stratified sampling.

DISCUSSION QUESTIONS AND PROBLEMS

6-22. A CPA's client is considering adoption of statistical sampling techniques. Accordingly, he has asked the CPA to discuss these techniques at a meeting of client employees. In connection with this presentation, the CPA prepared the following table, which shows the comparative characteristics of two populations and the samples to be drawn from each. For example, in Case 1, the variability of population 1 is smaller than that of population 2, whereas the populations are of equal size and the samples to be drawn from them have equal specified precisions (confidence intervals) and specified reliabilities (confidence levels).

	Population 1 relative to population 2		Sample from population 1 relative to sample from population 2	
	Size	*Variability*	*Specified precision*	*Specified reliability*
Case 1	Equal	Smaller	Equal	Equal
Case 2	Smaller	Equal	Equal	Higher
Case 3	Equal	Equal	Wider	Equal
Case 4	Larger	Equal	Narrower	Equal
Case 5	Equal	Greater	Equal	Higher

Using the table and the technique of unrestricted random sampling with replacement, meeting participants are to be asked to determine the relative required sample sizes to be drawn from the two populations. Each of the five cases is independent of the other four and is to be considered separately. Choose the best response for each.

a. The required sample size from population 1 in case 1 is:
  (i) Larger than the required sample size from population 2
  (ii) Equal to the required sample size from population 2
  (iii) Smaller than the required sample size from population 2
  (iv) Indeterminate relative to the required sample size from population 2

b. The required sample size from population 1 in case 2 is:
  (i) Larger than the required sample size from population 2
  (ii) Equal to the required sample size from population 2
  (iii) Smaller than the required sample size from population 2
  (iv) Indeterminate relative to the required sample size from population 2

c. The required sample size from population 1 in case 3 is:
  (i) Larger than the required sample size from population 2
  (ii) Equal to the required sample size from population 2
  (iii) Smaller than the required sample size from population 2
  (iv) Indeterminate relative to the required sample size from population 2

d. The required sample size from population 1 in case 4 is:
  (i) Larger than the required sample size from population 2
  (ii) Equal to the required sample size from population 2
  (iii) Smaller than the required sample size from population 2
  (iv) Indeterminate relative to the required sample size from population 2

e. The required sample size from population 1 in case 5 is:
  (i) Larger than the required sample size from population 2
  (ii) Equal to the required sample size from population 2
  (iii) Smaller than the required sample size from population 2
  (iv) Indeterminate relative to the required sample size from population 2

6-23. You are using statistical sampling to confirm accounts receivable of Pittance Manufacturing Company. The population of accounts receivable is as follows:

Number of accounts	8,150
Total recorded book value	$23,689,423

You review the accounts receivable trial balance and observe that there are several extremely large balances.

The sample is designed to include the 50 largest accounts, which total $6,843,902, and a random selection of 160 of the remaining amounts. This sample size is based on the following criteria:

Materiality (based on net income)	$400,000
Alpha risk	10%
Beta risk	10%

The sample when audited contains 24 errors, none of which are in the 50 largest accounts. These are detailed as follows:

Sample item error results

Item no.	Book amount	Audited amount	Difference
1	$ 864.75	$1,064.75	$ (200.00)
2	8,400.00	7,200.00	+ 1,200.00
3	1,612.10	1,640.10	(28.00)
4	1,489.05	–0–	+ 1,489.05
5	6,207.00	5,207.00	+ 1,000.00
6	120.00	–0–	+ 120.00
7	1,216.20	300.00	+ 916.20
8	1,150.08	1,250.08	(100.00)
9	3,744.19	3,417.10	+ 327.09
10	465.15	527.15	(62.00)
11	309.86	326.00	(16.14)
12	6,379.80	5,181.70	+ 1,198.10
13	824.86	618.86	+ 206.00
14	2,188.50	2,136.50	+ 52.00
15	603.36	461.36	+ 142.00
16	1,439.73	1,233.73	+ 206.00
17	976.56	982.56	(6.00)
18	1,032.00	904.00	+ 128.00
19	7,962.60	6,762.60	+ 1,200.00
20	856.36	652.36	+ 204.00
21	1,803.90	2,160.02	(356.12)
22	836.20	810.20	+ 26.00
23	795.56	786.56	+ 9.00
24	926.08	874.08	+ 52.00
			$7,707.18

Book amount for the 136 items containing no errors	$333,200
Book amount squared for the 136 items containing no errors	$625,000,000

REQUIRED:

a. Evaluate the results using difference estimation.

b. In inspecting the sample items in error, you notice ten of them are due to the late recording of credit memos. As a result, you examine all credit memos issued after year-end, determine the total applicable to the audit period, and enter the total ($201,615) on your schedule of possible adjustments. The ten credit-memo-related errors are items numbered 2, 5, 6, 9, 13, 16, 18, 19, 22, and 24. Recalculate the confidence limits for both ratio and difference estimation. Is the population now acceptable?

c. Evaluate the acceptability of eliminating a specific type of error by performing additional audit tests to determine the population value of these errors.

6-24. For each of the following populations concerning the valuation of raw-materials inventory, the auditor has established an allowable error for hypothesis testing using difference estimation. The auditor has also calculated actual statistical results after the audit tests have been conducted.

Population	Allowable error	Point estimate of the population error (Understated book value is in parentheses)	Computed precision interval
1	$25,000	$ (6,000)	$16,000
2	25,000	0	24,000
3	25,000	(14,000)	18,000
4	25,000	21,000	30,000
5	25,000	12,000	16,000
6	25,000	0	27,000

REQUIRED:

a. Show by means of a graph, using the appropriate decision rule, which of populations 1 through 6 should be accepted as fairly stated without audit adjustment.

b. Show with the same graph, which of populations 1 through 6 cannot be made acceptable by adjusting the client's book value.

c. What options does the auditor have for any sample result in part b?

d. Show with the same graph as for part a, which of populations 1 through 6 should not be accepted as fairly stated but can be made fairly stated by an adjusting entry. Prepare the minimum adjusting entry that can be made for each population.

6-25. For each of the following populations concerning the valuation of raw-materials inventory, the client and auditor have agreed to an adjustment of the client's recorded value equal to the amount of the point estimate if they can be confident that there will not be a material error after the adjustment. Difference estimation is being used.

Population	Allowable error	Point estimate of the population error (Understated book value is in parentheses)	Computed precision interval
1	$25,000	$ (6,000)	$16,000
2	25,000	0	24,000
3	25,000	(14,000)	18,000
4	25,000	21,000	30,000
5	25,000	12,000	16,000
6	25,000	0	27,000

REQUIRED:

a. Distinguish between interval estimation as used in this problem and hypothesis testing as used in 6-24.

b. For which of the populations would the population not be acceptable if the book value were adjusted?

c. Prepare the appropriate adjusting entries for the populations that would be acceptable after the adjustment.

6-26. For each of the following populations concerning the valuation of raw-materials inventory, the auditor has established an allowable error for hypothesis testing using ratio estimation. The auditor has also calculated actual statistical results after the audit tests have been conducted.

Population	Allowable error	Point estimate of the population error (Understated book value is in parentheses)	Computed precision interval
1	$50,000	$20,000	$35,000
2	50,000	25,000	55,000
3	50,000	35,000	10,000
4	50,000	(10,000)	30,000
5	50,000	(15,000)	60,000
6	50,000	15,000	45,000

REQUIRED:

a. Show with a graph, using the appropriate decision rule, which of populations 1 through 6 should be accepted as fairly stated without audit adjustment.

b. Show with the same graph which of populations 1 through 6 cannot be made acceptable by adjusting the client's book value.

c. What options does the auditor have for any sample result in part b?

d. Show with the same graph as for part a, which of populations 1 through 6 should not be accepted as fairly stated but can be made fairly stated by an adjusting entry. Prepare the adjusting entry.

e. How would your answers compare if all information were identical, but difference estimation were being used instead of ratio estimation?

6-27. For each of the following populations concerning the valuation of raw-materials inventory, the client and auditor have agreed to an adjustment of the client's recorded value equal to the amount of the point estimate if they can be confident that there will not be a material error after the adjustment. Ratio estimation is being used.

Population	Allowable error	Point estimate of the population error (Understated book value is in parentheses)	Computed precision interval
1	$50,000	$20,000	$35,000
2	50,000	25,000	55,000
3	50,000	35,000	10,000
4	50,000	(10,000)	30,000
5	50,000	(15,000)	60,000
6	50,000	15,000	45,000

REQUIRED:

a. Distinguish between the use of interval estimation as used in this problem and hypothesis testing as used in 6-26.
b. Which of the populations would not be acceptable if the book value were adjusted?
c. Prepare the appropriate adjusting entries for the populations that would be acceptable after the adjustment.
d. How would your answers compare if all information were identical, but difference estimation were being used rather than ratio estimation?

6-28. Rebecca Downs, CPA, is doing the audit of Berlup Gun and Rack Shop, a national wholesaler of rifles and related equipment and supplies. She is surprised at the results found in the testing to this point in sales and sales returns. There are large numbers of errors in the sales tests, which were done using a judgmental sample. There are a variety of types of errors, including pricing, extensions, footings, failure to record, and duplicate recording in sales returns and postings to subsidiary records. The confirmation of accounts receivable also indicates numerous errors. Upon analysis of the errors, she concludes that the problem is extremely sloppy bookkeeping rather than intentional errors.

When Downs informs management of the problem, she is told that they are not too surprised. Customers have been complaining about their bills in recent months, and the bookkeeper has been having personal problems. He has now been discharged, and the company is in the process of hiring a new bookkeeper. The owner states that he does not feel the problem is serious from a financial statement point of view, because the errors mostly offset each other.

Downs is not convinced that the problem of overall financial statement errors is as minor as the owner states. She decides that additional confirmation of accounts receivable is required under the circumstances. Further thought leads her to conclude that there are two problems: The positive confirmation response has been only approximately 25% to 30% in the past, and it is now 45 days after the balance sheet date. After considerable deliberation, Downs decides to select a combined sample of sales and sales returns and determine the effect of the errors on net sales and earnings. She has concluded that a misposting of a sale or return to the wrong customer is not an error, because gross sales are correctly stated. The owner assures Downs that failure to bill a customer even for a period of several months is not likely to make the receivable uncollectible.

Total recorded sales amount to $14,625,416, and recorded returns are $1,421,711. Downs concludes that an error of $200,000 affecting net earnings would be material. She decides to use a Beta risk of 10% and an Alpha of 100%. She has no basis for estimating the standard deviation or a point estimate. She decides to select 100 items to calculate these two figures.

The sales invoices for the year started with 18,624 and ended with 32,041. They are recorded in the sales journal in the order of issue rather than sequentially. Sales returns and allowances, which are sequentially recorded in the returns journal, start with 671 and end with 3,621.

Based upon the sample size of 100 items, of which 26 were sales returns and allowances, the following error information was noted:

Type of error	Recorded value	Audit value	Error (Understated net sales are in parentheses)
Sales			
Pricing	$ 98.50	$ 95.50	$ 3.00
	333.00	310.00	23.00
	25.30	25.10	.20
	1,147.40	1,117.04	30.36
	789.10	758.90	30.20
	615.00	605.00	10.00
	542.25	539.25	3.00
	2,040.40	2,000.00	40.40
	998.00	948.00	50.00
	478.50	432.50	46.00
	13.12	131.20	(118.08)
	883.20	890.20	(7.00)
	629.50	653.40	(23.90)
	174.39	194.39	(20.00)
Extensions & footings	921.00	901.00	20.00
	292.80	278.50	14.30
	448.50	430.50	18.00
	168.20	155.00	13.20
	1,515.15	1,499.00	16.15
	2,750.50	2,570.50	180.00
	7,137.00	7,173.00	(36.00)
	111.10	125.10	(14.00)
	727.20	772.20	(45.00)
	10.00	100.00	(90.00)

Type of error	Recorded value	Audit value	Error (Understated net sales are in parentheses)
Sales returns			
Posting to subsidiary	(510.00)	(810.00)	300.00
record	(890.90)	(590.90)	(300.00)
	(152.00)	(1.52)	(150.48)
Failure to record	–0–	(725.00)	725.00
sales returns	–0–	(700.00)	700.00
	–0–	(515.00)	515.00
	–0–	(1,219.50)	1,219.50
	–0–	(353.00)	353.00
	–0–	(777.00)	777.00
	$24,402.01	$28,397.20	$4,282.85

The value of the 68 items in the sample that have no errors is $77,280. The sum of these items squared is $104,830,000.

REQUIRED:

a. Evaluate the approach Downs is taking.
b. Explain how she should select the random numbers using a random number table.
c. Calculate the confidence limits for the population of sales and sales returns combined using ratio estimation.
d. How large would the sample need to be to meet Downs' confidence limits requirements?
e. What would the confidence limits be if all errors were included except for the failure to record sales returns errors? Why is the difference between your answers in c and e so large?
f. Suggest a strategy for Downs to follow at this point.

6-29. Reynolds Products Inc. buys large amounts of raw materials and parts from approximately 600 different vendors. Individual raw-materials purchases range from less than $100 to more than $10,000.

All acquisitions of goods and services transactions, except payroll, are recorded on a computer listing. The listing shows the purchase order number, date received, vendor's invoice number, vendor, amount of the acquisition at gross, and the account distribution. When more than one account is involved for a transaction, each account number and the amount assigned to each account are also shown.

During the past three years, the cash position of Reynolds Products has been exceptionally adverse. The result has been an inability to make timely payments to vendors. It has been impractical to take discounts for timely payment of purchases.

The cash position of Reynolds has now improved somewhat. Currently, management is negotiating with banks and several potential major investors to improve the cash position further. One type of information management wants is the potential savings that could be achieved by taking all discounts on a timely basis. Management has decided it wants an accurate estimate of all discounts lost from the purchase of raw materials and parts for each of the past three years. The information for the past three years can then be used as primary information to estimate future potential savings. Management has decided that it would like the estimate of the total discounts lost to be accurate within 10% of the true value of the lost discounts.

The raw-materials and purchased-parts information is no longer in machine-readable form. All computer printouts for the past three years are readily available. Vendors' invoices and related documentation are readily available for the preceding year. The documents for the two years before are available, but will be somewhat expensive to obtain because of this filing system. Management has pledged total cooperation in finding all the necessary documentation.

REQUIRED:

a. Which statistical method—ratio or difference estimation—would probably be more desirable in this situation? Explain your answer.
b. Considering the large variation in the size of the raw-materials and purchased-parts inventory, would unstratified sampling be appropriate in this situation? Explain your answer.
c. What is the likely sampling unit in this situation? Explain which alternatives are available and the advantages and disadvantages of each alternative.
d. Explain how you would estimate the point estimate of the discounts lost and the standard deviation for determining the sample size.
e. Does this situation call for interval estimation or hypothesis testing? How would you determine the appropriate confidence level or Beta and Alpha risks in this situation?

6-30. Roger Goodman, CPA, is doing a test of the cost of inventory of Spiller Spring Manufacturing Company. The decision is made to use both ratio and difference estimation to determine whether the raw-materials inventory is materially misstated. Roger decides that a population error of $25,000 or more would be a material misstatement of raw-materials inventory. Beta risk is set at 5%.

A random sample of 100 inventory items is selected and audited for the correct inventory cost as defined by company policy. The ratio estimation confidence interval for the raw materials errors was $13,000 ± $14,000 at a 5% Beta risk. The difference estimation confidence interval, based upon the same sample results, was $11,000 ± $13,000 at the same Beta risk.

REQUIRED:

a. Is it acceptable to use both ratio and difference estimation for one audit situation? Explain.
b. Explain the cause, to the extent possible from the information provided, for the difference in the confidence intervals for the two statistical methods.
c. Show graphically, using the appropriate decision rule, that a different decision is made about the acceptability of the population according to which statistical method is used.

d. Given the results in *c*, what is the appropriate course of action for the auditor to follow?

6-31. You are doing the audit of Baker Tool's valuation of inventory. The inventory is made up of 8,000 different kinds of items. The value of different kinds of inventory does not vary enough to justify stratification. You conclude that an error of $75,000 would be material, and you expect a point estimate of approximately $25,000 and a standard deviation of $75 using ratio estimation. You decide that you are willing to take a 10% Beta risk of accepting a population that is materially misstated and a 75% Alpha risk for rejecting a population that is not materially misstated.

REQUIRED:

a. Calculate the preliminary sample size for ratio estimation. What would the sample size be for difference estimation if the estimated standard deviation and point estimate were the same?

b. Assume you select a sample size of 200 and obtain the following results, which include 53 errors:

Item	Book value	Audit value	Recorded value squared
1	$ 125.00	$ 124.00	$ 15,625.00
2	34.70	35.00	1,204.09
3	417.00	401.09	173,889.00
.			
.			
.			
n = 200	64.30	64.30	4,134.49
Totals	$27,432.00	$26,674.00	$1,928.750.00

The total recorded value of the population is $730,625.00. The sum of the errors squared is $830,050. Other relevant information is $\sum e_j y_j = 93,256$. Calculate the confidence limits for ratio and difference estimation.

c. Is the population acceptable? Explain what you should do at this point.

6-32. In testing the cash discounts on vendors' invoices, the auditor did not expect to find any errors in the sample, and therefore he used attributes sampling techniques. Based upon the statistical requirements for the test, a sample size of 120 items was randomly selected and carefully tested. Much to the auditor's surprise, there were fifteen sample items where the client had failed to take the discount even though company policy clearly indicated one should have been taken. At this point, he decided to switch to variables estimation to measure the amount of the lost discounts.

REQUIRED:

a. Is it acceptable to change to variables estimation at this point? Explain.

b. What would be the purpose of making the calculations? Would the test be a hypothesis test or interval estimation? Explain.

c. If ratio estimation is used, explain how the auditor should proceed.

d. Calculate the confidence limits for the discounts not taken, assuming a confidence level of 90%, from the following information:

Item	Invoice amount	Discount lost	Invoice amount squared
1	$ 465.00	$–0–	$ 216,225.00
2	36.50	.72	1,332.25
3	123.45	1.23	15,239.90
4	1,505.00	–0–	2,265.025.00
.			
.			
.			
$n = 120$	231.00	–0–	53,361.00
Totals	$21,600.00	$27.00	$6,888,000.00

The population of vendors' invoices consisted of 6,000 invoices totaling $1,038,000. The sum of the discounts lost squared is $53.00. The sum of the discounts lost times the invoice amount is $5,530.

e. State in words the meaning of the confidence limits calculated in *d*.

6-33. In auditing the valuation of inventory, the auditor, Claire Butler, decided to use difference estimation. She decided to select an unrestricted random sample of 80 inventory items from a population of 1,840 that had a book value of $175,820. Butler had decided in advance that she was willing to accept a maximum error in the population of $6,000 at a Beta risk of $2\frac{1}{2}\%$. There were eight errors in the sample, as follows:

	Audit value	Book value	Sample errors
	$ 812.50	$ 740.50	$(72.00)
	12.50	78.20	65.70
	10.00	51.10	41.10
	25.40	61.50	36.10
	600.10	651.90	51.80
	.12	0	(.12)
	51.06	81.06	30.00
	83.11	104.22	21.11
Total	$1,594.79	$1,768.48	$173.69

REQUIRED:

a. Calculate the point estimate, the computed precision interval, the confidence interval, and the confidence limits for the population. Label each calculation.

b. Demonstrate by the use of a graph whether Butler should accept the book value of the population.

c. Assume the population is not acceptable given the sample results, and the client is unwilling to accept an adjustment. Calculate the additional sample size required. If the additional sample items are selected and tested, will the result be a conclusion that the population is fairly stated? Explain.

d. Evaluate whether ratio or difference estimation is apt to be a better statistical method in this situation.

6-34. a. Calculate the preliminary sample size using ratio estimation for a to e from the following information provided:

	a	b	c	d	e
Population size	5,000	10,000	5,000	10,000	5,000
Alpha risk	20%	49%	20%	25%	5%
Beta risk	5%	5%	$\frac{1}{2}$%	10%	5%
Allowable error	$50,000	$80,000	$50,000	$80,000	$50,000
Estimated standard deviation	100	150	100	150	100
Estimated point estimate	$20,000	$30,000	$20,000	$30,000	$20,000

b. Compare your answers in a to the ones for problem 5-31, part a. Explain why the answers are similar or different.

c. In general, what is the effect on the preliminary sample size (increase, decrease, no effect, or cannot determine without additional information) of each of the following independent changes, assuming the other components of sample size are held constant?

	Effect on preliminary sample size
1. Increase Beta risk.	
2. Increase Alpha risk.	
3. Increase estimated point estimate.	
4. Increase population size.	
5. Increase Alpha risk and decrease Beta risk.	
6. Increase allowable error and increase estimated standard deviation.	

6-35. You are in charge of the audit of the United Widget Workers of America, a labor union that your firm has been auditing for several years. In performing the audit for the year ended June 30, 198X, you note that the union signed a new contract with all employers as of January 1, 198X. The new contract requires that increased medical benefits be paid to those who retire after 1/1/8X. These benefits are to be paid for by additional employer contributions of 1% of gross wages.

Under the contract, the union was required to set up a separate trust for the employees covered for the additional benefits. Those covered by the old contract were to remain under the previous trust. These are referred to below as the "old trust" and the "new trust."

In conducting the audit, you note that the books have not been kept by trust. The client informs you that there has been a lack of communication between its legal and its accounting department. After discussion with the client, you conclude that it will be easy to make the adjustment for the income that should be in each trust and for the administrative expenses that should be charged to each trust. However, the volume of medical benefits is such that it is not practical to analyze each benefit payment to determine whether it applies to the old or the new trust. Accordingly, the client wishes your advice on whether an appropriate sampling scheme is feasible.

During the six months ending June 30, the client wrote 7,000 checks for benefits, which totaled $38 million. Medical benefits are paid mainly through doctors' consulting arrangements. The doctor lists on a form (voucher) the patient seen, the Social Security number, the service rendered, and the charge, and submits the form for payment once a month. Each form and related check will generally have several hundred line items. The client has an index file of employees by Social Security number. This will permit it to identify which trust the employee belongs to.

You decide that the proper technique is either ratio or difference estimation. The sampling unit is defined as the check, since the population size for the line items is not determinable. You define the total payment as the book value and the amount applicable to the new trust as the audited value.

You decide to randomly select 75 items to obtain more information about the population. The sample information is included below. In addition, you and the client agree on a confidence level of 95% and an allowable error of $1,900,000.

REQUIRED:

a. Is the appropriate statistical test an interval estimate or a hypothesis test? Explain.
b. Calculate the required sample size using difference estimation.
c. Calculate the required sample size using ratio estimation.
d. Compare your answers and explain the reason for the difference.
e. Based on the results of the sample size calculation, 25 additional items were selected. Using all 100 sample items, calculate the confidence limits using difference and ratio estimation.
f. Prepare an entry to adjust the recorded book value if the allowable error requirements are satisfied. After the adjustment is made, use the statistical method resulting in the lowest computed precision interval.

Details of sample values used

Item no.	Audited value	Book value
1	$ 22.22	$ 300.00
2	125.60	313.88
3	679.00	1,568.00
4	3,912.00	11,100.58
5	512.78	1,000.00
6	1,800.00	2,800.00
7	54.55	63.55

Item no.	Audited value	Book value
8	791.00	1,363.00
9	1,313.00	2,000.00
10	712.40	2,000.00
11	1,002.45	1,876.90
12	308.50	664.50
13	3,440.64	5,000.00
14	451.64	500.00
15	3,218.60	6,000.00
16	2,283.00	10,000.00
17	1,600.00	3,550.00
18	614.00	4,120.00
19	2,437.00	5,912.00
20	784.00	4,759.00
21	2,437.74	7,896.47
22	784.50	2,356.78
23	539.00	1,029.00
24	3,827.00	7,748.00
25	8,533.00	25,250.00
26	350.00	600.00
27	219.00	500.00
28	350.00	700.00
29	40,460.00	77,750.00
30	522.66	2,950.00
31	644.22	1,300.00
32	1,314.00	6,000.00
33	680.00	805.00
34	805.22	2,000.00
35	125.00	904.00
36	460.00	2,240.00
37	441.78	1,350.00
38	2,530.00	5,150.00
39	208.30	1,500.00
40	405.00	1,029.50
41	505.00	3,447.00
42	210.00	740.00
43	79.50	337.50
44	1,042.00	2,000.00
45	23.40	1,100.00
46	243.78	330.00
47	509.30	1,250.00
48	527.34	1,732.00
49	716.96	1,029.68
50	411.00	2,000.00
51	335.00	1,240.00
52	1,734.00	3,200.00
53	70.00	180.00
54	1,864.75	13,076.71
55	922.95	2,750.00
56	70.50	180.00
57	334.00	944.00
58	7,038.80	17,597.75
59	421.27	484.57
60	2,684.00	4,200.00

Item no.	Audited value	Book value
61	182.38	1,056.93
62	2,445.00	9,723.00
63	1,071.00	2,031.00
64	17,809.00	28,900.00
65	1,071.25	2,030.79
66	11,969.60	29,924.00
67	1,256.40	6,300.00
68	12.50	12.50
69	397.17	750.00
70	1,119.50	1,349.50
71	15.00	242.00
72	31.65	1,027.39
73	266.68	5,000.00
74	160.00	605.00
75	672.36	1,500.00
Totals	$149,921.84	$362,221.48

Item no.	Audited value	Book value
76	$ 172.00	$ 3,662.00
77	726.96	790.00
78	275.88	450.00
79	380.00	4,531.50
80	55.00	135.00
81	53.60	135.00
82	628.18	1,000.00
83	2.70	89.20
84	590.85	1,750.00
85	1,616.90	2,000.00
86	1,109.49	5,000.00
87	1,216.44	3,100.00
88	60.45	750.00
89	2,464.40	4,000.00
90	428.40	1,000.00
91	1,060.40	2,000.00
92	3,200.00	7,500.00
93	641.01	1,300.00
94	93.00	537.50
95	329.16	1,300.00
96	250.00	832.00
97	5492.98	21.862.41
98	70.40	844.80
99	3,473.55	8,683.87
100	3,900.00	10,000.00

6-36. When your supervisor reviews the audit working papers for Maylo Supply Company (see problem 5-45), he concludes that difference estimation may not have been the most appropriate statistical method. He believes that ratio estimation may be preferable for the circumstances.

REQUIRED:

a. Would the Alpha and Beta risks be different for ratio estimation than difference estimation? Explain reasons for your answer.

b. Calculate the sample size required using ratio estimation, assuming there is no basis for changing the expected error or standard deviation. Explain why your answer is the same as or different from the one you determined for difference estimation.

c. Calculate the confidence limits for ratio estimation using the same sample results that were used for difference estimation. The 82 items containing no errors had a total book value of $5,269. The sum of the squared book values for the 82 items was $676,888. The audited and recorded values for the eighteen differences are as follows:

Inventory tag number	Audited value	Recorded value	Difference
51	$ 420	$ 450	$ 30
73	130	135	5
104	200	210	10
167	85	79	(6)
171	93	113	20
245	510	520	10
300	38	48	10
363	0	50	50
463	60	68	8
478	190	175	(15)
481	110	135	25
692	107	110	3
711	315	345	30
735	170	190	20
790	225	245	20
821	305	345	40
854	152	150	(2)
862	76	86	10
	$3,186	$3,454	$268

d. Is the population acceptable or not acceptable? Explain the reason for the difference in confidence limits using ratio and difference estimation.

7

mean-per-unit estimation

INTRODUCTION

The calculations of sample size and confidence intervals for mean-per-unit (also frequently called simple extension) estimation are made in the same manner as for difference estimation. The only distinction is that whereas all calculations for difference estimates are made from *errors in the sample,* the calculations for mean-per-unit estimates are made from the *audited values in the sample.*

Although the calculations of mean-per-unit and difference estimation are almost the same, the uses of the two methods are usually different. An understanding of difference estimation should make the study of mean-per-unit easier.

There are only two situations in which unstratified mean-per-unit estimation would be used in auditing. The first situation is one in which there is no recorded book value for individual population items—for example, where the client has estimated the amount of inventory obsolescence write-off in total. The auditor wants to determine the reasonableness of the total by sampling the inventory and applying a known obsolescence criterion to each sample item. Previous chapters have shown that ratio and difference estimation require a recorded and an audit value. Mean-per-unit requires only an audited value.

The second case is one in which the auditor concludes that ratio and difference estimation are unreliable estimators. The lack of reliability could be due to the low rate of errors in the population or to the fact that the errors are primarily in one direction.

It is unlikely that an auditor would use unstratified mean-per-unit estimation even in the two circumstances described. It will be shown in Chapter 8 that stratified mean-per-unit may be more appropriate in both these situations. In Chapter 9 it will be shown that dollar unit sampling may be the most appropriate method. Nevertheless, in a few circumstances, unstratified mean-per-unit is the most useful statistical method.

The reason unstratified mean-per-unit estimation is infrequently used in auditing is the large standard deviation that exists. Ratio and difference estimation and stratified mean-per-unit almost always result in a smaller standard deviation and therefore smaller required sample sizes.

An important reason for studying unstratified mean-per-unit estimation is as a background for stratified mean-per-unit, which is studied in the next chapter. Stratified mean-per-unit is emerging as one of the most useful of all statistical methods.

For mean-per-unit estimation, the following outline will be used:

1. Calculation of statistical results for mean-per-unit
2. Calculation of required sample size and statistical results and the use of the results
3. Efficiency, sample selection and calculation costs, and reliability
4. Appropriate uses of mean-per-unit estimation
5. Illustrations of typical applications of mean-per-unit estimation

CALCULATION OF STATISTICAL RESULTS

The calculation of confidence limits for mean-per-unit estimation can be illustrated by means of the same inventory example used for difference estimation in Chapter 5 and ratio estimation in Chapter 6. The purpose is to identify the appropriate formulas and methodology for mean-per-unit, illustrate the calculations, and show how mean-per-unit results in inefficient sampling results under some circumstances. Later, a situation in which mean-per-unit is more likely to be used will be illustrated.

Assume that the auditor selects 130 sample items to test inventory costing errors where the inventory has been priced using FIFO. The auditor has decided on a Beta risk of 10 percent and an allowable error of $80,000. There are 2,700 inventory items in the population, and the client's recorded book value is $3,600,000.

The audit tests on the 130 sample items are done in exactly the same manner as for difference and ratio estimation. The only difference is that the auditor is concerned only about the *audit value* of each sample item. The client's recorded value and error in the sample have no other relevance. The sample results are in Figure 7-1. The audit results are shown in the same format as those in Chapters 5 and 6 only to aid in comparing the three methods.

Sample item	Recorded value	Error	Audit value	Audit value squared
7	$ 2,611	$ 203	$ 2,408	$ 5,798,464
9	87	(49)	136	18,496
21	890	439	451	203,401
30	501	(110)	611	373,321
36	1,208	105	1,103	1,216,609
41	3,150	168	2,982	8,892,324
42	2,493	382	2,111	4,456,321
53	216	(243)	459	210,681
59	511	460	51	2,601
62	1,821	(642)	2,463	6,066,369
69	660	660	0	0
73	1,408	(113)	1,521	2,313,441
96	3,408	1,241	2,167	4,695,889
101	799	48	751	564,001
106	1,293	172	1,12!	1,256,641
109	181	(630)	811	657,721
114	3,415	(611)	4,026	16,208,676
121	2,117	308	1,809	3,272,481
127	315	(100)	415	172,225
130	136	44	92	8,464
All others	150,372	0	150,372	255,827,185
	$177,592	$1,732	$175,860	$312,215,311

FIGURE 7-1 Results of sample

Calculate Point Estimate of the Audited Value

The point estimate is a direct extrapolation from the audited values in the sample to the audited value of the population. The calculation of this amount is shown in Figure 7-2. The point estimate is $3,652,479 for the inventory example being used. The point estimate for mean-per-unit is calculated in the same way as for difference estimation (see Figure 5-2), except that audited values are used instead of errors. Naturally, it is much larger than the point estimate of the errors shown for difference estimation, because audited values are ordinarily larger than the related errors.

It is unlikely for the actual but unknown population value to be exactly the same as the point estimate. It is necessary to calculate the precision interval to get a useful estimate of the actual population value. First, the standard deviation must be calculated.

$$\bar{x} = \frac{\sum x_j}{n}$$

$$N = N \cdot \bar{x} \quad \text{or} \quad N \cdot \frac{\sum x_j}{n}$$

where:

x_j = the audited value of an individual item in the sample
n = sample size
N = population size
$\bar{x}$ = mean audited value of the sample items
$\hat{X}$ = point estimate of the population total audited value

$$\bar{x} = \frac{\$175,860}{130} = \$1,352.77$$

$$\hat{X} = 2,700 \cdot 1,352.77 = \$3,652,479$$

or

$$\hat{X} = 2,700 \cdot \frac{175,860}{130} = \$3,652,479$$

FIGURE 7-2   Point estimate of the audited value

Compute an Estimate of the Population Standard Deviation

The formula for calculating the standard deviation of the mean-per-unit is the same as for difference estimates except that audited values are used instead of error values. The formulas and calculation of the mean-per-unit standard deviation for the inventory example are shown in Figure 7-3. The standard deviation is 758.6 for the example.

$$SD = \sqrt{\frac{\sum x_j^2 - n(\bar{x})^2}{n-1}}$$

where:

SD = standard deviation
x_j = the audited value of an individual item in the sample
n = sample size

$$\bar{x} = \frac{\sum x_j}{n}$$

$$SD = \sqrt{\frac{312,215,311 - 130(1,353)^2}{130-1}}$$

$$SD = \$758.6$$

FIGURE 7-3   Estimated standard deviation of the population audited values

Why is the standard deviation 758.6 for mean-per-unit when it was 175.9 for the same sample items for difference estimation? The answer can be seen by examining the audited values and errors in Figure 7-1. The range of the absolute value of the errors is $1,241 (0 to 1,241), and most of the errors are zero. The range of the audit values for the 20 sample items shown is $4,026 (0 to 4,026), and almost all items have a value of more than zero. Except in rare cases, where the errors in the sample are larger than the audited values, the standard deviation of unstratified mean-per-unit will be larger than difference or ratio estimation.

Compute the Precision Interval

The mean-per-unit precision interval is also calculated the same way as for difference estimation, except that a different standard deviation is used. The formula and calculation of the precision interval for mean-per-unit are shown in Figure 7-4. A confidence level of 80 percent is used (Beta risk is 10 percent). The precision interval is $225,376.

$$CPI = \frac{N \cdot Z(1 - 2\beta) \cdot SD}{\sqrt{n}} \cdot \sqrt{\frac{N - n}{N}}$$

where:

$\quad CPI$ = computed precision interval
$\quad N$ = population size
$Z(1 - 2\beta)$ = confidence coefficient (two-sided) for the confidence level desired
$\quad SD$ = estimated population standard deviation of the audited values
$\quad n$ = sample size
$\sqrt{\dfrac{N - n}{N}}$ = finite correction factor

$$CPI = \frac{2,700 \cdot 1.28 \cdot 758.6}{\sqrt{130}} \cdot \sqrt{\frac{2,700 - 130}{2,700}}$$

$$CPI = \frac{2,621,722}{11.40} \cdot .98$$

$$CPI = 225,376$$

FIGURE 7-4 The computed precision interval at the desired confidence level

The difference between the precision interval of $52,258 for difference estimation, as calculated on page 149, and mean-per-unit estimation of $225,376 is caused entirely by the standard deviation of 175.9 for difference estimation and 758.6 for mean-per-unit.

Compute the Confidence Interval
and the Confidence Limits

The confidence interval and limits are also calculated the same way as for difference estimates, but they have a different meaning. The confidence limits of a difference estimate are the upper and lower bounds at a given confidence level of the errors in a population. The confidence limits of a mean-per-unit estimate are upper and lower bounds at a given confidence level of the *audited value of a population*. The confidence limits for mean-per-unit are shown in Figure 7-5. The upper limit is $3,877,855 and the lower limit is $3,427,103.

$$CI = \hat{X} \pm CPI$$
$$UCL = \hat{X} + CPI$$
$$LCL = \hat{X} - CPI$$

where:

CI = computed confidence interval
$\hat{X}$ = point estimate of the population total audited value
CPI = computed precision interval
CI = $3,652,479 $\pm$ $225,376
UCL = $3,652,479 + $225,376 = $3,877,855
LCL = $3,652,479 - $225,376 = $3,427,103

The auditor can state with an 80% confidence level that the true value of the population is between $3,427,103 and $3,877,855

FIGURE 7-5 The confidence limits at the desired confidence level

Confidence intervals of difference and mean-per-unit have different meanings, but it is easy to convert from one to the other if there is a recorded value. The audited value of the population being used in the example determined from a difference estimate is

$$\frac{\text{Confidence interval}}{\text{of the audited value}} = \text{Book value} - \text{Point estimate of the errors} \pm \text{Precision interval}$$

$$= 3,600,000 - 35,972 \pm 52,258$$

$$= 3,564,028 \pm 52,258$$

$$= 3,511,770 \text{ to } 3,616,286$$

compared to 3,427,103 to 3,877,855 from a mean-per-unit estimation.

The estimated value of the errors in the same population determined from mean-per-unit estimation is

$$\begin{array}{l} \text{Confidence interval} \\ \text{of the errors} \end{array} = \text{Book value} - \begin{array}{l} \text{Point estimate of} \\ \text{the audited value} \end{array} \pm \begin{array}{l} \text{Precision} \\ \text{interval} \end{array}$$

$$= 3{,}600{,}000 - 3{,}652{,}479 \pm 225{,}376$$

$$= -52{,}479 \pm 225{,}376$$

$$= -277{,}855 \quad \text{to} \quad 172{,}897$$

compared to 16,286 to 88,230 from a difference estimation.

The Audit Decision

The decision rule for a hypothesis test is the same for mean-per-unit as for difference estimation except that the materiality limits are set plus and minus the client's book value rather than plus and minus zero. The decision rule for mean-per-unit estimation is:

If the two-sided confidence interval is completely within the book value plus and minus the amount considered material, accept the hypothesis that the book value is not misstated by a material amount.

The decision rule is applied to the ongoing example as follows:

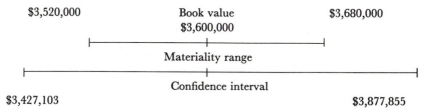

Both sides of the confidence interval are outside the materiality limits. Therefore, the hypothesis that the book value is not misstated by a material amount must be rejected. It is not possible to adjust the book value for the estimated error in the population, because both sides of the confidence interval are outside the materiality limits. Considering the large standard deviation and confidence interval, it is not surprising that the book value cannot be accepted.

The amount by which the upper precision limit exceeds the upper materiality range is so large ($197,855) that it may be impractical to increase the sample size to determine the amount of the error. In other words, an inordinate number of additional items would have to be tested to get the precision interval small enough to accept the population as stated or determine the amount of the adjusting entry to correct the population.

Summary

The previous example was meant to show:

1. How to calculate the confidence limits of the results of an audit test using mean-per-unit estimation, assuming the sample size is given.
2. The similarities and differences between difference and mean-per-unit estimation.
3. The effect of using an excellent statistical method (mean-per-unit) in a situation where it was probably the wrong method to use. Difference or ratio estimation is far more efficient and is apt to be sufficiently reliable in this situation. A sample size far greater than 130 items is needed for mean-per-unit estimation to provide a satisfactory audit result.

CALCULATION OF REQUIRED SAMPLE SIZE AND ILLUSTRATION OF USE

Let us show an example of a situation where mean-per-unit is a logical statistical method, in order to illustrate its use. The example includes calculating the proper sample size for the circumstances, calculating the confidence limits, and using the statistical results in the audit.

Description

The client, Marshall Implement Dealers, is a farm-implement dealer with a large number of parts for sale at retail. The inventory includes tractors, combines, and other equipment, but these are counted separately and are not a part of this problem. The parts inventory is stored in bins attached to 60 walls in a large warehouse. Each wall is ten bins high and 80 bins across, for a total of exactly 48,000 bins. The bins are marked in part-number sequence to facilitate finding the parts. The unit selling price is also attached to each bin. When the company has stock in addition to what will fit into the bin, the quantity is indicated on the appropriate bin and the items are stored in a second warehouse.

The client does not want to take a complete physical count in the year under audit because of cost. Instead, it plans to take a sample of parts inventory and determine the book value on the basis of the sample. The decision is made to count all parts in the second warehouse, because they are of significantly higher average cost than those in the primary warehouse. In addition, ten bins in the primary warehouse have a known high value and are also counted.

Based on prior years and results of approximations from gross margin calculations, the controller estimates that the book value of parts is about $3,500,000. The client's intention is to record as the book value the point estimate of the statistical sample. Management decides that it is willing to accept an estimate of inventory based on a statistical test as long as it is not misstated by more than $200,000 from the point estimate. Management is willing to accept a risk of 10 percent of a misstated population.

The client estimates that the standard deviation is approximately 55. The estimate is based on last year's inventory listing. It is not too important that this estimate be accurate, because the average cost per item of sampling is not large, and additional items can be tested if necessary.

Statement on Auditing Standards permits the client's determining inventory values using statistical methods. There are audit requirements that must be met in these circumstances:

> ... the independent auditor must satisfy himself that the client's procedures or methods are sufficiently reliable to produce results substantially the same as those which would be obtained by a count of all items each year. The auditor must be present to observe such counts as he deems necessary and must satisfy himself as to the effectiveness of the counting procedures used. If statistical sampling methods are used by the client in the taking of the physical inventory, the auditor must be satisfied that the sampling plan has statistical validity, that it has been properly applied, and that the resulting precision and reliability, as defined statistically, are reasonable in the circumstances.[1]

The auditor agrees with the precision ($200,000) and reliability (90 percent).

Determining Sample Size

There is no need to consider the Alpha risk for this statistical application, because an estimate is being made, rather than a hypothesis test. There is also no estimate of the expected error in the population. The book value will be adjusted to the point estimate. The expected error is therefore zero.

The sample size is therefore:

$$n = \left(\frac{N \cdot Z \cdot SD^*}{AE}\right)^2$$

where:

n = sample size
N = population size
Z = confidence coefficient (two-sided)
  for the confidence level desired
SD^* = advance estimate of standard deviation
AE = acceptable error

$$n = \left(\frac{48,000 \cdot 1.64 \cdot 55}{200,000}\right)^2 = \left(\frac{4,329,600}{200,000}\right)^2$$

$$n = (21.65)^2 = 469$$

Instead of the client's counting and costing all 48,000 inventory items, it will be necessary to count and cost only 469 items plus all items in ware-

[1]SAS 1, Section 331.11.

house 2 and the ten large items already identified by the client. (The population size is actually 47,990, but we use 48,000 for ease of calculation.)

The only thing that can cause the sample size to be too small to meet the allowable error requirements is a standard deviation that is larger than 55. The standard deviation will be calculated from the sample results.

Random Selection

The sampling unit could be defined as either a part number or a storage bin. The part number is an impractical sampling unit in this case, because it includes letters. Besides, many letters and numbers are not used in identifying the parts. With storage bins used as the sampling unit, the sample items can be identified by wall number (60 walls), row number (80 rows), and column number (10 columns). Identifying selected storage bins can be facilitated by the client's identifying each wall and row with a number. The likelihood of selecting the wrong bin is also reduced.

The easiest way to select the random number is with a computer terminal. Random selection could also be done with a random number table by using a five-digit number whose first two digits are the wall number, the third and fourth digits the row, and the last digit the column (0 equals column 10). Any random number larger than 60809 or smaller than 01010 is a discard. All numbers whose third and fourth digits exceed 80 are also discards.

Using the random number table on page 26 with a starting point of line 1027, column 1, the first random bin numbers are:

	Wall number	Row number	Column number
1	16	62	3
2	56	64	10
3	54	72	5
4	25	65	8
5	51	63	7

After all numbers are randomly selected, they may be put into a sequence to minimize the time spent doing the actual counting. Wall numbers should be the most important consideration in putting the numbers in sequence, to facilitate simultaneous work by several inventory count teams. Putting row numbers and column numbers in sequential order is a secondary consideration. When the numbers are put in sequence, it is necessary to keep all five digits for a given number exactly as they were when they were selected from the random table. Otherwise, bias exists.

Physical Count and Pricing

Care must be used to avoid errors in counting the inventory and pricing it. The population point estimate will be the actual ending balance on the balance sheet. Any errors in the physical counts or pricing will be reflected on the statements more than a hundredfold $\left(\dfrac{N}{n} = \dfrac{48,000}{469} = 102\right)$.

The client, rather than the auditor, is responsible for supervising and taking the physical inventory and doing the actual costing of the inventory. The auditor is responsible for reviewing the internal controls over the physical count and inventory costing and performing tests to determine the fairness of the results.

The audit time for the physical count is apt to be greater than it would be if the client took a complete physical. The client's sample size is larger than the auditor would usually find necessary for difference estimation, which might be practical if a 100 percent count had been taken. More careful planning and control are essential at every point, because the consequences of an error by the client or auditor are so significant.

The additional audit time, however, may well be more than offset by savings to the client. The cost of taking a physical count and pricing 469 items is far less than it would be for 48,000 items. Also the actual inventory will probably be more accurate with a well-supervised statistical sample than with a 100 percent count, because there is less likelihood of mistakes caused by such things as boredom and fatigue.

Actual Results of the Sample

The client's results of the physical count and costing of the sample the auditor has verified are shown in Figure 7-6. Only the first ten items are included, to avoid unnecessary detail.

Sample items in sequential order	Physical count in units	Unit costs	x_j Total cost	x_j^2 Total cost squared (nearest $)
01064	21	$ 12.60	$ 264.60	$ 70,013
01147	3	26.58	79.74	6,358
01271	126	.18	22.68	514
01425	0		0	0
01509	29	3.76	109.04	11,890
01730	1	156.20	156.20	24,398
02036	35	.81	28.35	804
02112	7	8.98	62.86	3,951
02294	0		0	0
02297	2	81.30	162.60	26,439
			$ 886.07	$ 144,367
Additional 459 sample items			33,785.52	3,841,261
Total (sample size 469)			$34,671.59	$3,985,628

FIGURE 7-6   Sample results for inventory example

Calculate the Point Estimate

The point estimate is:

$$\hat{X} = N \cdot \frac{\sum x_j}{n}$$

$$\hat{X} = 48,000 \cdot \frac{34,671.59}{469} = 48,000 \cdot 73.93$$

$$\hat{X} = 3,548,640$$

The inventory items that were separately counted on a 100 percent basis must also be added to the point estimate to determine the book value of the inventory. For convenience, it is assumed here that these inventories are recorded on the books separately, and are disregarded in the remainder of the illustration. That is, the point estimate of $3,548,640 will be the amount on the balance sheet, and it will be a determinant of cost of goods sold if the computed precision is less than $200,000.

Calculate the Standard Deviation

The standard deviation is:

$$SD = \sqrt{\frac{\sum x_j^2 - n(\bar{x})^2}{n-1}}$$

$$SD = \sqrt{\frac{3,985,628 - 469(73.93)^2}{468}} = \sqrt{3039} = 55.1$$

The standard deviation is very close to that expected. It is therefore likely that the actual computed precision interval will be close to the $200,000 that is allowed.

Calculate the Precision Interval

The computed precision interval is:

$$CPI = \frac{N \cdot Z \cdot SD}{\sqrt{n}} \cdot \sqrt{\frac{N-n}{N}}$$

$$CPI = \frac{48,000 \cdot 1.64 \cdot 55.1}{\sqrt{469}} \cdot \sqrt{\frac{48,000 - 469}{48,000}} = \frac{4,337,472}{21.66} \cdot .995$$

$$CPI = \$199,251$$

What causes the computed precision interval to be less than the materiality limit of $200,000 when the actual standard deviation is slightly larger than expected? The computed precision interval is smaller because the finite correction factor was omitted from the sample-size calculation but included in determining precision.

If the computed precision interval had been larger than $200,000 by any significant amount, it would have been necessary to increase the sample size. The additional sample items can be determined by recalculating the sample size using the formula on page 225. The only thing that would change is the standard deviation, which would be the amount determined from the actual sample. The new required sample, less the items already tested, would be the number of additional sample items needed. After the additional items are counted and costed, it would be necessary to recalculate the computed precision interval combining both the first and second sample results.

Calculate the Confidence Limits

The confidence limits are:

$$CI = \hat{X} \pm CPI$$
$$CI = \$3,548,640 \pm \$199,251$$
$$UCL = \$3,548,640 + \$199,251 = \$3,747,891$$
$$LCL = \$3,548,640 - \$199,251 = \$3,349,389$$

The client and auditor can conclude that there is a 90 percent likelihood that the true balance in inventory is between $3,349,389 and $3,747,891. This is shown as follows in a decision framework, assuming that the book value will be adjusted to the point estimate.

Materiality range with the book value equal to the point estimate is:

$3,348,640	$3,548,640	$3,748,640
$3,349,389	Confidence interval	$3,747,891

The entire confidence interval falls within the materiality range after the book value has been adjusted to the point estimate; therefore, the population should be accepted.

Accepting a Population Materially Different from the Point Estimate

The auditor's greatest concern in this instance is the possibility of adjusting the book value to a point estimate when the actual, but unknown, inventory value is more than $200,000 different from the point estimate. What are the possible causes of this occurrence?

1. The confidence interval indicates that there is a 5 percent Beta risk of the inventory's being misstated by $200,000 or more (there is a 5 percent risk of over-

statement and a 5 percent risk of understatement, but it cannot be both at the same time; therefore, Beta risk is 5 percent). If the auditor is unwilling to accept a risk that high, a higher confidence level should have been used.

2. Errors were made in calculating the point estimate. The errors could arise, for example, from selecting the wrong random numbers, wrongly converting the random numbers into bins, incorrectly counting quantities in a bin, costing mistakes —including possible obsolescence—and incorrect calculations of the point estimate or computed precision interval.

3. The estimator was not sufficiently reliable considering the population. If the population included a few inventory items of unusually large value, unstratified mean-per-unit estimation may not be a desirable statistical method. Care must be used before the sampling begins, to avoid use of the wrong method. (In fact, in this illustration, certain high dollar items were counted 100%.)

EFFICIENCY, SAMPLE SELECTION AND CALCULATION COSTS, AND RELIABILITY

Efficiency

It has already been demonstrated that unstratified mean-per-unit is likely to result in larger sampling than is difference or ratio estimation. The reason is the larger standard deviation for audited values.

The only time unstratified mean-per-unit is likely to result in a reasonably small sampling is when the population is made up of items of approximately the same size (the standard deviation is small). Otherwise, it is ordinarily the least efficient method studied in this book.

Sample Selection and Calculation Costs

There is no significant difference between the selection and calculation costs for mean-per-unit, difference, or ratio estimation. Naturally, if the sample size for mean-per-unit is larger, that will have an effect on sample selection and calculation costs.

The costs for all three methods are affected by the degree to which a computer is available as an aid. The effect of computer costs was discussed in earlier chapters.

Reliability of the Estimator

The *skewness* of the book values is the most important determinant of the reliability of mean-per-unit estimation. When the population skewness is high, the reliability is usually sufficiently low to require stratification or an alternative statistical method.

Skewness is a term representing the characteristic of nonsymmetry in the population. When a population distribution is perfectly symmetrical about its mean, its skewness is zero. When there are extreme values in the population, they influence the mean more than the median, and the values of these two characteristics diverge, providing skewness. Most accounting populations are positively skewed, having a mean value greater than the median because of the existence of a relatively few high-value items.

There are several measures of skewness available. One such measure is the coefficient of skewness developed by Karl Pearson:

$$Sk = \frac{3(\bar{X} - \text{Median})}{s}$$

where $\bar{X}$ is the population mean, and s is the population standard deviation. This coefficient will range from minus to plus 3. Whenever an amount is significantly different from zero, stratification of extreme values should be considered (see Chapter 8), or sample size should be increased beyond minimum levels. Unfortunately, where unstratified mean-per-unit estimation is to be used, data to determine skewness may not be available and must be estimated from sample results. Also, a specific application rule on degree of skewness as it concerns reliability of unstratified mean-per-unit is not currently available.

A comparison of the actual and nominal confidence coefficients between difference and mean-per-unit estimation for the populations tested in the Neter and Loebbecke research study is shown in Figure 7-7. The only error rates illustrated are for 1 percent (populations 1–4) and 30 percent (populations 13–16).

The following conclusions are drawn from the comparison in Figure 7-7:

| | | | | | *Actual reliability* | | | |
| | | | | | *Difference estimation* | | *Mean-per-unit estimation* | |
Population number	*Error rate*	*Size of errors*	*Direction of errors*	*Skewness of book values*	*Sample size of 100*	*Sample size of 200*	*Sample size of 100*	*Sample size of 200*
1	1%	small	both	very high	37.3%	53.0%	81.8%	87.5%
2	1%	large	both	moderate	41.8%	54.5%	93.7%	95.5%
3	1%	moderate	over	high	36.8%	57.0%	82.5%	87.7%
4	1%	large	over	moderate	30.0%	47.0%	92.7%	95.2%
13	30%	small	both	very high	96.3%	93.7%	81.7%	87.2%
14	30%	large	both	moderate	95.5%	96.0%	93.0%	95.5%
15	30%	moderate	over	high	90.8%	92.2%	82.5%	87.7%
16	30%	large	over	moderate	74.8%	87.5%	93.3%	94.7%

FIGURE 7-7 Comparison of actual to nominal 95.4% confidence coefficient under varying conditions, difference and mean-per-unit estimation

1. Sizes of the errors in the population have no effect on the reliability of the mean-per-unit estimator. (Compare the actual reliability of populations 1 and 13, 2 and 14, etc., to reach this conclusion.) That conclusion should be expected, inasmuch as mean-per-unit measures the audited values and ignores the errors in the population.

2. An increase of sample size from 100 to 200 increased the reliability in every case.

3. Sample sizes of 200 from populations of moderate skewness resulted in high actual reliability. Even sample sizes of 100 resulted in actual reliability of 92% or better for moderate skewness.

4. High and very high skewness resulted in approximately 80% actual reliability for sample sizes of 100 and 87% for sample sizes of 200. These results imply the need for care in evaluating the skewness of populations when the use of mean-per-unit estimation is planned.

Naturally, even if an auditor selects a sample of 200 from a moderately skewed population, it does not mean that the sample size is sufficient. It may, and often does, result in a computed precision interval larger than the auditor is willing to allow. On the other hand, if a sample of 200 is selected from a moderately skewed population and the confidence interval satisfies the auditor's materiality standards, the actual reliability level is likely to be high.

APPROPRIATE USES
OF MEAN-PER-UNIT ESTIMATION

The authors believe that unstratified mean-per-unit is rarely the most desirable statistical method for auditors. When it is practical to use ratio or difference estimation and these are believed to be reliable, one of them should be used, since mean-per-unit is usually more costly. Even when ratio or difference estimation is not reliable, unstratified mean-per-unit may not be the best method. Frequently, dollar unit sampling or stratified mean-per-unit is more reliable, more efficient, and less costly than unstratified mean-per-unit.

The only type of situation where unstratified mean-per-unit is likely to be used is one in which no recorded values exist for a population determined by mean-per-unit estimation, and the point estimate is to be used as the recorded value. An example was shown in this chapter. It is not possible to use difference or ratio estimation in that situation. Even then, it may be less costly to use stratified mean-per-unit estimation if criteria for identifying strata can be determined. More will be said about stratification and when it should be used in the next chapter.

A SECOND APPLICATION OF UNSTRATIFIED MEAN-PER-UNIT ESTIMATION

The following is a second audit situation in which unstratified mean-per-unit was found to be a reliable statistical method and less costly than alternative statistical methods.

Background and Circumstances

ABC Leasing Corporation leases trucks and automobiles, both on a fleet basis (with each vehicle on a separate lease), and individually. For internal purposes, the company follows the practice of computing interest earned on leases by a straight-line method. For statement purposes, it makes an adjustment to accrue additional interest income on a "rule of 78s" basis. This is a very material adjustment, and a major audit objective is to determine that the amount is computed accurately.

The crux of the rule of 78s adjustment is average vehicle lease life, which the company contends is 35 months. Of course, there is no way of directly establishing the lease life of a vehicle on the road, but this can be estimated by observing the time period of terminated leases. An appropriate approach is to determine the average life of all leases terminated during the past two years and compare the average to the 35-month period as a test of its reasonableness. The appropriateness of this method is based on the fact that the number of vehicles leased and the rate of turnover have remained reasonably stable over the past several years.

The approach will be as follows:

1. Select a preliminary sample of 50 leases, using a random number generator.
2. Evaluate the results of the preliminary sample in order to:
   a. Obtain data for computing final sample size
   b. Gain a preliminary indication of the reasonableness of the client's assumption
3. Select and evaluate the final sample to determine whether the company's figure is accurate within ±1.5 months.

The population characteristics are as follows:

- There are 15,000 leases currently active.
- There are 14,000 leases terminated during the two-year period.
- Data concerning the leases terminated are available on an EDP listing consisting of 280 pages with 50 leases (lines) per page. (Since these leases originated at various times over the past several years, the lease identification numbers are not consecutive; also, the listing is in sequence by lessee, not by lease ID number.)
- There are no unusual lives shown on the EDP listing.

Approach to Sample Selection

The preliminary sample of 50 leases is selected from the EDP listing, using a computer time-sharing-based random number generator specifying the following parameters:

1. Numbers are to be five digits, broken into two sets of three digits and two digits respectively.
2. The parameters for set 1 are 1 through 280, representing the number of pages.
3. The parameters for set 2 are 1 through 50, representing the number of items on a page.

The 50 leases are then located on the company's listing, and the vehicle number, lease date, termination date, and lease life are recorded. These data are verified by tracing to appropriate lease files.

Approach to Sample Evaluation

The evaluation method used is unstratified mean-per-unit because only one value is available for each sample unit.

A hypothesis test is made because the objective is to determine that the company's figure of 35 months is not materially misstated.

A low Beta risk of 5 percent is chosen because this is a critical audit area and this is the primary test being performed. However, since sample size can be easily expanded, a high Alpha risk of 40 percent is used. Materiality of 21,000 lease months is used (1.5 months × 14,000 leases), since the objective is to determine whether the company's figure is accurate within ±1.5 months.

Sample Results

The preliminary sample of 50 items yields the following results:

Sum of the audited values (actual lease months per sampled vehicle)	1,620
Sum of the squares of the audited values	58,309.2

From this, the following computations are made:
Sample mean:

$$\bar{x} = \frac{\sum x_j}{n} = \frac{1,620}{50} = 32.4$$

Sample standard deviation:

$$SD^* = \sqrt{\frac{\sum x_j^2 - n(\bar{x})^2}{n - 1}} = \sqrt{\frac{58,309.2 - 50(32.4)^2}{49}}$$

$$SD^* = \sqrt{118.8}$$

$$SD^* = 10.9$$

Acceptable precision interval:

$$API^* = \text{Materiality} \cdot \frac{Z(1 - 2\beta)}{Z(1 - 2\beta) + Z(1 - \alpha)}$$

$$API^* = 21,000 \cdot \frac{Z(1 - .10)}{Z(1 - .10) + Z(1 - .40)}$$

$$API^* = 21,000 \cdot \frac{1.64}{1.64 + .84}$$

$$API^* = 13,887$$

Required sample size:

$$n = \left(\frac{N \cdot Z(1 - 2\beta) \cdot SD^*}{API^*}\right)^2$$

$$n = \left(\frac{14,000 \cdot 1.64 \cdot 10.9}{13,887}\right)^2$$

$$n = 325$$

Based on the calculations above, the auditor selects 275 additional leases and repeats the steps for the entire sample of 325. If the confidence interval obtained falls within the materiality range of 35 ± 1.5 months, the client's figure will be accepted as reasonable for purposes of the interest-earned computation. If the confidence interval falls outside these limits, the 35-month figure must be challenged.

SUGGESTED READINGS AND REFERENCES

HALL, WILLIAM D., "Inventory Determination by Means of Statistical Sampling Where Clients Have Perpetual Records," *Journal of Accountancy*, March 1967, pp. 65–71.

REVIEW QUESTIONS

7-1. Distinguish between mean-per-unit and difference estimation in terms of methodology and when each method should be used.

7-2. Identify the two situations in which unstratified mean-per-unit is most apt to be used. Explain why they are the only two situations where mean-per-unit is a likely estimation.

7-3. Explain why an auditor is more likely to use mean-per-unit estimation for interval estimates than difference or ratio estimation.

7-4. Assume that an auditor decides to use unstratified mean-per-unit estimation to estimate the value of inventory in cooperation with a client. The client has not taken a complete physical inventory because of the high cost of doing it. Why is mean-per-unit preferable to difference and ratio estimation in this situation?

7-5. Answer as true or false the following four questions about question 7-4 and give reasons for each answer.
   a. A hypothesis test is more appropriate than an interval estimation.
   b. It is unnecessary to make an estimate of the point estimate to determine the preliminary sample size.
   c. It is unnecessary to make an estimate of the standard deviation to determine the preliminary sample size.
   d. It is unnecessary to make a materiality decision about the allowable error to determine the preliminary sample size.

7-6. What are the probable consequences of taking a preliminary sample size that is smaller than actually needed in the circumstance described in 7-4? What are the probable consequences of taking a preliminary sample size that is larger than actually needed? Draw a general conclusion from your answers.

7-7. In question 7-4, the population size is 10,000 and the estimated standard deviation is 40. Last year's recorded book value was $2,000,000, and the client believes this year's will be approximately the same. The auditor decides that a material misstatement of inventory would be $50,000 at a 95% confidence level. Calculate the required sample size.

7-8. Assume that a reasonable advance estimate of the standard deviation was impractical in 7-7. How should the auditor determine an appropriate estimate?

7-9. The auditor took a sample of 250 items based on the answer to question 7-7 and calculated the standard deviation as $44. The summation of the inventory values at cost in the sample was $52,500. Calculate the point estimate of the inventory and the precision interval. Explain what caused the sample results to be unacceptable.

7-10. Assume the same results as in question 7-9 except that the standard deviation was $39. Calculate the adjusting entry for inventory if inventory is now stated at last year's ending balance of $2,000,000.

7-11. Under what circumstances is mean-per-unit estimation likely to be more efficient than difference or ratio estimation? What are the implications of your conclusions?

7-12. Under what circumstances is mean-per-unit likely to be a more reliable estimation than difference or ratio estimation? What are the implications of your conclusions?

7-13. The reliability of mean-per-unit estimation is not affected by either the rate of error in a population or the magnitude of the errors. Explain why.

7-14. An auditor wants to use unstratified mean-per-unit estimation if he can be confident that the statistical conclusions are reliable. At what point will the population be so skewed that reliable statistics are unlikely? What factor other than skewness will affect your answer?

7-15. Under what circumstances is it appropriate to use unstratified mean-per-unit estimation?

DISCUSSION QUESTIONS AND PROBLEMS

7-16. An audit partner is developing an office training program to familiarize his professional staff with statistical decision models applicable to the audit of dollar-value balances. He wishes to demonstrate the relationship of sample sizes to population size and variability and the auditor's specifications as to precision and confidence level. The partner prepared the following table to show comparative population characteristics and audit specifications of two populations.

	Characteristics of population 1 relative to population 2		*Audit specifications as to a sample from population 1 relative to a sample from population 2*	
	Size	*Variability*	*Specified precision*	*Specified confidence level*
Case 1	Equal	Equal	Equal	Higher
Case 2	Equal	Larger	Wider	Equal
Case 3	Larger	Equal	Tighter	Lower
Case 4	Smaller	Smaller	Equal	Lower
Case 5	Larger	Equal	Equal	Higher

R EQUIRED :

In items *a* to *e* below, you are to indicate for the specified case from the table above the required sample size to be selected from population 1 relative to the sample from population 2. Your answer choice should be selected from the following responses:

(i) Larger than the required sample size from population 2

(ii) Equal to the required sample size from population 2

(iii) Smaller than the required sample size from population 2

(iv) Indeterminate relative to the required sample size from population 2

a. In case 1, the required sample size from population 1 is

b. In case 2, the required sample size from population 1 is

c. In case 3, the required sample size from population 1 is

d. In case 4, the required sample size from population 1 is

e. In case 5, the required sample size from population 1 is

7-17. The following is a set of sample and related data taken from a population of 1,000 items that have a recorded book value of $498,000. Even though only 20 items are used to simplify the problem, compute the sampling results as indicated.

Sample data

Sample item no.	Audited amount	Book amount	Difference
1	$ 90	$ 100	$ 10
2	120	120	—
3	130	150	20
4	200	180	(20)
5	250	250	—
6	260	260	—
7	315	300	(15)
8	200	310	110
9	390	390	—
10	450	450	—
11	500	525	25
12	610	600	(10)
13	705	695	(10)
14	710	710	—
15	760	760	—
16	820	820	—
17	900	900	—
18	920	1,020	100
19	1,100	1,100	—
20	1,400	1,400	—
	$10,830	$11,040	$210

REQUIRED :

a. Calculate each of the following:

	Mean-per-unit estimation	Difference estimation
1. Sample mean	_____	_____
2. Point estimate of total audited amount	_____	_____
3. Estimated population standard deviation	_____	_____
4. Finite population correction factor	_____	_____
5. Standard error of the total estimate	_____	_____
6. Computed precision interval at a 95% confidence level	_____	_____
7. Confidence interval at a 95% confidence level	_____	_____

b. Why is the computed precision interval so much smaller for difference than for mean-per-unit estimation?

c. Convert the difference estimation confidence interval of the errors into a confidence interval of the audited values. Why is the point estimate different from that calculated under mean-per-unit estimation?

d. Given the results in *a*, explain why an auditor would ever choose difference estimation rather than mean-per-unit, or vice versa.

7-18. An inventory has a book value of $1,829,000. An auditor obtains a random variables sample and projects the result. The point estimate is $1,425,000. The interval estimate is from $1,325,000 to $1,525,000 at the 95% confidence level. Assume that a material error is defined as $110,000.

REQUIRED:

a. Since the auditor doubted the validity of the book value, the auditor suggests that the client adjust the book value. The client asks how much of an adjustment is necessary. How would you respond to the client?

b. Suppose there were no book value and the purpose of the sample were to establish the value for the financial statements. What value would you recommend the client use?

c. The client wants your advice on how to make the adjustment in the perpetual inventory records and in the general ledger. How would you respond?

d. Suppose that the purpose of the sample were to establish a purchase price at which to buy the entire inventory from someone else. What figure would you recommend the client use?

7-19. In each of the following situations, an auditor used the mean-per-unit estimation direct projection method of variables sampling. The method used was inefficient because of the great variability in the data.

(1) The auditor was sampling accounts receivable to determine the total dollar amount of accounts receivable that were more than 120 days past due. For each account selected, the auditor recorded the dollar amount past due. Then the direct projection method was used to determine the average dollar amount past due and to make a projection to the population.

(2) In order to assist the client in adjusting its records from the FIFO to the LIFO inventory method (using the indexing method for dollar-value LIFO), the auditor suggested that the client sample from a run of parts as of the year-end date. For each part selected, the LIFO value was calculated from a point estimate and the computed precision interval of the LIFO value was also calculated.

(3) An auditor was testing the reasonableness of the client's cost of goods sold. A sample of sales invoices was selected, and for each invoice, the cost of sales was recorded. The auditor then used the direct projection method to obtain an average cost of sales and a total for cost of sales.

(4) The auditor wanted to test the reasonableness of the client's accruals for warranties for a company that manufactures air conditioners. The warranty period is one year. After selecting a sample of sales invoices from a twelve-month period, the auditor recorded the warranty expense for each

sample item. Then, using the direct projection method, the auditor calculated the average warranty expense per sales invoice.

REQUIRED:

Indicate how difference or ratio estimation could have been used to increase the sampling efficiency in each situation.

7-20. Mean-per-unit estimation is being used in the audit of inventory to determine confidence intervals for the following independent populations:

Population number	Population size	Sample size	Total sample value	Recorded book value	Computed precision interval	Materiality
1	4,500	500	10,000	100,000	40,000	50,000
2	940	60	30,000	450,000	35,000	50,000
3	800	60	24,000	300,000	25,000	40,000
4	1,500	75	25,500	500,000	55,000	50,000
5	1,000	100	47,500	500,000	70,000	100,000
6	800	125	15,625	100,000	60,000	50,000

REQUIRED:

a. Using a hypothesis test at a 5% Beta risk, identify which of the six populations are acceptable as stated.
b. Using a hypothesis test at a 5% Beta risk, identify which populations can be adjusted to make the population acceptable. Calculate the minimum adjustment.
c. Using an interval estimation test, identify which population will be acceptable at a 95% confidence level after the recorded value is adjusted. Calculate the appropriate adjustment.
d. Compare your conclusions in a and b and the adjustment in b with the conclusion and adjustment in c.

7-21. Owing to data processing problems and a shortage of accounting personnel at the King Cleaning Supply Company, management has neither records of the balances in accounts payable at the balance sheet date nor a listing of accounts payable in total or by vendor. An audit for the current year is essential. Management has asked its auditor to help come up with a balance in accounts payable.

Chuck Nelson, the engagement manager, has decided to use unstratified variables estimation (mean-per-unit, difference, or ratio estimation) to make a statistical estimate of the balance in accounts payable.

The first step Chuck takes is to obtain a complete list from management of every vendor King Cleaning has done business with in the preceding three years, regardless of whether or not a balance was owed at the balance sheet date. Steps are taken to make sure the listing is complete.

REQUIRED:

a. Which of the three statistical methods should Chuck use in this situation? Explain your answer.

b. Explain why it is essential that the list of vendors with a balance owed be complete. What are the audit implications if several vendors with zero balances were unintentionally excluded from the list?

c. Assume the auditor selects a random sample of 200 vendors for confirmation and related audit procedures. Explain how an audited balance of zero should be treated.

d. Explain the steps the auditor will follow to determine the accounts payable to record on the client's statements.

e. Assume that the auditor is confident that all accounts payable at the balance sheet date were paid and recorded in the subsequent-period cash disbursement journal. Many of the subsequent payments were also for subsequent-year transactions. In this situation, why is it likely to be preferable to define the sample unit for accounts payable verification as subsequent-period check numbers rather than vendors on the list?

7-22. Armandy Discount Stores is a large department store catering primarily to low-income people. More than 20,000 different products are kept in inventory and sold by the store. Management has followed the practice of using the retail inventory method in previous years. A team of outside professional counters came into the store after closing and took a complete physical count of units and prices at retail by the use of tape recorders. The information on the tape recorders was then keypunched. The inventory value at retail was determined by means of the computer. Additional calculations were made to convert the retail inventory to cost. Management feels that this entire process is more costly than is desirable, considering the need to have staff members of the CPA firm involved at every step.

A partner in the CPA firm believes it may be possible to use statistical sampling to determine the inventory value at cost. Further discussion with Armandy's management indicates that no perpetual records exist, but all merchandise purchases are computerized at the time of acquisition, including product description and unit cost. The decision is made to use a line item on the product-description computer output list as the sampling unit for mean-per-unit estimation. There are 24,856 lines on the list.

The recorded value of last year's inventory was $1,852,627. The audit partner and management decide they are willing to accept the point estimate as the recorded value if it is within $75,000 of the true value. They do not want more than a 5% risk that it is misstated by more than $75,000. Based on last year's recorded inventory, the standard deviation is estimated as $55.

REQUIRED:

a. Evaluate the use of unstratified mean-per-unit estimation in this situation. What other alternatives should be considered?

b. Evaluate the decision to use line items on the product-description computer output list as the sampling unit. What problems is the auditor likely to encounter?

c. Should interval estimation or hypothesis testing be used in this situation? Explain.

d. Calculate the appropriate sample size, given the information provided to this point.

e. For approximately 10% of the items included in the random sample, there was no actual inventory on hand. How should these items be included in (or excluded from) the statistical results?

f. Assume that a random sample of 1,100 items was selected. The total value of the inventory at historical cost was $87,203. The total of the individual values squared was $9,871,405. Calculate the confidence interval for the population. Is an adjusting entry appropriate at this point? If so, state what the entry should be. If not, what action is necessary?

7-23. Jay Smith, CPA, is doing the audit of accounts receivable of Jones Wholesale Stationery and Office Supplies. There are 820 accounts receivable, totaling $887,500. Total current assets are $1,450,000, and total assets are $2,200,000.

Jay makes no effort to determine the appropriate sample size statistically. Owing to the high expectation of errors in accounts receivable, he decides to select a random sample of 200 accounts receivable for positive confirmation. He plans to evaluate the results statistically, using several different statistical methods.

REQUIRED:

a. Is it acceptable to statistically calculate confidence limits from a random sample without having determined the appropriate sample size with the use of appropriate formulas? Explain. Why should anyone ever use statistical formulas in determining the sample size?

b. Explain how Smith should handle nonresponses to first and second requests for confirmation. What can he do to minimize the likelihood of including a confirmation response value at the wrong amount due if a respondent states that a confirmation is correct when it is actually wrong?

c. Assume that all 200 confirmations were returned by customers or alternate procedures were followed by Smith to determine the audited value of each account. The audited value of the 200 confirmations was $216,512, and the client's recorded value was $237,416. There were 34 errors discovered. An analysis of the 34 errors indicated that 22 were overstatements and 12 were understatements. The size of individual errors appeared closely related to the size of the recorded balance. Calculate the point estimate of the audited value of the population using mean-per-unit, difference, and ratio estimation. Explain the reason for the differences in the three answers.

d. Which of the three methods is likely to result in the smallest computed precision interval at a given confidence level? Which method is likely to result in the largest precision interval? Explain why you answered as you did.

7-24. (AICPA adapted) You desire to evaluate the reasonableness of the book value of the inventory of your client, Draper, Inc. You satisfied yourself earlier as to inventory quantities. During the examination of the pricing and extension of the inventory, the following data were gathered using appropriate unrestricted random sampling without replacement procedures:

Total items in the inventory (N)	12,700
Total items in the sample (n)	400
Total audited value of items in the sample ($\sum x_j$)	$38,400

$$\sum_{j=1}^{400} (x_j - \bar{x})^2 = 312{,}816$$

Formula for estimated population standard deviation:

$$S_{x_j} = \sqrt{\frac{\sum_{j=1}^{j=n} (x_j - \bar{x})^2}{n-1}}$$

Formula for estimated standard error of the mean:

$$SE = \frac{S_{x_j}}{\sqrt{n}}$$

Confidence coefficient of the standard error of the mean at a 95% confidence (reliability) level: ± 1.96.

REQUIRED:

a. Based on the sample results, what is the estimate of the total value of the inventory? Show computations in good form where appropriate.

b. What statistical conclusion can be reached regarding the estimated total inventory value calculated in *a* above at the confidence level of 95%? Present computations in good form where appropriate.

c. Independent of your answers to *a* and *b*, assume that the book value of Draper's inventory is $1,700,000 and, based on the sample results, the estimated total value of the inventory is $1,690,000. The auditor desires a confidence (reliability) level of 95%. Discuss the audit and statistical considerations the auditor must evaluate before deciding whether the sampling results support acceptance of the book value as a fair presentation of Draper's inventory.

7-25. Your client, Motor Leasing Corporation, leases trucks and automobiles, both by fleet (with each vehicle on a separate lease) and individually. For internal purposes, the company computes interest earned on leases on a straight-line basis; for statement purposes, it makes an adjustment to accrue additional interest income by the "rule of 78s," contending that the average vehicle lease life is 48 months. One of your major audit objectives is to determine that the amount is computed accurately.

The most critical part of the "rule of 78's" adjustment is average vehicle lease life, which the client contends is 48 months. There is no way of directly establishing the lease life of a vehicle on the road, but it can be estimated by observing the time period of terminated leases.

You decide to determine the average life of all leases terminated during the past two years, and to compare the average to the 48-month period as a test of its reasonableness. The number of vehicles leased and the rate of turnover have remained reasonably stable over the past several years.

You decide your approach will be as follows:

(1) Select a preliminary sample of 50 leases, using a random number table.
(2) Calculate the confidence limits of the average life of all leases on the basis of the preliminary sample in order to (a) obtain data for computing the final sample size, and (b) gain a preliminary indication of the reasonableness of the client's assumption.
(3) Determine the final sample size and select the sample. Evaluate the final sample to determine whether the client's figure is accurate within ± 2.0 months.

You determine the population characteristics to be as follows:

- There are 20,000 leases currently active.
- There are 18,000 leases terminated during the two-year period.
- Data concerning the leases terminated are available on an EDP listing consisting of 300 pages with 60 leases (lines) per page. The lease identification numbers are not consecutive, and the listing is in sequence by lessee, not by lease ID number.

REQUIRED:

a. Determine and describe how you will identify and select the preliminary sample.
b. Indicate the evaluation method you will use and whether you will make an interval estimate or a hypothesis test. Specify precision and reliability or Alpha and Beta risks and materiality you consider appropriate.
c. Assume you have selected the preliminary sample, reviewed the leases, and summarized the sample data as follows:

Size of preliminary sample	50 leases
Sum of the audited values	2,331 lease-months
Sum of the squares of the audited values (squared before summing)	115,341

(i) Determine the confidence limits of the average life of all leases from the results of the preliminary sample, using the assumptions you made in part b.
(ii) Describe the results of this evaluation in terms of the apparent reasonableness or unreasonableness of the client's assumption of the average lease life.
(iii) Calculate the final sample size, given the results of the preliminary sample results, population facts, audit decisions that were stated in the problem, and judgments you have made.

8

stratified sampling

INTRODUCTION

Stratified sampling is an extension of variables sampling in which all the elements in the total population are divided into two or more subpopulations. Each subpopulation is then independently audited and statistically measured in the manner described for variables estimation. After the results of the individual parts have been completed, they are combined into one overall population estimate in terms of a confidence interval and confidence limits.

The following outline is used for this chapter:

1. Purpose of stratification
2. Calculation of confidence intervals using stratified mean-per-unit estimation
3. Determination of number of strata, stratum boundaries, and sample size
4. Illustration of stratification—difference estimation
5. Efficiency, sample selection and calculation costs, and reliability
6. Appropriate uses of stratified mean-per-unit estimation

PURPOSE OF STRATIFICATION

Stratification is used for two reasons. The first and most common is that stratification often reduces the sample size needed to achieve a desired level of precision and reliability. Population items with similar characteristics are combined into separate strata, thereby resulting in sampling efficiency. The standard deviation of the population of items and the computed precision interval within each stratum are thereby reduced. When the computed precision intervals for each stratum are combined, the total population confidence interval is also reduced. A simple example will show how the standard deviation can be reduced through stratification:

Inventory elements in the population	Book value
1	$ 10
2	1,900
3	1,950
4	14
5	18
6	1,850

An examination of this population indicates that its standard deviation is large because there is a large variation between the smallest and the largest items. In this case, when the population is properly divided into a stratum of large items (elements 2, 3, and 6) and another stratum of small items (elements 1, 4, and 5), the variations in the individual strata are greatly reduced.

Second, the auditor may want a separate estimate of a particular sub-population. For example, management may want information about a population by location for decision purposes, or a separate audit opinion may be desired for one subsidiary in addition to the consolidated statements.

CALCULATION OF CONFIDENCE INTERVALS USING STRATIFIED MEAN-PER-UNIT ESTIMATION

The sequence followed for stratified sampling is as follows:

1. Select the statistical method.
2. Decide on the number of strata.
3. Establish criteria for putting population items into particular strata.
4. Determine the sample size for each stratum.
5. Select the sample items and perform the audit tests.
6. Calculate confidence intervals.

The calculation of confidence intervals is shown at the beginning of the chapter to help the reader understand better what the auditor accomplishes by stratification. Each of the other five aspects of stratification is then discussed. Mean-per-unit is used to illustrate stratification, because it is frequently used in practice.

The selection of sample items and the calculation of confidence limits for stratified mean-per-unit follow the methodology used for unstratified mean-per-unit except that a separate random sample, point estimate, and standard error must be calculated for each stratum. The results of each stratum are then combined into a confidence interval for the entire population.

The example used to illustrate the calculation of statistical results is the same population of inventory used in Chapters 5 through 7 for unstratified difference, ratio, and mean-per-unit estimation. The population has been divided into four strata and a sample size selected from each stratum such that the total equals 130, the sample size used in the previous examples. The data are as follows:

Stratum number	Strata limits	Number per stratum	Total book value per stratum	Sample size per stratum
1	10–1,000	1,200	$ 421,600	20
2	1,001–2,500	900	1,320,400	40
3	2,501–4,000	580	1,653,200	50
4	>4,000	20	204,800	20
		2,700	$3,600,000	130

Random Selection

An independent random sample must be selected for each stratum. The auditor will therefore select 20 items from the population elements in stratum 1, 40 from stratum 2, 50 from stratum 3, and all stratum 4 population elements.

The random selection will be easy if the population elements have been separated by stratum on the inventory listing. More commonly, however, elements from the four strata are intermingled. Random selection can be time-consuming in that situation.

Let us illustrate one way to obtain the independent random samples reasonably efficiently with an example in which there are 45 pages of inventory with 60 lines per page. Random numbers are selected from the random number table on the basis of page and line number, the same way that has been shown for unstratified sampling. However, for stratified sampling, if an element is for a population item that fits into the stratum 1 criterion, use it as a sample item for stratum 1. The same is true for strata 2 and 3. For cxample, if a line item selected has a total value of $912.17, it is identified as a stratum 1 sample item. If a number selected has a recorded book value of over $4,000, discard it, since all numbers for those items are included in the sample. Continue selecting random numbers until sufficient sample items have been selected to meet the sample size requirement of any stratum (20 items for stratum 1). It is likely that stratum 1 sample size requirements will be met first, since a larger portion of population items than sample items are from stratum 1. Keeping in mind that now a sample item that is for a population item falling into either stratum 1 or 4 is a discard, continue selecting until the required number of sample items have been selected for a second stratum. This process is continued until sufficient sample items are selected for all strata.

Perform Audit Tests to Determine the Audit Value

The audit tests are performed identically for stratified and unstratified sampling. The sample results for the first seven of the 20 items from stratum 1 are shown in Figure 8-1. Only the totals for the other three strata are shown.

	Sample item	Recorded value	Audited value	Sample size
Stratum 1	1	$ 217	$ 217	
	9	87	136	
	16	343	343	
	21	890	451	
	30	501	611	
	37	212	212	
	53	216	459	
	etc.			
Totals		$ 7,024	$ 6,505	20
Stratum 2 Totals		$ 61,296	$ 61,084	40
Stratum 3 Totals		$138,105	$137,104	50
Stratum 4 Totals		$204,800	$204,800	20

FIGURE 8-1   Audited results of inventory tests

In the determination of sample audited values, it may happen that the sample book value is in one stratum and the sample audited value in another. In this case, the book value dictates. The stratum that a particular sample item belongs to *must be determined before the random numbers are selected* to avoid bias in the results. The reason is that it is necessary to know the population size for each stratum. It is not possible to determine the population size for a stratum on the basis of audited values unless every population item is audited. Therefore, the stratum to which a sample item is assigned is based on recorded values, not audited values.

Calculate the Point Estimate for each Stratum and the Total

The point estimate for each stratum in mean-per-unit estimation is calculated the same way as for the point estimate of unstratified mean-per-unit estimation. The point estimate of the total population is determined by adding the point estimates of each stratum. The formula and calculations for the example are shown in Figure 8-2.

$$\bar{x}_t = \frac{\sum x_{tj}}{n_t}$$

$$\hat{X}_t = N_t \bar{x}_t \quad \text{or} \quad N_t \cdot \frac{\sum x_{tj}}{n_t}$$

$$\hat{X} = \sum \hat{X}_t = \sum N_t \bar{x}_t$$

where:

$\bar{x}_t$ = mean point estimate of the audited values for a stratum ($\bar{x}_1$ = mean point estimate for stratum 1; $\bar{x}_2$ = mean point estimate for stratum 2)

x_{tj} = an individual item in the sample for a stratum at the audited value (x_{26} = 6th sample item in the 2nd stratum)

n_t = sample size for a stratum

N_t = population size for a stratum

$\hat{X}_t$ = point estimate of the audited value for a stratum

$\hat{X}$ = point estimate of the audited value for all strata combined

Stratum	$\sum x_{tj}$ (Fig. 8-1)	n_t	$\bar{x}_t$	N_t	$\hat{X}_t$
1	$ 6,505	20	$ 325.25	1,200	$ 390,300
2	61,084	40	1,527.10	900	1,374,390
3	137,104	50	2,742,08	580	1,590,406
4	204,800	20	10,240.00	20	204,800
$\hat{X}$					$3,559,896

FIGURE 8-2 Point estimate of the audited value for a stratified sample (mean-per-unit)

The point estimate for the population is $3,559,896 using stratified sampling, compared to $3,652,479 using unstratified mean-per-unit. Neither of these is a better estimate of the actual audited population value. The important thing is the computed precision interval for any given point estimate.

Calculate the Standard Deviation for Each Stratum

The standard deviation is calculated for each stratum in the same manner as for the total population in unstratified mean-per-unit. The formula and calculations for the ongoing example are shown in Figure 8-3.

$$SD_i = \sqrt{\frac{\sum x_{ij}^2 - n(\bar{x}_i)^2}{n_i - 1}}$$

where:

SD_i = standard deviation of a stratum (SD_1 is the standard deviation for stratum 1, etc.)

x_{ij} = an individual item in the sample for a given stratum at the audited value

n_i = sample size for a stratum

$$\bar{x}_i = \frac{\sum x_{ij}}{n_i}$$

	$\sum x_{ij}^2$	$-$	$n(\bar{x}_i)^2$	$\div$	$n_i - 1 =$	$\dfrac{\sum x_{ij}^2 - n(\bar{x}_i)^2}{n-1}$	$\sqrt{\dfrac{\sum x_{ij}^2 - n(\bar{x}_i)^2}{n-1}}$
1	3,786,269	$-$	2,115,751	$\div$	19 =	87,922	296.5
2	102,427,578	$-$	93,281,376	$\div$	39 =	234,518	484.3
3	389,809,100	$-$	375,950,136	$\div$	49 =	282,836	531.8
4[a]							

[a] *Not necessary to calculate. The standard error and computed precision interval equal zero when all population items are audited.*

Note to reader: *Up to this point, the data in this illustration have been completely consistent with the information given in the earlier chapters. Here, however, we have a departure, in the values of* $\sum (\bar{x}_j)^2$, *because it is assumed that all 20 items over $4,000 were sampled. This assumption was not present in the earlier chapters because of unrestricted random sampling. The difference does not adversely affect the statistical aspects being illustrated.*

FIGURE 8-3 Estimated standard deviation of the population audited values (mean-per-unit)

It is unnecessary to calculate the standard deviation for stratum 4, because every sample item has been audited. The only purpose of calculating the standard deviation is to determine the computed precision interval. The computed precision interval is always zero when $n = N$, because of the effect of the finite correction factor $(\sqrt{N - n/N})$.

Now compare the standard deviations for the unstratified and stratified samples for the example being used:

Stratum	Stratified mean-per-unit	Unstratified mean-per-unit (Figure 7-3)	Unstratified difference estimation
1	296.5	758.6	175.9
2	484.3		
3	531.8		
4	*Not calculated*		

The reduction in standard deviation by using stratified rather than unstratified mean-per-unit resulted from grouping similar population items and calculating the standard deviations separately. An even smaller standard deviation for each stratum could have been accomplished in this example with more strata. Note that the smallest standard deviation for any stratum in this example is still larger than for unstratified difference estimation. The use of a larger number of strata would probably have made the standard deviation for some of the strata smaller than for difference estimation.

Compute the Standard Error of Each Stratum

The standard error of a population is the computed precision interval at a confidence coefficient of 1. It is therefore calculated in the same way as the computed precision interval without including the confidence coefficient. The only reason for not including the confidence coefficient at this point is calculation convenience. The confidence coefficient is included in the calculations of the combined computed precision interval for all strata.

The standard error formula is shown in Figure 8-4. The calculations for each stratum are the same as for the overall population in unstratified mean-per-unit.

$$SE_t = \frac{N_t SD_t}{\sqrt{n_t}} \sqrt{\frac{N_t - n_t}{N_t}}$$

where:

SE_t = standard error of the population for a stratum
N_t = population size for a stratum
SD_t = estimated population standard deviation of the audited values for a stratum
n_t = sample size for a stratum

Stratum	N_t	SD_t	n_t	$\frac{N_t SD_t}{\sqrt{n_t}}$	$\sqrt{\frac{N_t - n_t}{N_t}}$	SE_t
1	1,200	296.5	20	79,597	.99	78,801
2	900	484.3	40	68,967	.98	67,588
3	580	531.8	50	43,627	.96	41,882
4[a]						

[a]SE_t equals zero when $n = N$.

FIGURE 8-4 Computed standard error of the population for each stratum (mean-per-unit)

It is easy to also calculate the computed precision interval for any stratum. The standard error for any stratum (SE_i) is multiplied by the confidence coefficient (Z). In stratum 3, the computed precision interval at a confidence level of 90 percent is $68,686 (41,882 × 1.64). This means that there is a 5 percent risk that the point estimate for stratum 3 ($1,590,406) is more than $68,686 larger than the correct total value of the population, and a 5 percent risk that it is at least $68,686 smaller than the correct value. There is no need to calculate the computed precision interval for each stratum when the auditor is interested only in the estimate of the total population.

Calculate the Precision Interval for the Population

Two calculations take place at this point: The standard errors of each stratum are combined, and the confidence coefficient effect on the estimate of the population is included. The calculations are shown in Figure 8-5.

$$CPI = Z\sqrt{\sum SE_i^2}$$

where:

CPI = computed precision interval for the population
Z = confidence coefficient for the confidence level
SE_i = standard error of the population for a stratum

$$CPI = 1.64\sqrt{(78,801)^2 + (67,588)^2 + (41,882)^2 + 0^2}$$
$$CPI = 1.64\sqrt{12,531,837,305}$$
$$CPI = 1.64(111,946) = 183,591$$

FIGURE 8-5 Computed precision interval of the population (mean-per-unit)

The combined standard error of the population ($111,946) is smaller than the sum of the standard errors but larger than the largest standard error for any stratum. This is always the case; it is a reflection of the fact that increasing the population size increases the standard error, but increasing the sample size decreases it.

To illustrate this important concept, assume that the auditor has a population of 1,000 items with a population standard deviation of 5. The auditor samples 25 items. The standard error is 1,000 [(1,000 × 5)/$\sqrt{25}$]. Now assume a population four times as large but proportionately identical to the first population. Assume also that the auditor samples four times as many items (100). The standard error is now 2,000 [(4,000 × 5)/$\sqrt{100}$]. A stratified sample of the four populations, each of which is identical to the first population, yields identical results ($\sqrt{4(1,000)^2}$ = 2,000). This example illustrates two points about stratification:

1. Stratification is simply a weighted average of unstratified sampling. The effect of any changes in sample size, population size, and standard deviation is the same as for unstratified sampling.
2. The worst effect on the precision interval that can ordinarily happen is to have the same size combined CPI as with unstratified sampling. CPI will be smaller for stratified sampling if similar-sized items are kept in separate strata.

Additional insight into stratification is possible by examining the result of the calculations in Figure 8-5. First consider what the effect would be if the standard error for stratum 1 had equaled that of stratum 2. Assume that result was caused by having tested more sample items in stratum 1 but less than 100 percent of stratum 4 (calculations are not shown for the standard error for stratum 4). The change in the combined standard error is shown in Figure 8-6. Note that the combined computed precision interval decreased.

Stratum	Standard error for actual stratification results (*see Figure 8-5*)	Assumed stratification results when Stratum 1 standard error equals Stratum 2	Assumed stratification results when standard error is the same for each stratum
1	78,801	67,588	40,000
2	67,588	67,588	40,000
3	41,882	41,882	40,000
4	0	11,320	40,000
Combined standard error	111,946	104,969	80,000

FIGURE 8-6 Effect of changing the standard error for each stratum

The decrease in total resulted from decreasing the stratum with the largest standard deviation.

Second, consider the effect of having stratified the population and selected sample sizes in a manner that would have resulted in an identical standard error for each stratum. A larger standard error for each of strata 3 and 4 would have resulted, but the standard error for each of strata 1 and 2 would have been smaller. Assuming that the standard deviations of the four strata are still the same as in the original sample, the combined computed precision interval is shown in Figure 8-6.

Finally, consider the effect of increasing the number of strata to ten, but still testing only a sample size of 130 items in total. The strata and sample size for each stratum are determined in such a manner as to minimize the standard error for each stratum and to have an equal standard error for each stratum. Assume the standard error is $11,000 for each stratum. The combined standard error is therefore $34,785 ($\sqrt{10(11,000)^2}$). By the use of ten strata and reduction of the standard error to $11,000 per stratum, the combined standard error for the example is less than it was for either difference or ratio estimation (see Chapters 5 and 6).

From the discussion above, three additional conclusions about stratification are now evident:

1. The combined standard error can be reduced most easily by reducing the standard error of the stratum with the largest standard error.
2. For any given number of strata, the combined standard error will be reduced by having the same size standard error for each stratum.
3. The combined standard error can usually be decreased for a given sample size by increasing the number of strata. There is, however, a limit to the number of strata that can be used to reduce the combined standard error.

Compute the Confidence Interval and Confidence Limits

There is no difference between calculating confidence intervals and limits for stratified and for unstratified mean-per-unit. The formula and calculations are shown in Figure 8-7.

$$CI = \hat{X} \pm CPI$$
$$UCL = \hat{X} + CPI$$
$$LCL = \hat{X} - CPI$$

where:

CI = computed confidence interval
$\hat{X}$ = point estimate of the population
CPI = computed precision interval
UCL = upper confidence limit
LCL = lower confidence limit

$$CI = 3,559,896 \pm 183,591$$
$$UCL = 3,559,896 + 183,591 = 3,743,487$$
$$LCL = 3,559,896 - 183,591 = 3,376,305$$

FIGURE 8-7 90% confidence interval and limits of the population (mean-per-unit)

It is also possible to calculate the confidence interval for a given stratum. The auditor may want to reach a separate audit opinion for a particular stratum—for example, when one stratum is the entire population of an account, such as the inventory of a subsidiary that requires a separate opinion.

The confidence interval (90 percent reliability) for stratum 2 is shown below. The information for the calculation is taken from Figures 8-2 and 8-4.

$$CI_2 = \hat{X}_2 \pm Z\,SE_2$$
$$CI_2 = 1{,}374{,}390 \pm (1.64)(67{,}588)$$
$$CI_2 = 1{,}374{,}390 \pm 110{,}844$$

The Audit Decision

The decision rule for a hypothesis test is the same for stratified as for unstratified mean-per-unit. If the two-sided confidence interval is completely within the book value plus and minus the amount considered material, accept the hypothesis that the book value is not misstated by a material amount. Otherwise, reject that hypothesis.

The decision rule is applied to the ongoing example, utilizing a Beta risk of 10 percent (that is, an 80 percent confidence interval), as follows:

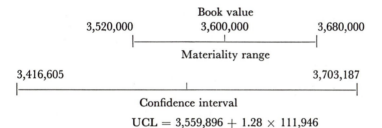

Book value

| 3,520,000 | 3,600,000 | 3,680,000 |

Materiality range

3,416,605   3,703,187

Confidence interval

$$\text{UCL} = 3{,}559{,}896 + 1.28 \times 111{,}946$$
$$\text{LCL} = 3{,}559{,}896 - 1.28 \times 111{,}946$$

The stratified mean-per-unit results in narrower confidence limits than does the unstratified example, but both sides of the confidence interval are outside the materiality limits. Therefore, the hypothesis that the book value is not misstated by a material amount must be rejected.

Assume that the statistical results had yielded a standard error of $34,785 as illustrated for the use of ten strata (a standard error of $11,000 per stratum and a point estimate the same as the four-strata example). The hypothesis would still have been rejected. This is shown as follows:

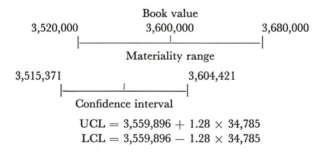

Book value

| 3,520,000 | 3,600,000 | 3,680,000 |

Materiality range

3,515,371   3,604,421

Confidence interval

$$\text{UCL} = 3{,}559{,}896 + 1.28 \times 34{,}785$$
$$\text{LCL} = 3{,}559{,}896 - 1.28 \times 34{,}785$$

The Alpha risk associated with this conclusion is 30 percent (computation is not shown).

DETERMINING THE NUMBER OF STRATA, STRATUM BOUNDARIES, TOTAL SAMPLE SIZE, AND SAMPLE SIZE FOR EACH STRATUM

These four audit decisions are discussed in the order listed, but the reader should be aware of their interrelationship. For example, the number of strata affects the stratum boundaries, total sample size, and sample size for each stratum. At the same time, the standard deviation of each stratum, which cannot be determined until after the boundaries have been selected, is affected by the number of strata. When the data are in computer-readable form, the four decisions can be made most efficiently by the use of computer programs. Less-than-optimal decisions are likely when calculations are made manually.

Number of Strata

Research about stratification indicates that the combined population standard error is ordinarily not reduced significantly by increasing the number of strata beyond 20. There are usually significant reductions in sample size for up to five strata. Therefore, between five and ten strata are common for most accounting populations when a computer is not available. It is not unusual to use up to 20 strata when the client's data is in machine-readable form and a computer is available for making calculations.

A major factor in deciding the number of strata is the cost of separating the population items into strata and random selection. When a population is set up in a manner that makes stratification easy, it would generally be desirable to have a reasonably large number of strata—for example, where the client has prepared a listing of recorded values of populations in descending order of size. A second consideration affecting the number of strata is the range of the recorded values of population elements. The larger the range, the greater the need for more strata.

Stratum Boundaries

Three methods of identifying the boundary for each stratum will be discussed. Regardless of the method, every population element must be associated with only one stratum after the boundaries are set. The boundaries are based on the recorded value rather than the audited value. A sample item is therefore associated with a stratum on the basis of the recorded value regardless of the audited value.

Judgmentally Selected Boundaries. Under this method, the auditor selects boundaries by reviewing the population and arbitrarily deciding on the boundary locations in any manner that seems appropriate. The four stratum boundaries for the inventory example used in the early part of the chapter were judgmentally selected. This method is acceptable, but it often results in larger sample sizes than the other two alternatives because the standard error for different strata is likely to vary considerably.

Equal-Recorded-Value Boundaries. First, the largest recorded values in any stratum that the auditor is going to audit 100 percent are eliminated. The remaining recorded book value is divided by the number of strata (excluding the one audited 100 percent). The result is the total recorded dollar value of each stratum. The boundaries are then set so that each stratum has a cutoff to include approximately that total recorded value. A frequency distribution of population values is desirable for allocation by this method, but reasonable approximations are still possible without such a frequency distribution.

For example, using the inventory example from the early part of the chapter, the approximate book value indicated in each of the three strata would be $1,131,733 [($3,600,000 − 204,800) ÷ 3]. Compared to the actual boundaries used in the example, setting boundary limits in this manner would have increased the number of population items in stratum 1 and decreased the number in strata 2 and 3.

Equal-Cumulative-Square-Root-of-Frequency Boundaries. A more complicated method, requiring a frequency distribution of recorded values, usually results in more efficient stratification. First, the population items to be audited 100 percent are eliminated. The remaining items are set up in a frequency distribution such as in the following example:

Recorded amount	Width of interval	Number of accounts	Width times number of accounts	Square root of width times number of accounts	Cumulative square root
$0–$49.99	50	4,620	231,000	481	481
$50–$199.99	150	3,610	541,500	736	1,217
$200–$499.99	300	2,480	744,000	863	2,080
$500–$999.99	500	1,274	637,000	798	2,878
$1,000–$2,999.99	2,000	567	1,134,000	1,065	3,943
$3,000–$9,999.99	7,000	167	1,169,000	1,081	5,024
$10,000–$25,000.00	15,000	38	To be audited 100%		

The total cumulative square root is now divided by the number of strata not audited 100 percent to arrive at a planned square root per stratum. Assuming four strata, with the widest interval audited 100 percent, the planned square root interval is 1,675 and the desired boundaries are 1,675, 3,350, and 5,024. The cumulative square roots coming closest to those numbers are 2,080, 2,878, and 5,024. The boundaries for the four strata are therefore:

Stratum	Recorded value	Frequency
1	$0– $499.99	10,710
2	$500– $999.99	1,274
3	$1,000– $9,999.99	734
4	$10,000–$25,000.00	38

This method of determining stratum boundaries is intended to keep the population size multiplied by the standard deviation approximately the same for each stratum. It will be shown shortly that doing this will reduce the required sample size.

It would be difficult to manually perform the calculations required for setting boundaries by the use of the equal cumulative square root of frequency. When a computer is used to make the calculations, the method is common.

Determining Sample Size

The auditor must have certain information to determine the appropriate sample size for stratified mean-per-unit for a hypothesis test.

1. Total allowable error. This concept is identical to unstratified mean-per-unit. In a given set of circumstances, the allowable error in the population would be the same for stratified or unstratified sampling.
2. Beta risk. Beta risk is the same for stratified and unstratified methods.
3. Alpha risk. Alpha risk is the same for stratified and unstratified sampling.
4. Population size for each stratum.
5. Population standard deviation for each stratum.
6. The method of allocating the sample to the strata. There are two methods that will be discussed shortly—proportional to recorded amounts, and optimum allocation. A different sample-size formula must be used for each method.

The formula and an example of determining the sample size for optimum allocation are shown in Figure 8-8. The inventory example, used earlier in this chapter and in chapters 5 through 7, is continued to illustrate the formula's use. The allowable error is set at $80,000, Beta risk 10 percent, Alpha risk 40 percent, and the estimated population error $12,000. The population size is 2,700. These amounts are the same as were used with this example previously.

The four strata and their boundaries identified at the beginning of the chapter are used for determining the sample. The standard deviations calculated in Figure 8-3 are used with straight upward rounding. A standard

$$\text{API*} = (\text{AE} - \text{E*})\frac{Z(1 - 2\beta)}{Z(1 - 2\beta) + Z(1 - \alpha)}$$

$$n = \frac{[Z(1 - 2\beta)]^2(\sum N_i \text{SD}_i^*)^2}{(\text{API*})^2 + [Z(1 - 2\beta)]^2 \sum N_i \, \text{SD}_i^{*2}}$$

where:

API* = allowable precision interval including Alpha and Beta risk

AE = acceptable error in the population

E* = estimated point estimate of the population error

$Z(1 - 2\beta)$ = confidence coefficient for $1.0 - $ two times Beta risk

$Z(1 - \alpha)$ = confidence coefficient for $1.0 - $ Alpha risk

n = sample size

N_i = population size for a stratum

SD_i^* = estimated standard deviation for a stratum

$$\text{API*} = (80,000 \quad 12,000) \times \frac{1.28}{1.28 + .84} = 41,100$$

$$n = \frac{(1.28)^2[(1200 \times 300) + (900 \times 485) + (580 \times 550) + (20 \times 750)]^2}{(41,100)^2 + (1.28)^2[(1200 \times 300^2) + (900 \times 485^2) + (580 \times 550^2) + (20 \times 750^2)]}$$

$$n = 831$$

Note: this formula for sample size includes adjustment for the finite correction factor within each stratum.

FIGURE 8-8 Sample size determination for stratified sampling—optimum allocation

deviation is also estimated for stratum 4 (750), as previously discussed. The stratification design is not likely to result in as small a sample size as would be possible with more strata and more sophisticated setting of boundaries.

The sample size of 831 items is considerably larger than the sample of 130 required for difference estimation as shown in Chapter 5. This is caused by the relatively large standard deviation of each stratum compared to the combined standard deviation of the total population for difference estimation. Stratum 1 had the smallest estimated standard deviation (300), whereas the overall standard deviation for the same population using difference estimation was 135. The required sample size of 831 items is also affected by the small number of strata used and the judgmentally selected boundaries. If more strata were being used and the stratum boundaries had been selected by one of the two nonjudgmental methods, the required sample size would have been considerably smaller.

On the other hand, the sample size using stratified mean-per-unit is considerably smaller than if unstratified mean-per-unit had been used. The conclusion reached in Chapter 7 using unstratified mean-per-unit with the previous example was that the sample size would have been extremely large.

Allocation of the Sample to Strata

The final step is to determine how the total sample size is to be allocated to each stratum. The allocation can be done on an arbitrary basis, as was illustrated at the beginning of the chapter. The disadvantage of arbitrary allocation is that it is likely to result in a larger combined computed precision interval than would occur if some kind of formula were used. Keep in mind that the objective of deciding on the number of strata and the boundary limits is to minimize the standard deviation as a means of minimizing the computed precision interval.

Two common methods of allocating are *allocation in proportion to recorded value* and the *Neyman allocation* method. In both these methods, any stratum tested on a 100 percent basis can be ignored. Allocation in proportion to recorded value is the simpler of the two methods and is done in the manner implied by its name. The allocation is shown in Figure 8-9.

$$n_i = \frac{Y_i n}{Y}$$

where:

n_i = sample size for a stratum where the total sample size is known
Y_i = recorded value of a stratum
n = total sample size
Y = recorded value of the total population = $\sum Y_i$

Stratum	Recorded values	Percent	Allocation of total sample
1	$ 421,600	12.4%	101
2	1,320,400	38.9	315
3	1,653,200	48.7	395
4[a]	N/A	N/A	20
	$3,395,200	100.0%	831

[a]*Initially, the total sample was 20 for stratum 4. Since the population size is only 20, that sample size was used, and the percent and allocation were recalculated.*

FIGURE 8-9 Allocation of a sample to strata in proportion to the recorded-value method

The Neyman method allocates the total sample in proportion to the product of the number of population items per stratum times the standard deviation of the stratum. The allocation is shown in Figure 8-10.

These methods for allocation of sample sizes to strata closely parallel the three methods for determination of stratum boundaries. The relationship between each method for determining stratum boundaries and allocation of the sample size to strata is illustrated in Figure 8-11.

$$n_i = \frac{N_i \mathrm{SD}_i n}{\sum N_i \mathrm{SD}_i}$$

where:

n_i = sample size for a stratum where the total sample size is known
N_i = population size for a stratum
SD_i = standard deviation for a stratum
n = total sample size

Stratum	Population size	Estimated standard deviation	Population size × standard deviation	Percent	Sample size
1	1,200	300	360,000	32.3	262
2	900	485	436,500	39.1	317
3	580	550	319,000	28.6	232
4	N/A	N/A	N/A	N/A	20
	2,680		1,115,500	100.0	831

FIGURE 8-10 Allocation of a sample to strata, Neyman method

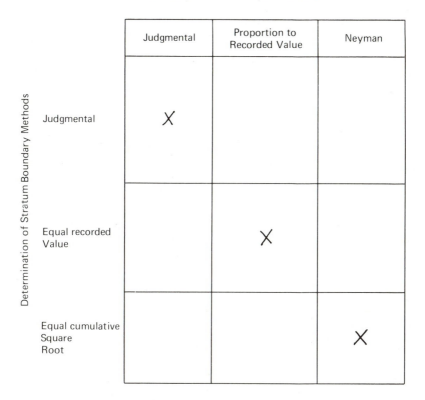

FIGURE 8-11 Relationships between methods of determining stratum boundaries and allocation of sample size to strata

It would, for example, be inefficient to determine stratum boundaries judgmentally and then allocate by the Neyman method. The sample size would probably end up being larger than necessary. Similarly, if the boundaries were determined by the equal cumulative square root method and the sample was allocated to individual strata judgmentally, there is a high likelihood of ending up with confidence limits that are rejected by the decision rule.

The increased cost of using the progressively more complex method of determining stratum boundaries and allocating the sample to strata must be compared to the cost reductions from reducing the sample size.

Summary

A list of the steps followed in a typical use of stratified mean-per-unit estimation is now provided as a summary. It may be useful to compare the steps to the ones followed for the major illustration used for difference estimation, starting on page 146.

Step 1	Decide on the objective of the test.
Step 2	Decide on the net total error that would be considered material for the audit test.
Step 3	Decide on the acceptable Beta risk.
Step 4	Decide on the acceptable Alpha risk.
Step 5	Decide on the sampling unit.
Step 6	Decide on the number of strata (may be done in conjunction with steps 7–9).
Step 7	Decide on the boundaries for each stratum (may be done in conjunction with steps 6, 8, and 9).
Step 8	Estimate the standard deviation for each stratum (may be done in conjunction with steps 6, 7, and 9).
Step 9	Estimate the total population error and the population size per stratum (may be done in conjunction with steps 6–8).
Step 10	Calculate the acceptable precision interval, considering both the Alpha and Beta risks.
Step 11	Calculate the required total sample size.
Step 12	Allocate the total sample among the strata.
Step 13	Select a random sample from each stratum and perform the audit tests.
Step 14	Calculate the point estimate for each stratum and the combined point estimate.
Step 15	Calculate the estimated standard deviation for each stratum, except any stratum for which all population items were tested.
Step 16	Calculate the standard error for each stratum.
Step 17	Calculate the precision interval for all strata combined, at a two-sided confidence level equal to $1 - 2\beta$.
Step 18	Calculate the confidence limits.
Step 19	Decide on the acceptability of the population.

EFFICIENCY, SAMPLE SELECTION AND CALCULATION COSTS, AND RELIABILITY

Efficiency

Stratified mean-per-unit is a highly efficient statistical method if a reasonably large number of strata are used, the boundaries are set by the use of the equal cumulative square root frequency method, and the allocation of sample size is done by the Neyman method. The only time all three of these approaches to stratification are likely to be followed is when the client's data are in machine-readable form and the auditor has a computer available to make the calculations. Stratified mean-per-unit will always be more efficient than unstratified mean-per-unit in these circumstances. It is likely to be somewhat less efficient than difference or ratio estimation except when there are a great many errors of reasonably large magnitude.

When computer-aided calculations are not available, the efficiency of mean-per-unit stratification is likely to drop considerably for most populations. It is still apt to be considered more efficient than unstratified mean-per-unit, except when the population is highly homogeneous. Stratified mean-per-unit is likely to be less efficient than difference or ratio estimation in most audit situations.

Sample Selection and Calculation Costs

The cost of determining the number of strata, stratum boundaries, sample size, and sample allocation, and the cost of random selection and calculation are not a significant consideration when a computer is used in all facets of the statistical methods. Costs become significant when these functions are performed manually. Not only is the use of these methods costly, but the risk of making an arithmetic error is usually high.

The costs of manual calculation are not so high that stratified sampling should be ignored except when a computer is used. The calculation costs are just one consideration, along with efficiency and reliability, in selecting the most desirable statistical method.

Reliability

Stratified mean-per-unit estimation can usually be considered a highly reliable statistical method. When a large number of strata, such as 20, are used in an efficient boundary and sample allocation method, the statistical results will probably be reliable. Again, this high level of reliability is most likely when a computer is used.

The Neter and Loebbecke research on the reliability of statistical estimators showed excellent reliability when 15 to 20 strata were used and the sample sizes were anywhere from 100 to 200. No statistical method tested resulted in a higher level of reliability than stratified mean-per-unit. This research did not consider the effect of using a small number of strata and arbitrary strata design. Based on the relatively high reliability of unstratified mean-per-unit, it seems likely that arbitrary-strata-designed mean-per-unit is reliable.

APPROPRIATE USES
OF STRATIFIED MEAN-PER-UNIT

Based upon the discussions in this chapter and the results of the Neter and Loebbecke research, the following conclusions are reached:

1. Stratified mean-per-unit is one of the most useful of all statistical methods when the auditor has a computer at his disposal and the client's data are in machine-readable form. The estimator is likely to be highly reliable when a large number of strata are properly used. The calculation and selection costs are not a major consideration. Reasonable efficiency of the estimator is also likely.

2. Unstratified difference and ratio estimation will be more efficient in many circumstances, even when a computer is used. The advantage of stratified mean-per-unit tends to be its reliability. Whenever the auditor is concerned about the reliability of ratio or difference estimation, stratified mean-per-unit is a likely alternative.

3. The desirability of stratified mean-per-unit decreases considerably when a computer cannot be used to aid in strata design and calculation. The reliability of the estimator is still apt to be higher. The efficiency is apt to be lower than in ratio and difference estimation, but high relative to unstratified mean-per-unit. Calculation and selection costs will probably be high.

4. The auditor who decides to use mean-per-unit estimation is almost certain to use stratified rather than unstratified. The only exception, which is rare, will occur when the population is highly homogeneous. Stratified mean-per-unit, when a computer is not available, is most apt to be used when difference and ratio estimation are considered unreliable estimators, or when recorded values of individual population items are not available.

5. When a computer is available and is doing the calculation and random selection, there is usually little to be gained by having more than 15 strata. Neither efficiency nor reliability tends to increase.

STRATIFIED DIFFERENCE AND
RATIO ESTIMATION

The requirements for using stratified difference and ratio estimation closely parallel those for stratified mean-per-unit. It is still necessary to decide on the number of strata, stratum boundaries, total sample size, and sample size for each stratum. For simplicity, only stratified difference estimation will be discussed here.

The calculations of required sample size are the same for stratified difference and mean-per-unit estimation, except for the estimated standard deviation. The mean-per-unit sample size is based on the estimated standard deviation of the audited values for each stratum. The sample size for difference estimation is based on the estimated standard deviation of the errors in each stratum. The sample size determination formulas and the allocation of the sample to strata for difference estimation are the same as those shown in Figures 8-8, 8-9, and 8-10.

Except when exceptionally large errors are expected, the standard deviation for a given stratum will be smaller for difference than for mean-per-unit estimation. Smaller sample sizes are therefore ordinarily needed for difference than for mean-per-unit estimation.

The calculations of the confidence limits for difference estimation also follow the same concept as for mean-per-unit estimation. First, the point estimate and the standard error are calculated independently for each stratum, using difference-estimation statistics. The point estimate is calculated the same as shown in Figures 5-1 and 5-2. The standard deviation is calculated for each stratum the same as shown in Figure 5-3. The standard error is calculated for each stratum as shown in Figure 5-4 except that the confidence coefficient (Z) is excluded from the formula. The combined error $(\hat{E})$ for all strata is calculated in the same manner as for stratified mean-per-unit except for the substitution of the point estimate of the error $(\bar{e}_i, \hat{E}_i, \text{ or } \hat{E})$ for the point estimate of the audit values $(\bar{x}_i, \hat{X}_i, \text{ or } \hat{X})$. The formula for mean-per-unit is shown in Figure 8-2.

The total population computed precision interval for difference estimation is calculated with the same formula as for mean-per-unit. The formula is shown in Figure 8-5. The standard errors in this case refer to the ones calculated from the errors instead of the audited values. The confidence interval and confidence limits for difference estimation also parallel those for mean-per-unit as shown in Figure 8-7.

Stratified difference estimation results in a smaller total sample size than unstratified difference estimation only when the auditor can predict which segments of a population have more errors or larger errors than other segments. If error frequency and magnitude occur randomly in all segments of the population, the expected standard deviation for a given segment is the same as for all other segments and the total population. Therefore, no sample size reductions result from stratification.

Frequently, auditors can make reasonable predictions of error frequency and magnitude. For example, larger errors are often expected in larger accounts receivable balances than in smaller ones. Similarly, more errors are frequently expected in accounts receivable that have been outstanding for more than 120 days than in current accounts. Stratification can provide additional efficiency and reliability when error frequency and magnitude are predictable.

The number of strata and stratum boundaries must be decided before the audit tests are performed. These two decisions should be based on the expected frequency and magnitude of errors in different segments of the population. The objective is to stratify in such a way that errors of similar size are in the same stratum. If no reasonable prediction is possible, or if there is no special interest in a particular subpopulation, stratified difference estimation should not be used. In the example that follows, the auditor has attempted to differentiate as to the expected frequency and magnitude of errors:

Stratum	
1	All accounts with a recorded debit balance exceeding $10,000 where a part of any balance has been outstanding more than 90 days
2	All accounts with a recorded debit balance exceeding $10,000 not included in stratum 1
3	All accounts with a recorded debit balance between $2,000 and $10,000 where a part of any balance has been outstanding more than 90 days
4	All accounts with a recorded debit balance between $2,000 and $10,000 not included in stratum 3
5	All accounts with a recorded debit balance less than $2,000
6	All credit balances

Efficiency

As stated earlier, stratified difference estimation results in smaller sample sizes for a given confidence level than unstratified only when the auditor can predict which segments of a population are likely to have a higher frequency of errors or larger errors than other segments. In most audits, there is an expectation of larger errors in accounts with large recorded balances than in those with small recorded balances. There is typically an expectation of a higher frequency of errors in accounts in which there is a high volume of transactions, the amounts have been there for a long time, there is a dispute about the amount, or the transaction was complex. To the extent the auditor can identify and separate segments that have these characteristics, there are efficiency benefits from stratification.

Sample Selection and Calculation Costs

The same conclusions about the additional costs of designing strata, random selection, and making calculations are appropriate for stratified compared to unstratified difference estimation as were discussed for mean-per-unit. The additional costs are not a significant consideration when a computer is available, but they may be for manual calculations.

Stratification without the availability of a computer is not likely to be as serious a problem with difference estimation as with mean-per-unit. There will usually be only a few strata used for difference estimation; therefore, the calculations are not as significant. Still, the calculation costs are greater than for unstratified.

Reliability

Stratified difference estimation will result in a more reliable estimate than unstratified difference estimation when the auditor can predict which segments of population are likely to have a higher frequency of errors or larger errors than other segments. This conclusion about improving reliability by stratification is the same as for improving efficiency.

The study of the reliability of unstratified difference estimation for selected populations by Neter and Loebbecke did not indicate significant improved reliability when stratification was used for difference estimation. Figure 8-12 shows the reliability for different population conditions when stratified or unstratified difference estimation is used.

An improvement in reliability is relevant only in those situations where the actual reliability is reasonably high, such as 85 percent or more. For sample sizes of 100 and 200, each with 15 strata, there was no trend of consistent improvement of reliability through stratification for difference estimation.

Study Pop.	Error rate	Size of errors	Direction of errors	Skewness of book value	Sample size = 100		Sample size = 200	
					Unstratified difference estimation	15 strata difference estimation	Unstratified difference estimation	15 strata difference estimation
1	1%	small	both	very high	37.3	55.2	53.0	81.7
2	1	large	both	moderate	41.8	43.0	54.5	65.2
3	1	moderate	over	high	36.8	14.8	57.0	29.3
4	1	large	over	moderate	30.0	39.7	47.0	60.2
9	10	small	both	very high	94.0	92.3	93.5	94.7
10	10	large	both	moderate	97.2	97.2	97.0	98.3
11	10	moderate	over	high	80.3	67.3	87.7	81.2
12	10	large	over	moderate	62.0	86.2	70.7	91.7
13	30	small	both	very high	96.3	95.3	93.7	92.7
14	30	large	both	moderate	95.5	95.5	96.0	93.8
15	30	moderate	over	high	90.8	86.8	92.2	92.8
16	30	large	over	moderate	74.8	95.2	87.5	95.0

FIGURE 8-12 Comparison of actual to nominal 95.4% confidence coefficient under various circumstances for stratified and unstratified difference estimation

When a small number of carefully selected strata are used, the Neter and Loebbecke research results may not be applicable. For example, in the illustration where six strata are used for confirming accounts receivable, the reliability of the estimator is likely to be improved by stratification, assuming there is a 10 percent or more rate of error in the population.

Appropriate Use of Stratified Difference and Ratio Estimation

Based upon the discussion in this chapter and the results of the Neter and Loebbecke research, the following conclusions are reached regarding the use of stratified difference or ratio estimation:

1. Stratification will result in improved efficiency only in those cases where it is possible to predict which segment of a population will have a higher error rate or magnitude than other segments.

2. Ordinarily, the efficiency and reliability of difference and ratio estimation are improved when judgmentally selected boundaries are used. The objective in selecting the number of strata and stratum boundaries is to keep expected errors of similar size in the same stratum. Judgment is required in predicting which population items will be in error.

3. Stratified difference or ratio estimation should be used only when the auditor expects a large percentage of the population items to be in error *in each stratum*. Unreliable results are likely otherwise. Arbitrarily, the authors recommend the use of stratified difference or ratio estimation only if there are at least ten errors in each stratum. This rule does not apply to any stratum where all population items are audited.

4. Difference or ratio estimation is more likely to be used when the auditor cannot practically use stratified mean-per-unit owing to the lack of computer availability.

5. The decision to use stratified ratio compared to stratified difference estimation should be based on the auditor's expectation of the relationship between individual errors and the related recorded balance. The same conclusions hold that were discussed in Chapter 6.

POST-STRATIFICATION

Assume that an auditor is using unstratified difference estimation and has already calculated the confidence limits for an audit test. Given the allowable error, the decision results in a population that is unacceptable. The auditor analyzes the errors and concludes that an identifiable portion of the population has larger errors than the rest of the population. Is it acceptable to stratify the population at this point and recalculate the confidence limits using stratified difference estimation? The answer is yes, as long as all the requirements for stratification are met. For example, stratum boundaries must be clearly defined, the population size for each stratum must be determined, and, most important, the sample items associated with a given stratum must be determined on the basis of recorded rather than audited values. When this is done, it is called post-stratification, and this technique can be similarly applied to other variables sampling estimators.

COMBINING CONFIDENCE LIMITS
FOR DIFFERENT AUDIT TESTS

The same methodology is followed in combining two or more statistical estimates from different audit tests as was used for combining the point estimates and standard errors of individual strata. An example is used to illustrate the concept.

Assume variables sampling was used for the following three tests:

Audit area	Statistical method used	Confidence interval at a 95% confidence level
Accounts receivable	Stratified difference estimation	15,000 ± 26,000
Inventory	Unstratified ratio estimation	−8,000 ± 22,000
Accounts payable	Stratified mean-per-unit	360,000 ± 41,000

The accounts receivable and inventory can be combined using the following formula, which is essentially the same one used for combining strata:

$$\hat{E} = \sum \hat{E}_i$$
$$\text{CCPI} = \sqrt{\sum \text{CPI}_i^2}$$

where:

$\hat{E}$ = combined point estimate of the errors
$\hat{E}_i$ = point estimate of the errors in a given audit test
CCPI = combined computed precision interval
CPI_i = computed precision interval in a given audit test

The combined confidence interval is as follows:

$$\hat{E} = 15,000 - 8,000 = \$7,000$$
$$\text{CCPI} = \sqrt{(26,000)^2 + (22,000)^2} = \$34,060$$

The confidence interval for the combined total of receivables and inventory is therefore $7,000 ± $34,060.

It is also possible to combine accounts payable in the same manner with a minimum change in the way mean-per-unit is stated. First, a point estimate of the error for accounts payable is needed. Assume the recorded value for accounts payable is $375,000. The estimated error is $15,000 (375,000 less 360,000).

The confidence interval can now be calculated in the same manner as previously shown. The point estimate of the net asset error in the accounts receivable, inventory, and accounts payable is −8,000 (7,000 − 15,000; an overstatement of a liability is treated as an understatement of an asset), and the combined computed precision interval is $53,300.

Use of this method requires that all confidence intervals being combined use the same confidence level. Where this is not the case, the confidence intervals will have to be recalculated on the same basis before the above formula is applied.

SUGGESTED READINGS AND REFERENCES

COCHRAN, WILLIAM G., *Sampling Techniques*, 2nd ed. New York: John Wiley, 1963.

REVIEW QUESTIONS

8-1. Define *stratified sampling*.

8-2. What are the purposes of stratification?

8-3. Explain why stratification with three or four strata is more likely to be used for mean-per-unit estimation than for difference or ratio estimation.

8-4. Explain how the point estimate for the total population is calculated using stratified sampling. Calculate the point estimates for mean-per-unit, difference, and ratio estimation from the following information:

Stratum	Population size	Sample size	Recorded total population value	Recorded total sample value	Audited total sample value
1	400	50	1,000,000	130,000	128,000
2	600	100	500,000	85,000	84,000

8-5. Explain how the standard deviation is calculated when stratified mean-per-unit sampling is used. What information is needed before the calculation can be made?

8-6. Explain why the standard error rather than the computed precision interval is calculated for each stratum when stratified sampling is used. Would the same combined computed precision interval result if the computed precision interval were calculated for each stratum? Explain.

8-7. Calculate the combined standard error of the population if the standard deviation in question 8-4 is 500 in stratum 1 and 300 in stratum 2. (Ignore the finite correction factor.)

8-8. Explain in what ways the decision-rule graph used in Chapter 7 to evaluate whether a population is materially misstated is similar to and different from the appropriate graph for stratified mean-per-unit estimation. Assuming a total allowable error of $60,000, a Beta risk of 5%, and an Alpha risk of 100% for the population used in questions 8-4 and 8-7, prepare the decision-rule graph. Prepare the minimum adjusting entry required to make the population fairly stated.

8-9. What are the two most important criteria in deciding on the appropriate number of strata that should be used in an audit situation?

8-10. Explain why recorded values are ordinarily used as the basis for determining the number of strata and stratum boundaries, when stratification on the basis of audited values would ordinarily result in a smaller combined computed precision interval.

8-11. What basis other than recorded values could be used to determine stratum boundaries? Under what circumstances should a basis other than recorded values be used?

8-12. Explain the difference in methodology of each of the following three methods of determining stratum boundaries: judgmental, equal recorded value, and equal cumulative square root of frequency. Under which circumstances should each method be used?

8-13. What is the difference between the formulas for sample size determination for stratified mean-per-unit and for stratified difference estimation?

8-14. Determine the required sample size using stratified mean-per-unit estimation for the population in questions 8-4, 8-7, and 8-8.

8-15. Assume a calculated sample size of 200 for question 8-14. Allocate this sample size to the two strata by the two methods described in the chapter.

8-16. Under what circumstances should stratified mean-per-unit be considered a more desirable alternative than ratio and difference estimation?

8-17. What are the most appropriate circumstances in which to use stratified mean-per-unit estimation?

8-18. What are the most appropriate circumstances in which to use stratified difference or ratio estimation?

8-19. Define what is meant by post-stratification. When is it appropriate to post-stratify?

8-20. Explain the methodology for combining two or more statistical estimates from different audit tests. Calculate the combined confidence limits for two asset accounts whose separate confidence intervals at a 95% confidence level are:

Account 1: 20,000 ± 16,000
Account 2: (14,000) ± 12,000

DISCUSSION QUESTIONS AND PROBLEMS

8-21. The following problems apply to stratified sampling. Choose the best response.

a. Mr. Murray decides to use stratified sampling. The basic reason for using stratified sampling rather than unrestricted random sampling is to

(i) Reduce as much as possible the degree of variability in the overall population

(ii) Give every element in the population an equal chance of being included in the sample

(iii) Allow the person selecting the sample to use his own judgment in deciding which elements should be included in the sample

(iv) Reduce the required sample size from a nonhomogeneous population

b. What is the primary objective of using stratification as a sampling method in auditing?

(i) To increase the confidence level at which a decision will be reached from the results of the sample selected

(ii) To determine the occurrence rate for a given characteristic in the population being studied

(iii) To decrease the effect of variance in the total population

(iv) To determine the precision range of the sample selected

c. From prior experience, a CPA is aware of the fact that cash disbursements contain a few unusually large disbursements. In using statistical sampling, the CPA's best course of action is to

(i) Eliminate any unusually large disbursements that appear in the sample

(ii) Continue to draw new samples until no unusually large disbursements appear in the sample

(iii) Stratify the cash disbursements population so that the unusually large disbursements are reviewed separately

(iv) Increase the sample size to lessen the effect of the unusually large disbursements

Problems *d* through *h* apply to an examination by Robert Lambert, CPA, of the financial statements of Rainbow Manufacturing Corporation for the year ended December 31, 1983. Rainbow manufactures two products, A and B. Product A requires raw materials that have a very low per-item cost, and product B requires raw materials that have a very high per-item cost. Raw materials for both products are stored in a single warehouse. In 1982, Rainbow established the total value of raw materials stored in the warehouse by physically inventorying an unrestricted random sample of items selected without replacement.

Lambert is evaluating the statistical validity of alternative sampling plans Rainbow is considering for 1983. Lambert knows the size of the 1982 sample and that Rainbow did not use stratified sampling in 1982. Assumptions about the population, variability, specified precision (confidence interval), and specified reliability (confidence level) for a possible 1983 sample are given in each of the following five items. You are to indicate in each case the effect upon the size of the 1983 sample as compared to the 1982 sample.

d. Rainbow wants to use stratified sampling in 1983. (The total population will be divided into two strata, one each for the raw materials for product A and product B.) Compared to 1982, the population size of the raw materials inventory is approximately the same, and the variability of the items in the inventory is approximately the same. The specified precision and specified reliability are to remain the same.

Under these assumptions, the required sample size for 1983 should be
(i) Larger than the 1982 sample size
(ii) Equal to the 1982 sample size
(iii) Smaller than the 1982 sample size
(iv) Of a size that is indeterminate based upon the information given

e. Rainbow wants to use stratified sampling in 1983. Compared to 1982, the population size of the raw materials inventory is approximately the same, and the variability of the items in the inventory is approximately the same. Rainbow specified the same precision but desires to change the specified reliability from 90% to 95%.

Under these assumptions, the required sample size for 1983 should be
(i) Larger than the 1982 sample size
(ii) Equal to the 1982 sample size
(iii) Smaller than the 1982 sample size
(iv) Of a size that is indeterminate based upon the information given

f. Rainbow wants to use unrestricted random sampling without replacement in 1983. Compared to 1982, the population size of the raw materials inventory is approximately the same, and the variability of the items in the inventory is approximately the same. Rainbow specifies the same precision but desires to change the specified reliability from 95% to 90%.

Under these assumptions, the required sample size for 1983 should be
(i) Larger than the 1982 sample size
(ii) Equal to the 1982 sample size
(iii) Smaller than the 1982 sample size
(iv) Of a size that is indeterminate based upon the information given

g. Rainbow wants to use unrestricted random sampling without replacement in 1983. Compared to 1982, the population size of the raw materials inventory has increased, and the variability of the items in the inventory has increased. The specified precision and specified reliability are to remain the same.

Under these assumptions, the required sample size for 1983 should be
(i) Larger than the 1982 sample size
(ii) Equal to the 1982 sample size
(iii) Smaller than the 1982 sample size
(iv) Of a size that is indeterminate based upon the information given

h. Rainbow wants to use unrestricted random sampling without replacement in 1983. Compared to 1982, the population size of the raw materials inventory has increased, but the variability of the items in the inventory has decreased. The specified precision and specified reliability are to remain the same.

Under these assumptions, the required sample size for 1983 should be
  (i) Larger than the 1982 sample size
  (ii) Equal to the 1982 sample size
  (iii) Smaller than the 1982 sample size
  (iv) Of a size that is indeterminate based upon the information given

8-22. Assume that an auditor is using stratified ratio estimation in the confirmation of accounts receivable. There are 940 accounts with a recorded value of $250,000. They are listed on ten pages, with a maximum of 100 lines per page in alphabetical order. The auditor has decided to use three strata. The first stratum has 20 items and includes all recorded values over $5,000; the second, 200 items that include all recorded values between $1,000 and $5,000; and the third, 720 items with recorded values of less than $1,000. The sample sizes of 20, 40, and 50 are to be selected from the first, second, and third strata respectively.

REQUIRED:

Describe in detail an efficient plan for selecting the random numbers using a random number table. Your description should include a definition of all discards.

8-23. Your client is a wholesaler of automobile and truck parts. The parts come in two sizes: loose parts, which are in bins, and bulk parts, which are in sealed packages arranged in pallets.

You are considering using statistical sampling to test the perpetual inventory records, which are kept by price and quantity, for correct physical count, unit cost, and extensions. The client produces a run of the perpetuals on a monthly basis. Perpetual records are maintained separately for bulk and for loose parts. The client uses a minicomputer and is willing to produce the run in any order you believe necessary (including descending or ascending dollar amounts).

There are 20 parts in the inventory that account for roughly 15% of the total inventory. The balance of the inventory comprises approximately 8,000 parts. Parts which the client believes are obsolete are coded "0" on the run of the perpetuals and are not valued.

REQUIRED:

  a. Discuss whether stratification should be used. If so, how should the auditor decide on the number of strata and the stratum boundaries, assuming there is no computer available for making calculations?
  b. How should the auditor decide whether to use mean-per-unit, difference, or ratio estimation in this situation?
  c. Identify the major problems that have to be solved in implementing a statistical sampling plan of this type.
  d. You define the sampling unit as a line item in the listing of inventory from the perpetuals. The selection is made using a computer terminal. The counting of the inventory is done by the client, with you observing the counts. At the physical, one of the items selected is item 1234. The plant manager indicates that 1234 is a member of a family that includes 1234A, 1234B, and 1234C. Because of the way the goods are stored, the plant manager believes it is necessary to count the entire family (i.e., 1234A, 1234B, 1234C) rather

than the individual item selected. The other items in the family are scattered throughout the run of the perpetuals, but can be easily located by the client. You believe that the plant manager's comment about the necessity to count the entire family is valid. How should you modify your sampling plan, assuming that every inventory item that is a part of an inventory family is coded A, B, C, etc.? The client cannot rerun the inventory listing at this point.

8-24. Your client has three locations. You visit each to test the perpetual inventory records. You take a sample at each and obtain count data and check prices and extensions. You also test 100% all items over $10,000. You calculate results for each sample, including all items tested 100%, using ratio estimation. A summary of the results is as follows:

	Location A	Location B	Location C
Point estimate of the population errors	10,643	−18,012	43,119
Standard error of the estimate	9,887	14,463	8,794

REQUIRED:

a. Explain how the results of those sample items that were tested on a 100% basis have been incorporated in the summary of results above.
b. Calculate the point estimate of the population error and the confidence interval at a 95% confidence level.
c. Explain the meaning of the negative number in the lower confidence limit.
d. Assume you are willing to accept a $55,000 error in the total inventory with a Beta risk of 5%. What is the minimum acceptable adjustment to the client's recorded value you would be willing to accept?
e. Describe a different way the population could have been subdivided to end up with six strata. (The present method was to use two strata for each location.) What are the likely advantages and disadvantages of your stratification design?

8-25. You are using stratified mean-per-unit estimation in the confirmation of accounts receivable. You have already decided to use five strata, and the stratum boundaries have been set. A sample size of 250 positive confirmations has already been determined.

The following data have been determined from analyzing population data or by estimating:

Strata	Population size	Estimated standard deviation	Recorded population value
1	4,000	120	400,000
2	2,000	200	300,000
3	1,000	350	600,000
4	500	600	500,000
5	50	2,000	200,000

REQUIRED:

a. Allocate the total sample to strata by using the "proportion to the recorded value" method.
b. Allocate the total sample to strata by using the Neyman method.
c. Explain which method is preferable under the circumstances.

8-26. You are doing the audit of Virginia Tire and Parts, a wholesale auto parts dealer. Unstratified mean-per-unit estimation has been used to calculate statistical information for accounts receivable and inventory. The following data have been calculated or taken from the client's records:

	Accounts receivable	Inventory
Recorded values	$12,000,000	23,000,000
Statistical values		
Point estimate of total audited value	12,000,000	22,300,000
Standard error of the estimate	204,000	306,000

You consider the following amounts to be material:

Accounts receivable (Beta risk 5%)	$400,000
Inventory (Beta risk 5%)	800,000
Combined (Beta risk 2½%)	1,000,000

REQUIRED:

a. State whether each account is misstated by a material amount, using a Beta risk of 5%.
b. Determine whether the combined amount is misstated by a material amount, using a Beta risk of 2½%.
c. What are the auditor's options at this point? Be as specific as possible.
d. Justify using a different Beta risk for errors in the individual accounts and for the combined error.

8-27. Label Products, Inc., produces badges, stickers, posters, etc., to be used for promotional purposes. It caters to a few big customers, but it also accepts a lot of small orders for certain types of badges.

The accounts receivable balances are to be audited by your firm. You have reviewed the internal controls (the bookkeeping system is a manual one) and performed tests of compliance, but you intend to rely primarily on positive confirmations.

There are 9,500 balances with a total recorded value of $2,005,000; 50 balances account for $1,755,000 of this total.

You decide to audit the 50 large balances 100%, and to sample the remaining 9,450. You require a materiality of 2.5% ($50,125) and low Beta risk.

The sampling objective is to test the hypothesis that receivable balances are not misstated by a material amount. You have also decided to use a 5% Beta risk and a relatively low Alpha risk (10%), since it is inconvenient to expand the test due to timing constraints.

Difference and ratio estimation are rejected as sampling methods because of your concern for their reliability in the circumstances. You decide to use stratified mean-per-unit. You decide to use two strata, with a 100% test of the 50 population items in stratum 1. The estimated standard deviation is $850 in stratum 1 and $134 in stratum 2.

REQUIRED:

a. Calculate the required sample size for stratum 2.
b. The 50 large accounts, plus a sample of 100 of the smaller balances, were circularized requesting confirmation. The results of the confirmation procedures (or alternative procedures in the case of nonreplies) are as follows:

	100% stratum	Sampling stratum
No. of accounts	50	100
Total audited value ($\sum x_{tj}$)	1,722,150	2,500
Total recorded value ($\sum y_{tj}$)	1,755,000	2,538
Total audited values squared	–	1,837,810
Total recorded values squared	–	1,840,002
Total products, audited × recorded	–	1,838,652
Difference between recorded and audited values squared	–	624

Calculate the confidence limits of the population, using stratified mean-per-unit estimations.

c. Draw conclusions about the population, using the proper decision rule. What factors cause the auditor to reject the population? What should the auditor do at this point?
d. Assume you decide, after examining the errors, that difference estimation would result in a reliable estimate. Is the population acceptable using difference estimation? Make calculations to support your answer.

8-28. You are using stratified mean-per-unit estimation in the confirmation of accounts receivable for the audit of Johnstone Lumber Company. You are trying to decide on the number of strata and stratum boundaries for each stratum. The client provides you with the following frequency distribution information for your analysis:

Range of recorded value of accounts (rounded to nearest dollar)	Frequency of each recorded value
1– 199	87
200– 399	136
400– 599	275
600– 799	241
800– 999	146
1,000– 1,199	47
1,200– 1,399	51
1,400– 1,599	26
1,600– 1,799	4
2,600– 2,799	2
14,000–14,199	1

REQUIRED:

a. Using a judgmental basis for selecting stratum boundaries, decide on the number of strata and the cutoff for each boundary.
b. Assume you have decided to use four strata, with the largest population items all being included in one stratum and being 100% sampled. Determine the stratum boundaries, using the equally recorded value method.
c. Use the same assumptions as in part *b* and determine the boundaries by the equal cumulative square root of frequency method.
d. Identify the circumstances under which each of the three methods is preferable.

8-29. You are doing the audit of inventory pricing of Western Engine and Supply. The company follows the policy of valuing year-end inventory at standard cost. The standards were last revised 19 months ago, but they are adjusted monthly for inflation by the same percentage as the change in the National Wholesale Price Index. The financial statement indicates that inventory is valued at FIFO. You realize that every recorded value is likely to be misstated.

The decision was made earlier by the engagement partner to use stratified variables estimation to determine whether the recorded inventory is materially misstated from a FIFO inventory valuation. Statistical results are to be calculated for difference, ratio, and mean-per-unit estimation. You plan to use the statistical method resulting in the most favorable audit result. Three strata have been selected based on recorded dollar value of inventory items. All inventory items over $10,000 constitute stratum 1, those under $1,000 are included in stratum 3, and all others in stratum 2. Sample sizes of 40 have been selected from each stratum. The partner has decided to use a Beta risk of 5% and an allowable error of $350,000. The following are the calculated results of the audit tests:

Stratum	Population size	Recorded value of the population	Total recorded value of the sample items (y)	Total audited value of the sample items (x)
1	100	$1,832,500	$678,000	$675,000
2	350	1,599,000	198,000	190,500
3	7,500	4,258,000	22,800	23,000

Stratum	Sum of errors squared (e^2)	Sum of y^2	Sum of x^2	Sum of ey
1	$ 238,000	$12,284,700,000	$11,108,000,000	$50,000,000
2	1,619,000	942,676,000	929,800,000	38,570,000
3	6,350	22,985,000	23,225,000	13,750

REQUIRED:

a. Calculate the population point estimate and computed precision interval for each of the three statistical methods.
b. Explain the causes of the difference in the results for the three statistical methods. Explain whether the causes seem reasonable, considering the nature of the audit tests.

c. Using the proper decision rule, determine whether the recorded value should be accepted for each of the three statistical methods.

8-30. Jake Jones, CPA, is price-testing the inventory for the Concord Jar Company. A listing of inventory that includes description, quantity determined by a physical count, unit cost, and extended cost is prepared on the client's computer system. The listing includes 45 lines per page in part-number order. There are 63 pages, but some pages do not have 45 inventory items, because the description takes two lines. Whenever that happens, the extended dollars for the inventory description are on the second line. There are 2,271 extended inventory items in the inventory.

The auditor has decided to select a stratified sample of the following size:

Stratum	Description (as recorded by client)	Population size	Sample size
1	Extended inventory, $\geq$ $5,000	23	23
2	Extended inventory, < $5,000 and $\geq$ $1,000	411	25
3	Extended inventory, < $1,000	1,837	50
		2,271	93

REQUIRED:

a. Design a random selection plan to obtain the 93 sample items in an efficient manner that also meets the requirements of randomness for stratified sampling. Include definition of sampling units, population definition, and all decision rules.

8-31. Before the sample of inventory for pricing was selected for Armandy Department Stores (see problem 7-22), a new staff member, Joe Krebbs, who had taken statistical sampling in auditing in college, came up with two ideas that he felt were more efficient than unstratified mean-per-unit.

The first idea was to use stratified rather than unstratified mean-per-unit. He took the position that the use of stratification would reduce the standard deviation of the population by putting items of similar value in the same stratum. After looking at last year's inventory listing, he concluded that the following three strata should be used:

Stratum 1 : Any inventory item, after extension of price times quantity, valued in excess of $3,000

Stratum 2 : Any inventory item valued between $1,000 and $3,000

Stratum 3 : Any inventory item valued at less than $1,000

The partner on the engagement felt that the idea was good but that it was not possible, because of the rule that the population size for each stratum had to be known. Since inventory had not been extended yet, the population size for each stratum could not be determined.

Joe is somewhat discouraged by now but has decided to explore the second idea further anyway. His plan is to use stratified difference or ratio estimation. He wants to use last year's listing at retail as the recorded value because there are individual values and a total. The audited value will be this year's historical cost value, and the difference for a sample item will be the difference between last year's retail value and this year's audited value. He wants to use stratified difference or ratio estimation to reduce the standard deviation.

The partner, who prides himself on shooting holes in other people's plans, informs Joe that the second idea won't work either. He says, "Some of last year's inventory items are no longer being stocked, and there are new items that weren't stocked last year. It wouldn't be practical to find a sampling unit that would properly define the population. Unstratified mean-per-unit is the best way to go in this case. Joe, you are now learning the difference between theory and practice."

REQUIRED :

a. Devise a plan for using stratified mean-per-unit sampling that would answer the partner's objections and meet the requirements of stratified sampling. Evaluate implementation problems you might encounter. Under what circumstances is the plan apt to be an improvement over unstratified mean-per-unit estimation?

b. Devise a plan for using stratified difference or ratio estimation that would answer the partner's objections and meet the requirements of stratified sampling. Identify potential implementation problems. Under what circumstances is the plan apt to be an improvement over both stratified and unstratified mean-per-unit estimation?

8-32. The data from problem 7-17 are used in this problem to make calculations in part *a*. All inventory items valued at more than $700 are considered a part of stratum 1. All those valued at $700 or less are considered a part of stratum 2, which includes 640 population items with a recorded value of $170,000. Even though only 20 items in total are used to simplify the problem, compute sampling results as indicated.

REQUIRED :

a. Calculate each of the following. (Where a blank should not be completed because it is inappropriate to do so, indicate by NA.)

	Stratified mean-per-unit estimation			Stratified difference estimation		
	Strata			Strata		
	1	*2*	*Overall*	*1*	*2*	*Overall*
1. Sample mean						
2. Point estimate of the total audited amount						
3. Estimated population standard deviation						
4. Finite population correction factor						
5. Standard error of the total estimate						
6. Computed precision interval at a 95% reliability						
7. Confidence interval at a 95% confidence level						

b. Compare the stratified mean-per-unit results to the unstratified mean-per-unit results in problem 7-17. Explain why the overall point estimate is similar in size and the precision interval is so different.

c. Compare the stratified difference results to the unstratified difference results in problem 7-17. Explain why there is so little difference in the point estimate and precision interval.

8-33. Mary Obrien, CPA, is using stratified mean-per-unit to determine whether the client's recorded inventory is correctly stated. The decision has been made to use mean-per-unit rather than difference or ratio estimation because a low error rate is expected.

Inventory has been stratified by two criteria: inventory location, and the recorded value of individual inventory items. There are six strata and three inventory locations.

The audit tests for a sample item include comparing the recorded count to the perpetual record at the balance sheet date, comparing the perpetual record on the audit date to the inventory on hand, testing the unit costs by reference to vendors' invoices, and extending the price times quantity. The client did not take a physical at year-end, but inventory is counted annually and the records are considered excellent. No adjusting entries are likely to be accepted by the client unless a large error is discovered.

The following information is available from the accounting records and estimates of the population data:

Stratum	Population size	Recorded value	Estimated standard deviation
1	600	$ 300,000	750
2	3,500	800,000	500
3	800	400,000	400
4	2,900	450,000	300
5	500	500,000	1,200
6	4,700	700,000	200
	13,000	$3,150,000	

The following specifications are set:

Alpha risk	100%
Beta risk	10%
Allowable error	150,000
Expected point estimate	3,150,000

REQUIRED:

a. Calculate the total required sample, using the optimum allocation method. Use the finite correction factor where it is appropriate.

b. Allocate the total sample size in *a* to each stratum in proportion to the recorded value.

c. Suggest two ways the auditor might have designed the strata to have a smaller required sample size and still meet the audit requirements. What problems could exist for each way suggested?

d. Assume Mary calculated the required sample size in *a* and allocated the sample to the strata in part *b*. She decided to use the following sample size and ended up with the following results after performing all audit tests. Calculate the confidence limits for the inventory valuation.

Stratum	Sample size	Audited value	Standard deviation
1	100	52,000	730
2	350	80,500	530
3	150	77,250	380
4	200	30,000	320
5	200	210,000	1,400
6	300	45,000	210

e. Evaluate the acceptability of the population, using the appropriate decision rule.

f. Mary is considering two alternatives at this point:
   (i) Divide one of the strata into two strata and recalculate the results without changing the sample size.
   (ii) Increase the sample size in one stratum.

   Evaluate each of these two alternatives. If she decides to follow one of these two approaches, which stratum should she take? Explain your answer.

8-34. The ARC Leasing Co. leases both trucks and autos. You have decided to test the client's assertion that the average combined useful life for all leases is 35 months.

The client has 12,000 auto leases and 2,000 truck leases. You believe that the truck leases have a different variability from the auto leases and therefore decide to use stratified sampling. You decide on a confidence level of 95%. You desire a precision of $\pm$ 1.5 months; thus, in determining sample size, you use 21,000 lease months as the total precision for the population.

You select a pilot sample of 50 auto leases and 50 truck leases, with the following results:

	Population size	Sample size	Sample mean	Sample std. dev.
Auto leases	12,000	50	32 months	10.1
Truck leases	2,000	50	38 months	16.2
	14,000	100		

REQUIRED:

a. Calculate the required sample size.

b. Assume that the sample, including the pilot sample of 100, yielded the following results (using the sample size calculated in *a* above):

	Sample mean	Sample std. dev.
Auto leases	33 months	9.5
Truck leases	38 months	16.2

The sample size was divided evenly between the strata. Calculate an appropriate interval estimation at the desired confidence level for the life of the leases.

c. Evaluate, using an appropriate decision rule, the client's assertion that the combined useful life for all leases is 35 months.

9

dollar unit sampling

INTRODUCTION

Dollar unit sampling, which was introduced in Chapter 2, is a method of sampling in which the probability of selecting any given item is proportional to its dollar value. For example, assume that there is one account receivable recorded at $25,000 in a population of 100 accounts receivable with a total value of $250,000. Using unstratified sampling of physical units, the probability of selecting the population item in question using a sample size of 1 is 1 percent (1/100). Using dollar unit sampling, the probability is 10 percent ($25,000/$250,000). It was shown in Chapter 8 that by using stratified sampling, the probability of selecting that account receivable could be 100 percent, depending on the stratification design.

In Chapter 2, four methods of selecting dollar unit samples were discussed. These were random number table cumulative amounts, random number table noncumulative, systematic sampling, and computer techniques.

Regardless of the selection method, dollar unit samples can be evaluated statistically. Four evaluation methods will be discussed in this chapter:

- Simple attributes evaluation
- Combined attributes-variables evaluation
- Multinomial bound evaluation
- Dollar unit difference estimation

Each of these methods, and the conditions required for their use, will be discussed and illustrated in the following sections.

SIMPLE ATTRIBUTES EVALUATION

A random sample of dollar units can be evaluated using attributes sampling principles in the same way that attributes sampling is applied to a random sample of physical audit units. Using simple attributes, the auditor selects a sample on the basis of dollar units rather than physical units. Any of the four dollar unit selection methods described in Chapter 2 can be used. For any given dollar unit, the auditor first identifies the physical unit containing the dollar unit. The methodology for identifying the physical unit was explained in Chapter 2. The auditor then determines, for each attribute of interest, whether the physical unit does or does not contain an error. If the physical unit contains an error, the sample dollar units in it are also presumed to contain an error. The portion of sample dollar units that contains errors is used as the basis for estimating the maximum portion of dollars in the population that contains errors. The maximum portion of dollars is estimated separately for each attribute. There is a difference in the calculations and conclusions for compliance and substantive tests. These are discussed separately below.

It is common in simple attributes to separate extremely large population items for 100 percent testing in the same manner as for stratified sampling. A common cutoff is automatic selection of any population items with a recorded value larger than the allowable error specified by the auditor. Larger dollar items are automatically selected if dollar unit systematic selection is used and the interval is smaller than the allowable error. All larger dollar items may or may not be included with random selection.

It is less important to separate larger recorded values for separate testing when simple attributes is used than for physical unit sampling, because there is a high likelihood of their inclusion anyway. When larger items are separated and audited, the combined value of those items is treated in the same way as a stratum in stratified sampling where all population items are audited.

Compliance Tests

The simple attributes approach for compliance tests can be illustrated by a common application of attributes sampling. A sample of 100 dollar units is selected at random as a test of cash disbursements transactions, using a dollar unit selection method from the total dollar value of all vouchers recorded during the year. Cash disbursements for the year total $1,200,000.

The 100 vouchers containing the random dollars are audited and no compliance deviations are found.

The upper precision limit in dollars is determined by using a table such as the one used for physical unit attributes sampling. Using a 95 percent confidence level in the table in Figure 3-2, a sample size of 100 and an occurrence rate of zero results in an upper precision limit of 3 percent. This percentage is applied to the dollars in the population; i.e., the upper precision limit is the upper precision limit in percent times the recorded value of the population.

In the illustration, the upper precision limit is $36,000 (3 percent of $1,200,000). The auditor can conclude at a 95 percent confidence level that no more than $36,000 of the recorded cash disbursements contain a compliance deviation of the type defined by the attribute being tested. The auditor can then evaluate whether he or she is satisfied with the controls in a population of $1,200,000 when no more than $36,000 of that total is likely to contain compliance deviations.

Is the information stated in terms of dollars more useful than when it is stated in terms of percentages? That is for the auditor to decide. In both cases, the upper precision limit deals with compliance deviations, not dollar errors.

The same concepts discussed for the situation where there were no errors can be applied when compliance deviations are found. For example, if there were two compliance deviations in a sample of 100, the upper precision limit in percent is 6.2 percent (see the table in Figure 3-2). The upper precision limit in dollars is therefore $74,400 (6.2 percent of $1,200,000).

Differences Between Dollar Unit Simple Attributes and Physical Unit Attributes Sampling

To summarize, there are only three differences between dollar unit simple attributes and physical attributes sampling as it was studied in Chapter 3:

- *The selection of sample items.* For dollar unit simple attributes, those physical units with large recorded values have a higher probability of being selected than those with small recorded values. All physical units, regardless of the recorded value, have the same probability for physical unit attributes selection.
- *Calculation of the upper precision limit.* One additional step is needed for dollar unit simple attributes. The upper precision limit in percent is multiplied by the total population recorded value to obtain an upper precision limit in dollars.
- *Evaluation of the computed upper precision limit.* For both methods, the auditor evaluates whether the upper precision limit is low enough for the controls to be relied upon. In dollar unit simple attributes, the upper precision limit is the amount of dollars in the population that may contain compliance deviations. The upper precision limit for physical unit attributes is the rate of error in the number of population items.

Determining Sample Size

Sample size determination is much as it was for physical unit attributes sampling. The auditor must specify or know four things:

- Allowable dollar value of the population containing compliance deviations (judgment based on materiality)
- Confidence level (judgment)
- Expected rate of compliance deviations (prior experience)
- Recorded value of the population (obtained from appropriate records)

The sample size is determined by first calculating the maximum percentage of the recorded population value that the auditor is willing to allow to have compliance deviations (allowable upper precision limit). The allowable upper precision limit is the allowable dollar value of the population containing compliance deviations divided by the recorded population value. After the allowable upper precision limit in percent is determined, the sample size is obtained from the appropriate table in the same manner as for physical unit attributes sampling.

Determining the preliminary sample size is illustrated by assuming that the auditor in the previous example is willing to allow, at a 95 percent confidence level, compliance deviations for population items totaling $50,000. He expects a 2 percent sample error rate for the compliance test. The preliminary sample size determined from Figure 3-2 is approximately 250 ($50,000 ÷ $1,200,000 = 4.2%; an allowable upper precision limit of 4.2 percent, an expected error rate of 2 percent, and a 95 percent confidence level requires a sample of 250).

Substantive Tests

Simple attributes is applied to substantive tests much as it is to compliance tests, with four major differences:

- Simple attributes should be used for substantive tests only when there are no errors found in the sample.
- A separate evaluation is made for overstatement errors and for understatement errors.
- In order to make the evaluation, the auditor must make an assumption about the maximum amount of error that might exist in the average population dollar unit.
- The projected values are referred to as upper and lower error *bounds* rather than confidence or precision limits.

These four differences are discussed in this and the next section.

Illustration. The same illustration of cash disbursements tests of transactions used previously is employed to show the use of simple attributes for substantive tests. A sample of 100 items is tested from a population with a recorded value of $1,200,000. No errors are uncovered in the sample.

The upper and lower error bounds are determined by applying the upper precision limit in percent to the total recorded population value. The upper precision limit is determined from the same attributes sampling table as was followed for compliance tests (3.0 percent in the illustration). Since there were no errors in the sample, the precision limit is a precision interval (0 + 3%) and can therefore be used to determine both an upper and lower precision limit (0 ± 3%).

The error bounds in dollars depend on the assumption of the *average percent of error for population items that contain an error.* To illustrate the concept of average percent of error three cases will be assumed: (1) Overstatements and understatements both equal 100 percent errors; (2) overstatements and understatements both equal 10 percent errors; and (3) overstatements equal 20 percent errors and understatements equal 200 percent errors.

Assumption 1. Overstatements 100 percent; understatements 100 percent; error bounds at a 95 percent confidence level.

$$\text{Upper error bound} = \$1,200,000 \times 3\% \times 1 = \$36,000$$
$$\text{Lower error bound} = \$1,200,000 \times 3\% \times 1 = \$36,000$$

The assumption is that, on average, those population items in error will be misstated by the full dollar amount of the recorded value. Since the upper precision limit is 3 percent, the dollar value of the error is not likely to exceed $36,000. If all the errors are overstated, there will be an overstatement of $36,000. If they are all understated, there will be an understatement of $36,000.

The assumption of 100 percent errors is extremely conservative, especially for overstatements. Assume that the actual population error rate is 3 percent, using simple attributes. The following conditions would have to exist before the $36,000 properly reflected the upper precision limit:

- All errors would have to be overstatements. Offsetting errors would reduce the amount of the overstatement.
- All population items in error would have to be 100 percent misstated. There could not, for example, be an error such as a check written for $262 that was recorded at $226.[1]

---

[1]Conceptually, some errors could be only partially overstated and, on average, errors could still be overstated 100 percent if other population items were stated as a positive value when the amount should have been a negative value. For example, if a cash receipt of $250 was included as a cash disbursement of $250, that recorded cash disbursement would be overstated by 200 percent (500/250).

Because of the extreme conservatism, the upper and lower limits are referred to as error bounds rather than confidence limits. The risk inherent in confidence limits is highly unlikely when 100 percent errors are assumed.

Assumption 2. Overstatements 10 percent; understatements 10 percent; error bounds at a 95 percent confidence level.

$$\text{Upper error bound} = \$1,200,000 \times 3\% \times .1 = \$3,600$$
$$\text{Lower error bound} = \$1,200,000 \times 3\% \times .1 = \$3,600$$

The assumption is that, on average, those items in error will be misstated by no more than 10 percent. If all items were misstated in one direction, the error bounds would be between $-\$3,600$ and $+\$3,600$. The change in assumption from 100 percent errors significantly affects the error bounds.

Assumption 3. Overstatements 20 percent; understatements 200 percent; error bounds at a 95 percent confidence level.

$$\text{Upper error bound} = \$1,200,000 \times 3\% \times .2 = \$7,200$$
$$\text{Lower error bound} = \$1,200,000 \times 3\% \times 2.0 = \$72,000$$

The justification for a larger percent for understatements is the larger potential percent error. For example, a disbursement recorded at $20 that should have been recorded at $200 is understated by 900 percent $[(200 - 20)/20]$, whereas one that is recorded at $200 that should have been recorded at $20 is overstated by 90 percent $[(200 - 20)/200]$.

Items containing larger understatement errors may have a very small recorded value, due to those errors. As a consequence, because of the mechanics of dollar unit sampling, very few of them will have a chance of being selected in the sample. Because of this, some auditors select an additional sample of small items to supplement the dollar unit sample wherever understatement errors are an important audit concern.

Appropriate "Percent of Error" Assumption

The appropriate assumption to make regarding the overall percent of error in those population items containing an error is an auditor's decision. The auditor must set these percentages based on personal judgment in the circumstances. In the absence of convincing information to the contrary, many auditors believe it is reasonable to assume a 100 percent error for both over- and understatements. This approach is considered highly conservative, but it is easier to justify than any other assumption. Unless stated otherwise, the 100 percent error assumption is used in the chapter and problem materials.

Determining Sample Size

Sample size for simple attributes is determined for substantive tests much as for compliance tests and physical unit attributes sampling. Four things must be known or specified:

- Allowable upper and lower error bounds (judgment based on materiality).
- Assumption of the average percent of error for population items that contain an error. There may be a separate assumption for the upper and lower bounds (judgment based on auditor's knowledge of client and past experience).
- Confidence level (judgment).
- Recorded value of the population (obtained from general ledger).

The auditor must first determine the allowable upper precision limit in percent. The preliminary sample size is then determined, using the conventional attributes sampling tables. The allowable upper precision limit is determined separately for the upper and lower bounds independently by the following three steps:

1. Divide each allowable bound by the average percent of error assumption.
2. Divide each quotient by the recorded population value to obtain an upper precision limit.
3. Use as the upper precision limit the result in step 2 with the smaller absolute value.

For example, assume the auditor has obtained or decided the following in the audit of sales transactions, where no errors are expected in the substantive tests:

Allowable error bounds (each)	$100,000
Average percent of error assumption—overstatements	50%
Average percent of error assumption—understatements	100%
Confidence level	90%
Sales per general ledger	6.6 million

The sample size is:

	Upper	Lower
Error bound	100,000	100,000
Average percent of error assumption	÷ .50	÷ 1.00
	200,000	100,000
Recorded population value	÷ 6,600,000	÷ 6,600,000
Allowable upper precision limit	3%	1.5%
Required sample size from the attributes table—90% confidence level	Not applicable	150

If 150 sample items are selected and there are no errors in the sample, the upper bound requirements will be easily satisfied and the lower bound will be exactly met. If there are monetary errors, the combined attributes-variables evaluation method discussed below is used.

Shortcut Method
of Sample Size Determination

A shortcut method for determining the required sample size is available when no errors are expected and the 100 percent error assumption is followed. It is:

$$n = \frac{Y \times \text{Factor}}{\text{Smaller allowable error bound}}$$

where:

n = required sample size
Y = recorded population value
Factor = factor obtained from the table for the appropriate confidence level
Smaller allowable error bound = the smaller of the upper or lower allowable error bound

Table of factors

Confidence level	Factor
95	3.00
90	2.30
85	1.93
80	1.60
75	1.40
70	1.33

To illustrate, using a 100 percent error percent assumption in the previous example, the sample size is determined as follows:

$$n = \frac{6,600,000 \times 2.3}{100,000} = 152$$

The difference in sample size between 152 and the previously determined 150 is caused by rounding. It may be noted that the factor for the shortcut method is 100 times the upper precision limit, at a zero occurrence rate and the appropriate confidence level, for a sample size of 100.

COMBINED ATTRIBUTES-VARIABLES EVALUATION

The illustration for substantive tests provided in the preceding section was of a sample containing no monetary errors. This section presents the evaluation method when there are monetary errors in the sample. The same illustration is continued; the only change is the assumption about the errors. The sample size remains at 100 and the recorded value is still $1,200,000, but now five errors in the sample are assumed. The errors are shown in Figure 9-1.

Voucher no.	Recorded voucher amount	Audited voucher amount	Error	Error ÷ recorded amount
2073	$ 6,200	$ 6,100	100	.016
5111	12,910	12,000	910	.07
5206	4,322	4,450	(128)	(.03)
7642	23,000	22,995	5	.0002
9816	8,947	2,947	6,000	.671

FIGURE 9-1 Illustrative errors

When there were no errors in the sample, an assumption was required as to the average percent of error for the population items in error. The error bounds were calculated showing several different assumptions. Now that errors have been found, sample information is available to use in determining the error bounds. The error assumption is still required, but it can be modified.

Using the attributes table again, the upper precision limit can be determined for any error rate the auditor desires. Since the error bounds are calculated independently for overstatement and understatement errors, the error rate for overstatements is 4 percent (4/100) and understatements 1 percent (1/100).

Using the attributes sampling table for a sample size of 100, the upper precision limits for different error results at a confidence level of 95 percent are shown in Figure 9-2. (The last column will be used later.)

As with simple attributes, there are several different assumptions the

Number of errors	Upper precision limit	Increase in precision limit resulting from an additional error
0	.03	
1	.047	.017
2	.062	.015
3	.076	.014
4	.089	.013

FIGURE 9-2 Upper precision limits (from Figure 3-2) for different error results (confidence level 95%; sample size 100)

auditor can make in calculating the error bounds. For example, the auditor could assume that all population overstatement errors are 100 percent overstated and all population understatement errors are 100 percent understated. Following that assumption and using simple attributes, the error bounds would be:

$$\text{Upper error bound} = \$1,200,000 \times .089 \times 1.0 = \$106,800$$

$$\text{Lower error bound} = \$1,200,000 \times (.047) \times 1.0 = (\$56,400)$$

This assumption is exceptionally conservative, and it is not consistent with the error results.

Another assumption that is far more appealing is the assignment of each portion of the upper precision limit to the actual error results found. The actual error results are thereby reflected in the error bounds. This is the method followed by combined attributes-variables evaluation.

To assure a conservative error bound, the assumption to make is that the largest error results, as measured by the errors for each dollar unit, are assigned to the largest segment of the upper precision limit. This requires a ranking of the unit errors in Figure 9-1 as follows:

Overstatements	
Largest error	.671
Second largest	.07
Third largest	.016
Smallest	.0002

The calculations of the upper and lower error bounds using the described assumptions are shown in Figure 9-3.

Notice that the portion of the upper precision limit associated with no errors (.03) is based on a 100 percent error assumption. Thus, based on a sample of 100 items containing five errors, the auditor is at least 95 percent certain that population overstatement errors do not cxceed $51,220 in total, and that population understatement errors do not cxceed $36,612 in total. The usefulness of these bounds depends on the circumstances of the test. For cxample, the audit objectives and procedures used, other planned tests, and materiality considerations all affect their usefulness. The combined attributes-variables evaluation method does not provide a point estimate of net error amount or a confidence interval about that amount that would be suitable for estimating an adjustment to the books. Where an adjustment is likely, some other approach is generally required. Often, the nature of the errors located by the dollar unit sample is investigated and measurements

Number of errors	Upper precision limit portion (see Figure 9-2, "increase in precision limit resulting from an additional error")	Recorded value	Unit error assumption (see Figure 9-1, "error ÷ recorded amount")	Error bound portion (columns 2 × 3 × 4)
0	.03	$1,200,000	1.0	$36,000
1	.017	1,200,000	.671	13,688
2	.015	1,200,000	.07	1,360
3	.014	1,200,000	.016	269
4	.013	1,200,000	.0002	3
Upper precision limit	.089			
Upper error bound				$51,220

FIGURE 9-3A Illustration of upper error bound with 4 errors at a confidence level of 95%

Number of errors	Upper precision limit portion	Recorded value	Unit error assumption	Error bound portion
0	.03	$1,200,000	1.0	$36,000
1	.017	1,200,000	.03	612
Upper precision limit	.047			
Lower error bound				$36,612

FIGURE 9-3B Illustration of lower error bound with 1 error at a confidence level of 95%

are made judgmentally. In other cases, the dollar unit sample can be evaluated using dollar unit difference estimation, which will provide data in a format suitable for adjustment purposes. This statistical method will be discussed later.

Formulas

Formulas for calculating error bounds for simple attributes and combined attributes-variables evaluation are shown below. Each formula is illustrated with the example that has already been shown in the text.

The following symbols are used:

$D(i)$ = maximum total population error bound when i errors are found (D_0 for overstatement errors and D_u for understatement errors)

Y = total population recorded dollars

$Pu(i)$ = upper precision limit from the one-sided attributes table for i errors

$E(i)$ = amount of a dollar unit error number i [$E_0(i)$ for overstatement error number i, and $E_u(i)$ for understatement error number i]

M = assumed maximum amount of error in any population dollar unit (M_0 for overstatement error and M_u for understatement error)

Simple attributes—No errors

Formula

$$D(0) = Y \cdot Pu(0) \cdot M$$

Illustration. Assumes 100 percent error assumption; 95 percent confidence level; sample size 100.

$$\text{Upper bound} = \$1,200,000 \times .03 \times 1 = \$36,000$$

There is no lower bound for a compliance test. The lower bound is $36,000 for a substantive test.

Simple Attributes—Compliance—Errors

Formula

$$D(i) = Y \cdot Pu(i) \cdot M$$

Illustration. Assumes 100 percent error assumption; two errors; 95 percent confidence level; sample size 100.

$$\text{Upper precision limit} = \$1,200,000 \times .062 \times 1 = \$62,000$$

Combined Attributes-Variables Evaluation—Errors

Formula

$$D(i) = Y \cdot [Pu(0) \cdot M + (Pu(1) - Pu(0)) \cdot E(1) + (Pu(2) - Pu(1)) \cdot E(2) \\ + \cdots + (Pu(i) - Pu(i-1) \cdot E(i)]$$

Illustration. Assumes 100 percent error assumption; four overstated errors and one understated error; errors are ordered from the largest dollar unit error to the smallest; 95 percent confidence level, sample size 100. Therefore:

$$E_0(1) = .671$$
$$E_0(2) = .07$$
$$E_0(3) = .016$$
$$E_0(4) = .0002$$
$$E_u(1) = .03$$

The 95 percent bound for maximum total population overstatement error is:

$$
\begin{aligned}
D_0(4) = {} & (1,200,000)(.03)(1.00) + (1,200,000)(.047 - .03)(.671) \\
& + (1,200,000)(.062 - .047)(.07) + (1,200,000)(.076 - .062)(0.16) \\
& + (1,200,000)(.089 - .076)(.0002) \\
= {} & 36,000 + 13,688 + 1,260 + 269 + 3 \\
= {} & 51,220
\end{aligned}
$$

and the 95 percent bound for maximum total population understatement error is:

$$D_u(1) = (1,200,000)(.03)(1.00) + (1,200,000)(.047 - .03)(.03)$$
$$= 36,000 + 612$$
$$= 36,612$$

Computational Shortcut

Combined attributes-variables evaluation is particularly useful when a computer is not available to make calculations. (When a computer is available, multinomial bound evaluation can be used.) A computational shortcut method is shown in this section using a special table developed to save computation time. Any difference in results from those obtained using the formulas should not be significant.

The computation consists of the following steps, which are illustrated using the same example previously used:

1. Rank the errors in descending order of magnitude:

$$E_0(1) = .671 \qquad E_u(1) = .03$$
$$E_0(2) = .07$$
$$E_0(3) = .016$$
$$E_0(4) = .0002$$

2. For each error, obtain the appropriate adjustment factor from the desired reliability column from Figure 9-4. Since the desired reliability level in the example is 95 percent, the adjustment factors to be used are:

$$E_0(1) \text{ and } E_u(1) = 1.75$$
$$E_0(2) \qquad\qquad = 1.56$$
$$E_0(3) \qquad\qquad = 1.46$$
$$E_0(4) \qquad\qquad = 1.40$$

3. Multiply the adjustment factor by the amount of each error, add the factor for zero errors, and sum the results:

$E_0(1)$:	$1.75 \times$	$.671$	$= 1.1740$
$E_0(2)$:	$1.56 \times$	$.07$	$= .1090$
$E_0(3)$:	$1.46 \times$	$.016$	$= .0230$
$E_0(4)$:	$1.40 \times$	$.0002$	$= .0003$
$E_0(0)$:	$3.00 \times$	1.00	$= 3.0000$
			4.3063
$E_u(1)$:	$1.75 \times$	$.03$	$= .0525$
$E_u(0)$:	$3.00 \times$	1.00	$= 3.0000$
			3.0525

4. Divide the total population dollars by the sample size and multiply the quotient by the summed results obtained in step 3 to obtain the population maximum total error bounds:

$$D_0(4) = (1,200,000 \div 100)(4.3063) = 51,676$$

$$D_u(1) = (1,200,000 \div 100)(3.0525) = 36,630$$

Note that these results are very close to those obtained previously.

Rank of errors	Reliability level					
	70%	75%	80%	85%	90%	95%
0	1.33	1.40	1.60	1.93	2.30	3.00
1	1.25	1.32	1.39	1.50	1.59	1.75
2	1.19	1.24	1.28	1.37	1.44	1.56
3	1.16	1.20	1.24	1.30	1.36	1.46
4	1.14	1.17	1.21	1.26	1.32	1.40
5	1.13	1.16	1.19	1.24	1.29	1.36
6	1.12	1.14	1.17	1.22	1.26	1.33
7	1.11	1.13	1.16	1.20	1.24	1.31
8	1.10	1.12	1.15	1.19	1.23	1.29
9	1.09	1.12	1.14	1.18	1.22	1.28
10	1.09	1.11	1.14	1.17	1.21	1.26
Over 10	1.09	1.11	1.13	1.16	1.20	1.25

FIGURE 9-4 Combined attributes-variables evaluation error adjustment factors

Note that the zero error factors agree with those given for simple attributes sample size determination.

Sample Size Determination

Sample size determination is a difficult problem for combined attributes-variables evaluation, because it is very hard to predict the amounts of errors that will be found, let alone the sample error rate. Frequently, some arbitrary and conservative approach is used. One possibility is to assume a high error rate and that all errors will be 100 percent. The problem is that this often results in large sample sizes, which defeats the purpose of sampling efficiency.

Another more commonly followed alternative is to determine the sample size assuming a zero rate of error and the same maximum amount of error in the dollar units that will be used if no errors are found. Of course, if errors are found, an increase in the sample size or some alternative audit approach is required. This procedure should not be followed when it is impractical to expand the sample size if the audit requirements are not met.

MULTINOMIAL BOUND EVALUATION

Simple attributes and combined attributes-variables evaluation are based on the binomial distribution. They assume no more than two possible outcomes for any population item. The combined attributes-variables evaluation approach goes on to make some adjustment where error information is available, but the primary underlying distribution of all population items is the binomial.

Multinomial bound evaluation is based on a different distribution. It assumes that the true population distribution comes from a very broad set of possible outcomes. Based on the error information obtained, a specific subset of those possibilities is used to determine upper and lower error bounds, much as for the combined attributes-variables approach.

The multinomial bound evaluation approach is far more complex to describe and to apply than the combined attributes-variables evaluation approach. A detailed study of the methodology is beyond the scope of this book. It can be used only with the help of a computer time-sharing program. Such a program makes it easy to apply. The advantage of this approach is that it always produces both overstatement and understatement bounds that are at least as narrow as combined attributes-variables evaluation bounds. In most cases, the bounds are considerably narrower and therefore more useful for audit purposes.

DOLLAR UNIT DIFFERENCE ESTIMATION

When a sample of dollar units is audited and errors are found, a variables sampling type of evaluation can also be made, much as for difference and ratio estimation. The statistical method is called dollar unit difference estimation, and the statistical result is in the form of a confidence interval of the errors at a specified confidence level. This method is called estimation rather than evaluation because the reliability of the estimator is much like that of ratio and difference estimation, that is, it is based on the normal distribution.

The error conditions for dollar unit difference estimation must be much like those for difference or ratio estimation as discussed in Chapters 5 and 6 before the estimator is considered reliable. The Neter and Loebbecke study, as shown in earlier chapters, indicates that for difference and ratio estimation to be reliable, the error rate should be at least 10 percent for a sample of 300 and 5 percent for a sample in excess of 300, with no more than approximately 75 percent of the errors in one direction. The error rate must be considerably higher when all errors are in one direction. No similar research has been done for dollar unit difference estimation, but the conclusions are likely to be similar.

Dollar unit difference estimation results in a point estimate and a confidence interval at a specified confidence level. The formulas for calculating the confidence limits are shown in Figures 9-5 to 9-8. Calculations of the confidence limits are illustrated by using the example with five errors that was followed for combined attributes-variables evaluation. Keep in mind that the example followed is not consistent with the number of errors required for a reliable estimate using dollar unit difference estimation. In studying the calculations, notice how closely the formulas correspond to those followed for difference estimation.

$$\hat{E} = Y\left(\frac{\sum (e_i/y_i)}{n}\right) = Y\bar{w}$$

$$\bar{w} = \frac{\sum (e_i/y_i)}{n} \quad \text{or} \quad \frac{\sum w_i}{n}$$

$$w_i = e_i \div y_i$$

where:

$\hat{E}$ = point estimate of the population error
Y = client-recorded population value
e_i = error in a sample item
y_i = recorded balance of a sample item
w_i = ratio of error in a sample item to the recorded balance
$\bar{w}$ = average ratio of errors to recorded balance of all sample items
n = sample size

Error	e_i		y_i		w_i
1	100	÷	6,200	=	.016
2	910	÷	12,910	=	.070
3	(128)	÷	4,322	=	(.030)
4	5	÷	23,000	=	.000
5	6,000	÷	8,947	=	.671
	$\sum w_i$				.727

$\bar{w} = .73 \div 100 = .0073$
$\hat{E} = 1,200,000 \cdot .0073 = 876$

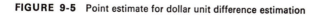

FIGURE 9-5 Point estimate for dollar unit difference estimation

$$SD = \sqrt{\frac{\sum (w_i)^2 - n(\bar{w})^2}{n-1}}$$

where:

SD = standard deviation (All other symbols are defined in Figure 9-5.)

Error	w_i	$(w_i)^2$
1	.016	.003
2	.070	.0049
3	(.030)	.0009
4	.000	.0
5	.671	.4502
	$\sum (w_i)^2$	.4563

$$SD = \sqrt{\frac{.4563 - 100(.0073)^2}{100 - 1}} = .068$$

FIGURE 9-6 Standard deviation for dollar unit difference estimation

$$CPI = \frac{Y \cdot Z \cdot SD}{\sqrt{n}}$$

where:

CPI = computed precision interval
Z = confidence coefficient

$$CPI = \frac{1,200,000 \times 1.96 \times .068}{\sqrt{100}} = 15,994$$

FIGURE 9-7 Computed precision interval for dollar unit difference estimation

$$CI = \hat{E} \pm CPI$$
$$UCL = \hat{E} + CPI$$
$$LCL = \hat{E} - CPI$$

where:

CI = confidence interval
UCL = upper confidence limit
LCL = lower confidence limit

$$CI = 876 \pm 15,994$$
$$UCL = 876 + 15,994 = 16,870$$
$$LCL = 876 - 15,994 = -15,118$$

FIGURE 9-8 Confidence interval and confidence limits for dollar unit difference estimation

The following are the key terms for which formulas are needed and the calculated totals determined from the formulas for the ongoing illustration:

Figure	Formula	Calculated amount as shown in the figure
9-5	Point estimate $(\hat{E})$	876
9-6	Standard deviation (SD)	.068
9-7	Computed precision interval (CPI)	15,994
9-8	Confidence limits (LCL and UCL)	−15,118 to 16,870

Notice that the confidence limits for the dollar unit difference estimation are −15,118 to 16,870, whereas the error bounds for combined attributes-variables evaluation are −36,612 and 51,220. Although, as indicated, the dollar unit difference estimation cannot be considered reliable, because of the small number of errors, this does illustrate how highly conservative the error bounds are.

Determining Sample Size

Determining sample size for dollar unit difference estimation is done in much the same way as for difference estimation. First, the auditor must decide whether the estimator is reliable. Next, the auditor must decide whether the intent is to use a hypothesis test or an interval estimate. After these two decisions are made, the following information must be obtained or decisions made:

- Estimated point estimate
- Estimated standard deviation
- Recorded book value
- Confidence level or Beta and Alpha risk
- Allowable error

The formula for sample size is in the same form as for difference estimation. (All the terms in the formula have been previously defined.)

$$n = \left(\frac{Y \cdot Z(1 - 2\beta) \cdot SD^*}{AE - E^*} \right)^2$$

If the auditor wants to consider Alpha in determining sample size, the adjustment is made to $AE - E^*$, the same as was done for difference and ratio estimation.

AUDIT USES OF DOLLAR UNIT SAMPLING

The four evaluation techniques discussed in this chapter have become known collectively as dollar unit sampling, because of the method of selecting the samples they are designed to evaluate. Dollar unit sampling is particularly appealing to auditors for at least four reasons. First, it automatically increases the likelihood of selecting high-dollar items from the population being audited. Auditors make a practice of concentrating on these items because they generally represent the greatest risk of material misstatements. Stratified sampling, discussed in Chapter 8, can also be used for this purpose, but dollar unit sampling is often easier to apply.

A second related advantage is the frequently reduced cost of doing the audit testing because several sample items are tested at once. For example, if one large item makes up 10 percent of the total recorded dollar value of the population and the sample size is 100, the dollar unit sampling selection method is likely to result in approximately 10 percent of the sample items from the large population item. Naturally, that item needs to be audited only once, but it counts as a sample of ten. If the item is in error, it is also counted as ten errors. Larger population items may be eliminated by auditing them 100 percent, in the manner described earlier, if the auditor so desires.

Third, dollar unit sampling is appealing because of its ease of application. Dollar unit samples can be evaluated using simple attributes or combined attributes-variables by the application of simple tables. Multinomial bound evaluation requires computer time-sharing, but the method is not difficult if a computer is available. Dollar unit difference estimation is no more difficult than difference or ratio estimation. It is easy to teach and to supervise the use of dollar unit techniques.

Finally, dollar unit sampling always gives the statistical conclusion as a dollar amount. This provides a definite advantage over the use of attributes sampling, where the result is in terms of frequency of the number of items in error.

The primary disadvantage of dollar unit sampling is that the total error bounds resulting from the combined attributes-variables evaluation and multinomial bound evaluation methods when errors are found may be too high to be useful to the auditor. This is because these evaluation methods are inherently conservative when errors are found and often produce bounds far in excess of materiality. At the same time, there may be too few errors to use dollar unit difference estimation. In order to overcome these problems, large samples may be required.

For all the reasons above, dollar unit sampling is most commonly used where zero or very few errors are expected and a dollar result is desired (that is, where attributes sampling is not completely helpful). One such situation is the testing of transactions for compliance purposes. Another is testing the details of year-end asset account balances, such as accounts receivable.

Another common use of dollar unit sampling is made when a large number of errors is expected, the auditor does not want to use an unstratified sampling method, and the client's data are not in machine-readable form. Dollar unit difference estimation is frequently more convenient than stratified difference or ratio estimation in such a situation.

SUGGESTED READINGS AND REFERENCES

ANDERSON, ROD, and A.D. TEITLEBAUM, "Dollar-Unit Sampling: A Solution to the Audit Sampling Dilemma," *CA Magazine*, April 1973, pp. 30–38.

GOODFELLOW, JAMES L., JAMES K. LOEBBECKE, and JOHN NETER, "Perspectives on CAV Sampling Plans," *CA Magazine*, Part I, October 1974, pp. 23–30; Part II, November 1974, pp. 47–53.

LESLIE, DONALD A., A.D. TEITLEBAUM, and RODNEY J. ANDERSON, *Dollar-Unit Sampling: A Practical Guide for Auditors.* Toronto: Copp Clark Pitman, 1979.

NETER, J., R.A. LEITCH, and S.E. FEINBERG, "Dollar-Unit Sampling: Multinomial Bounds for Total Overstatement and Understatement Errors," *Accounting Review*, January 1978, pp. 77–93.

REVIEW QUESTIONS

9-1. Explain the difference in methodology and statistical conclusions between compliance tests using attributes sampling (physical unit) and those using simple attributes (dollar unit).

9-2. A sample size of 150 items is selected in a test of purchase transactions to determine whether the receiving report is attached to the related vendors' invoices. The population size is 5,000 items and the recorded purchases for the year are $1,800,000. Three of the vendors' statements did not have a receiving report attached. Calculate the statistical results for attributes (physical unit) and simple attributes (dollar unit) at a 90% confidence level.

9-3. You are testing for the client's failure to record purchases in the accounts payable journal by sampling receiving reports. No errors are expected. Explain how you would conduct the tests. Why would simple attributes not be appropriate in this situation?

9-4. What is the difference between error bounds as used for dollar unit sampling and confidence limits? Explain why the term *upper and lower error bounds* is used for dollar unit sampling instead of the term *confidence limits*.

9-5. Explain why error bounds are calculated for substantive tests using simple attributes, whereas an upper precision limit in dollars is calculated for compliance tests.

9-6. An auditor is determining the appropriate sample size for testing inventory valuation using dollar unit sampling. The population has 2,620 inventory items valued at $12,625,000. The allowable understatement or overstatement is $500,000 at a 90% confidence level. No errors are expected in the population. Calculate the preliminary sample size using a 100% average error assumption.

9-7. The 2,620 inventory items described in question 9-6 are listed on 44 inventory pages with 60 lines per page. There is a total for each page. The client's data are not in computer-readable form, and the CPA firm does not have a computer terminal available. Describe the three ways in which a dollar unit sample can be selected in this situation. Explain which method is most likely to be followed here.

9-8. The auditor decided to select a sample of 100 items using the random number table noncumulative method for verifying the inventory valuation in question 9-6. In the selection of the 100 random numbers, none of the dollar units were duplicates, but after the dollar units had been associated with the inventory items, it was found that 23 inventory items had been included for testing as previous sample items. One population item was included four times. Explain how this could happen. How should these 23 items be handled?

9-9. No errors were uncovered in the sample of 100 items for question 9-6. Calculate the error bounds and draw audit conclusions based upon the results. How would the error bounds be affected if you used a 50% error assumption?

9-10. What is meant by the "percent of error assumption" in those population items that are in error? Why is it common to use a 100% error assumption when it is almost certain to be highly conservative?

9-11. Explain the difference between simple attributes and combined attributes-variables evaluation. When should each be used?

9-12. Instead of no errors in question 9-9, assume that the following three errors were found:

Error	Recorded value	Audited value
1	897.16	609.16
2	47.02	0
3	1621.68	1522.68

Calculate error bounds for the population, using both the attributes tables and the shortcut method. Draw audit conclusions based on the results.

9-13. Assume that in question 9-12, the population item that included error 1 was included in the sample twice as two separate dollar units. How should the auditor treat this item?

9-14. Why is it difficult to determine the appropriate sample size for combined attributes-variables evaluation? How should the auditor determine the proper sample size?

9-15. What options does the auditor have when an error bound for combined attributes-variables evaluation is larger than the allowable error? When should each option be followed?

9-16. Explain what is meant by multinomial bound evaluation. What are the advantages and disadvantages of multinomial bound evaluation compared to combined attributes-variables evaluation? When should it be used?

9-17. Explain what is meant by dollar unit difference estimation. What are the advantages and disadvantages of dollar unit difference estimation compared to physical unit difference or ratio estimation?

9-18. Under what circumstances is there a risk that dollar unit difference estimation is a biased estimator? Under what circumstances is it apt to be an unreliable estimator?

9-19. What are the circumstances in which dollar unit difference estimation should be used rather than one of the other three dollar unit sampling methods described in the chapter? When would it be inappropriate to use dollar unit difference estimation?

9-20. Taken as a group, what are the primary advantages and disadvantages of the dollar unit sampling methods described in this chapter?

DISCUSSION QUESTIONS AND PROBLEMS

9-21. The following questions concern the determination of the proper sample size in simple attributes sampling using dollar unit sampling.
   a. For each column, 1 through 5, determine the initial sample size needed to satisfy the auditor's requirements from the appropriate table.

	1	2	3	4	5
Confidence level	90%	95%	95%	95%	95%
Maximum dollars in the population that can contain compliance deviations before a control is considered unreliable	$120,000	$6,000	$240	$30	$50,000
Estimated population error rate	3%	3%	3%	3%	0%
Book value	$2,000,000	$100,000	$6,000	$500	$1,000,000

   b. Explain why the finite correction factor is not used for simple attributes, whereas it sometimes is used for physical unit attributes.
   c. Using your understanding of the relationship between the factors above and sample size, state the effect on the initial sample size (increase or decrease) of changing each of the following factors while the other three are held constant:

      (i) An increase in confidence level
      (ii) An increase in the desired upper precision limit
      (iii) An increase in the estimated population error rate
      (iv) An increase in the population value

   d. Compare your answers in part *c* with the results you determined in part *a*. Which of the four factors appears to have the greatest effect on the initial sample size? Which one appears to have the least effect?

   e. Why is the sample size referred to as the initial sample size?

   f. Compare your answers in parts *a* and *c* to the corresponding questions in problem 3-20. Explain why the answers are the same or different.

9-22. The following questions relate to determining the computed upper precision limit in simple attributes.

   a. For each column, 1 through 5, determine the computed upper precision limit from the appropriate tables.

	1	*2*	*3*	*4*	*5*
Confidence level	95%	95%	95%	95%	95%
Book value	$5,000	$5,000	$50,000	$500	$5,000
Sample size	200	50	200	400	100
Number of error occurrences	4	1	4	8	0

   b. Using your understanding of the relationship between the four factors above and the computed upper precision limit, state the effect on the computed upper precision limit (increase or decrease) of changing each of the following factors while the other three are held constant:

      (i) A decrease in the confidence level
      (ii) A decrease in the population value
      (iii) A decrease in the sample size
      (iv) A decrease in the number of occurrences in the sample

   c. Compare your answers in part *b* with the results you determined in part *a*. Which of the four factors appears to have the greatest effect on the computed upper precision limit? Which one appears to have the least effect?

   d. Why is it necessary to compare the computed upper precision limit in dollars with the acceptable upper precision limit in dollars?

   e. Compare your answers in parts *a* and *b* to the corresponding questions in problem 3-21. Explain why your answers are the same or different.

9-23. You are planning to use dollar unit sampling to evaluate the results of accounts receivable confirmation for the Meridian Company. You have already tested internal controls for sales, sales returns and allowances, and cash receipts, and they are considered excellent. Owing to the quality of the controls, you decide to use a confidence level of 90%. There are 3,000 accounts receivable with a gross value of $6,800,000. An overstatement or understatement of more than $150,000 would be considered material.

REQUIRED:

a. Calculate the required sample size at a confidence level of 90%.

b. Calculate the required sample size if the confidence level was 70%. (Hint: Use the combined attributes-variables evaluation error adjustment factors table.)

c. Explain the methodology of obtaining sample items for confirmation. Your explanation should include how to select the random numbers and the receivable items to be confirmed.

d. Assume the sample size you selected for part *a* was 150 items. Twenty-five of the random numbers were for accounts that had already been selected by other random numbers. Calculate the error bounds, assuming no errors were found in the sample.

e. What conclusion can you reach about the population?

9-24. You intend to use dollar unit sampling as a part of the audit of several accounts for Roynpower Manufacturing Company. You have done the audit for the past several years, and there has rarely been an adjusting entry of any kind. Your audit tests of all tests of transactions cycles were completed at an interim date, and the controls have been evaluated as excellent. You therefore decide to use a confidence level of 75% for all direct tests of balances.

You intend to use dollar unit sampling in the audit of the three most material asset balance-sheet account balances: accounts receivable, inventory, and marketable securities. You feel justified in using the same confidence level for each audit area because the controls in each area are excellent.

The recorded balances and related information for the three accounts are as follows:

	Recorded value
Accounts receivable	$ 3,600,000
Inventory	4,800,000
Marketable securities	1,600,000
	$10,000,000

Net earnings before taxes for Roynpower are $2,000,000. You decide that a combined error of $100,000 is allowable for the client.

The audit approach that will be followed is to determine the total sample size needed for all three accounts. A sample will be selected from all $10 million, and the appropriate testing for a sample item will depend on whether the item is a receivable, inventory, or marketable security. The audit conclusions will pertain to the entire $10,000,000, and no conclusion will be made about the three individual accounts unless significant errors are found in the sample.

REQUIRED:

a. Evaluate the audit approach of testing all three account balances in one sample.

b. Calculate the required sample size for all three accounts.

c. Calculate the required sample size for each of the three accounts assuming you decide that the allowable error in each account is $50,000.

d. Assume you select the random sample using a seven-digit random number table. How would you identify which sample item in the population to audit for the number 4,627,871? What audit procedures would be performed?

e. Assume you select a sample of 200 sample items for testing and you find one error in inventory. The recorded value is $987.12, and the audit value is $887.12. Calculate the error bounds for the three combined accounts, and reach appropriate audit conclusions.

9-25. You want to select a dollar unit sample from a population of cash disbursements. The parameters are:

Recorded population value	$26,800,768
Population characteristics	Voucher register with 634 pages, 50 items per page

Assume a confidence level of 90% and an allowable error of $1,000,000.

REQUIRED:

a. What is the sampling interval if you plan to use systematic sampling?

b. How might you identify physical audit units containing the random dollars selected without computer assistance?

c. Assume that in your audit tests, you selected a sample of 120 dollar units. The four errors listed below were found. Compute upper and lower error bounds at a confidence level of 90%.

Voucher no.	Recorded book amount	Audited amount	Error amount
03-764	$ 2,017.62	$1,817.62	$ 200.00
06-112	9,463.12	4,500.00	4,963.12
07-462	514.10	614.10	(100.00)
09-807	16,843.00	6,843.00	10,000.00

d. Are cash disbursements materially misstated? Given the sample size determined in part *a* and the actual sample size in *c*, explain your answer.

9-26. Phil Murphy is using simple attributes in the audit of sales transactions. The system of internal control is excellent in all regards except for the internal verification of unit prices, extensions, and footings of sales invoices. Phil expects to find no errors in the sales tests.

The recorded population value is $2,600,000, and materiality is defined as $5,000 at a 95% confidence level.

REQUIRED:

a. Calculate the required sample size using a 100% average error assumption for both overstatements and understatements.

b. Calculate the required sample size using a 50% average error assumption for both overstatements and understatements.

c. Calculate the required sample size using a 25% average error assumption for overstatements and a 50% average error assumption for understatements.

d. Assume Phil took a sample size of 100 dollar units and found no errors in the audit tests. Calculate the error bounds using the following:
   (i) 100% average error assumption
   (ii) 50% average error assumption for overstatement and understatements
   (iii) 25% average error assumption for overstatements and 50% error assumption for understatements

e. Assume Phil took a sample size of 100 dollar units and found one error in the audit tests. The error was an extension error on a sales invoice, in which the amount billed to the customer was $62.18 when it should have been $642.18. Calculate the error bounds using the following:
   (i) 100% average error assumption
   (ii) 50% average error assumption for overstatement and understatements
   (iii) 25% average error assumption for overstatements and 50% error assumption for understatements

f. What do you believe is the appropriate average error assumption in a situation such as this? Justify your answer.

9-27. In the audit of Price Seed Company for the year ended 9/30, the auditor set a maximum allowable error of $50,000 at a Beta risk of 10%. A sample size of 100 was selected from a population of 1,850 that had a recorded accounts receivable balance of $1,975,000. The following differences were uncovered in the confirmation:

Accounts receivable per records	Accounts receivable per confirmation	Follow-up comments per the confirmation auditor
1. $2,728.00	$2,498.00	Pricing errors on two invoices.
2. $5,125.00	–0–	Customer mailed check 9/26; company received check 10/3.
3. $3,890.00	$1,190.00	Merchandise returned 9/30 and counted in inventory; credit was issued 10/6.
4. $791.00	$815.00	Footing error on an invoice.
5. $548.00	$1,037.00	Goods were shipped 9/28; sale was recorded on 10/6.
6. $3,115.00	$3,190.00	Pricing error on a credit memorandum.
7. $1,540.00	–0–	Goods were shipped on 9/29; customer received goods 10/3; sale was recorded on 9/30.

REQUIRED:

a. Calculate the upper and lower error bounds on the basis of the client errors in the sample.
b. Is the population acceptable as stated? If not, what options are available to the auditor at this point? Which option should the auditor select? Explain.

9-28. Refer to problem 2-29, at the end of Chapter 2. Instead of using stratified estimation, assume Ronson intends to use dollar unit sampling.

REQUIRED:

a. Compare the ease of selection using dollar unit sampling with random number tables to selection using stratified sampling for parts *a* and *c*.
b. Compare the ease of selection using dollar unit sampling with systematic sampling to selection using stratified systematic sampling for parts *a* and *c*.
c. Explain how credit balances in accounts receivable would be treated using dollar unit and physical unit sampling.
d. What are the advantages and disadvantages of using dollar unit sampling compared to stratified sampling in the circumstances described?

9-29. Refer to problem 3-18, at the end of Chapter 3, concerning audit tests of control on shipments. The auditor in that case has now decided to use simple attributes.

REQUIRED:

a. Given the sampling unit that was used for part *a* in problem 3-18, do you believe dollar unit sampling would be desirable in this situation? Explain your answer.
b. Given the sampling unit that was used for part *d* in problem 3-18, do you believe dollar unit sampling would be desirable in this situation? Explain your answer.

9-30. Refer to problem 6-23, at the end of Chapter 6, concerning the confirmation of accounts receivable of Pittance Manufacturing Company. You are now considering using dollar unit sampling in the audit of accounts receivable.

REQUIRED:

a. Is it acceptable to audit the 50 largest accounts when dollar unit sampling is being used? How would these 50 items be treated in evaluating the results if they were selected and audited separately?
b. Would the same sample items have been selected if dollar unit sampling had been used? How would the characteristics of the sample probably differ?
c. Assume the sample items as shown in the sample error results for problem 6-23 had been obtained using dollar unit sampling. Calculate the statistical results using combined attributes-variables evaluation and dollar unit difference estimation.
d. Explain why your answers in *c* are different from or similar to the ones obtained in part *a* of problem 6-23 using difference estimation.
e. Would it be acceptable to follow the practice described in part *c* of problem

6-23 if combined attributes-variables evaluation or dollar unit difference estimation was used?

9-31. Refer to problem 6-26, concerning decision rules for variables sampling. Instead of using ratio estimation, the auditor is using dollar unit difference estimation. Assume that the allowable error, point estimate, and computed interval using dollar unit difference estimation are as stated in the problem.

REQUIRED:

Do parts *a* through *d* in problem 6-26.

9-32. Refer to problem 6-28, concerning the audit of sales and sales returns. For this problem, assume that Rebecca is using dollar unit sampling.

REQUIRED:

a. Would it be practical to use combined attributes-variables estimation in this situation? Why would she have to use a different sampling method (statistical or judgmental) to test for unrecorded sales returns and allowances, even if she did use combined attributes-variables evaluation?

b. Explain how the random numbers would be selected using dollar unit sampling with systematic selection.

c. Calculate the confidence limits for the population of sales and sales returns combined, using dollar unit difference estimation, assuming the sample results shown in problem 6-28 but excluding the unrecorded sales returns and allowances.

d. How large would the sample need to be to satisfy Rebecca's requirements as they were specified in problem 6-28, assuming dollar unit difference estimation is used?

9-33. Refer to problem 6-29, concerning discounts on raw materials and purchased parts. As an alternative to ratio or difference estimation, the CPA is considering dollar unit difference estimation.

REQUIRED:

a. Would the total sample size for dollar unit difference estimation probably be larger than for ratio estimation? Explain the reasons for your answer.

b. Would the number of invoices that would need to be examined to calculate the discounts not taken be larger or smaller for dollar unit difference estimation than for ratio estimation?

c. What are the advantages and disadvantages of dollar unit difference estimation compared to unstratified ratio estimation in this situation?

9-34. Refer to problem 8-26, concerning the audit of accounts receivable and inventory. You have decided to use simple attributes instead of mean-per-unit estimation because no errors are expected in the sample. You are concerned about the combined amount of error in accounts receivable and inventory, but not the individual balances.

REQUIRED:

a. Calculate the required sample size using simple attributes, assuming a Beta risk of 5% and an allowable error of $34,500.

b. How would you approach selecting a random sample for inventory and accounts receivable in this situation, using systematic selection?

c. Assume you selected the required sample size in part *a* and found no errors in your audit tests. What would be your statistical and audit conclusions?

d. Assume you selected the required sample size in part *a* and found four errors in your audit tests. What would you do at this point?

9-35. Refer to problem 8-33, concerning the audit of inventory. Mary now decides to use dollar unit sampling rather than mean-per-unit.

REQUIRED:

a. Would it be acceptable to use dollar unit difference estimation in this situation? Explain your answer.

b. Calculate the required sample size using simple attributes at the 90% confidence level. Compare your answer to part *a* in problem 8-33.

c. Under what circumstances will the auditor conclude that the population is acceptable if the sample size selected using dollar unit sampling is the same as the one calculated in part *b*?

d. What options does the auditor have if several errors are found in the sample using dollar unit sampling?

10

use of
statistical techniques
in analytical tests

INTRODUCTION

As mentioned in Chapter 1, analytical tests involve the examination of trends and relationships of data for several purposes: to improve the auditor's understanding of the client's business and results of operations in relation to the general planning process; to determine if there is any indication that the client is in or is moving toward financial difficulty; to search for audit areas that appear to contain financial statement errors and should receive special attention; and to obtain additional evidence about the fairness of financial statement balances in audit areas where indications of possible errors are not found.

Analytical tests are used extensively in all audits and for review services as a part of compilation and review. The most commonly used techniques include computing financial ratios and percentages for comparison with both industry data and internal data. These traditional analytical tests are simple in concept and application, involving few and generally simple computations.

Several factors in recent years have motivated auditors to seek more effective analytical testing techniques:

1. *Audit Costs.* Auditing is based on the assumption of efficiency. As salaries of staff and number of hours have increased owing to changes in the auditing environ-

ment, it has become necessary to find procedures that provide useful audit evidence at a low cost. Analytical tests do not require a great deal of time to perform and are therefore attractive in terms of reducing audit costs.

2. *Lawsuits.* Many of the lawsuits against CPA firms have directly or indirectly concerned such things as management fraud, misstatements resulting from management policies, and the failure to disclose important information, rather than the extent of the auditor's detailed tests. To uncover these types of errors, many auditors believe a thorough understanding of the client's business and industry is essential before performing and evaluating detailed audit procedures. Analytical tests are a major tool in gaining this understanding.

3. *Quantitative Approach.* With the development of the computer and increased emphasis on mathematical and statistical methods in college curricula, many auditors enter the profession with a favorable view toward problem solving and the use of quantitative methods. Naturally, these auditors will attempt to use their skills. The area of analytical testing offers opportunities for using quantitative methods.

4. *Quarterly Reviews.* In 1976, the Securities and Exchange Commission adopted a requirement under which CPAs must perform formal reviews of their publicly held clients' published interim financial statements. The data in these financial statements must be included in the audited annual financial statements as an *unaudited* footnote. Although the data are unaudited, the auditor is by statute *associated* with the data as a result of his review. Certain review procedures must be performed to fulfill the auditor's responsibilities with regard to this association. These are presented in SAS 24, *Review of Interim Financial Information.* One of these procedures is directly concerned with analytical review:

> Analytical review of interim financial information by reference to internal financial statements, trial balances or other financial data, to identify and inquire about relationships and individual items that appear to be unusual. An analytical review consists of (i) a systematic comparison of current financial information with that anticipated for the current period, with that of the immediately preceding interim period, and with that of the corresponding interim period of the previous fiscal year; (ii) a study of the interrelationships of elements of financial information that would be expected to conform to a predictable pattern based on the entity's experience; and (iii) a consideration of the types of matters that in the preceding year or quarters have required accounting adjustments.

The SAS 24 requirements do not include the examination of details of account balances and transactions. Only this set of general analytical procedures is required. Auditors must believe these procedures are an effective means of uncovering errors, particularly in the light of a lack of definition by the SEC of the term *associated with* as it applies to the reviewed data.

Although the use of advanced quantitative or statistical methods in performing analytical tests is today in a developmental stage, several useful techniques have been tried and proven effective. Three techniques are discussed in this chapter, and their use in analytical tests is illustrated. They are *regression analysis*, *Markov chain processes*, and *discriminant analysis*. In studying these techniques, the reader must realize that each technique is actually a complex area in itself. The presentation given is accurate and provides an appropriate degree of understanding, but it is at a rudimentary level. The application of these techniques in practice requires greater study and usually is accomplished with the assistance of time-sharing-based computer programs.

REGRESSION ANALYSIS

Regression analysis is used to make inferences of what financial balances *should be* for comparison to *recorded* balances.[1] By making this comparison, the auditor can identify those balances that, based on the analysis, appear to be out of line. The audit work can then be allocated so that more effort is spent investigating and substantiating the out-of-line balances than those supported by the analysis.

Regression analysis is commonly applied in two general audit situations. One is when inferences must be made about a specific account balance. For example, an inference can be made about the reasonableness of selling expense for a particular period, based on selling expense and its relationship to sales during other periods. The second use is to infer reasonable results of a subunit of an entity as of an audit date, based on the results of all other similar subunits as of the same date. An example would be the net operating income of an individual store in a large retail chain.

This section will present the technical aspects of making these inferences and illustrate their application.

Relationships as a Basis for Inference

Regression analysis as an inference tool is based on the notion that the data it deals with have some pattern and reliability. There are frequently *relationships* within data that can be identified and relied upon to produce useful inferences. These relationships are expressed in terms of *variables*. Variables are the identity of the various types of data being considered in the analysis. For example, in inferring current-year selling expense, the variables to consider might include current sales, previous year's selling expense, the number of products, and the number of salesmen.

The identification of variables allows the auditor (inferrer) to define the relationships that exist among them. These relationships will never be exact,

---

[1]Note that the term *inference* is used rather than *prediction*. *Prediction* refers to future values. Although regression analysis can be used to make predictions, as in forecasting, in auditing it is used to estimate what existing values should be, given other relevant data. *Inference* is considered a more appropriate term to indicate this use and to avoid confusion with use in prediction.

and they will differ at various times. Thus, the definition of the relationships among variables will be *statistical* in nature. As long as the relationships indicate that a relatively stable pattern exists, useful inferences are possible.

Variables for a particular analysis, in order to be defined, must be classified into two types: *independent* variables and *dependent* variables. Independent variables are associated with *cause*, and dependent variables are associated with *effect*. For example, if sales were the independent variable and selling expense the dependent variable, the analysis made would define how selling expense relates to sales over time and infer what selling expense should be as of the audit date, given sales for the corresponding operating period. The value the auditor intends to make inferences about is the dependent variable. The independent variable or variables are used to determine the expected value of the dependent variable.

Common statistical notation for variables is as follows:

$$X = \text{independent variable}$$

$$Y = \text{dependent variable}$$

Thus, in our example, if selling expense is defined as 10 percent of sales, the relationship between the two would be expressed as:

$$Y = .1X$$

LINEAR REGRESSION

Linear regression is a technique that defines the relationship between variables in terms of a straight line. This technique analyzes the relationships among the variables and determines the straight line that best fits the pattern of the data. The criterion for best fit is the line that results in the minimum aggregate squared difference between the regression line and the amount of each data item. This is commonly known as the *method of least squares*. This method has two useful results: (1) a definition of the straight-line relationship, which can be used for inference; and (2) a measure of the goodness of fit—the *coefficient of correlation*—which indicates the strength of the relationships being used for inference.

Several steps are needed when regression analysis is used to make inferences about a recorded value. Briefly summarized, the steps are these:

1. Define the dependent and independent variables. The standard formulation for simple linear regression is $Y = a + bX$.

2. Decide on the number of data sets desired to determine the confidence limits.
3. Calculate the values, given the data sets, for *a* and *b*.
4. Calculate the coefficient of correlation.
5. Calculate the point estimate of the value from $\hat{Y}_x = a + bX$.
6. Determine the standard deviation of the observed data sets $(S_{Y.x})$.
7. Determine the standard error of the point estimate $(S_{\bar{Y}_x})$.
8. Calculate the precision interval $(tS_{\bar{Y}_x})$.
9. Calculate the confidence interval $(\hat{Y}_x \pm tS_{\bar{Y}_x})$.
10. Compare the recorded value to the confidence interval and investigate outliers.

Define the Dependent and Independent Variables

These two terms have been previously defined. The example that will be used in the discussion of regression analysis includes one dependent and one independent variable. The dependent variable is selling expense, and the independent variable is sales.

Since the regression line under the least squares method is a straight line, it is always defined by the following standard formulation:

$$Y = a + bX$$

where *a* is the value of Y when $X = 0$, and *b* is the slope of the regression line—that is, the value by which Y changes for each additional unit of X. The sign associated with *b* will be positive if Y increases as X increases, and negative if Y decreases as X increases.

Suppose that monthly selling expense in our example is $1,000 even when sales are zero, because a sales office and one salesman must be maintained. Salesmen are added as volume goes up. For each dollar of sales, $.02 is added to selling expense. This relationship would be defined as:

$$\text{Selling expense } (Y) = \$1{,}000(a) + [.02(b) \text{ Sales}(X)]$$

If sales were $100,000, one would expect selling expense for the month to be $3,000 [$1,000 + (.02 × $100,000)] under the defined relationship.

Data Sets

It is necessary to decide on the number of sets of data to be used to determine the regression estimate of the dependent variable. In auditing, the number of data sets is frequently equal to the number of prior periods' account balance information used to estimate the current period's account balance. The number of data sets has the same effect on the precision interval for regression as sample size does for variables sampling. If all other things are assumed equal, the larger the number of data sets, the smaller the precision interval.

Frequently, the causal relationship of the independent variable and the dependent variable changes over time. If the causal relationship is believed to have changed significantly, the older data sets should not be used.

The example of selling expenses and sales uses as the data sets the current year's twelve months' recorded selling expenses and sales. There are therefore twelve data sets, as follows:

Month	Selling expense Y	Sales X
January	$ 3,000	$ 100,000
February	4,000	180,000
March	3,500	180,000
April	4,200	170,000
May	4,100	200,000
June	3,900	190,000
July	3,200	140,000
August	2,400	100,000
September	3,000	120,000
October	2,900	110,000
November	3,300	140,000
December	3,800	170,000
Total	$41,300	$1,800,000

It would have been possible to use both this year's and last year's sales and selling expense (24 data sets), or only last year's. It is the auditor's choice to select the number of data sets.

Calculate the Values for a and b

Under the regression technique, the problem is to find *the* straight line that best fits the data sets for the two or more variables. This is done by calculating values for *a* and *b* from the data in such a way that the resulting line minimizes the sum of the squares. This is done using the following two formulas:

$$b = \frac{\sum XY - \dfrac{\sum X \sum Y}{n}}{\sum X^2 - \dfrac{(\sum X)^2}{n}}$$

$$a = \frac{1}{n}\left(\sum Y - b \sum X\right)$$

where n is the number of data sets of X and Y used. There are twelve data sets for the ongoing example.

Use of the three formulas presented up to this point is illustrated by continuing our selling expense example in Figure 10-1.

Month	Selling expense Y	Sales X	XY	Y^2*	X^2
January	$3,000	$100,000	$300,000,000	$ 9,000,000	$10,000,000,000
February	4,000	180,000	720,000,000	16,000,000	32,400,000,000
March	3,500	180,000	630,000,000	12,250,000	32,400,000,000
April	4,200	170,000	714,000,000	17,640,000	28,900,000,000
May	4,100	200,000	820,000,000	16,810,000	40,000,000,000
June	3,900	190,000	741,000,000	15,210,000	36,100,000,000
July	3,200	140,000	448,000,000	10,240,000	19,600,000,000
August	2,400	100,000	240,000,000	5,760,000	10,000,000,000
September	3,000	120,000	360,000,000	9,000,000	14,400,000,000
October	2,900	110,000	319,000,000	8,410,000	12,100,000,000
November	3,300	140,000	462,000,000	10,890,000	19,600,000,000
December	3,800	170,000	646,000,000	14,440,000	28,900,000,000
Totals	$41,300	$1,800,000	$6,400,000,000	$145,650,000	$284,400,000,000

Mean $\bar{Y} = 3,441.67$; $\bar{X} = 150,000$*

$$b = \frac{6,400,000,000 - \dfrac{(1.800,000)(41,300)}{12}}{284,400,000,000 - \dfrac{(1,800,000)^2}{12}} = \frac{205,000,000}{14,400,000,000}$$

$$b = .0142$$

$$a = \frac{1}{12}[41,300 - (.0142)(1,800,000)] = 1,311.67$$

These values are not used to compute the regression line, but will be used later.

FIGURE 10-1 Computation of regression line—selling expense example

Thus, the regression line for these data is defined as:

$$Y = 1,311.67 + .0142X$$

Figure 10-2 expands on this example by presenting the data graphically.

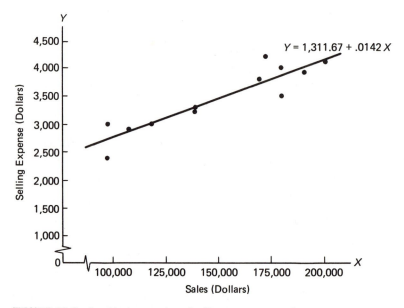

FIGURE 10-2 Graphic presentation of selling expense example

Calculate the Coefficient of Correlation

The visual impression given by Figure 10-2 is that the regression line represents a good definition of the relationship of selling expense to sales. Most of the data sets result in points that are close to the regression line, and none are a long way out. The question this raises is: How consistent is the pattern of data as represented by the regression line? This is answered by computing the coefficient of correlation.

The coefficient of correlation will always be a signed number with an absolute value between 0 and 1. The sign indicates the slope of the regression line it is associated with. For a group of data in which all sets result in a point directly on the regression line, the coefficient will be plus or minus 1. This indicates an exact and unvarying relationship between the variables in all instances. Where there is no clear relationship between the variables represented, the coefficient will be 0. Decimal fractions between these extremes represent degrees of usefulness of X in inferring Y. There are no standards for an acceptable level of correlation in practice; the auditor must determine the level he or she would accept as a matter of judgment.

The following formula is used to compute the coefficient of correlation, which is represented by the symbol r:

$$r = \frac{\sum XY - \dfrac{\sum X \sum Y}{n}}{\sqrt{\sum X^2 - \dfrac{(\sum X)^2}{n}} \sqrt{\sum Y^2 - \dfrac{(\sum Y)^2}{n}}}$$

The coefficient of correlation for the ongoing example of selling expenses is calculated as follows:

$$r = \frac{6,400,000,000 - \frac{(1,800,000)(41,300)}{12}}{\sqrt{284,400,000,000 - \frac{(1,800,000)^2}{12}} \sqrt{145,650,000 - \frac{(41,300)^2}{12}}}$$

$$= \frac{205,000,000}{\sqrt{14,400,000,000} \sqrt{3,509,167}}$$

$$= .912$$

Since this is a value close to 1, it indicates a close correlation between the two variables. This was expected after viewing Figure 10-2. The positive value of r indicates that selling expense can be expected to increase as sales increase.

Calculate the Point Estimate

The expected value of selling expense for any month can now be determined from the formula $Y = 1311.67 + .0142X$. For example, the expected value of July selling expense is \$3,299.67 [1311.67 + .0142(140,000)]. Is the difference between \$3,200 actual and \$3,299.67 significant and something to be concerned about?

As we have established, the data sets analyzed with the regression technique are rarely, if ever, perfectly correlated. Thus, if inferences are to be made from the data for comparison to recorded amounts, the estimated amount and the recorded amount would not be expected to be exactly the same, even when the recorded amount is correct. Thus, for these comparisons to be useful, the auditor must be able to judge whether the difference between the amounts is *reasonable*—that is, due only to the imperfection inherent in defining the relationships among the variables—or *unreasonable*—that is, due to a possible significant error in the recorded amount.

The technique used to make this judgment is to determine a *confidence interval* about the regression line. This confidence interval is similar to that used in making variables estimates. It is based on normal distribution theory. The auditor uses the confidence interval by concluding that a recorded amount falling outside the confidence interval requires additional investigation.

Determine the Standard Deviation

Recall that, in Chapter 4, where variables estimation was first introduced, a confidence interval was defined as:

$$\text{CI}\,(\bar{X}) = \hat{X} \pm Z \frac{\text{SD}}{\sqrt{n}}$$

where $\hat{\bar{X}}$ is the estimated average audited value of the population sampled, Z is the area of the normal (sampling) distribution relating to the reliability level desired, SD is the standard deviation of the sample data, and n is the sample size. The finite correction factor has been omitted only for the sake of this illustration.

With regression analysis, the process is basically the same, but the formulation is somewhat more complex because there is more than one variable involved (in the variables case shown here, the only variable is audited value). In regression analysis, the values of the two or more variables must be considered, as well as the correlation among the variables.

An unbiased point estimate of the standard deviation of the sampling distribution of Y—that is, $S_{\bar{Y}_X}$, the standard error of $\bar{Y}_X$—is obtained using the observed data of X and Y.

As for variables estimation, the standard deviation must be calculated first. $S_{Y.X}$ is the standard deviation of the observed data sets, determined by:

$$S_{Y.X} = \sqrt{\frac{1}{n-2}\left[\left(\sum Y^2 - \frac{(\sum Y)^2}{n}\right) - \frac{\left(\sum XY - \frac{\sum X \sum Y}{n}\right)^2}{\sum X^2 - \frac{(\sum X)^2}{n}}\right]}$$

All the terms in the formula have been previously defined. To illustrate the calculation, return to our previous example. Recall the following values:

$\sum X$	(sales for twelve periods)	1,800,000
$\sum Y$	(selling expense for twelve periods)	41,300
$\sum XY$		6,400,000,000
$\sum Y^2$		145,650,000
$\sum X^2$		284,400,000,000
n		12

Note that the three major expressions under the square root sign are identical to those used in calculating either or both b and r. Using these values and the formula for $S_{Y.X}$:

$$S_{Y.X} = \sqrt{\frac{1}{12-2}\left\{\left[145.65(10^6) - \frac{(41,300)^2}{12}\right] - \frac{\left(6.4(10^9) - \frac{1.8(10^6)41,300}{12}\right)^2}{284.4(10^9) - \frac{(1,200,000)^2}{12}}\right\}}$$

$$= \sqrt{\frac{1}{10}\left[3,509,167 - \left(\frac{(205,000,000)^2}{14,400,000,000}\right)\right]}$$

$$= 243.05$$

Determine the Standard Error of the Point Estimate

The standard error for variables estimation is determined by the formula $SD/\sqrt{n}$. In regression analysis, the standard error $(S_{\bar{Y}_x})$ is as follows:

$$S_{\bar{Y}_x} = \frac{S_{Y.x}}{\sqrt{n}} + S_{Y.x}\sqrt{\frac{(X - \bar{X})^2}{\sum X^2 - \frac{(\sum X)^2}{n}}}$$

All the terms in the formula have been previously defined. The standard deviation computed from a series of observations (twelve, in this case) will be constant for the inferences drawn about the data; however, the standard error will vary depending on the particular value of X assumed. For instance, in the example case where sales are \$140,000, the standard error—$S_{\bar{Y}_x}$—would be as follows (as with $S_{Y.x}$, note that the expression of the denominator under the square root sign was derived in the earlier computations):

$$S_{\bar{Y}_{140,000}} = \frac{243.05}{\sqrt{12}} + 243.05\sqrt{\frac{(140,000 - 150,000)^2}{14,400,000,000}}$$

$$= 40.51$$

Calculate the Precision Interval

Using the standard error, we can construct a precision interval for selling expense predicted from sales of \$140,000. This is done by multiplying the standard error by the number of standard errors associated with the confidence level desired, and then adding and subtracting the result to and from the selling expense obtained from $Y = 1,311.67 + .0142X$, where $X = 140,000$.

As noted earlier, under classic variables estimation, the Z value is used to determine the precision interval. The Z value represents the number of standard errors along the horizontal axis about the mean under the normal distribution, which includes a specified area of the distribution. For purposes of the regression confidence interval, the procedure is the same, but a different distribution—the *t-distribution*—is used. The t-distribution, like the normal distribution, is symmetrical and unimodal, but it is flatter and varies with different sample sizes. At the point of sample sizes of about 30 and larger, the t-distribution and the normal distribution are the same. The t-distribution is often used in estimation sampling when small sample sizes (below 30) are used. A table of t-distribution values is given in Figure 10-3.

	Total area in both tails			Total area in both tails	
Degrees of freedom	*.10*	*.05*	*Degrees of freedom*	*.10*	*.05*
1	6.314	12.706	16	1.746	2.120
2	2.920	4.303	17	1.740	2.110
3	2.353	3.182	18	1.734	2.101
4	2.132	2.776	19	1.729	2.093
5	2.015	2.571	20	1.725	2.086
6	1.943	2.447	21	1.721	2.080
7	1.895	2.365	22	1.717	2.074
8	1.860	2.306	23	1.714	2.069
9	1.833	2.262	24	1.711	2.064
10	1.812	2.228	25	1.708	2.060
11	1.796	2.201	26	1.706	2.056
12	1.782	2.179	27	1.703	2.052
13	1.771	2.160	28	1.701	2.048
14	1.761	2.145	29	1.699	2.045
15	1.753	2.131	30	1.697	2.042
			Normal distribution	1.645	1.960

Source: Abridged from Table III of Fisher and Yates, *Statistical Tables for Biological, Agricultural, and Medical Research*, 6th ed., 1974, published by Longman Group Ltd., London, and by permission of the authors and publishers.

FIGURE 10-3 Table of t-distribution

In the use of the t-distribution in regression analysis, the number of data sets determines the degrees of freedom that apply. Specifically, t_{n-2} is used. Thus, in our example, since twelve observations were made, ten degrees of freedom are used.

The table presented in Figure 10-3 has columns that relate to the following confidence intervals, which show the value of t, assuming twelve data sets.

	Confidence level		
	90%	*95%*	*97½%*
One-sided interval	–	1.812	2.228
Two-sided interval	1.812	2.228	–

Thus, in our example, the precision interval for a two-sided 90 percent confidence interval estimate of selling expense for sales of $140,000 would be:

$$t_{10}S\hat{Y}_{140,000} = 1.812 \times 40.51$$
$$= 73.40$$

Calculate the Confidence Interval

The point estimate at $X = 140,000$, using $Y = 1,311.67 + .0142X$, is 3299.67. Given this result and the precision figure above, the 90 percent confidence interval to be constructed is:

$$3,299.67 \pm 73.40$$
$$= 3,226.27 \text{ to } 3,373.07$$

Compare the Recorded Values to the Confidence Interval

Recall from Figure 10-1 that the recorded amount of selling expense for July and November, months when sales were $140,000, was $3,200 and $3,300 respectively. November selling expense falls within the confidence interval above; however, July selling expense does not. This may lead the auditor to concentrate more effort in inspecting transactions relating to July than to November.

Of course, a more complete analysis would be to determine a confidence interval about each observation point and follow up on all outliers. The results of this analysis are shown in Figure 10-4, which is an extension of the graphic analysis of the regression line presented earlier.

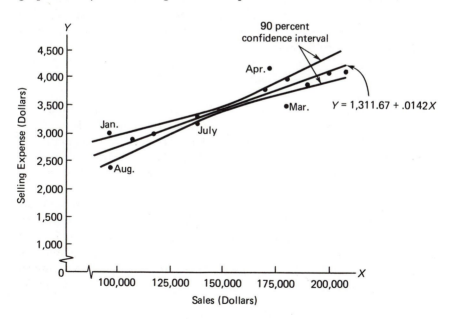

FIGURE 10-4 90% confidence interval for selling expense

Figure 10-4 indicates that three months—March, April, and August—have selling-expense amounts that are considerably outside expected amounts, and two months—January and July—might be considered borderline. On the basis of this more complete analysis, the auditor would emphasize the three primary outlying months in investigating the selling expense and sales accounts.

COMPLEX APPLICATIONS

The preceding presentation on regression analysis discusses basic concepts and provides a methodology for evaluating the reasonableness of accounting information in either of the two situations introduced at the outset. The example used corresponds to determining the reasonableness of a particular account for a particular period based on a trend over time. The observations could as easily have been of similar subunits to identify outliers at a particular time.

In the application of regression analysis to practice, two complexities are frequently added to this basic approach. The first of these is consideration of more than one independent variable in determining the value of the dependent variable Y. For example, in analyzing selling expense, number of products and number of salesmen might be used as independent variables, as well as sales dollars. This situation is referred to as *multiple regression analysis*. In multiple regression analysis, the regression line must be determined by the general formula:

$$Y = a + b_1X_1 + b_2X_2 \ldots + b_mX_m$$

where the independent variables are $X_1 \ldots X_m$ and the quantities that define the best fit (on the basis of the least squares method) are $b_1 \ldots b_m$.

Where there are two or more independent variables, the computation of a and $b_1 \ldots b_m$, as well as the coefficient of correlation and inferential data, becomes quite cumbersome. In such cases, the computer should be used to make the calculations.

The second complexity is the use of a curved rather than a straight line to represent the relationship between variables. In business situations, straight-line relationships have obvious limits. For example, in cost-volume relationships, cost efficiencies may occur beyond a minimum volume and then reach a point where they disappear. There are many types of curvilinear equations that may be used to represent sets of correlated data. For example:

$$Y = a + bX + X^2$$

Computer programs are often used to analyze data in order to identify a definable curvilinear relationship. The least squares method is applied in the same manner as with straight-line regression analysis.

The overriding consideration in applying regression analysis in audit applications is establishing logical causal relationships between variables. If changes in the independent variables chosen do not actually *cause* changes in the dependent variable, but change with the dependent variable by coincidence, the regression analysis, even though it might appear useful based on the data, in actuality may not be useful, or may even be misleading.

MARKOV CHAIN PROCESSES

Markov chain processes are used to describe a situation in which there is a series of events that have a number of possible outcomes, and the probability that a particular outcome of one event will occur is dependent on the actual outcome of a preceding event. Several authors have recognized that the aging of accounts receivable can be described in this way and the reasonableness of the allowance for doubtful accounts can be tested by auditors using a Markov chain process.[2]

Illustration—Determining Allowance for Doubtful Accounts

Consider the following:

1. ABC Company has the following accounts receivable aging as of year-end:

Current	$2,500,000
30 days	1,000,000
60 days	600,000
90 days	300,000
Over 90 days	400,000
Total	$4,800,000

2. There are 24,000 accounts; the average account balance is $200. Balances range from $1 to $1,200.

[2]See, for example, Springer, Herlihy, Mall, and Beggs, *Probabilistic Models* (Homewood, Ill.: Richard D. Irwin, 1968), pp. 82–100; and J. D. Barrington, "Accounting Models for Managing Credit," *The Canadian Chartered Accountant*, May 1971.

3. A sample of accounts is taken by the auditor from each aging category at different points throughout the year to determine whether they were collected in the ensuing month, with the following results:

Aging category	Percent collected in ensuing month
Current	85%
30 days	65
60 days	45
90 days	55
Over 90 days	40

4. A further sample of accounts over 90 days also indicates that 5 percent of such accounts are written off as uncollectible in the ensuing month.

Given these data, what should be the allowance for doubtful accounts as of year-end, pertaining to total accounts receivable of $4,800,000?

First, consider that at any point in this situation, the accounts fall into five possible states, corresponding to the aging categories. As an accounting cycle (one month, in this case) occurs, each account receivable will change to another state, or move out of the aging altogether through either *collection* or *write-off*. Collection and write-off are referred to as *absorption* states, because they eliminate items from the process.

The investigation of what has actually been happening to accounts in various aging categories throughout the year, expressed in items 3 and 4, provides a set of *probabilities* concerning the movement of accounts between states. These data can be summarized in terms used in describing Markov chain processes as a *partitioned matrix of transitional probabilities*. This is done in Figure 10-5. This matrix shows that each account must, during the accounting cycle, either be paid, be written off, or enter the next aging category. One of these events must occur, and no more than one can occur for the same account. Thus, the combined probability of their occurrence is 1.0, or 100 percent. The body of the matrix shows the probabilities of the separate events occurring for each aging category based on data gathered. These probabilities are therefore established by the audit process. They could be adjusted by the auditor based on new evidence, or they could be expressed as ranges of "best" and "worst" expected experience, as the auditor's judgment dictates.

Armed with this information, the auditor is in a position to determine at a given point the amount of each aging category that will eventually be uncollectible (written off) if the probabilities selected hold true. For example, of the current accounts receivable totaling $2,500,000, 85 percent are

Possible state	Probability of being absorbed		Probability of moving into next nonabsorption state				
	Paid	Written off	Current	30	60	90	Over 90
Paid	100	0	0	0	0	0	0
Written off	0	100	0	0	0	0	0
Current	85	0	0	15	0	0	0
30	65	0	0	0	35	0	0
60	45	0	0	0	0	55	0
90	55	0	0	0	0	0	45
Over 90	40	5	0	0	0	0	55

FIGURE 10-5 Partitioned matrix of transitional probabilities

expected to be collected in the first ensuing month. This means only 15 percent, or $375,000, will be 30 days old at the end of that month. In the second ensuing month, 65 percent of that amount should be collected, leaving only $131,250 to enter the 60-day aging category, and so forth. Eventually, after five months, some residual will be written off, and this amount should be reserved. This process is summarized for the current accounts in Figure 10-6.

Period	Amount due at beginning of period	Expected to be collected during period		Expected to be written off during period		Residual
		Percent	Amount	Percent	Amount	
1	$2,500,000	85	$2,125,000	0	0	$375,000
2	375,000	65	243,750	0	0	131,250
3	131,250	45	59,062	0	0	72,188
4	72,188	55	39,703	0	0	32,485
5	32,485	40	12,994	5	$1,624	17,867
6	17,867	40	7,147	5	893	9,827
7	9,827	40	3,931	5	491	5,405
8	5,405	40	2,162	5	270	3,073
9	3,073	40	1,229	5	154	1,690
10	1,690	40	676	5	84	930
.	.	.	.	.	.	.
.	.	.	.	.	.	.
.	.	.	.	.	.	.
.	.	.	.	.	.	.
Totals			$2,496,391		$3,609	
Percent of original amount			99.86		.14	

FIGURE 10-6 Summary of expected collection or write-off of current accounts receivable

Thus, it is seen here that if an account is current as of the evaluation date, it has a high likelihood of eventually being collected and a low likelihood of being written off. When similar computations are made for all aging categories, the results in Figure 10-7 are obtained, which indicate that the allowance for doubtful accounts should be approximately $90,000.

Aging category	Account balances	Expected percent to be:		Expected amount of write-offs
		Collected	Written off	
Current	$2,500,000	99.86%	.14%	$ 3,609
30	1,000,000	99.04	.96	9,625
60	600,000	97.25	2.75	16,500
90	300,000	95.00	5.00	15,000
Over 90	400,000	88.89	11.11	44,444
	$4,800,000			$89,178

FIGURE 10-7 Summary of expected eventual write-off of accounts receivable

Direct Computation

A simplification of the Markov process described in this illustration is that by the use of *matrix algebra* and computer techniques, the expected write-off percentages used can be calculated directly, avoiding the cumbersome computations shown in Figure 10-6. This is done by representing the matrix of transitional probabilities in mathematical terms as shown in Figure 10-8, and solving for the "expected loss factor"—the expected percent of each aging category to be written off, using the formulation given below.

Possible state	Probability of being absorbed		Probability of moving into next nonabsorption state				
	Paid	Written off	Current	30	60	90	Over 90
Paid Written off	I				O		
Current 30 60 90 Over 90	R				Q		

FIGURE 10-8 Matrix of transitional probabilities

On this basis, each component in the matrix in Figure 10-8 is represented by a symbol:

I is the probability of an absorbed account's entering an absorption state. This must always either be zero or 100%.

O is the probability of an absorbed account's moving between nonabsorption states. This must always be zero.

R is the probability of an unabsorbed account's being absorbed in the next cycle.

Q is the probability of an unabsorbed account's moving into the next nonabsorption state.

As was illustrated in Figure 10-6, the expected loss factor is equal to the probability of an item's entering every ensuing state without being collected, until it is finally absorbed by being written off.

This will be done for each aging category. For example, for the aging category 90 days, in period 1 there is no write-off, but 45 percent of the accounts become over 90 days old. In the second period, 40 percent of those items are collected and 5 percent are written off. Thus, the expected loss after two periods is:

$$0 + (.05)(.45)$$
$$= .0225$$

Of the original 90-days' amount of $300,000, 2.25 percent = $6,750. The proof of this amount is:

1. Amount becoming over 90 days old = $300,000 × .45 = $135,000
2. Amount of residual written off = $135,000 × .05 = $6,750

At the beginning of the third period, the residual is 55 percent of 45 percent of the original amount, and the amount written off is 5 percent of that amount, or:

$$R \cdot Q \cdot Q$$
$$= R \cdot Q^2$$

Thus, for periods 1, 2, and 3, the expected loss factor is:

$$R + R \cdot Q + R \cdot Q^2$$

This process will be continued until the entire amount is absorbed, and is defined mathematically as:

$$R + R \cdot Q + R \cdot Q^2 + \ldots R \cdot Q^n$$

or, equivalently:

Expected loss factor for each aging category $= R(I - Q)^{-1}$

For the reader who is familiar with the conventions of matrix algebra, the expression $(I - Q)^{-1}$ is the inverse of the matrix $(I - Q)$ and is easily obtained using these conventions to process the contents of the transitional matrix (Figure 10-5) using common computer techniques. The results will be in the form of the "Expected Percent to Be Written Off" column in Figure 10-7.

DISCRIMINANT ANALYSIS

Discriminant analysis refers to a group of techniques used to develop a set of rules for classifying numerically represented situations into useful groups, usually for purposes of decision making. The rules for classification are developed from empirical data gathered over a broad set of actual outcomes of situations identical (or at least very similar) to those being classified. The results of discriminant analysis are often called *scoring systems*. Examples of uses of these are scores based on consumer attributes in granting credit by retail stores, and scores based on borrower attributes in giving loans by banks.

Illustration—Predicting Business Failure

The most common use of discriminant analysis in auditing is in judging whether a present or potential client company may be likely to become insolvent or bankrupt in future periods. This is extremely important to the auditor in accepting new clients and in setting required overall assurance levels for existing clients.

The most notable work completed in this area is that done by Edward Altman.[3] Altman developed a scoring system related to bankruptcy by studying financial statement data and various ratios developed from those data for a sample of companies that included equal numbers of healthy companies and companies that had actually become bankrupt. All the companies were in manufacturing industries. Using discriminant analysis, the author was able to develop a satisfactory formula for developing scores and a set of scoring decision rules. The formula is:

$$Z = .012X_1 + .014X_2 + .033X_3 + .006X_4 + .010X_5$$

---

[3]See Edward I. Altman, *Corporate Bankruptcy in America* (Lexington, Mass.: Heath Lexington, 1971); and Edward I. Altman and Thomas P. McGough, "Evaluation of a Company as a Going Concern," *Journal of Accountancy*, December 1974.

where:

Z = the determined score

X_1 = working capital $\div$ total assets

X_2 = retained earnings $\div$ total assets

X_3 = earnings before interest and taxes $\div$ total assets

X_4 = market value of equity $\div$ book value of total debt

X_5 = sales $\div$ total assets

In computing the Z score in this instance, the percentages computed in X_1 through X_5 are expressed as whole numbers; that is, 10 percent would be expressed as 10, and so forth.

Altman's data revealed that the following scoring system would be a reasonable basis for discrimination:

Z score	Discrimination
Less than 1.81	Company will go bankrupt within a year or two.
1.81 to 2.675	Company will probably go bankrupt, but there is a chance it will not.
2.676 to 2.99	Company will probably not go bankrupt, but there is a chance it will.
2.99 or over	Company will not go bankrupt.

Although the use of a scoring system such as this is relatively straightforward, the development of the scoring model itself is complex and beyond the level of this text. However, our purpose here is to give the reader an appreciation for the types of tools and techniques entering the auditor's world. Once such models are developed through sound research and development efforts, they can be of invaluable assistance to the auditor who has this basic understanding.

SUGGESTED READINGS AND REFERENCES

ALTMAN, EDWARD I., *Corporate Bankruptcy in America*. Lexington, Mass.: Heath Lexington, 1971.

ALTMAN, EDWARD I., and THOMAS P. McGOUGH, "Evaluation of a Company as a Going Concern," *Journal of Accountancy*, December 1974.

BARRINGTON, J. D., "Accounting Models for Managing Credit," *The Canadian Chartered Accountant*, May 1971.

DEAKIN, EDWARD B., and MICHAEL H. GRANOF, "Directing Audit Effort Using Regression Analysis," *The CPA Journal*, February 1976, pp. 29–33.

KINNEY, W.R., JR., "ARIMA and Regression in Analytical Review: An Empirical Test," *The Accounting Review*, January 1978, pp. 48–60.

SPRINGER, HERLIHY, MALL, and BEGGS, *Probabilistic Models*, pp. 82–100. Homewood, Ill.; Richard D. Irwin, 1968.

TOUCHE ROSS & CO., *Financial Analysis as an Audit Tool*. 1975.

REVIEW QUESTIONS

10-1. What are the purposes of analytical tests from an auditor's point of view?

10-2. Identify the major factors motivating auditors to seek more effective analytical testing techniques.

10-3. What is meant by regression analysis? Describe two audit situations in which regression analysis might be used.

10-4. Distinguish between *inference* and *prediction* as each is used in regression. Which is a more appropriate term when the auditor is verifying the reasonableness of an account balance with regression?

10-5. What is meant by the term *variables* in regression? Distinguish between independent variables and dependent variables. Assume the auditor was using regression analysis to make inferences about total cost of sales. The variables being considered are commercial sales and wholesale sales. Identify the dependent and independent variables.

10-6. What are the characteristics of simple linear regression? Provide an example in which this method might be appropriate.

10-7. Distinguish between linear and curvilinear regression. What are the advantages and disadvantages of each?

10-8. Distinguish among the following three terms and define the standard formulation of independent and dependent variables for each term: *simple linear regression, simple curvilinear regression, multiple linear regression, and multiple curvilinear regression.*

10-9. Using simple linear regression, define each term for the formulation $Y = a + bX$. Use this formula to determine February's expected value of repair and maintenance expense for a rock crusher if there is $2,000 of repairs and maintenance monthly regardless of volume. The expense is expected to increase $12 for every hour of actual machine operating time. There are 180 hours of rock-crushing machine hours in February.

10-10. How would an auditor ascertain what information should be used to determine the values of a and b in question 10-9? Assuming the information is available, how would the values of a and b be determined?

10-11. What is meant by a data set in regression analysis? How many data sets would there be if 26 months of data were used to determine the value of a and b for each of four independent variables for purposes of estimating total sales?

10-12. What is meant by the coefficient of correlation in regression analysis? What do the values .9 and −.82 for two different coefficients of correlation indicate? How is the coefficient of correlation obtained in a particular situation?

10-13. What is meant by a confidence interval for a regression line? Compare in concept the confidence interval for regression analysis and for variables sampling.

10-14. Compare a t-distribution to a normal distribution. Which is used for regression analysis? Assume there were 20 data sets used to determine values for *a* and *b*. How many degrees of freedom should be used to determine the *t* value? What will be the *t* value for a two-sided interval at a 95% confidence level?

10-15. What is meant by an outlier in regression analysis? How would the auditor find which of the current year's monthly recorded repairs and maintenance expense totals are outliers? What would the auditor do with outliers?

10-16. What is meant by a Markov chain process? What might be the purpose of using a Markov chain in the audit of inventory? What information would be needed to make the calculations?

10-17. What is meant by the term *discriminant analysis*? How might discriminant analysis be used by auditors?

DISCUSSION QUESTIONS AND PROBLEMS

10-18. (AICPA adapted) During your examination of the 1980 financial statements of MacKenzie Park Co., which manufactures and sells trivets, you wish to analyze selected aspects of the company's operations.

Labor hours and production costs for the last four months of 1980, which you believe are representative for the year, were as follows:

Month	*Labor hours*	*Total production costs*
September	2,500	$ 20,000
October	3,500	25,000
November	4,500	30,000
December	3,500	25,000
	14,000	$100,000

Based upon the information above and using the least squares method of computation, select the best answer for each of the following questions:

a. The cost function derived by the least squares method:
   (i) Would be linear.
   (ii) Would have a negative slope.
   (iii) Would be parabolic.
   (iv) Would indicate maximum costs at the point of the function's point of inflection.

b. Monthly production costs could be expressed by
   (i) $Y = aX + b$
   (ii) $Y = a + bX$
   (iii) $Y = b + aX$
   (iv) $Y = (a + bX)$

c. Using the least squares method of computation, the fixed monthly production cost of trivets is approximately:
   (i) $10,000
   (ii) $ 9,500
   (iii) $ 7,500
   (iv) $ 5,000
d. Using the least squares method of computation, the variable production cost per labor hour is:
   (i) $6.00
   (ii) $5.00
   (iii) $3.00
   (iv) $2.00

10-19. Renolds Rims and Spokes manufactures a large variety of automobile and truck tire rims for sale to manufacturers and repair shops. The equipment used to manufacture the rims is expensive and requires considerable maintenance. Management has always followed the policy of doing preventive maintenance whenever possible.

You are doing late interim testing for the audit of Renolds and observe that considerable time was spent auditing repair and maintenance expense in the previous year, yet there were no significant errors uncovered. You decide to compare repair and maintenance expense as a percent of sales and find that there is considerable variation from year to year. You also discover considerable variation from month to month when the ratio is calculated on monthly data. When you discuss your findings with management, you are informed that a large portion of monthly maintenance is required regardless of volume and there is a significant large variation in volume from month to month and year to year.

You next decide to use regression analysis to see if your results are more meaningful. You decide to use data for the past ten months, because the transactions for the last two months of the year are not yet recorded.

Ideally, machine hours would be used as the independent variable. Total monthly machine hours are available, but they will not be audited by your CPA firm. You therefore decide to use direct labor dollars as the independent variable.

The information for the first ten months of the audit is as follows (in thousands):

	X direct labor	Y repair and maintenance		X direct labor	Y repair and maintenance
Jan.	10.0	3.8	June	20.0	4.0
Feb.	9.0	3.2	July	21.0	4.5
Mar.	14.0	3.3	Aug.	20.0	4.2
April	11.0	3.2	Sept.	17.0	4.0
May	18.0	3.9	Oct.	16.0	4.5

REQUIRED:

a. Plot the ten data points on a graph and draw, without making calculations, an estimate of the least squares regression line.
b. Calculate a and b for the regression line. State the regression line using the values for a and b in terms of $Y = a + bX$.
c. Draw the regression line in part b on the graph you prepared in part a. Compare the actual regression line to the estimate you made.
d. Calculate the coefficient of correlation between direct labor dollars and repairs and maintenance expense. What do your calculations indicate?
e. Determine the precision interval and confidence interval for the regression line at a 95% confidence level.
f. Include the confidence limits on the graph you prepared in item a.
g. Identify all outlying months on the graph. What is the appropriate action with regard to the outliers?

10-20. The graph below is a 97.5% confidence interval for a regression analysis. Eight data sets were used for the calculations. The following questions refer to the graph.

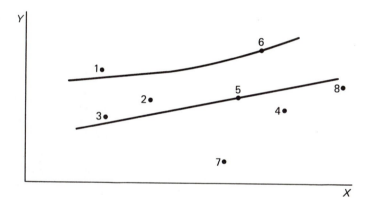

a. The two variables being used in the regression are monthly repairs and maintenance expense and monthly total factory machine hours. Label each axis. Explain why you labeled them as you did.
b. Identify the line on the graph that is defined by $Y = a + bX$.
c. Identify the amount of monthly fixed repair and maintenance expense that can be expected.
d. Does the graph show a one-sided or two-sided confidence interval?
e. Identify all data points (1–8) on the graph that are outliers.
f. Regraph the confidence interval using a two-sided interval at a 90% confidence level.
g. Using the confidence interval in f, which data points are outliers?
h. Which data point (1–8) shows the expected value of repairs and maintenance at a particular number of machine hours? Explain your answer.
i. Regraph the straight line and confidence interval assuming that there was

an error in the original calculation. The correct straight line has a slightly smaller fixed element and greater slope.

10-21. Tastee Dinner operates 14 family restaurants in the southwestern United States. All restaurants are centrally owned and controlled by a management group in Phoenix.

Every Tastee Dinner is built on an identical floor plan, has the same furniture, and uses the same menu. There is an ongoing attempt to standardize every possible aspect of each restaurant as a step in building additional restaurants throughout the United States.

A decision has been made by the CPA firm doing the audit of Tastee Dinner to use regression analysis as one factor in deciding which stores are to be extensively audited as a part of the current-year annual audit. The partner on the engagement decides to use sales as the independent variable and operating income as the dependent variable.

The following table shows the sales and operating income for each store (additional calculations needed for the case are also included):

Store	Y Operating income	X sales	XY	Y²	X²
1	$ 2,800	$ 58,000	$ 162,400,000	$ 7,840,000	$ 3,364,000,000
2	1,200	41,000	49,200,000	1,440,000	1,681,000,000
3	2,500	55,000	137,500,000	6,250,000	3,025,000,000
4	2,600	53,000	137,800,000	6,760,000	2,809,000,000
5	2,000	48,000	96,000,000	4,000,000	2,304,000,000
6	3,000	59,000	177,000,000	9,000,000	3,481,000,000
7	6,100	60,000	366,000,000	37,210,000	3,600,000,000
8	⟨3,000⟩	25,000	⟨75,000,000⟩	9,000,000	625,000,000
9	0	49,000	0	0	2,401,000,000
10	3,200	61,000	195,200,000	10,240,000	3,721,000,000
11	2,100	52,000	109,200,000	4,410,000	2,704,000,000
12	2,400	55,000	132,000,000	5,760,000	3,025,000,000
13	2,900	58,000	168,200,000	8,410,000	3,364,000,000
14	1,900	51,000	96,900,000	3,610,000	2,601,000,000
	$29,700	$725,000	$1,752,400,000	$113,930,000	$38,705,000,000
	$\bar{X} = \$51,785$		$\bar{Y} = \$2,121$		

REQUIRED:

a. Evaluate the auditor's decision to select the restaurants to audit extensively partially on the basis of the results of the regression analysis.

b. Calculate the operating income regression line for the 14 restaurants.

c. Calculate the coefficient of correlation. Interpret the meaning of the results.

d. Calculate the confidence interval for the operating income regression line at a 90% confidence level.

e. Identify which stores are outliers. What are possible causes of a store's being an outlier?

f. Plot the data points, regression line, and confidence limits on a graph. What do you conclude from examining the graph?

g. Recalculate the correlation, regression line, and confidence limits, excluding the two most extreme outliers. Plot the results on the same graph as *f.* Explain the difference.

10-22. Below are three graphs showing data points for independent and related dependent variables.

a. Draw a rough approximation of the regression line for each, A to C $(Y = a + bX)$.

b. Identify the graph with a coefficient of correlation near zero. What causes a coefficient to be near zero?

c. Identify the graph with a negative slope. Provide an example where regression could be used in auditing in which there is likely to be a negative slope.

d. Assuming both the X and Y axes for all three graphs use the same scale, which graph is likely to have the largest standard deviation? Which is likely to have the smallest precision interval? Explain the reasons for your answers.

e. In which graph is a, in the straight-line formula $Y = a + bX$, likely to be near zero? Provide an example where regression could be used in auditing in which a is likely to have a zero value.

f. Identify the graph in which curvilinear regression is likely to provide a significantly improved coefficient of correlation.

g. Identify the graph in which multiple correlation provides the greatest application for a smaller confidence interval.

10-23. George Mayer, CPA, is auditing the allowance for uncollectible accounts. The client has always had collection problems, but management has been uncooperative about booking recommended adjustments to the allowance. Every year there is disagreement between the auditor and management about the appropriate amount of the allowance. Accounts receivable is the largest account in the financial statements, and the allowance is large.

George has already tested the aging of outstanding accounts receivable on the aged trial balance and has concluded there are no significant errors. A calculation was also made of the relative percentage of each age category in total accounts receivable for the current year. Accounts receivable has increased in the current year, and the percent of total receivables in the more-than-90-days category has also increased relative to previous years.

George has decided to use regression analysis to help him decide whether the allowance is misstated in the current year. The dependent variable in George's intended approach is the percentage of allowance for uncollectible accounts divided by accounts receivable. An independent variable is the number of days' receivables outstanding. If the current year's allowance account is materially different from the regression line, George intends to insist on an adjustment to the allowance account.

The following are the data sets (all in thousands) George decides to use for the calculations:

Year	Sales	Recorded allowance for uncollectible accounts	Accounts receivable
Current year	430.0	37.0	200.0
Preceding year	425.0	43.0	174.0
2 years ago	390.0	40.0	156.0
3 years ago	400.0	40.0	155.0
4 years ago	380.0	39.0	137.0
5 years ago	350.0	35.0	135.0

REQUIRED:

a. Evaluate the use of simple linear regression conclusions in this situation.
b. Calculate the regression line, coefficient of correlation, and the confidence interval at a 90% confidence level for the information provided.
c. Plot the data points on a graph and draw the regression line and confidence interval.
d. What conclusions do you reach about the current-year balance in allowance for uncollectible accounts in this situation? Recommend an adjusting entry if you consider one appropriate.
e. Explain why the results of the regression analysis might not be meaningful in this situation.
f. What additional information would be needed to use a Markov chain process to evaluate the reasonableness of the allowance in this situation?

11

strategy development in the use of statistical sampling

INTRODUCTION

Previous chapters have dealt with the use of the primary statistical methods available to auditors. Each chapter was organized around the uses of the particular statistical method reported.

This chapter approaches the application of statistical sampling to auditing by examining the alternative types of statistical methods for each major type of audit test. The emphasis will be on the conditions and circumstances that should be considered in selecting the appropriate statistical method for each type of test.

The authors' opinions regarding appropriate confidence levels, upper precision limits, minimum sample sizes, and other auditor judgments are included more frequently in this chapter than in previous ones. These are meant to be more illustrative of the kind of judgment auditors make than representative of all auditors' judgments.

TYPES OF AUDIT TESTS

Chapter 1 included a review of the basic types of audit tests used by auditors: compliance observations, compliance tests of transactions, substantive tests of transactions, analytical review, and direct tests of details of balances.

The auditor uses these types of audit tests jointly to provide the level of assurance needed for each particular situation. Chapter 1 dealt with determining the normal level of assurance for a given audit client.

There are alternative approaches that can be followed to satisfy a given level of assurance, depending on such factors as the reliance the auditor intends to place on internal control, cost and reliability of alternative types of evidence, and auditor preference.

Alternative audit approaches can be illustrated schematically. Each of the four blocks shown below represents the same level of overall audit assurance for a particular objective. Each shows how the audit work can be allocated among the various types of procedures. Each section in a box represents the percentage of total fieldwork time spent doing that type of test. (Obviously, the total number of possible combinations is almost endless.)

Situation No. 1: Internal control excellent and heavily relied upon; direct tests of balances concentrated at year-end.

COMPLIANCE OBSERVA- TIONS AND COMPLIANCE TESTS OF TRANS.	SUBS. T OF T	ANALYTICAL REVIEW	DIRECT TESTS OF DETAILS OF BALANCES

Situation No. 2: Internal control excellent and heavily relied upon; substantive tests spread throughout the year.

COMPLIANCE OBSERVA- TIONS AND COMPLIANCE TESTS OF TRANS.	SUBSTANTIVE TESTS OF TRANS.	ANALYT- ICAL REVIEW	DIRECT TESTS OF DETAILS OF BALANCES

Situation No. 3: Internal control only fair and not heavily relied upon; direct tests of balances work spread throughout the year.

COMP. OBS. AND COMP. T OF T	SUBSTANTIVE TESTS OF TRANS.	ANALYT- ICAL REVIEW	DIRECT TESTS OF DETAILS OF BALANCES

Situation No. 4: Internal control adequate, but heavy year-end substantive approach taken.

COMP. OBS. AND COMP. T OF T	SUBS. T OF T	ANALYTICAL REVIEW	DIRECT TESTS OF DETAILS OF BALANCES

Although such a case is not shown above, there may be extreme situations in which *no* compliance tests of transactions or substantive tests of transactions are performed. Analytical review procedures and substantive tests of details of balances are always necessary.

SAMPLE DESIGN FOR JUDGMENTAL SAMPLES

Judgmental sampling is any method whereby sampling items are selected in an arbitrary or nonprobabilistic fashion. The idea of a judgmental sample is to obtain desired information about the population by examining the minimum number of items.

The auditor's knowledge about the population items is the key to effective sample design of judgmental samples. For example, if the auditor wants a representative sample of vouchers written during the year, he or she might design the sample so as to obtain one or two from each of the following groups: months processed, type of purchase (inventory, fixed asset, services, payroll), dollar value of voucher (larger, medium, small), and plant location.

When judgmental samples are meant to substantively test an account balance, the auditor usually tries to test a reasonably large percentage of the population dollar amount.

Figure 11-1 presents a summary of the various factors affecting judgmental samples and their effect on sample size.

COMPLIANCE TESTS OF TRANSACTIONS

Compliance tests of transactions are intended to obtain evidence about compliance with or deviations from one or more internal controls.

The statistical methods that are most applicable for testing compliance are unstratified attributes sampling using physical units and simple attributes using dollar units. Variables methods are generally not applicable because

Part I: Compliance tests of transactions

Factor	Conditions leading to	
	Smaller sample sizes	Larger sample sizes
Planned degree of reliance on internal controls being tested	Lesser reliance	Greater reliance
Nature of planned substantive tests	Stronger substantive tests (e.g., direct observation)	Weaker substantive tests (e.g., negative confirmation)
Extent of planned substantive tests	Lesser reduction in substantive tests (e.g., maximum or large)	Greater reduction in substantive tests (e.g., moderate or minimum)
Timing of planned substantive tests	Closer to balance sheet date	Further from balance sheet date
Quality of evidence about compliance available (i.e., effectiveness of audit procedure)	Higher-quality evidence	Lower-quality evidence. Where quality of evidence is low, either entire test or reliance on control should be reconsidered.
Expectation of errors (i.e., deviations from prescribed control procedures)	Zero expected errors (or very close to zero)	Errors expected. When a high frequency of errors is expected, reliance on control should be reconsidered.
Nature of population Diversity of types of items Materiality of items Sensitivity	Homogeneous type, source, etc. Homogeneous in amount of items Lack of sensitive items	Highly diverse Skewed—contains large items Presence of sensitive items
Presence of individually material or critical population items (key items)	No key items; entire sample representative items	Presence of key items—which must be examined in addition to representative items
Size of population	Size of population may or may not directly affect sample size, depending on its skewness and qualitative characteristics.	

FIGURE 11-1 Factors influencing judgmental sample sizes

Part II: Substantive tests of transactions and details of balances

	Conditions leading to	
Factor	*Smaller sample sizes*	*Larger sample sizes*
Reliance on internal control	Greater reliance	Lesser reliance
Extent of compliance deviations	No or few compliance deviations	Significant compliance deviations found
Quality of compliance evidence	Higher quality	Lower quality
Measure of audit materiality	Larger measure of materiality	Smaller measure of materiality
Significance of accounts being audited directly or affected by transactions being audited	Accounts less significant	Accounts more significant
Strength of other substantive procedures relating to same transactions and accounts and objectives (including analytical review procedures)	Stronger other substantive procedures	Weaker (or no) other substantive procedures
Quality of evidence in this test	Higher-quality evidence	Lower-quality evidence. Where quality of evidence is low, reconsider performing test.
Expectation of errors (i.e., monetary errors)	Zero expected errors (or very close to zero)	Errors expected. Where high frequency of large-magnitude errors is expected, reconsider performing test.
Nature of population	Size of population may or may not directly affect sample size, depending on its skewness and qualitative characteristics.	

FIGURE 11-1 (continued)

they are concerned with dollar values, not rates of procedural deviations. Other dollar-unit methods apply to high error rate situations, not generally the case where controls are to be relied upon.

Both of these methods use the binomial distribution and are therefore always reliable. The decision as to when each is more appropriate is based on three criteria: expected error rate, availability of computer assistance, and the type of information desired.

Attributes sampling with physical units (studied in Chapter 3) is usually efficient and easy to apply. The biggest disadvantage is the absence of stratification. In many applications of attributes sampling, the auditor may be more interested in the deviations from control procedures for large populations than for small ones. Stratified attributes sampling using physical units is not studied in this book, but it is sometimes used. The problem is that it is relatively inefficient compared to unstratified attributes. The auditor can use unstratified attributes sampling and in addition judgmentally select key items such as large transactions or unusual transactions for the circumstances. Dollar unit sampling would ordinarily be used when stratification is desired.

The most important advantages of dollar unit sampling for compliance tests are automatic stratification and the statement of results in terms of the maximum portion of dollars in the population that is likely to contain errors. Simple attributes sampling is efficient when no errors are expected or found in the sample; otherwise it is inefficient. Keep in mind that when many deviations are expected for compliance tests, the auditor should evaluate whether compliance tests are appropriate. A final problem with dollar unit sampling is the difficulty of sample selection without a computer.

The decision to select dollar or physical unit attributes sampling can be made using the matrix in Figure 11-2.

Error-rate condition and computer availability	Desire an estimate in percent of recorded dollars in error	Desire an estimate of frequency of error occurrence
High expected error rate	Dollar unit sampling; the use of compliance testing should be reevaluated	Physical unit sampling; the use of compliance testing should be reevaluated
Low expected error rate; no computer availability	Dollar unit sampling; cost of selection will be high	Physical unit sampling
Low expected error rate; computer availability	Dollar unit sampling	Physical unit sampling

FIGURE 11-2 Appropriate use of dollar and physical unit sampling for compliance testing

The auditor should be aware that dollar unit sampling requires that recorded values be available before selection is possible. There is also no way to test compliance deviations for omitted transactions.

When physical unit selection is followed, the auditor should also judgmentally select any population items that are considered material individually or items that are considered important for reasons other than size.

The auditor still has two decisions after he decides to use attributes sampling and chooses between physical units and dollar units. An appropriate reliability level and acceptable upper precision limit must be selected for each attribute. Figure 11-3 illustrates guidelines for deciding on the appropriate reliability level and upper precision limit.

Factor	*Judgment*	*Guideline*
		Reliability level:
Planned degree of reliance on internal	High reliance	95% reliability level
controls being tested. Consider:	Moderate reliance	90% reliability level
Nature, extent and timing of	Low reliance	80% reliability level
substantive tests; i.e., greater		
substantive tests, lesser reliance		
on internal control and vice		
versa		
Quality of evidence about		
compliance available; i.e., the		
lower the quality of evidence,		
the lesser the reliance on internal		
control will be		
		Upper precision limit:
Significance of the transactions and	Highly significant	4%
related account balances the internal	balances	
controls are intended to affect	Significant balances	5%
	Less significant	6%
	balances	

Notes: *1. The guidelines should also recognize that there may be variation in reliability levels based on overall audit assurance considerations. The guidelines above are the most conservative that should be followed.*

2. Reliability levels are for one-sided estimates.

3. Certain significant items may be judgmentally selected in addition to the statistical sample.

FIGURE 11-3 Illustrative guidelines for statistical sample sizes—compliance tests of transactions

SUBSTANTIVE TESTS OF TRANSACTIONS

Substantive tests of transactions are meant to obtain evidence about the presence or absence of monetary errors that will affect account balances. They are frequently done in conjunction with compliance tests of transactions. These are termed dual-purpose tests.

The following are the most common methods used for substantive tests of transactions:

To express an error-rate conclusion:
  Evaluation Method: *Types of Samples:*
  1. Attributes sampling   Unrestricted random sample
                                         of physical audit units
                                       Systematic sample of
                                         physical audit units

To express a dollar-amount conclusion:
  Evaluation Methods: *Types of Samples:*
  1. Simple attributes   Unrestricted random sample
  2. Combined attributes-variables   of dollar units
     evaluation   Systematic sample of dollar
  3. Multinomial bound evaluation   units

It is possible under some circumstances to use variables sampling methods for substantive tests of transactions—for example, to estimate the value of pricing errors in sales transactions when there are a large number of

	Information desired	
Error rate conditions and computer availability	*Desire an estimate of an upper bound of dollar values*	*Desire an estimate of frequency of error occurrence*
Zero expected error rate; no computer availability	Dollar unit, simple attributes; cost of selection would be high	Physical unit, attributes
Zero expected error rate; computer availability	Dollar unit, simple attributes	Physical unit, attributes
Other than zero expected error rate; no computer availability	Dollar unit, combined attributes-variables evaluation; cost of selection would be high	Physical unit, attributes
Other than zero expected error rate; computer availability	Dollar unit, combined attributes-variables evaluation, or multinomial bound evaluation	Physical unit, attributes

FIGURE 11-4 Appropriate use of dollar and physical unit sampling for substantive tests of transactions

sample errors. Usually there are insufficient errors for ratio or difference estimation or dollar unit difference estimation to provide a reliable estimate. Only stratified mean-per-unit is likely to result in both an efficient and reliable estimate. When the client's transaction data for the entire year are not available for computer analysis, stratified mean-per-unit estimation for transactions testing is not practical. It is uncommon for all transactions for the year to be available on the computer.

The statistical methods that are most likely to be followed for differing circumstances are shown in the matrix in Figure 11-4.

Figure 11-5 illustrates guidelines for deciding on reliability and precision for substantive tests of transactions. The guidelines are appropriate for physical unit and dollar unit samples, but the precision must be stated in terms of dollars for the latter method.

Planned reduction in substantive tests of details of balances	*Results of evaluation of internal control and compliance tests*	*Reliability level of substantive tests of transactions[c]*	*Precision of substantive tests of transactions*
Large	Excellent[b] Good Not Good	60% 80% 95%	Percent or amount based on materiality considerations for related accounts
Moderate	Excellent[b] Good Not Good	60% 75% 90%	
Small[a]	Excellent[b] Good Not Good	60% 70% 80%	

[a] *This situation is one in which little emphasis is being placed on the system at all. Neither compliance nor substantive tests of transactions are likely in this situation.*

[b] *This situation is one in which internal control and evidence about it are both good. Substantive tests of transactions are least likely to be performed at all in these cases.*

[c] *Reliability levels are for one-sided estimates.*

Note: *The guidelines should also recognize that there may be variations in reliability levels based on overall audit assurance considerations. The guidelines above are the most conservative that should be followed.*

FIGURE 11-5   Illustrative guidelines for statistical sample sizes—substantive tests of transactions

ANALYTICAL TESTS

Chapter 10 concerned the use of statistical methods for analytical tests. They will not be repeated here.

DIRECT TESTS OF BALANCES

Direct tests of details of account balances differ from tests of transactions in several pertinent ways:

1. The expected error rate and magnitude may be zero or low, or may be moderate or high for direct tests. Ordinarily, tests of transactions are performed only where the expected error rate is reasonably low.
2. Materiality has a direct impact on the precision of tests of details of account balances. It is a major consideration affecting sample size.
3. The results of internal control evaluation and testing, analytical review procedures, and perhaps other related tests of details of account balances are available in planning substantive tests of account balances.

There are a greater number of statistical methods available for use in direct tests of details of balances than in tests of transactions, particularly compliance attributes. Eleven methods have been discussed that are applicable in certain circumstances. These are:

UNSTRATIFIED SAMPLE OF PHYSICAL AUDIT UNITS:
1. Attributes sampling (Chapter 3)
2. Mean-per-unit estimation (Chapter 7)
3. Difference estimation (Chapter 5)
4. Ratio estimation (Chapter 6)

STRATIFIED SAMPLE OF PHYSICAL AUDIT UNITS:
5. Mean-per-unit estimation (Chapter 8)
6. Difference estimation (Chapter 8)
7. Ratio estimation (Chapter 8)

UNSTRATIFIED SAMPLE OF DOLLAR UNITS:
8. Simple attributes (Chapter 9)
9. Combined attributes-variables evaluation (Chapter 9)
10. Multinomial bound evaluation (Chapter 9)
11. Dollar unit difference estimation (Chapter 9)

None of these methods is best for every circumstance. The choice of method depends upon several considerations:

Consideration	*Comments*
1. The auditor desires to have an estimate of dollar values.	Attributes sampling of physical units does not provide this.
2. Recorded values for all population items are available.	Only attributes sampling and mean-per-unit estimation can be used when there are no recorded values.
3. A confidence interval is desired, or an audit adjustment is to be proposed.	Only mean-per-unit, ratio, difference estimation, and dollar unit difference estimation are applicable.
4. Expected error rates are high.	Dollar unit sampling is inefficient; difference and ratio estimation may be reliable and efficient.
5. Estimated error rates are low.	Only attributes, dollar unit sampling (except dollar unit difference estimation), and stratified mean-per-unit are likely to result in reliable and efficient estimations.
6. A computer is not available, a low rate of error is expected, and a decision based on dollars is desired.	Only dollar unit sampling (except dollar unit difference estimation) is likely to result in a reasonably efficient, reliable, and low-cost statistical estimate.

Figure 11-6 summarizes the most important considerations affecting the usefulness of each of the eleven methods.

Several observations can be made about Figure 11-6:

1. The reliability of methods relates to whether the reliability level associated with a confidence interval represents an accurate probability that the interval does contain the true population value being estimated. Where the binomial or multinomial distribution is used, this is never a problem. Thus, for attributes sampling, simple attributes, combined attributes-variables evaluation, and multinomial bound evaluation, there is no minimum sample size requirement.

Where the normal distribution is used, reliability is a problem and must be controlled with sample size.

There are two specific requirements that some firms use for variables estimates to assure reliable estimation. The first is a minimum sample size (not including 100 percent strata) of at least 100 items, and the second concerns minimum requirements about error conditions for ratio and difference estimation. The error rate for either method must be 10 percent for sample sizes up to 300. For sample sizes in excess of 300, there must be at least 30 errors plus 5 percent of the sample size in excess of 300. (For example, if the sample size is 400, there must be at least 35 errors.) In addition, no more than 75 percent of errors can be in only one direction, unless the error rate is greater than 50 percent. If these conditions for requirement 2 do not exist, ratio and difference estimation cannot be used. The existence of these conditions means that there are *qualifying errors*.

	Value characteristic of sample used for population estimate	Reliability of method	Efficiency of method	Ease of application	Other advantages/disadvantages
Unstratified sample of physical audit units					
Attributes sampling	Error occurrence rate	Always reliable	Usually very efficient	Very easy to apply	Does not provide estimate in terms of dollars.
Mean-per-unit estimation	Audited value	Usually reliable	Seldom efficient	Easy to apply	Can be used when no recorded value per sample item exists.
Difference estimation	Error amounts	Requires high error rate	Usually very efficient	Easy to apply	Requires two values per sample item.
Ratio estimation	Error amounts divided by values	Requires high error rate	Usually very efficient	Easy to apply	Requires two values per sample item. Can be used to directly estimate a ratio (e.g., for LIFO).
Stratified sample of physical audit units					
Mean-per-unit estimation	Weighted average of audited values	Always reliable	Usually very efficient	Very difficult without computer	Unless very few strata are used, a special computer program is required to select and evaluate sample.
Difference estimation	Weighted average of error amounts	Requires high error rate	Usually very efficient	Difficult without computer	
Ratio estimation	Weighted average of error amounts divided by values	Requires high error rate	Usually very efficient	Difficult without computer	

Method	Basis	Reliability	Efficiency	Sampling/Evaluation	Comments
Unstratified sample of dollar units Simple attributes	Error occurrence rate	Always reliable	Very efficient with zero errors, otherwise inefficient	Difficult to draw sample without computer; easy to evaluate	Sample units must have dollar value to be selected.
Combined attributes-variables evaluation	Error occurrence rate with modification for error amounts	Always reliable	Very efficient with zero or close to zero errors, otherwise inefficient	Difficult to draw sample without computer; easy to evaluate	Although results are expressed in terms of dollars, provides a bound and not an interval estimate usable for audit adjustment.
Multinomial bound evaluation	Error occurrence rate with modification for error amounts	Always reliable	Very efficient with zero or close to zero errors; sometimes efficient with more	Difficult to draw sample without computer; computer required to evaluate.	
Dollar unit difference estimation	Error amounts	Requires high error rate	Usually very efficient	Easy to apply	Sample units must have dollar value to be selected.

FIGURE 11-6 Summary of statistical sampling methods available for direct tests of details of balances

2. Most methods appear to be relatively efficient, except for unstratified mean-per-unit estimation. Dollar unit sampling methods are also not efficient to varying degrees, where errors are found.

3. Stratified sampling appears generally reliable and very efficient; however, it is difficult to apply without computer assistance. Similarly, dollar unit samples are difficult to obtain when selected manually, and a computer must be used for multinomial bound evaluation.

4. There are two additional problems with dollar unit sampling. First, it produces a bound and not a confidence interval. Second, sampling units must have a dollar value to be selected.

5. Mean-per-unit estimation is the only method that will provide a confidence interval expressed in dollars (or other quantitative terms) when only an audit value for each sample item exists. Typically, only unstratified mean-per-unit can be used when it is necessary to stratify in terms of dollars that are unknown. It may be possible to stratify by some other criterion, such as type of customer, location of inventory, or type of inventory. The population size for each stratum must be determinable.

6. Establishing a cutoff point above which all items will be audited and below which items will be sampled, is a means to control skewness. This is important for the reliability of estimates made with mean-per-unit estimation.

Establishing a high-dollar cutoff also gives the auditor protection against large infrequent errors that could invalidate his statistical test. The highest concern, particularly in difference and ratio estimation, is overlooking a small number of large errors. These are most likely in large population items.

Some items are of particular audit interest regardless of amount. Examples are old accounts receivable, slow-moving inventory items, and specific locations.

Based on the information about the eleven statistical methods and the previous observations, a specific set of decision recommendations has been developed for guidance in selecting the best statistical sampling method to use. These recommendations are presented in a flowchart in Figure 11-7.

Recommendation No. 1: If a dollar estimate is not needed to satisfy the audit objectives of the test, use attributes sampling. If a dollar estimate is needed, apply recommendations 2 through 6 as appropriate.

Recommendation No. 2: If only one value per sample item is available, use mean-per-unit estimation. Ordinarily, unstratified mean-per-unit must be used, because recorded values are not available as a means to stratify. If it is practical to stratify on a different basis, stratified mean-per-unit should be considered. That option is omitted from the flowchart to keep it simple. Otherwise, apply recommendations 3 through 6.

Recommendation No. 3: If "qualifying errors" are expected, use difference or ratio estimation. Use stratified sampling if there is reason to believe that certain identifiable segments of the population are likely to contain larger errors than the overall population.

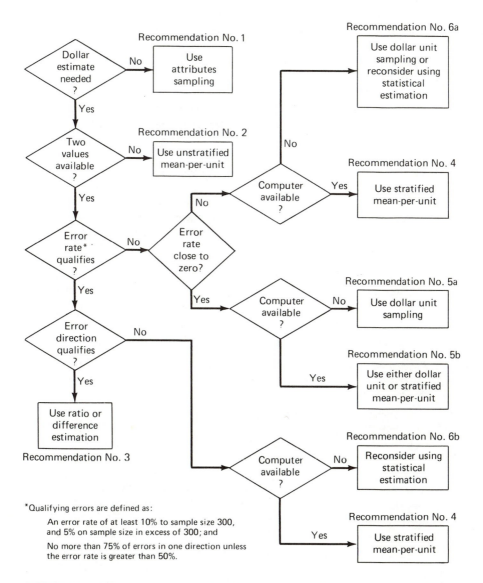

FIGURE 11-7 Selection of a statistical sampling method for substantive tests of details of account balances

Recommendation No. 4: If qualifying errors are *not* expected, yet the error rate is *not* close to zero, and the computer *is* available, use optimally stratified mean-per-unit estimation.

Recommendation No. 5: If qualifying errors are *not* expected and the error rate *is* close to zero:

- a. If computer is not available, use dollar unit sampling.
- b. If computer is available, use either dollar unit sampling or optimally stratified mean-per-unit.

When dollar unit sampling is used, the evaluation method will depend on the number of errors found.

1. Where no errors are found, use simple attributes.
2. Where one or a few errors are found, use combined attributes-variables evaluation.
3. Where more than a few but less than "qualifying" errors are found, use multinomial bound evaluation.
4. Where "qualifying" errors are found, use dollar unit difference estimation.

However, if dollar unit sampling is used, determine sample size based on a conservative assumption of expected error findings.

Recommendation No. 6: If errors do *not* qualify for difference or ratio estimation, the error rate is *not* close to zero, and the computer is *not* available:

- a. Dollar unit sampling might be used if the expected error rate is not too high; however
- b. It may be most prudent to reconsider the use of statistical estimation and instead use a judgmental approach.

In this situation, it is likely that there are material errors, yet applying appropriate statistical methods manually may be difficult. Dollar unit sampling may suffice but will require a very large sample size to be helpful, and then may indicate a material error without providing a sound basis for an adjustment. In such situations, a judgmental sample designed to cover problem areas and large dollar amounts may be the most effective approach.

Summary of Recommendations A given statistical method may be appealing from the standpoint of reliability and efficiency, but its use or non-use may be affected by practical considerations. Chief among these are information and computer availability. Information availability concerns what the auditor knows about a population. Does the auditor know the skewness or frequency of recorded values? What error experience has there been? What is the population size and variability? Lacking this information, the auditor will often choose the statistical method he or she feels "safest" with—not necessarily the most efficient. For example, on a first-year audit, the auditor may select a sample that is satisfying judgmentally and conservative statistically, in order to obtain planning data for the next year.

Computer availability reduces computation cost. It is a major practical consideration for most auditors. Whereas computer time-sharing is almost always available, two methods require batch-processing computer programs: optimally stratified mean-per-unit selection and evaluation, and dollar unit selection. These methods select sample items based on an analysis of the recorded values of the population. They can be done manually, but this is cumbersome with large populations.

Large Population Items

A general recommendation that applies to all statistical methods for direct tests of balances deals with identifying items that should be judgmentally sampled on a 100 percent basis. The authors recommend as an arbitrary rule that the following items always be stratified and audited on a 100 percent sample basis:

1. All population items recorded at ten times the mean recorded value
2. All population items recorded at an amount equal to or more than the allowable error for the test

Fallback Methods

The appropriate statistical method depends upon the appraisal of error conditions and population characteristics and computer availability. Whenever the error conditions or population characteristics differ from the original expectations, the statistical result will also differ. Such differences can render the statistical conclusions unacceptable.

Fallback procedures should be provided for times when unexpected results occur. There are three common types of fallback procedures:

1. Perform other audit procedures, probably in follow-up to specific types of errors found. The use of other audit procedures is almost always applicable. Where errors are found, they will often provide new insights into problem areas, which can then be audited as appropriate.

For example, assume several large errors are found in comparing perpetual records to the physical count in one inventory section. A complete physical count can be done of that segment to make sure that inventory is accurate.

2. Expand the sample and evaluate the larger sample with the same or another statistical method. In certain situations, such as confirmation of receivables, it may not be practicable to reopen the audit test. In considering sample expansion, the auditor should assume that the sample results in the additional sample will approximate those obtained in the first sample. The costs and benefits of increasing the sample should be calculated.

3. Reevaluate the sample with another, more suitable statistical method.

Considerable cost savings can occur by planning for an alternative method at the time the original sample method is selected. If there is a high likelihood of the primary method's not being acceptable, the lack of a good secondary method may cause the auditor to use different statistical methods to start with.

When attributes estimation is used as a primary method, it is generally because a dollar estimate is not considered essential. This is often because zero or very few errors are expected. Where numerous errors are actually found, however, the auditor will often adopt a new objective of estimating the total error amount. Difference or ratio estimation may be used depending on the magnitude, direction, and rate of the errors found.

If difference or ratio estimation is used as a primary method and the errors obtained are too inadequate for it to be reliable, fallback is generally limited to other audit procedures, because (1) an increase in sample size is not apt to change the error rate, and (2) sample design is apt to be far from optimal for mean-per-unit purposes. This tends to restrict difference and ratio estimation to situations in which a very reliable appraisal of circumstances can be made.

Let us emphasize here that fallback consideration must be part of the planning process. It does no good to rely on sample expansion or other audit procedures for fallback if they are not available owing to the audit circumstances. Planning of fallback should be just as detailed as planning of primary methods. For example, other procedures should be specifically identified, expanded samples might be chosen in advance in case they are needed, and the sample size for the primary method might be increased to provide an adequate sample for fallback evaluation.

GUIDELINES FOR SAMPLE SIZES

Regardless of the statistical method selected, the auditor must make decisions about the reliability level for substantive tests of balances and allowable error. Figure 11-8 shows one decision approach that can be followed.

Likelihood of significant errors in financial statements based on systems evaluation, compliance T. of T., and substantive T. of T.	Results of analytical procedures	Reliability level for direct tests of details of balances[a]
Low	Positive	60%
	Not positive	70%
Moderate	Positive	70%
	Not positive	80%
High or unknown	Positive	90%
	Not positive	95%

Allowable error:
    Where no errors are expected and attributes sampling is used, 1% upper precision limit based on population sampled.
    Where a variables method is used, percentage or amount based on materiality considerations.

    [a]*Reliability levels are for one-sided tests. Beta risk is the complement of this percentage. Also, where more than one test is performed for a specific objective, this is the joint reliability of all the tests.*

FIGURE 11-8 Guidelines for statistical sample sizes, substantive tests of details of balances

SUGGESTED READINGS AND REFERENCES

BAILEY, A.D., JR., and D.L. JENSEN, "A Note on the Interface Between Compliance and Substantive Tests," *Journal of Accounting Research*, Autumn 1977, pp. 293–99.

KINNEY, W.R., JR., "Integrating Audit Tests: Regression Analysis and Partitioned Dollar Unit Sampling," Canadian Auditing Research Symposium, November 1977.

LOEBBECKE, JAMES K., and JOHN NETER, "Considerations in Choosing Statistical Sampling Procedures in Auditing," *Journal of Accounting Research*, Supplement 1975, pp. 38–69.

REVIEW QUESTIONS

11-1. Explain how it is possible to use different audit approaches to obtain a given level of assurance. Provide two examples of different audit approaches that would result in the same level of assurance.

11-2. Identify three circumstances in which it may be desirable to judgmentally select a sample size and sample items rather than use statistical sampling methods.

11-3. Identify five factors that are likely to affect judgmentally determined sample size for substantive tests of transactions and details of balances. Explain the relationship between the factors and the sample size.

11-4. Which two statistical methods are applicable to compliance tests of transactions? Identify the circumstances in which each of these two methods is likely to be favored.

11-5. Identify the major considerations affecting reliability level and upper precision limit for compliance tests. Explain how the auditor will decide when to use a reliability of 95% compared to 80%.

11-6. What four statistical methods are most commonly used for substantive tests of transactions? Identify the circumstances in which each of the methods is most likely to be used.

11-7. What are the factors affecting the reliability level of substantive tests of transactions? Under what circumstances is the auditor likely to use a high confidence level? When is a low confidence level or no substantive tests of transactions most likely?

11-8. Identify and distinguish among the eleven statistical methods that are available for direct tests of balances.

11-9. Explain why attributes sampling is unlikely to be used for direct tests of balances. Under what circumstances is attributes sampling likely to be used?

11-10. There are limited circumstances in which unstratified mean-per-unit is likely to be used. Why? What are the circumstances?

11-11. Identify the circumstances in which difference and ratio estimation can be used in auditing.

11-12. Identify the circumstances in which dollar unit sampling is most likely to be used. Also identify the circumstances in which an alternative method is likely.

11-13. Explain why it is desirable to select all larger items for audit testing, regardless of the statistical method used. What decision rule was recommended in the book to identify those large items?

11-14. What is meant by a fallback method? Describe the three fallback methods commonly used for statistical methods.

11-15. Identify the factors that affect the reliability level for direct tests of balances. What are the circumstances in which a high reliability level would be used?

DISCUSSION QUESTIONS AND PROBLEMS

11-16. The following are 13 factors that would probably affect the sample size for compliance tests of transactions:
   (1) Upper precision limit
   (2) Quality of compliance evidence available
   (3) Planned reliance on internal control

(4) Adequacy of the client's documentation and records

(5) Compliance deviations found in the previous year

(6) Number of financial statement users and their intended use of the statements

(7) Planned nature, extent, and timing of substantive tests

(8) Expected frequency of compliance deviations

(9) Confidence level

(10) Existence of material or sensitive items in the population

(11) Overall audit assurance desired

(12) Significance of the related transactions and account balances that the internal controls are intended to affect

(13) Expected cost of confirmations

REQUIRED:

a. Set up a schematic relationship, such as the partial one illustrated below, showing how the 13 factors affect the sample size.

Factor	*Smaller sample size*	*Larger sample size*
(1) Upper precision limit	Larger upper precision limit	Smaller upper precision limit
(2) Quality of compliance evidence available		

b. Identify five additional factors that would affect the sample size for compliance tests, and put them on the schematic relationship.

11-17. This is your first year in charge of the audit of the All-America Bank. All-America is a publicly held bank in excellent condition; it has been a client of the firm for several years. Two years ago, the bank installed a highly computerized system for processing transactions. The system and all related controls have been tested and relied upon in the audit each year. Prior years' audit tests of both transactions and balances revealed no monetary errors in the processing of transactions.

You are currently planning the approach and scope of the audit. You will use statistical sampling for tests of the proof and transit function controls relating to demand deposits and for tests of details of demand deposits as of an interim audit date. You expect demand deposits to be 40,000 accounts totaling $100,000,000. Earnings before taxes for the year are expected to be about $500,000.

REQUIRED:

Develop a plan for applying statistical sampling to tests of controls and confirmation of demand deposits. Be as specific as possible for all steps and judgments. Make any assumptions necessary.

11-18. Steadfast Wholesaling Company purchases a line of approximately 42,000 different items and wholesales to a variety of industries. The company utilizes an elaborate EDP perpetual inventory system as a basis for its operations (promising deliveries, etc.) as well as financial reporting.

You have been newly assigned as supervisor on the account, and during your initial meeting with management, you discover that the company has been troubled by a "large number" of unexpected stockouts. Your review of prior years' inventory tests of compliance reveals that several errors were detected in recording issues and receipts to stock.

Curious about how this problem was resolved, you turn to the year-end inventory workpapers and discover that no physical inventory was taken; rather, the audit team counted the 200 most expensive parts as determined from a client listing. Large numbers of errors were noted from this exercise, in both over- and understatement directions. However, because the net overstatement of inventory was only $4,219 compared to the total inventory of $17 million, the difference was passed and no further work was done.

You are troubled by the degree and nature of that testing and discuss the matter with Peter Pleistocene, the audit partner. Pleistocene has been on the engagement for 17 years and will not concede that there is a possible problem.

You propose to Pleistocene that a complete physical inventory be taken this year. Pleistocene laughs and explains that this is the way the inventory has been evaluated for the past 17 years and that the client would not stand for a full physical. However, he gives you permission to talk to the controller. Unfortunately, the meeting goes exactly as Pleistocene indicated.

Ultimately, you decide that by using a statistical test, you will be able to satisfy your own objectives of quantifying the possible error in the perpetuals while avoiding the full physical inventory to which the client objects. Accordingly, you return to Pleistocene with your ideas.

Pleistocene surprises you by getting very defensive; he indicates that he knows very well how to audit Steadfast's inventory and that his method has worked for years.

REQUIRED:

a. What sort of problems can you see with Pleistocene's approach?
b. What arguments can you muster in support of your position to convince the controller and Pleistocene?

11-19. Following are four situations in which you will use statistical sampling. Indicate what precision and reliability values you will use for each and justify your answer. Be sure to indicate whether reliability is one-sided or two-sided, and why.

a. You are performing a detailed compliance test in a situation where you believe the system of internal control is very good and is being complied with; you intend to rely on the system extensively. The related account balance is the largest in the financial statements.

Precision _____

Reliability _____

b. You are designing year-end detailed procedures for the positive confirmation of accounts receivable. You have found numerous errors in testing internal controls, and analytical procedures are not particularly effective. Thus, these detailed procedures will play a critical role.

Precision_____

Reliability_____

c. You are designing year-end detailed procedures for the positive confirmation of accounts receivable where internal control looks good and tests of transactions indicate a low likelihood of errors in the financial statements. Analytical procedures are also strong.

Precision_____

Reliability_____

d. You are designing year-end detailed procedures for the positive confirmation of accounts receivable. You found no errors in tests of transactions, but the analytical tests indicated potential problems.

Precision_____

Reliability_____

11-20. If you were to perform hypothesis tests in the situations described in 11-19 *c* and *d*, what Beta risks would you use?

11-21. Suppose you selected a dollar unit sample of 300 items, expecting to find zero errors, and evaluated the results using an upper precision limit of 1.0%. What actions would you take if you found:

a. 3 errors?

b. 10 errors?

c. 30 errors?

index